INDIGENOUS RI
IN THE AGE OF THE UN

CW00739837

This examination of the role played by the United Nations Declaration
on the Rights of Indigenous Peoples (UNDRIP) in advancing indigenous peoples' self-determination comes at a time when the quintessentially
Eurocentric nature of international law has been significantly challenged
by the increasing participation of indigenous peoples on the international
legal scene. Even though the language of human rights discourse has
historically contributed to delegitimizing the rights of indigenous peoples
to their lands and cultures, this same language is now upheld by indigenous peoples in their ongoing struggles against the assimilation and
eradication of their cultures. By demanding that the human rights and
freedoms contained in various UN human rights instruments be now
extended to indigenous peoples and communities, indigenous peoples
are playing a key role in making international law more "humanizing"
and less subject to state priorities.

ELVIRA PULITANO is an associate professor in the Ethnic Studies
Department at California Polytechnic State University (Cal Poly, San
Luis Obispo). Her research and teaching interests include indigenous
studies, African diaspora literatures, Caribbean studies, theories of race
and ethnicity, migration, diaspora and human rights discourse.

INDIGENOUS RIGHTS IN THE AGE OF THE UN DECLARATION

Edited by

ELVIRA PULITANO

With an Afterword by

MILILANI B. TRASK

CAMBRIDGE
UNIVERSITY PRESS

CAMBRIDGE
UNIVERSITY PRESS

University Printing House, Cambridge CB2 8BS, United Kingdom

Published in the United States of America by Cambridge University Press, New York

Cambridge University Press is part of the University of Cambridge.

It furthers the University's mission by disseminating knowledge in the pursuit of education, learning and research at the highest international levels of excellence.

www.cambridge.org
Information on this title: www.cambridge.org/9781107417014

© Cambridge University Press 2012

First published 2012
First paperback edition 2014

A catalogue record for this publication is available from the British Library

Library of Congress Cataloguing in Publication data
Pulitano, Elvira, 1970–
Indigenous rights in the age of the UN Declaration / Elvira Pulitano, Mililani B. Trask.
p.   cm.
Includes bibliographical references and index.
ISBN 978-1-107-02244-7 (hardback)
1. Indigenous peoples–Civil rights.   2. Indigenous peoples–Legal status,
laws, etc.   3. Indigenous peoples (International law)   4. United Nations. General
Assembly. Declaration on the Rights of Indigenous Peoples.   I. Trask, Mililani.   II. Title.
K3247.P85   2012
342.08′72–dc23
2012007318

ISBN 978-1-107-02244-7 Hardback
ISBN 978-1-107-41701-4 Paperback

This book is dedicated to the resurgence and flourishing of indigenous peoples around the world, whose vision and strength continue to enrich us all.

CONTENTS

NOTES ON CONTRIBUTORS

JONI ADAMSON is an associate professor of English and Environmental Humanities at Arizona State University and 2012 president of the Association for the Study of Literature and the Environment (ASLE). She is the author of *American Indian Literature, Environmental Justice, and Ecocriticism: The Middle Place* (2001). With Scott Slovic she coedited a special issue of *MELUS* on "Ecocriticism and Ethnic Literatures" (summer 2009). Her essays and reviews have appeared in *Globalization on the Line*, *The Blackwell Companion to American Literature and Culture*, *The American Quarterly*, *Teaching North American Environmental Literature*, *Reading the Earth*, and *Studies in American Indian Literatures*.

CLINT CARROLL is an enrolled citizen of the Cherokee Nation and is currently a post-doctoral associate in the Department of American Indian Studies, University of Minnesota. He completed his doctoral dissertation in the Department of Environmental Science, Policy, and Management, University of California, Berkeley.

SHEILA COLLINGWOOD-WHITTICK is a senior lecturer in the Department of Anglophone Studies at Stendhal University – Grenoble 3. Over the previous thirty years her field of research has been, broadly, that of postcolonial literatures, and she has published widely on fictional and autobiographical writings from several former British settler colonies. For the past twelve years, however, her scholarship has focused increasingly on indigenous and non-indigenous Australian fiction. During that time she has edited a collection of essays entitled *The Pain of Unbelonging: Alienation and Identity in Australasian Literature* (2007), as well as publishing several essays on the tortuous relationship between history and fiction in recent Australian literature. The scope of her research has also widened to encompass non-literary issues, and her most recent work has been devoted to the ongoing impact of the trauma of colonization on the lives, culture, and environment of Australia's indigenous peoples. Forthcoming publications include two book chapters (one on scientific racism and the museumization of indigenous remains, the other on the historical (in)visibility of Australia's Aboriginal peoples) and a jointly edited book on indigenous peoples and genetic research.

CARRIE GARROW (Akwesane Mohawk) is the Executive Director of the Center for Indigenous Law, Governance and Citizenship at Syracuse University College of Law, as well as an adjunct professor. She received her BA from Dartmouth College, JD from Stanford Law School, and has an MPP from the Kennedy School of Government. Ms. Garrow's writings include "Treaties, Tribal Courts, and Jurisdiction: The Treaty of Canandaigua and the Six Nations' Sovereign Right to Exercise Criminal Jurisdiction," 2 *Journal of Court Innovation* (2009); "Following Deskaheh's Legacy: Reclaiming the Cayuga Indian Nation's Land Rights in the Inter-American Commission on Human Rights," 35 *Syracuse Journal of International Law and Commerce* (2008); (with Joseph Thomas Flies-Away and Miriam Jorgensen) "Native Nation Courts: Key Players in Nation Rebuilding," in Miriam Jorgensen, ed., *Rebuilding Native Nations, Strategies for Governance and Development* (2007); (with Joseph Thomas Flies-Away and Miriam Jorgensen) "Divorce and Real Property on American Indian Reservations: Lessons for First Nations and Canada," 29:2 *Atlantis: A Women's Studies Journal* (2005); (with Sarah Deer) *Tribal Criminal Law and Procedure* (2004); (with Paul Robertson and Miriam Jorgensen) "Indigenizing Evaluation Research: Raising the Tipi in the Oglala Sioux Nation," 28 *American Indian Quarterly* (2004).

KUʻUALOHA HOʻOMANAWANUI is a Kanaka Maoli scholar, poet, artist, and mālama ʻāina advocate. She is an assistant professor of Hawaiian Literature at the University of Hawaii at Mānoa and is also a founding and current Chief Editor of *ʻŌiwi: A Native Hawaiian Journal*. She has widely published both critical essays and creative writing in Hawaii and abroad. She was born in Kailua, Oʻahu, and raised in Wailua Homesteads, Kauaʻi, and has been a "Koʻolau" east-side girl her whole life, currently dividing her time between Anahola, Kauaʻi, and Haʻiku, Oʻahu.

KATHLEEN MARTIN is an assistant professor at Cal Poly State University in the Ethnic Studies Department, where she teaches courses in Indigenous Studies. She is a mother of three and grandmother of five, and her German, Irish, and Dakota family is from Minnesota and South Dakota. She holds an MA in Native traditions and a PhD in educational leadership, with an emphasis on culture, language, and literacy, from the University of California, Santa Barbara. Her research investigates the social, cultural, political, and historical relationships of Native peoples with the United States, including issues of land, culture, language, and education in Native communities. Her work has appeared in journals such as *Teaching and Teacher Education, Journal of School Effectiveness, Santa Barbara Papers in Linguistics*, and the *Encyclopedia of Religion*. Her most recent edited volume, *Indigenous Symbols and Practices in the Catholic Church: Visual Studies, Missionization and Appropriation* (2010), presents a multidisciplinary discussion of appropriation and missionization, spiritual and religious traditions, and educational issues in the teaching of art and art history, as well as the effects of government sanctions on traditional practice and the artistic interpretation of symbols from Native and Indigenous perspectives. She is co-founder with the California Indian Education Association and the University of California, Santa Barbara of the Community of Scholars: Gatherings of American Indian and Indigenous Students and Mentors.

ELVIRA PULITANO is an associate professor in the ethnic studies department at California Polytechnic State University, San Luis Obispo. Her research and teaching interests include indigenous studies, African diaspora literatures, Caribbean studies, theories of race and ethnicity, migration, diaspora, and human rights discourse. A Fulbright scholar from Italy, Dr. Pulitano holds a PhD in English from the University of New Mexico, where she specialized in Native American literatures and postcolonial studies. She is the author of *Toward a Native American Critical Theory* (2003) and has published essays on the work of Gerald Vizenor, Louis Owens, V. S. Naipaul, Caryl Phillips, Jamaica Kincaid, and Edwidge Danticat. She is also the editor of *Transatlantic Voices: Interpretations of Native North American Literatures* (2007). She is currently completing a monograph exploring literary representations of diaspora in Caribbean-born writers living in the United States. Before her current appointment at Cal Poly, she taught postcolonial literatures and theory at the universities of Geneva and Lausanne.

ISABELLE SCHULTE-TENCKHOFF is a professor at the Graduate Institute for International and Development Studies, Geneva. Her research focuses on the rights of non-state groups, and favors a non-Eurocentric approach to the role of indigenous peoples in the history of international relations. She is the author of, *inter alia, La question des peuples autochtones* (1997) and its sequel, *Introduction au droits des peuples autochtones* (forthcoming 2012 in the same series). Her publications also include the edited volume *Altérité et droit* (2002), as well as numerous articles published in Switzerland, France, and Canada.

LEE SCHWENINGER is Professor of English at the University of North Carolina Wilmington, where he teaches American Indian literature and serves as coordinator for the Native American Studies minor. In addition to several essays in book collections, he has published essays in such journals as *Studies in American Indian Literatures, American Indian Quarterly,* and *American Indian Culture and Research Journal.* He has published a book-length study of N. Scott Momaday (2001), and most recently a study of several Native American writers and the environment, *Listening to the Land: American Indian Literary Responses to the Landscape* (2008).

MILILANI B. TRASK is a Native Hawaiian attorney with an extensive background in Native Hawaiian land trusts, resources, and legal entitlements. In 1993, Ms. Trask became a member of the prestigious Indigenous Initiative for Peace (IIP), a global body of indigenous leaders convened by Nobel laureate Rigoberta Menchu-Tum. In 1995, she was elected the second vice chair of the General Assembly of Nations of the Unrepresented Nations and Peoples Organizations (UNPO), an international body founded by his holiness the Dalai Lama as an alternative forum to the United Nations. Ms. Trask is an acknowledged peace advocate, and studied and worked for seven years with Mother Theresa of Calcutta. In 2001, Ms. Trask was appointed as the Pacific representative to the United Nations Permanent Forum on Indigenous Issues and is currently considered an indigenous expert to the United Nations in international and human rights law. She is recognized as one of the primary authors of the United Nations Declaration on the Rights of Indigenous Peoples.

SHARON H. VENNE is an Indigenous Treaty person (Cree) and by marriage a member of the Blood Tribe within Treaty 7 with one son. She worked at the United Nations prior to the establishment of the Working Group on Indigenous Peoples in 1982. The background research to the many clauses on the Declaration on the Rights of Indigenous Peoples is included in her book: *Our Elders Understand Our Rights: Evolving International Law Regarding Indigenous Peoples* (1998). In addition, Venne has written numerous articles and edited materials related to the rights of indigenous peoples. She has lectured on the rights of indigenous peoples in Australia, Canada, France, Hawaii, Italy, New Zealand, Norway, Sweden, and the United States. In addition to her work on the

Declaration, she worked to secure a UN Study on Treaties. From the first introduction of the resolution in 1983 until the report was finalized in 1999, Venne worked to ensure that the report reflected indigenous laws and norms. All her work internationally and domestically relates to the promotion of the rights of indigenous peoples, especially rights related to lands, resources, and treaties. Some of her works on laws of the Cree Peoples related to treaty making were published in *Aboriginal and Treaty Rights in Canada* (Michael Asch, ed.) and *Natives and Settlers – Now and Then* (Paul DePasquale, ed.).

IRENE WATSON belongs to the Tanganekald and Meintangk peoples, traditional owners of the Coorong in South Australia. She is currently employed as an Associate Professor at the University of South Australia and is the author of a number of articles and books on Aboriginal peoples and the law. She is currently completing a manuscript, "Raw Law," for publication.

SIEGFRIED WIESSNER is a Professor of Law at St. Thomas University School of Law, Florida, and the founder and director of its LL.M. and J.S.D. programs in intercultural human rights. He holds a law degree (1977) as well as a Dr. iur. (1989) from the University of Tübingen and an LL.M. from Yale (1982). He is the editor-in-chief of Martinus Nijhoff's Studies in Intercultural Human Rights. Since 2008, he has served as the chair of the International Law Association's Committee on the Rights of Indigenous Peoples. From 2007 to 2010, he was a member of the American Society of International Law's Executive Council. He teaches US constitutional law and international law, and has written extensively in the fields of indigenous rights, international law, and jurisprudence, including "Rights and Status of Indigenous Peoples," 12 *Harvard Human Rights Journal* (1999); "Indigenous Sovereignty," 41 *Vanderbilt Journal of Transnational Law* (2008); and (with W. Michael Reisman et al.) *International Law in Contemporary Perspective* (2004).

ACKNOWLEDGMENTS

Projects such as these usually rely on the insight, support, and encouragement of many people. While it is impossible to list all the individuals to whom I owe a debt of gratitude for helping me shape ideas, finding sources, and offering suggestions, I would like at least to express my sincere thanks to a few. Deborah Madsen at the University of Geneva believed in this project from the very early stages, and I would like to acknowledge her long-time friendship and support. Conversations about the potential that the UN Declaration on the Rights of Indigenous Peoples offered for an interdisciplinary volume such as this one initiated at an international symposium on Native literatures and cultures at California Polytechnic State University, in San Luis Obispo, in autumn 2008. Deborah's enthusiasm was contagious and together we began sketching ideas and setting up the project's goals. We were both firmly convinced that this was going to be an important and timely collection, and I trusted our judgment. My research on indigenous peoples' presence at the United Nations goes back to the years 2002–2005 during my appointment as an assistant professor at the universities of Geneva and Lausanne, and I would like to thank the English departments of both institutions for giving me the opportunity to teach some inspiring courses in the field of postcolonial and indigenous studies. Gerald Vizenor, a long-time friend and inspiration, provided generous support and encouragement. The title for this book originated in a conversation we had on indigenous peoples' rights and international law, and I would like to acknowledge his original ideas on Native literatures and narratives of survivance. Equally grateful am I to Gordon Henry, Jr., and Kimberly Blaeser, whose creative vision has continued to inspire me in ways they cannot possibly imagine. I also thank Gary Dunham for supporting my scholarship over the years and for his excellent editorial work on indigenous literary studies.

I owe a special note of thanks to Kēhaulani Kauanui at Wesleyan University, who proved to be a valuable source of information in terms of suggesting potential contributors and offering overall support for this collection. My department colleague and friend Kate Martin deserves special recognition for her insight and knowledge, and for always reminding me that this was a project worth pursuing.

Mililani Trask's work as a human rights advocate has been truly inspiring, and I would like to thank her for supporting this collection all the way through, for helping me navigate some of the complexities of international law as they relate to the rights of indigenous peoples, and for her generous comments and observations during our conversation in Honolulu, in April 2010. Special thanks to my research assistant, Nestor Veloz, for transcribing my interview with Ms. Trask. I also owe a note of gratitude to Dore Minatodani at the Manoa Library, University of Hawaii, for helping me locate the reviews of the Peoples' International Tribunal and for sending precious information prior to my trip to Honolulu. Joan Lander, of Nā Maka o ka 'Āina video production team, offered generous and insightful comments on some of my questions on the Tribunal, and I would like to acknowledge her willingness to participate in a few e-mail exchanges. Special thanks to Joan and Puhipau for all those excellent documentaries on Hawaii.

John Purdy, at Western Washington University, deserves special thanks for providing valuable feedback when needed, editorial wisdom, and good humor, and I would like to thank him for his friendship and mentorship over the years. On the other side of the Atlantic, Mario Corona, at the University of Bergamo, has been an inspiring scholar and teacher, and I would like to acknowledge his continuous support during my numerous transatlantic crossings.

I would also like to thank all the contributors for their enthusiastic response to the subject of the Declaration, for their patience, and for working hard to bring this book into completion. I owe a special note of gratitude to Siegfried Wiessner for supporting this project from the very beginning, for generously sharing his expertise in international law in response to my numerous questions, and for providing excellent feedback as I was completing my introductory chapter. My students at California Polytechnic State University raised intriguing comments on indigenous rights and the evolving discipline of indigenous studies, and I want to thank them for their willingness to stand up against injustice and discrimination and to work for a better world. I also thank all my colleagues in the ethnic studies department – Victor Valle, Grace Yeh, Denise Isom, Jane Lehr, Aaron Rodrigues, and Don Ryujin – for their sincere support and encouragement. Thanks to Yolanda Tiscareño for being such a pillar in that department. I am also thankful to Michael Lucas, Tom Trice,

Brian Kennelly, Christina Firpo, and George Cotkin for believing in my work, for supporting ethnic studies at Cal Poly, and for all those excellent interdisciplinary conversations.

However, my biggest debt of gratitude is to my family and dear friends in Italy, whose love, care, and unconditional support have guided me throughout these years. To my father, who left me halfway through this journey, I offer my most heartfelt thanks. May his spirit and wisdom continue to guide me as I find my way away from home. *Ti voglio bene papà.*

~

Indigenous rights and international law:
an introduction

ELVIRA PULITANO

The reality of human rights provisions is more literary irony than protection. Yet, the declaration is a profound source of endurance in native stories, creative literature, and the everlasting narratives of survivance.

Gerald Vizenor, "Genocide Tribunals"

On September 13, 2007, the United Nations General Assembly adopted the Declaration on the Rights of Indigenous Peoples (UNDRIP or the Declaration), bringing to a conclusion a period of negotiations between nation states and indigenous peoples which had lasted nearly twenty-five years. By a vote of 143 in favor, with 11 abstentions and 4 against (Australia, Canada, New Zealand, and the United States), the Declaration defines the individual and collective rights of millions of indigenous peoples worldwide, and underscores the General Assembly's crucial role in setting international standards and moral and political and, at times, legal guidelines for states.[1] Unanimously celebrated as a landmark achievement for indigenous peoples and the UN system, the Declaration represents a momentous success for international law as well. For Claire Charters and Rodolfo Stavenhagen, "the Declaration is the most comprehensive and advanced of international instruments dealing with indigenous peoples' rights," and the fact that indigenous peoples, the "right bearers themselves," played a crucial role in the negotiations over its content, makes it "a first

---

[1] According to the UN Permanent Forum on Indigenous Issues (UNPFII), "more than 370 million indigenous people [currently live] in some 90 countries worldwide" (About UNPFII). UN official figures, however, are approximate, as these numbers are based on information provided by states and do not account for indigenous peoples not included in official state censuses. I am indebted to Mililani Trask for this information. The UNPFII is one of the three UN bodies responsible for dealing with indigenous issues. Established in 2000 by United Nations Economic and Social Council (ECOSOC) Resolution 2000/22, it reflects the growing concern on the part of the human rights organs and bodies of the UN over the plight of indigenous peoples (About Us/Mandate).

in international law" ("UN Declaration" 10). In April 2009, at the Durban Review conference, 182 states from all regions of the world issued a document in which they "Welcome[d] the adoption of the UN Declaration on the rights of indigenous peoples which has a positive impact on the protection of victims and, in this context, urge[d] States to take all necessary measures to implement the rights of indigenous peoples in accordance with international human rights instruments without discrimination" (Outcome Document para. 73).

Since the moment of adoption, the four countries that originally voted against the Declaration have changed their position. In April 2009 Australia officially endorsed the Declaration, a decision considered an important symbolic step towards rethinking the relationship between indigenous and non-indigenous Australians. In April 2010 New Zealand declared its support for the Declaration, followed in November and December by Canada and the United States respectively. In a fifteen-page document explaining the US government's position on the Declaration and discussing recent initiatives on Native American issues, it is stated that the Declaration "expresses aspirations of the United States, aspirations that this country seeks to achieve within the structure of the US Constitution, laws, and international obligations, while also seeking, where appropriate, to improve our laws and policies" (Announcement).[2] While referring to the fact that the Declaration is not a legally binding document, the United States acknowledges its moral and political force and would appear to be open to the possibility for improvement in laws and policies regarding indigenous rights.[3] Within this context, supporters of the Declaration are correct in welcoming it as an unprecedented opportunity for the international community to promote and confirm the collective rights of indigenous peoples in the twenty-first century. Within a month of its adoption, S. James Anaya, at the time of writing UN Special Rapporteur on the rights of indigenous peoples, and Siegfried Wiessner, now chair of the International Law Association's Committee on the Rights of Indigenous Peoples, celebrated the Declaration as "a milestone in the re-empowerment of the world's aboriginal groups." In their influential op-ed piece in the *Jurist*, they also stated that, in important parts, such as the rights to culture, self-determination, and land, the

---

[2] A closer look at the language of the Announcement, however, invites a cautious response as to what exactly the United States' support of the Declaration means. See Glenn Morris's commentary in *Indian Country Today* ("Still Lying").

[3] I elaborate on the legal status of the Declaration later on in this chapter.

Declaration also "reaffirms customary international law in the field" (Anaya and Wiessner).

The importance of the Declaration as an instrument of international law has drawn further scholarly attention, thanks to a growing body of literature devoted to its critical assessment; *Making the Declaration Work*, published in 2009 by the International Working Group of Indigenous Affairs (IWGIA), based in Copenhagen, was the first collection of essays produced by some of the participants directly involved in the drafting and adoption of the Declaration. Edited by Claire Charters and Rodolfo Stavenhagen, the volume "tells the story of the Declaration from the inside" while reflecting on "its broader social, cultural, and political significance into the future" ("UN Declaration" 11). For Stavenhagen, the Declaration "has opened the door to indigenous peoples as new world citizens" ("Making the Declaration Work" 355); whereas for Claire Charters the legitimacy of the Declaration, as a result of procedurally legitimate processes, fair content, and level of engagement, will obligate states to effect its provisions ("Legitimacy" 280, 298). *Reflections on the UN Declaration on the Rights of Indigenous Peoples* (2011), edited by Stephen Allen and Alexandra Xanthaki, also situates the Declaration within the context of international law while offering an in-depth institutional, thematic, and regional analysis of its content. Both collections raise interesting questions with regard to implementation and reflect on the significance of the Declaration for the governance of states. In the words of Allen and Xanthaki, the adoption of the Declaration represents "the beginning of a new phase in the debate on indigenous rights. Having focused on the coherence of indigenous claims within current international law, discussions should now turn to the challenges that the Declaration faces as well as the ones that the Declaration poses" (*Reflections* 7).[4]

Indigenous Rights in the Age of the UN Declaration contributes to the ongoing scholarship on the Declaration by advancing some of the discussions aforementioned. Specifically the volume interrogates whether international law, as illustrated in UNDRIP, is an instrument that indigenous peoples can use effectively for their emancipation and cultural

---

[4] An additional collection, *Indigenous Voices: The Declaration on the Rights of Indigenous Peoples* (2011), edited by Claire Charters, Les Malezer, and Victoria Tauli-Corpuz, is forthcoming in 2013. For additional legal assessments of UNDRIP, see Wiessner, "Indigenous Sovereignty", Odham and Frank, and, most recently, the Interim Report issued by the International Law Association Committee on the Rights of Indigenous Peoples (hereafter ILA Interim Report). This committee is entrusted with the mandate to write an authoritative legal commentary on the Declaration and on indigenous peoples' rights in general.

flourishing, and whether or not the quintessentially Eurocentric nature
of international law can be changed upon considering indigenous epistemologies and perspectives. With an interdisciplinary orientation ran-
ging from legal to anthropological to literary perspectives and indigenous
worldviews, the volume targets both specialized academic audiences and
a general public, located mostly (but not necessarily) in North America
and/or Europe and whose knowledge of indigenous histories and cultures remains significantly limited. As Kathleen Martin points out in
her contribution when discussing specifically the United States context,
"the struggle between Western and Native views with regard to ownership and land use continues to reveal 'cultural differences and conflicts'"
(Chapter 7). In most cases, Martin suggests, these cultural misperceptions
originate from past governmental actions against indigenous peoples.
Even though it might be argued that the utmost disrespect for indigenous peoples' rights has been prompted by vested economic and political
interests, it is undeniable that a general lack of education on indigenous
histories and cultures as well as a public attitude based on individual
rights has resulted in governments' policies aimed at ignoring indigenous
peoples' claims to self-determination. As has been contended by the main
actors involved in the development of the Declaration, indigenous legal
perspectives and cultures need to be taken into account if international
law is to be reoriented away from its Eurocentric origins. Contributors
to this volume evaluate the extent to which the Declaration represents
the beginning of a new phase in the debate of indigenous rights and the
potential that this landmark document has in affirming indigenous self-
determination. Important as it is, they argue, the Declaration by itself will
not produce significant change in the everyday lives of the millions of
indigenous peoples whose rights it purports to affirm. Change will ultimately come only if states, the general public, and the international community join together with indigenous peoples themselves to make decisions
and carry out programs that might indeed benefit indigenous peoples at
the grassroots level.[5] Such positive decisions have already been made in
many parts of the world, by both domestic legislators and judges and by
international human rights bodies, and contribute to an ever denser global quilt of state practice and *opinio juris*. UN Special Rapporteur James

---

[5] A similar view was expressed by the Office of the High Commissioner for Human Rights
and the UN Special Rapporteur on the Situation of Human Rights and Fundamental
Freedoms of Indigenous Peoples at the 2008 International Day of the World's Indigenous
Peoples (International Day).

Anaya, in particular, without contestation, measures state conduct using the legal "yardstick" of the Declaration (ILA Interim Report 5).

Unlike previous studies, this book also includes the literary perspective of indigenous writers on some of the issues discussed in the Declaration, setting up an interesting conversation between literature and law, theory and practice, legal discourse and lived experience. In the North American context specifically, Gordon Henry, Jr. (Anishinaabe), Thomas King (Cherokee), and Gerald Vizenor (Anishinaabe) among others have written with unrelenting humor about questions of repatriation of remains, museum collections, and ownership (the subject of Articles 11 and 12 of the Declaration), always upholding the centrality of stories to affirm Native histories and identities.[6] Whereas Western legal discourse is skeptical of the validity of stories and oral testimony as admissible evidence, Vizenor forcefully contends that stories have allowed individuals such as Charles Aubid, during a dispute with the federal government over the regulation of wild rice in Minnesota, to affirm "his *anishinaabe* human rights and sovereignty" ("Genocide Tribunals" 131). "Stories are wondrous things," Thomas King also states. "And they are dangerous" (*Truth* 9). So many stories have been told about Natives in North America that it is difficult to distinguish between (real) Natives and imaginary Indians. Yet, King states, "for those of us who are Indians, this disjunction between reality and imagination is akin to life and death" (*Truth* 54). Native American writers have been challenging imaginative constructions of *indianness* with stories that assert the presence of Native people on the American continent.[7] Against Western narratives of assimilation, termination, and conquest, Native writers tell stories of resilience and survival, stories that interrogate the past, make sense of the present, and imagine the future. In the specific context of the Declaration, Native writers continue to tell stories that affirm "the inherent dignity" and "inalienable rights" of indigenous peoples. These stories are also part of the debate on indigenous rights that the Declaration has contributed to fueling. And they deserve to be heard.

[6] My use of the term "Native American" (capitalized) in this study reflects commonly accepted usage among the writers whose work is the subject of analysis. The term "American Indian" is also currently accepted in the United States and is the term that Lee Schweninger uses in his contribution on repatriation and museum ownership. As for the use of the term "indigenous," this study adopts the "working definition" of indigenous peoples contained in the study by Martínez Cobo. I discuss the contested nature of the definition (or lack thereof) of the term "indigenous" in the Declaration below.

[7] Vizenor challenges representation of Native identity as "*indian*" by insisting that the term be spelled lower case and in italics. The word "*indian*," he says, is "a colonial enactment ... [a] simulation that has superseded real tribal names" (*Manifest Manners* 11).

The reality of human rights, Vizenor argues in "Genocide Tribunals," quoted in the epigraph to this chapter, is a rather ironic discourse for indigenous peoples, upon considering that blatant violations and downright denial of the most basic human rights have characterized the lives and experiences of indigenous peoples throughout history. At the same time, however, human rights provisions, as they were enunciated in the Universal Declaration of Human Rights (UDHR) and as they have now been reaffirmed in the UNDRIP, have inspired indigenous peoples to fight for the right of self-determination against ongoing attempts at assimilation and the eradication of their cultures.

From a broad historical perspective there is indeed a certain irony in the fact that the Declaration is framed in the language of international human rights law, the same law that legitimized the superiority of imperial colonial powers and the destruction of indigenous cultures. But international law is not immune to change any more than any other system of legal norms. The irony that various commentators have detected upon assessing the idiom of the Declaration might instead be welcomed as a significant change of direction in the legal tradition of states. According to H. Patrick Glenn, the Declaration plays a key role in moving international law "away from its original founding purpose and more open to non-state priorities, a movement recently described as 'humanizing'" ("Three Ironies" 174). In this sense the Declaration represents a significant shift in "the nature and direction of international law itself" (ibid. 174). In juxtaposing different truths, the Declaration, Glenn concludes, points to the possibility of the existence of "different types of law in the world" (ibid. 182). By demanding that the same human rights and freedoms contained in various UN human rights instruments be now extended to indigenous peoples, indigenous peoples in or through the Declaration have written the latest chapter in what Vizenor calls "the everlasting narratives of survivance" ("Genocide Tribunals" 156).

Whereas the two previously published collections have drawn attention to discussions on indigenous peoples' rights in an international framework by addressing regions such as Africa, Asia, the Arctic, and northern Europe, this volume has more of a North American focus.[8] Yet it could be argued that the North American angle of the essays presented here is representative of the status of most indigenous peoples globally. Indigenous

---

[8] And yet even these previous studies are limited in the kind of "global" reach they cover. Allen and Xanthaki, for instance, made the decision to "give priority to regions that have not been the focus of the literature on indigenous rights to date" (*Reflections* 6).

peoples in North America comprise Federally Recognized Tribes and Status Tribes, unrecognized tribes and groups, some of which are mixed-blood (part white, Metis, Kanaka), while others are tribes recognized by states but not by the federal government.[9] Clearly the status issue is going to play a key role in the implementation of the Declaration. Moreover, given the fact that the strongest opposition to the Declaration came from the United States and Canada and that these two governments continue, despite the recently announced endorsement, to oppose implementation in critical international arenas such as economic development and natural resources, it is most likely that their policies, clearly determined by their vested interests, are going to have an impact on other indigenous peoples from other regions.[10]

A closer look at the language of the Announcement of US support for the Declaration reveals significant ambiguities about what exactly the United States' pronounced support of the Declaration means. For example, when it comes to strengthening the government-to-government relationship with tribes, the announcement states: "the United States recognizes the significance of the Declaration's provisions on free, prior and informed consent, which the United States understands to call for a process of meaningful consultation with tribal leaders, *but not necessarily the agreement of those leaders*, before the actions addressed in those consultations are taken" (Announcement, emphasis added). Yet the Declaration affirms the principle of participation of indigenous peoples in matters that concern their internal affairs by stating that their "free, prior, and informed consent" must be obtained before states can adopt legislative measures that affect them (Articles 19, 32).[11] In light of these ambiguities, the North American focus of this collection, both geographically and in terms of how international law and the Declaration are perceived, provides an essential context for considering ways in which the Declaration could in the near future be used to influence the development of national laws and policies on indigenous issues. Upon considering the regional orientation of the collection as a whole (including the important

---

[9] The Kanaka Maoli of Hawaii, for instance, belong to the category of unrecognized people without any authority to command land and/or other rights, a privilege which is granted to the other Federally Recognized Tribes in the country.

[10] I am indebted to Mililani Trask for pointing out the importance of the status issue for the indigenous peoples of North America and the way in which it factors into the Declaration (Message to the Author, 26 April 2011).

[11] On the political participation recognized by UNDRIP, see s. 4 of the ILA Interim Report.

contribution on Australia's Northern Territory's recent policies affecting Aboriginal people), it is all the more interesting to observe that three of the four major countries to have endorsed the Declaration lately are also those that continue to oppose broad claims to self-determination on the part of their indigenous peoples.

A long and complex document, with a preamble and 46 articles, the Declaration recognizes the wide range of basic human rights and fundamental freedoms of indigenous peoples. It addresses topics as diverse as the indigenous peoples' inalienable collective right to the ownership, use, and control of lands, territories, and natural resources; their right to maintain and develop cultural and religious practices; their right to establish and control their educational systems; their rights to traditional medicine and cultural and traditional knowledge (intellectual property rights). The Declaration also recognizes the controversial "right to redress," whether in the form of monetary or land compensation, for the lands, territories, and resources which indigenous peoples "have traditionally owned or otherwise occupied or used"; it affirms in Article 3 a broad right to self-determination although cabined by references to internal and local affairs (Article 4) and the territorial integrity of states (Article 46). Central to all these issues is the question of the indigenous peoples' right to self-determination under international law, an issue where the positions of government representatives and indigenous peoples may be seen as incommensurable.[12] Arguably, there is discrepancy between Article 3, which, as stated, affirms the right to self-determination, and Article 46, which safeguards the "territorial integrity or political unity of sovereign independent states." Originating in the language of the Declaration on the Granting of Independence to Colonial Countries and Peoples, the provisions of Article 46 are standard in international law. According to Mililani Trask, international law provides that "States have the right to exist as long as they recognize the right of self-determination of peoples" (Message, 3 April 2010).[13] For James Anaya the

---

[12] Although many of the rights set out in the Declaration are collective in nature, framed in the terms "indigenous peoples have the right ... ," references to the rights of individuals to enjoy all human rights and fundamental freedoms guaranteed in the UN Charter add to the controversy surrounding the nature and content of the Declaration. In most cases, as James Anaya notes, both sets of rights tend to coincide ("Right" 193). For Anaya and other prominent indigenous rights advocates, the Declaration substantiates the principle of self-determination and related human rights historically denied to indigenous peoples. See also Schulte-Tenckhoff's chapter in this volume.

[13] A renowned attorney with expertise in international and human rights law, Mililani Trask was appointed as the Pacific representative to the Permanent Forum on Indigenous

tension between self-determination and state sovereignty doctrine provides "an animating force for efforts toward reconciliation." He writes:

> While state sovereignty doctrine limits the application of self-determination norms through the international system, the limitations are conditional and should not be considered as incompatible with, or debilitating to, self-determination values. Ideally, sovereignty doctrine and human rights precepts, including those associated with self-determination, work in tandem to promote a stable and peaceful world. ("Right" 196)

Yet when it comes to the Declaration it is far from clear in what sense states are going to accept the right of self-determination for indigenous peoples. It is often reiterated that indigenous peoples do not seek secession but a degree of autonomy and self-government within the state in which they live. In other words, they are more interested in exercising the right of *internal* rather than *external* self-determination. This, however, does not preclude the argument that they might pursue secession in appropriate cases. As stated in the Interim Report of the International Law Association (ILA) Committee on the Rights of Indigenous Peoples (2010), "under general international law indigenous peoples who find themselves in such a condition have the right to pursue secession. In this and other self-determination-related-respects, indigenous peoples must be exactly considered as all other peoples" (10). Self-determination for indigenous peoples often entails the right to determine their own destiny and govern themselves or, in the words of Mme Erica Irene Daes, the former chair of WGIP, "to live well and humanly in their own ways" ("Concepts of Self-Determination").

Upon analyzing the language of Articles 3 and 4 in the Declaration, the nature and scope of the right of self-determination for indigenous peoples is indisputable. But when considering that the exercise of this right has to be interpreted in the light of other provisions – notably Article 46 – then it might be argued, as some of the contributors to this volume maintain, that the Declaration promotes a limited right to internal self-determination for indigenous peoples.[14] More significantly, the language of the Declaration,

---

Issues to serve a three-year term beginning in January 2002. As a member of the Working Group on Indigenous Populations (WGIP) in Geneva, Trask worked on the Draft Declaration along with Mme Erica Daes, chair of the WGIP, from the very beginning of the negotiations.

UNGA Resolution 1514 (XV) on the Granting of Independence to Colonial Countries and Peoples rejects "any attempt aimed at the partial or total destruction of the national unity and the territorial integrity of a country."

[14] See also Helen Quane's discussion in Allen and Xanthaki.

by stressing the benefits of collaboration between states and indigenous peoples when it comes to control over lands and natural resources, makes the overall question of internal self-determination much more difficult to resolve.

The ILA Interim Report concludes the section on self-determination with the following statement: "Because indigenous peoples are numerous and diverse, the implementation and application of Article 3 should not be uniform. But the language of Article 3 will be important in facilitating the ability of indigenous peoples, who have been marginalized for so long, to live their lives in conformity with the values that are important to them" (11–12). Siegfried Wiessner has recently concluded that this goal of safeguarding cultural diversity undergirds the entire Declaration:

> The threat to the survival of their culture ... underlies indigenous peoples' demands to live on their traditional lands, to continue their inherited ways of life, to self-government. Cultural preservation and flourishing is thus at the root of the claims as recognized by the states; this goal, not primarily political or economic objectives, inspires the positive law guarantees. In this broad sense, all the rights of indigenous peoples are cultural rights, and any interpretation of these rights, whether in UNDRIP or other instruments and prescriptions recognizing rights of indigenous peoples, ought to keep this *telos* in mind. ("Cultural Rights")

The conciliatory rhetoric envisioned by the Declaration and endorsed by its supporters might result in "a world that might someday be" (Sambo Dorough 264),[15] but as the contributors to this volume point out, as Trask argues in the afterword, and as Anaya himself recognizes throughout his impressive range of work and the interventions he has made in the role of Special Rapporteur on the rights of indigenous peoples, the reality is much more complex than what legal provisions might at first suggest.[16] The fact that all the existing literature on the Declaration to date has drawn attention to the necessity of implementing its provisions testifies to what Stavenhagen calls the "implementation gap between laws and practical reality" ("Making the Declaration Work" 367).

[15] Sambo Dorough's expression is borrowed from Margaret Wise Brown's *The Dream Book*.

[16] Created in 2001 by the Human Rights Council, the Special Rapporteur on the situation of human rights and fundamental freedoms of indigenous peoples, now designated as the Special Rapporteur on the rights of indigenous peoples, works to promote agreements between indigenous peoples and states, reports on human rights violations against indigenous peoples in selected countries, and engages states in constructive dialogue. Crucial also is his role in promoting UNDRIP. Professor Anaya was elected Special Rapporteur in 2008, replacing Rodolfo Stavenhagen (James Anaya – UNSR Website).

Skepticism also remains as to the capacity of the Declaration to reshape international law in the postcolonial era when it comes to the definition (or lack thereof) of the term "indigenous." Nowhere in UNDRIP do we find a clear definition of this term. Indigenous peoples themselves forcefully opposed the inclusion of an official definition by arguing that definitions and categorizations have determined indigenous peoples' lives since first contact with European settlement or other colonizing powers. In lieu of definitions, a series of criteria have been advanced within various international forums and most recently in the UN Permanent Forum on Indigenous Issues (UNPFII). As listed in the ILA's Interim Report, these criteria include self-identification (as both indigenous and a people); historical continuity with pre-settler societies; special relationship with ancestral lands; distinctiveness (having distinct, political, social, and economic systems, and distinct cultures); non-dominance (forming non-dominant groups within the current society); and perpetuation (desire to maintain and reproduce their distinct ways of life) (Interim Report 7–8).[17] The ILA's report explains that not all of these criteria have to be met for a community to be defined indigenous, a "flexible approach" in line with the diversity of the countless indigenous peoples living in different parts of the world. The report also clarifies that some conceptualization of the term "indigenous" might be necessary in preventing states from fulfilling their responsibility by arguing that the Declaration does not apply to their own country "in light of the assumed absence of indigenous peoples within their borders" (Interim Report 7).

The ambiguity over who can be considered indigenous according to the Declaration has prompted a number of "national minorities," also known as "stateless nations," and subaltern groups to look at the Declaration as a potential instrument to affirm their human rights and dignity in light of historic injustices.[18] In other words, by seeking the recognition of their status as "indigenous" in order to get international protection, these groups see in the Declaration a powerful instrument to advance their interests in maintaining their identity, their culture, and their language. This is a much contested debate and one that is beyond the scope of this chapter, or this volume for that matter. But it is a debate certainly worth initiating in the near future within the context of the challenges that the Declaration

---

[17] This understanding of the term draws on the UN Permanent Forum on Indigenous Issues' Factsheet of October 21, 2007. See also Wiessner, "Rights and Status."

[18] Groups such as the Crimean Tatars, the Roma, the Afro-Latino, Palestinians, Chechens, Dalits, and Tibetans along with the Kurds have recently debated the option of whether to identify themselves as "indigenous" (Kymlicka 205–06).

poses. According to Will Kymlicka the UN has erected "a firewall" between the rights of indigenous peoples and national minorities ("Beyond" 207), and it is quite unlikely that a broader rethinking of categories currently used in international law is going to take place in the near future. Even though differences between indigenous peoples and national minorities are obvious, the history of oppression, discrimination, and ongoing injustices that both groups have endured makes them, according to various experts, similar vulnerable groups searching for rights and international recognition. Within the specific UN context, Kymlicka also argues that the overlap in participation in the UN Working Group on Minorities and the UN Working Group on Indigenous Populations makes the distinction between minorities and indigenous peoples arguable ("Beyond" 185). A completely opposite view is held by those actors and commentators who rely on the above-mentioned criteria for understanding indigenousness, especially the relationship between indigenous peoples and their ancestral lands, in order to advance the rights of indigenous peoples under international law. In light of this principle, they contend, it would be hard to maintain the claim to indigenous status for groups such as the Roma, Celts, or immigrants in general.

Indigenous rights and the UN system

Article 40 of the UN Declaration on the Rights of Indigenous Peoples states:

> Indigenous peoples have the right to access to and prompt decision through just and fair procedures for the resolution of conflicts and disputes with States or other parties, as well as to effective remedies of all infringements of their individual and collective rights. *Such a decision shall give due consideration to the customs, traditions, rules, and legal systems of the indigenous peoples concerned and international human rights.* (UNDRIP 40, emphasis added)[19]

As various contributions to the present volume point out, the essentially Eurocentric nature of dominant state law (both the civil- and the common-law systems are deeply grounded in Western epistemology and Western legal thought) makes it difficult to reconcile the rights of indigenous peoples, rights originating in the customs, traditions, and rules of their legal systems, with European values and worldviews. The

---

[19] All the quotations from UNDRIP are from the online version posted on the UNPFII website. The page numbers refer to the PDF version also available on the website.

United States, along with Canada and New Zealand, have time and again disregarded their treaty obligations with regard to indigenous peoples, violating both domestic and international law in order to advance their interests. And Australia, to mention one more example among the European settler colonies which first originated in the fifteenth-century age of "discoveries," had never negotiated a single treaty with its indigenous inhabitants, the doctrine of *terra nullius* remaining in full force until 1992, when, in *Mabo* v. *Queensland (No. 2)*, the High Court of Australia finally recognized Native title.

At the onset of what would later become our current understanding of international law, indigenous peoples were not entitled to rights, a commonly held view that dates back to the sixteenth-century Council of the Indies in Valladolid, Spain, which concluded that indigenous peoples could not be granted legal status. The modern international community of states, whose origin is usually traced to the Treaty of Westphalia of 1648, simply carried on the Eurocentric idea held by sixteenth-century Spanish intellectuals that indigenous peoples could not be included in the judicial system of nation states. As Venne posits, "with the doctrine of discovery as a guiding principle – despite its lack of legal legitimacy – European countries began to carve up the world of Indigenous Nations" (*Our Elders* 8). Within the context of UNDRIP, this age-old debate continued in the attempt to deny indigenous peoples the status of "peoples" and therefore the right to self-determination guaranteed by the UN Charter and other UN-issued international instruments.[20] Even though the UN Draft Declaration on the Rights of Indigenous Peoples, developed by the UN Working Group on Indigenous Populations in 1993, expressly recognized the right of indigenous peoples to self-determination, governments participating in the early work of the United Nations originally did not reach a broad consensus over the affirmation of such a right. As noted by Anaya, "a misguided tendency to equate the word *self-determination* with decolonization procedures or with an absolute fight to form an independent state" inevitably conditioned these governments' response (*Indigenous Peoples* 110–11). Such a narrow understanding of the term "self-determination," Anaya argues, was strongly influenced

[20] Part 1 (Art. 1) of both the International Covenant on Civil and Political Rights and the International Covenant on Economic, Social, and Cultural Rights, UNGA Res. 2200 (1966), entered into force Jan. 3, 1976, contain a self-determination provision that reads: "all peoples have the right to self-determination. By virtue of that right they freely determine their political status and freely pursue their economic, social, and cultural development." See also Anaya, *Indigenous Peoples*, 97–103.

by attributes of statehood and sovereign boundaries, a reasoning that within our increasingly interconnected and interdependent network of human associations appears rather anachronistic. He writes:

> Properly understood, the principle of self-determination, commensurate with the value it incorporates, benefits groups – that is, "peoples" in the ordinary sense of the term – throughout the spectrum of humanity's complex web of interrelationships and loyalties, and not just peoples defined by existing or perceived sovereign boundaries … The term *peoples* in this context … should be understood to refer to all those spheres of community, marked by elements of identity and collective consciousness, within which people's lives unfold – independently of consideration of historical or postulated sovereignty. These include not just the aggregate populations of states and colonial territories but other spheres of community that define human existence and place in the world, including indigenous peoples as well as other groups. (*Indigenous Peoples* 103)

Anaya refers to the Haudenosaunee political philosophy expressed in the Great Law of Peace to point out how it is becoming more and more necessary, within the international community, to move beyond the parameters of classical Western liberalism in the attempt to understand the political development of a world no longer divided into "exclusive monolithic communities" (*Indigenous Peoples* 102). The Haudenosaunee envisioned "a great tree with roots extending in the four cardinal directions to all peoples of the earth" (ibid.). As noted by Paul Wallace, "all nations would see these roots … and, if they were people of goodwill, would desire to follow them to their source and take shelter with others under the tree" (*Iroquois Book of Life* 28).

The increasing direct participation of indigenous peoples in the international arena has played a significant role in transforming the nature and content of international law.[21] In December 1992, at the inauguration ceremony of the International Year of the World's Indigenous Peoples, representatives of indigenous communities and organizations conveyed the vision of a world in which indigenous nations are finally granted the

---

[21] Even though the Universal Declaration of Human Rights, usually considered the most influential instrument of contemporary human rights discourse, does not mention the rights of indigenous peoples specifically, references to indigenous rights in the post-World War II international legal scene go back to the 1957 ILO Convention on Indigenous and Tribal Populations (modified in 1969). However, according to Mary Lawlor, it was not until the 1966 International Covenant on Civil and Political Rights and the International Covenant on Economic Social and Cultural Rights that indigenous peoples could claim self-determination under international law (*Public Native America* 171–2). See also Anaya, *Indigenous Peoples* 49–94.

dignity and respect enunciated in the Universal Declaration of Human Rights. Addressing the international community, they called attention to concepts of indigenous law beyond the narrow parameters of Western legal thought. Chief Oren R. Lyons, faithkeeper of the Haudenosaunee, talked about his people's belief in "the seventh generation to come" with respect to the generation yet unborn which can only be implemented by obeying the law of life, the seed, within which is "the mysterious and spiritual force of life and creation" ("Living History" 175, 176). Williams A. Means of the International Indian Treaty Council referred to the web of life by quoting Chief Seattle of the Sequamish Nation who stated that even Europeans are a single strand on this web and that "injury to one part of the web does injury to the whole" ("Living History" 190). And Thomas Banyacya, the spiritual leader of the Hopi Nation, told about the Hopi prophecies that led to the creation of the current fourth world and of the fragile condition of our planet as a result of human neglect and greed. Mr. Banyacya spoke a message of peace and invited members of the UN to visit Hopiland and learn about "the spiritual vision and power of the elders" ("Living History" 219). "Indigenous Peoples – A New Partnership" was the theme of the 1993 Year of the World's Indigenous Peoples, a year which was later transformed into an International Decade (1995–2004) and is currently continuing into a second International Decade (2005–2015) (Second International Decade).

The most significant development of the Year of the World's Indigenous Peoples was undoubtedly the creation of the UN Permanent Forum on Indigenous Issues (UNPFII), which provides expertise to the United Nations Economic and Social Council (ECOSOC) in areas that affect indigenous peoples and raises awareness on indigenous issues within the UN system (UN Permanent Forum). The UNPFII met for the first time in 2002 and ever since has played an active role in negotiations.[22]

The adoption of the Declaration on the Rights of Indigenous Peoples has reinvigorated the debates over sovereignty, indigenous rights, and the international legal framework. From the perspective of the UNPFII, "The Declaration is the most comprehensive statement of the rights of indigenous peoples ever developed, giving prominence to collective rights to a degree unprecedented in international human rights law" (UN

---

[22] According to Lawlor, the role of the UNPFII within the UN member states is rather prestigious, its position comparable to the Human Rights Commission itself ("Indigenous Internationalism" 175). Watson and Venne, by contrast, argue in this volume that the power of the Permanent Forum to draft standards or hear complains "remains significantly limited" (Chapter 3).

Permanent Forum). Though not legally binding itself, the Declaration's norms, reflecting preexisting or later emerging customary international law, Siegfried Wiessner notes, "are binding on states that do not qualify as persistent objectors" ("Indigenous Sovereignty" 1165).[23] The ILA's Interim Report states:

> [E]ven though it cannot be maintained that UNDRIP as a whole can be considered as an expression of customary international law, some of its key provisions can reasonably be regarded as corresponding to established practices of general international law, therefore implying the existence of equivalent and parallel international obligations to which States are *bound* to comply with [*sic*]. (43, emphasis in original)

Pertinent state practice at both the domestic and international level, according to the authors of the report, unequivocally reflects the fact that certain norms that are necessary to safeguard the basic rights of indigenous peoples "are today crystallized in the realm of customary international law" (43).[24] Of the same opinion is UN Special Rapporteur S. James Anaya (*Indigenous Peoples* 49–72).

The most debated point of contention, however, in terms of the language of the Declaration, remains the interpretation of the concepts of sovereignty and self-government. The diverse perspectives offered in this volume on such fundamental principles attest to the complexity of reconciling contrasting worldviews and epistemologies between indigenous peoples and Western states, and raise compelling questions on the effectiveness of bringing the Declaration to life by way of implementing its provisions. According to Wiessner, the deliberately indeterminate nature of the range of self-government granted to indigenous peoples under the Declaration might ultimately be a positive factor, "given the diversity of indigenous peoples' lives, traditions, and aspirations" ("Indigenous Sovereignty" 1166). This indeterminacy, Wiessner suggests, ultimately

---

[23] For recent Supreme Court decisions and pertinent laws in individual countries that acknowledge or incorporate UNDRIP, see Wiessner, "Introductory Note." Among all the countries in the world, Bolivia was the first country to implement the full Declaration as federal law. See also Kēhaulani Kauanui's audio interview in 2009 with Andrea Carmen (Yacqui Indian Nation), Executive Director of the International Indian Treaty Council.

[24] More skeptical with regard to the Declaration's international legal status is Stephen Allen. He suggests that the Declaration should be considered as a "highly persuasive tool" to be utilized in municipal laws and policies within states rather than an instrument of international law which some indigenous rights advocates would like to force upon "ambivalent States" ("UN Declaration" 252). And yet one could argue that the "international legal project" that he advises abandoning is an essential vehicle for overcoming states' traditional divide-and-conquer policies vis-à-vis indigenous peoples.

plays in favor of indigenous peoples in that, as it is, the language of the Declaration pushes the boundaries of international law beyond the Eurocentric legal framework to embrace fundamental indigenous epistemologies. On indigenous sovereignty Wiessner quotes Vine Deloria, Jr., for whom a significant understanding of indigenous sovereignty needs to take into account the cultural integrity of the people. Deloria writes: "so long as the cultural identity of Indians remains intact no specific act undertaken by the United States government can permanently extinguish Indian peoples as sovereign entities" ("Self-Determination" 121–22). Implicit in an indigenous notion of sovereignty as intended by Deloria is the concept of justice as a principle that aims at maintaining the cultural cohesiveness of the people.

In the introductory essay to *Justice as Healing: Indigenous Ways* (2005), James Sákéj Youngblood Henderson and Wanda McCaslin equate the process of healing to a reclamation of indigenous heritage, culture, knowledge, and jurisprudence as founding elements to respond to the systemic ongoing domination and colonization of indigenous lands and cultures. Unlike European notions of justice as deterrence and punishment, the old indigenous tradition of justice as healing aims at achieving balance and harmony in families and communities. Rather than a mere abstract, universal theory of rational ideas about the right and the just, aboriginal understandings of justice as healing originate from the lived experience of people who feel deeply connected to their cultures and traditions (McCaslin 3–4). Similarly, Dalee Sambo Dorough argues that "within indigenous justice systems, there is more emphasis on duties, obligation and responsibilities within these collectivities rather than rights ("Significance" 274). The most distinct aspect of such a worldview, she claims, is "the intimate linkage between the natural world, spirituality, and collective relations, which stands in contrast to the separation of religion and governance" found in most Western states ("Significance" 274). Upon considering that the Declaration articulates an ambivalent tension between individual and collective rights, with the language of international human rights discourse not exactly translating into the fundamental principles of jurisprudence upheld by indigenous peoples, it remains to be seen how future interpretations of the Declaration mediate indigenous notions of sovereignty and justice with human rights discourse and elements of international law.

In the first of the chapters presented here, Siegfried Wiessner cuts to the heart of the debates generated by the Declaration by exploring the concept of indigenous sovereignty. Retracing the historical meaning of the traditional Western notion of sovereignty and its dynamization via the principle of self-determination, Wiessner guides us through the global indigenous political resurgence starting in the 1970s and the development of customary international law through very widespread, often novel state practice and *opinio juris*, to finally analyze the effect of the 2007 UN Declaration. Starting from the premise that "law, in essence, ought to serve human beings," Wiessner argues that any law directed to serve the needs and values of indigenous peoples should be based on their claims and aspirations, what he calls their "inner worlds." While acknowledging that the Declaration might ultimately not respond to all the needs and aspirations of indigenous peoples, Wiessner concludes by offering a preferred vision of the future shape of international and domestic laws, a vision that the parties interested in implementing the Declaration should unquestionably consider. "Indigenous and non-indigenous forces," he argues, "need to combine in order to realize all of these aspirations."

The next two essays take a closer look at the text of the Declaration pointing out some of its significant limitations. In Chapter 2, "Treaties, peoplehood, and self-determination: understanding the language of rights in the UN Declaration," Isabelle Schulte-Tenckhoff analyzes the twofold reductionism characterizing the debate over indigenous peoples' rights. Indigenous peoples are increasingly collapsed with minorities. As a result, indigenous rights are, more often than not, addressed as rights exercised by individuals in community with other members of their group, rather than peoples' rights. Upon examining the language of the Declaration, Schulte-Tenckhoff is concerned with the effects of distinguishing all at once collective (minority-type) rights and group rights from individual human rights. To argue her point, she refers to Article 37 of the Declaration, which addresses treaties between indigenous peoples and states, and explores on this basis the changing meanings of self-determination. Since the principle of non-discrimination is crucial to the discourse of international human rights, tensions inevitably occur between rights derived from the human rights framework, which applies to all individuals, and special rights claimed by non-state actors, especially indigenous peoples. In their understanding of self-determination as a group right, indigenous peoples, Schulte-Tenckhoff argues, continue to fight for their lands and treaty rights, seeking redress for centuries of injustices. But they must do so within a system that ironically deprives them "of the possibility to claim any form of legal standing as peoples under international law." Following Schulte-Tenckhoff's theoretical framework, in Chapter 3 Irene Watson and Sharon Venne engage in a close reading of some of the provisions of the Declaration and compare and contrast them with the earlier 1993 Draft Declaration agreed on by the Working Group on Indigenous Populations (WGIP) in Geneva. Watson and Venne argue that the current UN Declaration has visibly shifted the focus from "the rights of people to self-determination under international law to indigenous peoples as human rights issues within their respective colonial states." Clauses that made specific reference to the UN Charter and rights of self-determination were eliminated from the 2007 text, leaving the state as the ultimate "determiner" of all the major aspects of the life of the state, including of course the lives of indigenous peoples. Within this context, Watson and Venne read the provision of Article 46 (on states' territorial integrity and political unity) as significantly limiting the possibility for indigenous peoples to "[be] able to develop and articulate a de-colonized Aboriginal space." While acknowledging the possibility that the Declaration might be used to negotiate domestic reforms and assist in the interpretation of the terms used under human rights law, they argue that, both at local levels and within the UN forums, there is currently no effective mechanism by which indigenous peoples can draft standards and enforce measures reflecting the current position of indigenous peoples across the globe. Despite the good rhetoric of the Declaration, which proclaims to be a "standard of achievement to be pursued in a spirit of partnership and mutual respect" (Preamble), such spirit, Watson and Venne posit, remains rather idealistic.

In the light of Australia's endorsement, in April 2009, of the Declaration, the 2007 Northern Territory Emergency Response (NTER) package of draconian policies targeting Aboriginal communities and their rights to self-determination indeed raises the urgency of how states can be made to comply with the rights they have committed themselves to protect and promote. In Chapter 4 Sheila Collingwood-Whittick examines Australia's Northern Territory Intervention measures in terms of the biased ethno-historical constructions of indigenous violence and a "dystopian vision" of Aboriginal culture that has been present in Australia since colonial times. Decoding NTER discourse, Collingwood-Whittick argues that the policies the government is now implementing both in the Northern Territory and elsewhere in Australia derive not so much from a deep concern for the high level of alcoholism and sexual abuse among Aboriginal communities, but rather from a desire to affirm cultural homogeneity at the center of a nationalist discourse that cannot bear to imagine any other relationship with its indigenous peoples than forced assimilation. Reading the Northern Territory's post-NTER decision to dismantle bilingual education against Articles 14 and 15 of the Declaration, which uphold the rights of indigenous peoples "to control their educational systems and institutions" and to provide "education in their own languages," Collingwood-Whittick argues that "Australia has delivered what might well prove the *coup de grâce* to Aboriginal identity." It remains to be seen, she concludes, whether UNDRIP can be brought to bear on the former settler colony or whether Australia's endorsement remains indeed, as some commentators have put it, an empty gesture aimed at enhancing the country's international reputation.

In "Articulating Indigenous Statehood: Cherokee State Formation and Implications for UNDRIP," Clint Carroll in Chapter 5 looks at the overall dichotomy between indigenous peoples and "the states" as presented in the Declaration as a departure point for discussing newly forming indigenous states. Using the Cherokee Nation as "a springboard," he argues against the widespread notion that indigenous nations are the antithesis of states as is clearly suggested by the unwillingness on the part of the UN system to acknowledge the legitimacy of American Indian nations. In the light of recent indigenous political transformations, Carroll invites a re-vision of what constitutes an indigenous state. Indigenous states, he posits, have the ability to "play the game while contesting its terms." Drawing from historical and contemporary Cherokee political formations, Carroll demonstrates that indigenous states need not be viewed merely as replications of mainstream forms; rather, their uniqueness – as transculturated political entities and sites of indigenous articulation – affords them the potential to transform how we think about international relations and global politics. In conversation with other significant works on settler-state indigenous politics, Carroll argues that indigenous states, *as political structures*, have the ability to assert "difference and autonomy without implying secession" and thus effectively occupy a "political third space."

Carrie Garrow investigates in Chapter 6 whether the Declaration should be used to defend the rights of the Haudenosaunee to "freely pass and repass" the border between Canada and the United States established in 1794 by the Jay Treaty. Over two hundred years later, she argues, both countries have significantly altered the interpretations of the Haudenosaunee Treaty rights, as numerous court battles, fought on both sides of the border, clearly demonstrate. In the light of the fact that Haudenosauneee political philosophy understands the principles of rights and sovereignty in distinctively different terms from Western political philosophy, the question whether the Declaration, deeply grounded in Western understanding of human rights, can truly advance the rights of the Haudenosaunee remains. Focusing on Articles 36 and 37, which address the rights affecting indigenous peoples divided by international borders and the overall protection guaranteed by treaties, Garrow argues that the Declaration, in these specific provisions, is supportive of Haudenosaunee philosophy: "it is not simply the right of an individual to cross the border, but a right to exist as nations and as a confederacy." Yet, she argues, the Declaration cannot be the ultimate tool in defense of Haudenosaunee rights under the Jay Treaty. Political action and strategy will be all the more necessary as domestic courts clearly fail to protect the rights guaranteed by treaties. Using the Declaration as a framework, Garrow suggests that it is imperative for Haudenosaunee nations, along with other Indian nations, to negotiate with the United States and Canada to adopt legislation that supports the border-crossing rights guaranteed by the Jay Treaty. In the spirit of traditional Haudenosaunee diplomacy, she posits, such negotiations become the most viable solution to keeping the border "ten feet above our head."

The most contentious articles of the Declaration, Articles 25 and 26, which address the rights of indigenous peoples to lands, territories, and resources, are discussed by Kathleen Martin in Chapter 7, which focuses on the quintessential disparity between the general public's understanding of the natural world, usually conceived in terms of economic development, and indigenous peoples' philosophy of reciprocal relationships, intended as moral and ethical behavior toward the earth and its inhabitants. Focusing on the United States, Martin uses the response of non-Native university students to a survey she administered in one of her courses to demonstrate the visible contrast between the general public's notion of *rights* vis-à-vis Native understanding of *responsibilities* toward the earth and all its living creatures. The US legal system, she argues, "is built upon the rarified and idealized notion of the individual and individual rights," a view diametrically opposed to community rights and the responsibilities that come with them upheld by Native peoples in the United States. Contextualizing some of the Native views on responsibilities to land and places within ongoing disputes over public lands and sacred sites (such as, for instance, Mato Tipila, known as Devils Tower, and Bear Butte State Park in South Dakota), Martin argues that the definitions in the articles of the Declaration, while explicitly creating "conditions to address the wrongs of the past," implicitly "foster the idea that rights, once established and put into print, can alleviate misperceptions and bring about justice." The absence, from the language of the Declaration, of the quintessential view upheld by Native peoples about care and responsibility for their land constitutes, for Martin, a significant obstacle with regard to the possibility of educating a dominant public view to change attitudes and correct misperceptions. While the endorsement of the UN Declaration on the part of the United States is a significant step forward, Martin argues that furthering the education of the generations to come is all the more critical.

The next two chapters address specifically Native, North American writers' responses to some of the provisions set out in the Declaration. In the same year that UNDRIP was adopted by the UN General Assembly, indigenous groups from across the Americas convened in Iximché (Guatemala) and issued a Declaration in which they "reaffirmed their 'decision to defend the nutritional sovereignty and struggle against the trans-genetic invasion.'" Food sovereignty and Native literary studies are the subject of Chapter 8 by Joni Adamson. Focusing on the work of Diane Glancy and Leslie Marmon Silko, Adamson discusses "how literature can contribute to a better understanding of hemispheric American indigenous alliance-building" directed at protecting intellectual property rights. Positioning Gloria Anzaldúa as a "Native border writer" (and mindful of the controversy that such a critical gesture entails), Adamson posits that understanding the events experienced by Anzaldúa's family in the Lower Rio Grande Valley between the 1930s and the 1980s is essential to grasping some of the key arguments currently being advanced by indigenous and small-scale farmers around the world, who are building alliances across nations, identities, and cultures in order to protect their "nutritional sovereignty." Adamson's reading of noted Native American novels such as Leslie Marmon Silko's *Garden in the Dunes* (1999) and *Almanac of the Dead* (1991) provides her with a framework to discuss science, genetically engineered crops, intellectual property rights, and the overall threat that international trade laws which support powerful international corporations pose not only to indigenous peoples' cultural heritage and traditional knowledge but to our global food system as a whole. As explicit as the language of Article 31 of the Declaration is with regard to indigenous peoples' rights to protect and develop their "human and genetic resources, seeds, medicines, and knowledge of the properties of fauna and flora," Adamson argues that indigenous peoples "cannot rely on any one document to achieve their objectives." Rather, they are organizing at the hemispheric and global levels to create documents that provide indigenous groups and the countries in which they live with a basis in international law for the protection of property rights that are key to securing a more healthy and peaceful future. From food sovereignty and intellectual property rights the discussion turns to issues of repatriation and redress in American Indian literature. Lee Schweninger in Chapter 9 examines Articles 11 and 12 of the Declaration in the context of the Native American Grave Protection and Repatriation Act (NAGPRA), since both texts raise the question of the validity of relying on Western ideologies and Western ways of understanding notions of indigeneity and ownership – in this specific case, as they apply to the right to own material culture and to repatriate human remains. He argues that contemporary Native American Indian writers powerfully "represent and/or challenge the ideas of ownership," closing therefore "the gaps between notions of international law and indigenous rights." Starting from the premise that "human rights is after all a matter of storytelling," Schweninger discusses the work of Native American writers such as Greg Sarris, Gerald Vizenor, and Gordon Henry, while reminding readers that responses to issues of museum collections and repatriations by American Indian writers in some cases pre-date NAGPRA. These writers, Schweninger argues, in the act of telling stories, "are making manifest the importance of human and specifically indigenous rights in the contexts of museums and repatriation."

The importance of the Declaration in the past, present, and future of the Native Hawaiians (Kanaka Maoli) is the topic of the two concluding chapters in the collection. In Chapter 10, "Contested ground, 'āina, identity, and nationhood in Hawaii," ku'ualoha ho'omanawanui examines the current situation in Hawaii with regard to the Kanaka Maoli struggle for land, identity, and nationhood, and considers the impact that the UN Declaration could have in such a struggle. Since the illegal overthrow of the Hawaiian Kingdom on the part of the US government in 1893, the subsequent annexation in 1898 and finally statehood in 1959, the Kanaka Maoli, ho'omanawanui argues, have always fought a human rights struggle. As a human rights document that affirms the inherent rights of indigenous peoples, the Declaration, according to ho'omanawanui, "allows for the hopeful imagining of what is possible to further positive political and social transformation" for the Kanaka Maoli, a transformation, however, that the Kanaka Maoli have already begun through various sovereignty initiatives and movements for self-determination. Her commentary on selected articles of the Declaration explores potential strategies for implementation within the Kanaka Maoli context, first and foremost the contested question of land, which in Hawaii is often tied to the presence of US military forces. Among the most recent issues, ho'omanawanui discusses the repatriation of *iwi kupuna* (ancestors' remains) unearthed from construction sites and/or recovered from museums around the world. As the Kanaka Maoli continue to seek justice, ho'omanawanui considers the Declaration as a way for the United States to "meaningfully address the wrongs of the past." "It is a matter of *kuleana*," she says, "responsibility at the national level." In Chapter 11, "Kānāwai, International Law, and the Discourse of Indigenous Justice," Elvira Pulitano discusses a significant event in the history of the Kanaka Maoli, the 1993 Peoples' International Tribunal, in an attempt to demonstrate that any discussion of indigenous issues at the international level will remain substantially limited unless it takes into consideration principles of indigenous law. What happened at the Peoples' Tribunal in Hawaii, she argues, can become "a teachable moment for future directions and the work ahead in the implementation of the Declaration." In 1993, a panel of international judges convened for twelve days in the Hawaiian islands to listen to the testimony of the Kanaka Maoli with regard to their experience as a colonized people under the United States. The charges pressed consisted of illegal annexation, imposition of statehood, illegal appropriation of Kanaka Maoli lands, and acts of genocide and ecocide. The tribunal found the United States and the state of Hawaii guilty, and urged the international community to pressure the parties involved to pose remedies and restore justice to the Kanaka Maoli. Pulitano's discussion of the tribunal – both the video recording of it and the written records that ensued – focuses on what was perhaps the tribunal's most remarkable feature and guiding spirit: a distinctive Kanaka Maoli epistemology reflected in the notion of *kānāwai*, a term which in the Hawaiian language means "law," but a term which in its essential component, "*wai*" (water), suggests that law for the Kanaka Maoli is inextricably connected to land and water, the essence of life. Pulitano considers the Peoples' Tribunal in Hawaii "almost prophetic" in the way in which it charted the path that states will have to follow in order to implement the provisions of the Declaration.

In the Afterword, Mililani Trask provides pragmatic educational tools for indigenous advocates, as they attempt to force states to comply with the provisions set out in the Declaration. The collective interventions of the global indigenous caucus, endorsed by the majority of indigenous peoples during the debates when the Declaration was being drafted, constitute, according to Trask, excellent international human rights law material that might assist indigenous peoples as they advance their struggles on the most critical issues such as self-determination, lands, and resources. Education at the UN level, Trask further maintains, is also necessary (and is currently being advanced) in order to guarantee effective implementation of the Declaration.

Collections such as these present significant challenges and call for strategic decisions.

It is not the primary intent of this volume to provide a comprehensive critical assessment and/or legal interpretation of the Declaration, neither do these chapters offer a complete history of the indigenous peoples' presence at the United Nations.[25] As I stated at the beginning of my discussion, the purpose here is to investigate whether the Declaration can somehow close the gap between international law, law within the states, and indigenous peoples' views and concerns. While it would be virtually impossible, for any book, to present the perspective of all the indigenous peoples to whom the Declaration is addressed, the essays included here provide instructive examples of some of the challenges faced by indigenous communities in the age of the Declaration.

The literature on the Declaration to date, including the perspectives presented in this collection, has abundantly demonstrated that this landmark human rights instrument cannot magically resolve all the problems affecting indigenous peoples at present. Whereas some commentators strongly criticized the Declaration's provisions, deemed too weak and too conciliatory toward states, others praised its overall content and results. Still others remind us that international alliances beyond the UN are crucial for the struggles of indigenous peoples on a global scale. However, one factor remains: UNDRIP constitutes, with all its imperfections and among all the controversy, a significant achievement for indigenous peoples worldwide. The question of how to make it work is the challenge now confronting governments, civil society, and indigenous peoples themselves. As stated by Stavenhagen, "The Declaration provides an opportunity to link the global and local levels, in a process of *glocalization*" ("Making the Declaration" 357). Contributors to this volume draw attention to the fact that some countries have been incorporating the provisions of the Declaration into their own legislation – Bolivia being a case in point, since it was the first country in the world to make the Declaration, within only two months of its adoption, federal law[26] – whereas others

---

[25] Readings on these topics include among others Anaya (*Indigenous Peoples*), Venne (*Our Elders*), and Xanthaki (*Indigenous Rights*). For a brief history of indigenous peoples in the international system, see the UNPFII website.

[26] The Philippines also set a significant goal with its pre-2007 introduction of the then Draft declaration into domestic law. I am indebted to Siegfried Wiessner for bringing this fact to my attention.

have been referencing it in important court cases involving indigenous issues. Inspired by such political action, the authors of these chapters have mapped out possibilities on how the Declaration could be effectively implemented at the local level within their own communities. Even though some critics remain skeptical of the possibility of linking the global and the local, the views presented in this volume suggest that alliances among the various groups involved in affirming indigenous rights are key. And the role of human rights education along with indigenous peoples' cultures and histories is all the more critical.

According to Sambo Dorough, "the success of the Declaration largely depends on the extent to which human rights concepts are understood by those in a position to right wrongs" ("Significance" 275). But who is going to help those occupying such key roles, both at national and international level, to understand human rights, rights that have consistently been denied to indigenous peoples, as is clearly acknowledged in one of the Preambular paragraphs of the Declaration? Questions such as those Sambo Dorough raises are crucial in affirming a human rights education. She writes:

> Who constitutes the "self" in self-determination? Who are indigenous peoples? What constitutes an indigenous nation? Who are the beneficiaries of the political, collective right to self-determination? Do indigenous peoples view themselves as one or are they many nations? And furthermore, who are the members of the indigenous nation or nations and how do they operate within their nation or respective nations and homelands? ... Are human rights concepts and the content of the collective and individual human rights known and understood by the people who assert self-determination? Are human rights concepts integrated in the community? ... How do we promote human rights education as a tool for capacity building within indigenous communities? ("Significance" 275–6)

As I read these questions, I am reminded of some of my students, who often ask why indigenous peoples "need special rights." But they are not the only ones to uphold such views. Those of us who teach indigenous studies are aware that students' responses often reflect views and opinions shared by the general public. But that is why we continue to teach. Education, according to both Sambo Dorough and Trask, is the answer in promoting dialogue, dialogue with indigenous communities, with state governments, and with the various international forums (not just the UN) interested in promoting and affirming the rights of indigenous peoples.

Thomas King's *The Truth About Stories* (2003) contains an illuminating example suggesting that in life, the story we choose to believe is the one that determines our existence. After telling the story about Coyote and the ducks, a story in which Coyote, driven by his vanity and greed, tricks the ducks into giving him their most beautiful feathers with the end result that "the world is going to change and no one is going to be particularly happy" (127), King writes: "Take it. It's yours. Do with it what you will. Tell it to your children. Turn it into a play. Forget it. But don't say in the years to come that you would have lived your life differently if only you had heard this story. You've heard it now." (151). We have heard the story of the indigenous peoples' claim for their inalienable rights in front of the international community. They have been telling it for a long time. It has now become our story. We should use it for good. It is my hope that this book will create the possibility for this story to be disseminated and for us to continue to fight for a better and more just world.

Works cited

About UNPFII and a Brief History of Indigenous Peoples and the International System. Web. Accessed July 23, 2011. www.un.org/esa/socdev/unpfii/en/history.html.

About Us/Mandate. UN Permanent Forum on Indigenous Issues. Web. Accessed June 25, 2011. www.un.org/esa/socdev/unpfii/en/about_us.html.

Allen, Stephen. "The UN Declaration on the Rights of Indigenous Peoples and the Limits of the International Legal Project." Allen and Xanthaki 225–56.

Allen, Stephen and Alexandra Xanthaki, eds. *Reflections on the UN Declaration on the Rights of Indigenous Peoples.* Oxford: Hart Publishing, 2011.

Anaya, James. *Indigenous Peoples in International Law,* 2nd edn. Oxford University Press, 2004. Print.

"The Right of Indigenous Peoples to Self-Determination in the Post-Declaration Era." Charters and Stavenhagen 184–200. Print.

Anaya, James and Siegfried Wiessner. "The UN Declaration on the Rights of Indigenous Peoples: Towards Re-empowerment." *Jurist Forum,* October 3, 2007. http://jurist.law.pitt.edu/forumy/2007/10/un-declaration-on-rights-of-indigenous.php.

Announcement of US Support for the UN Declaration on the Rights of Indigenous Peoples, 2010, www.state.gov/documents/organization/153223.pdf.

Charters, Claire. "The Legitimacy of the UN Declaration on the Rights of Indigenous Peoples." Charters and Stavenhagen 280–304. Print.

Charters, Claire and Rodolfo Stavenhagen, eds. *Making the Declaration Work: The United Nations Declaration on the Rights of Indigenous Peoples.* Copenhagen: IWGIA, 2009. Print.

"The UN Declaration on the Rights of Indigenous Peoples: How It Came to Be and What It Heralds." Charters and Stavenhagen 10–14.

Charters, Claire, Les Melezer, and Victoria Tauli-Corpus, eds. *Indigenous Voices: The Declaration on the Rights of Indigenous Peoples*. Oxford: Hart Publishing, forthcoming 2013. Print.

Daes, Erica-Irene A. "The Concepts of Self-Determination and Autonomy of Indigenous Peoples in the Draft United Nations Declaration on the Rights of Indigenous Peoples." *St. Thomas Law Review*, 259 (2001). Web. Accessed July 23, 2011.

Deloria, Vine, Jr. "Self-Determination and the Concept of Sovereignty." *Native Americans and the Law: Contemporary and Historical Perspectives on American Indian Rights, Freedoms, and Sovereignty*. John R. Wunder ed. Lincoln, NE: University of Nebraska Press, 1996. 118–28. Print.

Glenn, H. Patrick. "The Three Ironies of the UN Declaration on the Rights of Indigenous Peoples." Allen and Xanthaki 171–82.

International Day of the World's Indigenous Peoples, 9 August 2008. Joint Statement. Web. Accessed 1 June 2011. www.un.org/events/indigenous/2008/hcmessage.shtml.

International Law Association, Committee on the Rights of Indigenous Peoples, Interim Report, 74th Biennial Meeting, The Hague (July 23, 2011), accessible as "Conference Report The Hague (2010)," available at www.ila-hq.org/en/committees/index.cfm/cid/1024.

James Anaya–UNSR Website. Accessed July 23, 2011. http://unsr.jamesanaya.org/.

Kauanui, Kēhaulani. The International Indian Treaty Council Implementing the UN Declaration. An Interview with Andrea Carmen. "Indigenous Politics: From Native New England and Beyond." Friday, February 13, 2009. Web. Accessed July 23, 2011. www.indigenouspolitics.com/?p=19.

King, Thomas. *The Truth About Stories: A Native Narrative*. Minneapolis: University of Minnesota Press, 2003. Print.

Kymlicka, Will. "Beyond the Indigenous/Minority Dichotomy?" Allen and Xanthaki 183–208.

Lawlor, Mary. "Indigenous Internationalism: Native Rights and the United Nations." *Public Native America: Tribal Self-Representations in Museums, Powwows, and Casinos*. New Brunswick: Rutgers University Press, 2006, 162–227. Print.

"Living History: Inauguration of the International Year of the World's Indigenous People." *Transnational Law and Contemporary Problems* 3 (1993): 165–22.

Martínez Cobo, José. *Study on the Problem of Discrimination against Indigenous Populations*, UN Doc. E/CN.4/Sub.2/1986/Add.4. Web. Accessed September 29, 2011. www.un.org/esa/socdev/unpfii/en/spdaip.html.

McCaslin, Wanda D., ed. *Justice as Healing: Indigenous Ways*. St. Paul, MN: Living Justice Press, 2005. Print.

Morris, Glenn. "Still Lying after All These Years." *Indian Country Today*, February 16, 2011. Web. Accessed September 29, 2011. http://indiancountrytodaymedia network.com/ict_sbc/still-lying-after-all-these-years/.

Odham, Paul and Miriam Anne Frank. "'We the peoples': The United Nations Declaration on the Rights of Indigenous Peoples." *Anthropology Today* 24.2 (2008): 5–9.

Outcome Document of the Durban Review Conference. UN Office of the High Commissioner for Human Rights, 24 April, 2009, www.un.org/esa/socdev/ unpfii/en/declaration.html.

Quane, Helen. "The UN Declaration on the Rights of Indigenous Peoples: New Directions for Self-Determination and Participatory Rights?" Allen and Xanthaki 259–87.

Sambo Dorough, Dalee. "The Significance of the Declaration on the Rights of Indigenous Peoples and its Future Implementation." Charters and Stavenhagen 264–78.

Second International Decade of the World's Indigenous People, 22 December 2004, available at www.un.org/esa/socdev/unpfii/en/second.html. Web. Accessed September 29, 2011.

Stavenhagen, Rodolfo. "Making the Declaration Work." Charters and Stavenhagen 352–71.

Trask, Mililani. Message to the author. 3 April 2010. E-mail.
   Message to the author. 26 April 2010. E-mail.

UNGA Resolution 1514 (XV), 14 December 1960. Web. Accessed July 23, 2011. www.un.org/documents/ga/res/15/ares15.htm.

United Nations Declaration on the Rights of Indigenous Peoples, Adopted by the General Assembly 13 September 2007. Web. Accessed September 29, 2011. www.un.org/esa/socdev/unpfii/documents/DRIPS_en.pdf.

UN Permanent Forum on Indigenous Issues. Web. Accessed September 29, 2011. www.un.org/esa/socdev/unpfii/.

Venne, Sharon Helen. *Our Elders Understand Our Rights: Evolving International Law Regarding Indigenous Peoples*. Penticton: Theytus Books, 1998. Print.

Vizenor, Gerald. "Genocide Tribunals." Vizenor, *Native Liberty: Natural Reason and Cultural Survivance*. Lincoln, NE: University of Nebraska Press, 2009. 131–58. Print.
   Manifest Manners: Narratives on Postindian Survivance. Lincoln, NE: University of Nebraska Press, 1999. Print.

Wallace, Paul A. W. *The Iroquois Book of Life: White Roots of Peace*. Santa Fe, NM: Clear Light Publishers, 1994. Print.

Wiessner, Siegfried. "The Cultural Rights of Indigenous Peoples: Achievements and Continuing Challenges," *European Journal of International Law* 22 (2011): 121–40. Web. Accessed July 23, 2011.

"Indigenous Sovereignty: A Reassessment in Light of the UN Declaration on the Rights of Indigenous Peoples." *Vanderbilt Journal of Transnational Law* 41 (2008): 1141–76.

"Introductory Note – The United Nations Declaration on the Rights of Indigenous Peoples." Web. Accessed July 23, 2011. http://untreaty.un.org/cod/avl/pdf/ha/ga_61–295/ga_61–295_e.pdf.

"Rights and Status of Indigenous Peoples: A Global Comparative and International Legal Perspective." *Harvard Human Rights Journal* 12 (1999): 57–128. Web. Accessed September 29, 2011. www.law.harvard.edu/students/orgs/hrj/iss12/wiessner.shtml.

Wise Brown, Margaret. *The Dream Book: First Comes the Dream*. New York: Random House, 1950. Print.

Xanthaki, Alexandra. *Indigenous Rights and United Nations Standards: Self-Determination, Culture and Land*. Cambridge: Cambridge University Press, 2007. Print.

1

Indigenous self-determination, culture, and land: a reassessment in light of the 2007 UN Declaration on the Rights of Indigenous Peoples

SIEGFRIED WIESSNER

September 13, 2007. The UN General Assembly, in an overwhelming vote of 144 states in favor to four against, adopts the UN Declaration on the Rights of Indigenous Peoples (UNDRIP).[1] Worked on for over a generation, this document signifies for many a milestone of re-empowerment of the First Nations of the Earth. Yet questions remain: What, exactly, does this accomplishment mean? Have the indigenous communities succeeded in their long way back from what seemed to be assured assimilation or, in some cases, downright extinction? Have they, in effect, managed to reverse colonialism? Are they sovereign again, masters of their own fate?

Section 1 of this chapter will briefly review the history of marginalization, exclusion, and often destruction of indigenous peoples. Section 2 will describe the way in which the traditionally static Western concept of sovereignty has been rendered dynamic by the modern right of self-determination, also elucidating the anti-indigenous function and effect of the concepts of *terra nullius* and *uti possidetis*. Section 3 will delineate the cross-border indigenous renascence starting in the late 1960s and the resulting state practice that led to treaties and customary international law in the field as well as the 2007 UN Declaration on the Rights of

---

[1] United Nations Declaration on the Rights of Indigenous Peoples, GA Res. 61/295, Annex, UN Doc. A/RES/61/295 (September 13, 2007), available at www2.ohchr.org/english/ issues/indigenous/declaration.htm. For a draft expert commentary on this Declaration and indigenous peoples' rights in general, see ILA Committee on the Rights of Indigenous Peoples, Interim Report to the 74th ILA Conference in The Hague, August 15–20, 2010, available at www.ila-hq.org/en/committees/ index.cfm/cid/1024 (hereinafter 2010 ILA Interim Report). See also S. James Anaya and Siegfried Wiessner, "The UN Declaration on the Rights of Indigenous Peoples: Towards Re-empowerment," *Jurist Forum*, October 3, 2007, available at http://jurist.law.pitt.edu/forumy/2007/10/un-declaration-on-rights-of-indigenous.php.

Indigenous Peoples, in particular, as it relates to the indigenous peoples' key claims to self-determination, culture, and land. Based on an assessment of the authentic aspirations of indigenous peoples – their "inner worlds" – Section 4 will appraise the progress made and outline the critical elements of a legal regime that would allow for the flourishing again of indigenous cultures and communities.

The setting

The juggernaut of modern society, by its nature and often by design, has moved to extinguish the indigenous voice.[2] Its language, institutions, and rituals have become dominant.[3] Modernity's law, in particular, has imprinted itself on indigenous peoples, following the sword of conquest and the *ratio* of innovation in the Western hemisphere and beyond.[4] Its domination of indigenous ways of life was, in some ways, to be expected. Its aggressive use of the Earth and its resources,[5] combined with sanctions to punish perceived transgressions,[6] its focus on "getting ahead" via technological and social "progress,"[7] its premium on Cartesian reason and logic,[8] and its emphasis on the individual[9] ran head-on into and rolled over the soft, unresisting indigenous concepts of oneness with Mother

---

[2] Franke Wilmer, *The Indigenous Voice in World Politics: Since Time Immemorial* (Newbury Park, CA: Sage, 1993) 54–55 (noting that "because modernization is believed to be a good in itself," communities have rationalized actions that "[remove] obstacles to modernization," thereby justifying the oppressive treatment of indigenous communities).

[3] Ibid., at 37.

[4] Ibid., at 49; see, e.g., Robert Yazzie, "Indigenous People and Postcolonial Colonialism," in Marie Battiste (ed.), *Reclaiming Indigenous Voice and Vision* (Vancouver: UBC Press, 2000) 39–41 (discussing the colonization of indigenous people in the United States, Canada, Africa, and Asia through technological advances in warfare).

[5] Based often, though controversially, on God's command to humans found in Genesis 1:28: "Be fruitful, and multiply, and replenish the earth, and subdue it: and have dominion over the fish of the sea and over the fowl of the air, and over every living thing that moveth upon the earth."

[6] Thomas G. Blomberg and Karol Lucken, *American Penology: A History of Control* (Hawthorne, NY: Aldine de Gruyter, 2000) 33 (noting that "[punishment] was ... considered to be a moral obligation of the community" in colonial America).

[7] See, e.g., Reinhart Kosselleck, *The Practice of Conceptual History: Timing History, Spacing Concepts*, trans. Todd Presner (Stanford University Press, 2002) 233 (noting that "[t]he concept of progress encompasses precisely that experience of our own modernity: again and again, it has yielded unforeseeable innovations that are incomparable when measured against anything in the past").

[8] Yazzie, *supra* note 4, at 66–67.

[9] Ibid., at 82–83, 92.

Earth and Father Sky, their focus on peace and reconciliation, on faith, on leaving nobody behind, on community.[10]

Still, the onslaught has not been completely successful. All the military, economic, and materialistic might of the modern world has not succeeded in silencing the indigenous voice.[11] Just as tender water ultimately erodes the hardest of rocks, indigenous cultures, peoples, and their values have persisted. Like many oppressed communities, they have had to adapt, go underground, avoid open confrontation.[12] Thus their withdrawal into niches of survival, areas at least not initially desired by the more dominant and aggressive part of humanity;[13] thus religious syncretism;[14] thus their participation in the preeminent economies, by way of tourism and the sale of handicrafts;[15] thus their enlistment in the armed forces of the conqueror.[16]

Paradoxically, modern communication technologies[17] have helped indigenous peoples to come together, sharing their stories across the crumbs of land that the conquerors left them, and asserting their voice.[18] An international movement has united those who have been systematically divided in the past.[19] Domestic and international decisions have resulted in freezing the processes of assimilation and the termination of indigenous voices and values, sometimes even in slightly turning back the clock.[20]

The *Awas Tingni* decision of the Inter-American Court of Human Rights[21] and the campaign of the Western Shoshone, rather successful

---

[10] Ibid., at 43, 92.   [11] Wilmer, *supra* note 2, at 32, 40, 149.

[12] Ibid. (describing the assimilation process of the American Indians).

[13] Ibid.

[14] E.g., Ella Shohat and Robert Stam, *Unthinking Eurocentrism: Multiculturalism and the Media* (London and New York: Routledge, 1994) 43–44.

[15] Ibid. (contrasting predominant US narratives with Native American interpretation that "Pocahontas learns English ways in order to become an ambassador for her community and thus rescue it").

[16] For an example of a country's facilitation of the enlistment of indigenous persons, see Indigenous Australian Servicemen, www.awm.gov.au/encyclopedia/aborigines/indigenous.asp.

[17] Jeff J. Corntassel and Tomas Hopkins Primeau, "Indigenous 'Sovereignty' and International Law: Revised Strategies for Pursuing 'Self-Determination,'" 17 *Human Rights Quarterly* 343 (1995), 360 ("Due to the unprecedented level of modern communication, indigenous populations around the world are uniting and acting in a concerted fashion").

[18] Ibid.   [19] Wilmer, *supra* note 2, at 18–19, 137–38.

[20] Ibid., at 32.

[21] *Mayagna (Sumo) Awas Tingni Community* v. *Nicaragua*, 31 August 2001, Inter-American Court of Human Rights, Ser. C, No. 79, reprinted as "The Case of the *Mayagna (Sumo)*

on the international plane, against the taking of their sacred lands[22] are just two examples reaffirming the original assessment, based on recent state practice, that the lands traditionally held by indigenous peoples are theirs as a matter of right.[23] Honoring the land rights of indigenous peoples is the first step toward preservation of their culture. The next step is to respect the structures of decision-making within traditional communities – a distant variant of the modern processes of decision-making in communities we proudly call "democratic."[24]

Cultural difference provides the context within which indigenous peoples' claims to self-government arise. Unlike the claims of other groups, indigenous peoples' claims are often couched in the verbiage of "sovereignty."[25] Vine Deloria, Jr., one of the modern-day prophets of Indian resurgence, spoke in terms of "indigenous sovereignty."[26] Even today, US courts use "tribal sovereignty" as a term of art when they analyze cases involving American Indian tribes, or, as they prefer to be called,

Awas Tingni Community v. *Nicaragua*," 19 *Arizona Journal of International and Comparative Law* 395 (2002), 430–31, 440 (hereinafter *Awas Tingni*).

[22] Julie Ann Fishel, "The Western Shoshone Struggle: Opening Doors for Indigenous Rights," 2 *Intercultural Human Rights Law Review* 41 (2007), 46 (referring to the December 2002 Final Report of the Inter-American Commission on Human Rights finding violations of the right to property, due process, and equality under the law; *Dann* v. *United States*, Case 11.140, Inter-Am. CHR, Report No. 75/02, OEA/Ser.L/V/II.117, doc. 1 rev. 1 (2002); and the March 10, 2006, decision of the United Nations Committee on the Elimination of All Forms of Racial Discrimination (CERD), which urged the United States to "freeze," "desist," and "stop" actions being taken, or threatened to be taken, against the Western Shoshone Peoples of the Western Shoshone Nation, UN Committee on the Elimination of Racial Discrimination, *Decision 1 (68): Early Warning and Urgent Action Procedure*, UN Doc. CERD/C/USA/DEC/1 (Apr. 11, 2006)).

[23] Siegfried Wiessner, "Rights and Status of Indigenous Peoples: A Global Comparative and International Legal Analysis," 12 *Harvard Human Rights Journal* 57 (1999), 127.

[24] For a discussion of the legitimacy of internal decision-making structures, see Steven Wheatley, "Indigenous Peoples and the Right of Political Autonomy in an Age of Global Legal Pluralism," 12 *Current Legal Issues* 351 (2009), and Siegfried Wiessner, "The United Nations Declaration on the Rights of Indigenous Peoples: Selected Issues," in Aristotle Constantinides and Nikos Zaikos (eds.), *The Diversity of International Law. Essays in Honour of Professor Kalliopi K. Koufa* (Leiden and Boston, MA: Martinus Nijhoff, 2009), 343, 353–54.

[25] See, e.g., Vine Deloria, Jr., "Self-Determination and the Concept of Sovereignty," in John R. Wunder (ed.), *Native American Sovereignty* (New York: Garland 1996), 118. See also the Special Issue, Eric Cheyfitz, N. Bruce Duthu, and Shari M. Huhndorf (eds.), "Sovereignty, Indigeneity, and the Law", 110:2 *South Atlantic Quarterly* 291 (2011).

[26] Deloria, *supra* note 25, at 121, 123. For biographical background, see Steve Pavlik, *In Honor of Vine Deloria, Jr. (1913–2005)*, available at www.nwic.edu/deloria/memoriam.pdf (last visited September 24, 2008).

Nations.[27] Other states around the world also face indigenous peoples' demands for their space, their existence, both physically and spiritually, their ways of life.[28] It is not the word "sovereignty" as such that is in issue but structures to ensure all the values of human dignity for indigenous peoples.

Self-determination and *uti possidetis*: their effect on indigenous peoples

One key concept of the order established in the wake of World War II was the principle of self-determination.[29] The legacy of colonial conquest was supposed to be dealt with by offering colonized peoples a UN-supervised process of decolonization through which they could arrive at their preferred solution to their political status, whether they

[27] For a recent case law summary, see David H. Getches et al., *Federal Indian Law*, 5th edn. (St. Paul, MN: Thomson West, 2005), 377–413. As to the original Marshall trilogy of cases, see ibid., at 104–27. Felix S. Cohen, in his seminal handbook of federal Indian law, referred to powers of Indian tribes as "inherent powers of a limited sovereignty which has never been extinguished." *Handbook of Federal Indian Law* 122 (Washington DC: US GPO, 1941), quoted in *United States* v. *Wheeler*, 435 US 313, 322 (1978). See also *Santa Clara Pueblo* v. *Martinez*, 436 US 49, 55–56 (1978), and *United States* v. *Lara*, 541 US 193, 196 (2004) (discussing the inherent tribal sovereignty of American Indian nations). North American indigenous peoples often style themselves as a "nation." See, e.g., The Navajo Nation, www.navajo.org; The Oneida Indian Nation, www.oneidaindiannation. com; The Shasta Indian Nation, www.shastaindiannation.org/index.html; and The Catawba Indian Nation, http://catawbaindiannation.com.

[28] See Kirsten Matoy Carlson, "Premature Predictions of Multiculturalism?," 100 *Michigan Law Review* 1470 (2002), 1475–76 (referring to Latin American states' recognition of indigenous sovereignty claims); see also Dianne Otto, "A Question of Law or Politics? Indigenous Claims to Sovereignty in Australia", 21 *Syracuse Journal of International Law and Commerce* 65 (1995), 79–80; cf. Benjamin A. Kahn, "The Legal Framework Surrounding Maori Claims to Water Resources in New Zealand: In Contrast to the American Indian Experience," 35 *Stanford Journal of International Law* 49 (1999), 81 (referring to the "importance of a confined resource base to the retention of indigenous sovereignty"); Gordon Christie, "Indigeneity and Sovereignty in Canada's Far North: The Arctic and Inuit Sovereignty," 110 *South Atlantic Quarterly* 329 (2011). See generally Corntassel and Primeau, *supra* note 17; Steven Curry, *Indigenous Sovereignty and the Democratic Project* (Aldershot and Burlington, VT: Ashgate, 2004).

[29] UN Charter Art. 1(2) ("The purposes of the United Nations are: ... To develop friendly relations among nations based on respect for the principle of equal rights and self-determination of peoples"); International Covenant on Civil and Political Rights, GA Res. 2200A (XXI), Art. 1, UN Doc. A/6316 (opened for signature December 16, 1966, entered into force March 23, 1976) ("All peoples have the right of self-determination. By virtue of that right they freely determine their political status and freely pursue their economic, social and cultural development").

desired independence, integration into the colonizing state, association, or any other status in between.[30] This decolonization process has been virtually completed.[31]

The problem with the UN's decolonization process was this: the choice as to the political future of colonized peoples was not given to the individual peoples conquered, but to the inhabitants of territories colonized by European conquerors, within the boundaries of the lines of demarcation drawn by the colonizers.[32] Thus the colonizers, via their constituting the new country's "people" under the new sovereign's control, continued to rule the colonized from their graves. The name of the game is *uti possidetis*, a Roman legal term that essentially means one should leave the place as one received it.[33]

The decolonization of Spanish lands in Latin America set the precedent that was followed in other areas of European conquest, particularly Africa.[34] There, the boundaries were drawn by rulers who often literally used rulers at the Berlin Congo Conference of 1884.[35] The straight lines drawn there cut right through the heartlands of very distinct linguistic and ethnic groups, creating problems that persist to the present day.[36] Pursuant to the principle of *uti possidetis*, the UN-effectuated return of lands retraced the borders drawn by the conquerors.[37] Even the dissolutions of European countries today did not dare violate *uti possidetis*, as confirmed

---

[30] GA Res. 1514, UN GAOR, 15th Sess., Supp. No. 16, UN Doc. A/4684 (December 14, 1960); GA Res. 1541, UN GAOR, 15th Sess., Annex, UN Doc. A/4651 (December 15, 1960).

[31] W. Michael Reisman et al., *International Law in Contemporary Perspective* (New York: Foundation Press, and St. Paul, MN: Thomson/West, 2004), 187.

[32] GA Res. 1514, *supra* note 30; Malcolm N. Shaw, "The Heritage of States: The Principle of *Uti Possidetis Juris* Today," 67 *British Year Book of International Law* 75 (1997), 119–25.

[33] See generally Shaw, *supra* note 32, at 97–151 (explaining the principle of *uti possidetis juris* and providing practical examples of its application). For critical evaluations see Steven R. Ratner, "Drawing a Better Line: *Uti Possidetis* and the Borders of New States," 90 *American Journal of International Law* 590 (1996), and Helen Ghebrewebet, *Identifying Units of Statehood and Determining International Boundaries: A Revised Look at the Doctrine of Uti Possidetis and the Principle of Self-Determination* (Frankfurt am Main and New York: P. Lang, 2006).

[34] *Case Concerning the Frontier Dispute (Burk. Faso v. Mali)*, 1986 ICJ 554, 565 (December 22).

[35] H. J. de Blij and Peter O. Muller, *Geography: Realms, Regions, and Concepts* (New York: Wiley & Sons, 1997), 340.

[36] Ibid. See also Makau Mutua, "Why Redraw the Map of Africa: A Moral and Legal Inquiry," 16 *Michigan Journal of International Law* 1113 (1995).

[37] See Shaw, *supra* note 32, at 128–41 (explaining that, given the concept of *uti possidetis juris*, the borders traced at the time the UN returned lands to the indigenous African peoples were those that were in evidence at the time of independence, which happened to be those arbitrarily drawn by European rulers at the Berlin Conference).

by the Badinter Commission, which formulated the conditions for EU recognition of breakaway entities of the former Yugoslavia.[38] Kosovo had to deal with the application of this principle – originally directed at the Republika Srpska, the Serbian part of Bosnia–Herzegovina – as a major obstacle in its quest for recognition as an independent state.[39]

This process of decolonization was assumed to be concluded, by and large, in the mid-1970s after the demise of Franco and Salazar, the dictators of Spain and Portugal respectively, the last European colonial powers.[40] The Western Sahara and East Timor controversies were just part of the cleanup of this relatively orderly process.[41]

Orderly as the decolonization process was, it did not account for the peoples who were not yet back on the agenda of the state-centered international decision-makers.[42] Quiet but determined, they subsisted not just as collections of individuals but as organic cultures with fervently held beliefs – indigenous peoples from around the world, numbering about 370 million, scattered in about seventy different nation states.[43] They live a predominantly subsistence-based, non-urbanized, sometimes nomadic lifestyle; often they farm or hunt for food for immediate use.[44] They are called the Fourth World, and they have become a factor not only in the

---

[38] "Conference of Yugoslavia Arbitration Commission: Opinions on Questions Arising from the Dissolution of Yugoslavia, Jan. 11, 1992, and July 4, 1992," 31 ILM 1488, 1503. For a thorough analysis see Matthew C. R. Craven, "The European Community Arbitration Commission on Yugoslavia," 66 *British Year Book of International Law* 333 (1995).

[39] Reisman et al., *supra* note 31, at 218–30; Jonathan I. Charney, "Self-Determination: Chechnya, Kosovo, and East Timor," 34 *Vanderbilt Journal of Transnational Law* 455 (2001). On February 17, 2008, Kosovo declared its independence, with major Western powers and other countries in support; Serbia and Russia, principally, remained opposed. "Kosovo MPs Proclaim Independence," BBC News, February 17, 2008, http://news.bbc.co.uk/2/hi/europe/7249034.stm. An advisory opinion by the International Court of Justice, solicited by the UN General Assembly, affirmed that this declaration did not violate international law. ICJ, *Accordance with International Law of the Unilateral Declaration of Independence in Respect of Kosovo*, Advisory Opinion, July 22, 2010, paras. 121–123, at www.icj-cij.org/docket/index.php?p1=3&p2=4&k=21&case=141&code=kos&p3=4&PHPSESSID=fe6fb324388f4ce29bb59bdba24a78d9. As of July 23, 2011, Kosovo has been recognized by eighty-one states. Republic of Kosova, Ministry of Foreign Affairs, "Countries that Have Recognized the Republic of Kosova," www.mfa-ks.net/?page=2,33 (last accessed October 2, 2011).

[40] Reisman et al., *supra* note 31, at 187.

[41] Ibid., at 154–87.

[42] Shaw, *supra* note 32, at 119–25; see also GA Res. 1514, *supra* note 30.

[43] Official Website of the United Nations Permanent Forum on Indigenous Issues, www.un.org/esa/socdev/unpfii/en/history.html.

[44] Wiessner, *supra* note 23, at 58–60, 93, 101–04.

world's social process but also in its constitutive process.[45] They have risen like a phoenix from the ashes.

Indigenous renascence and the 2007 United Nations Declaration on the Rights of Indigenous Peoples

Prior to the 1970s in the United States, and even today in Europe, indigenous peoples were not known to textbooks on international law as actors of any significance in the field; if anything, they were viewed as legal units of domestic law, as one arbitral tribunal characterized the Cayuga Nation in 1926.[46] Their numbers had decreased: in the census of 1960, only 523,591 people in the United States identified themselves as American Indian.[47] The conquerors' policies of assimilation and termination had had a significant effect.

The 1960s and 1970s, however, were characterized by a revolutionary fervor that fueled a remarkable resurgence of the First Nations that continues today.[48] The American Indian Movement militantly protested the treatment of indigenous peoples in the United States.[49] In 1973, they ended up in a memorable seventy-one-day standoff with federal authorities near Wounded Knee in South Dakota, the site of the last major battle between white soldiers and Native Americans – as one view of history would have it – or the site of a massacre of over three hundred Sioux men, women, and children – as another opinion would hold.[50] It evoked the memory of other flashpoints of degradation, and physical and cultural extermination of

---

[45] See, e.g., Center for World Indigenous Studies, Fourth World Documentation Program, www.cwis.org/fwdp/index.php.

[46] *Cayuga Indians (Gr. Brit.)* v. *United States*, 6 *Review of International Arbitral Awards* 173 (1926), 176 (stating that an Indian tribe "is not a legal unit of international law"); see also *Island of Palmas Case (US* v. *Neth.)*, 2 *Review of International Arbitral Awards* 829 (Permanent Court of Arbitration, 1928). For an argument for international Cayuga land rights today, see Carrie E. Garrow, "Following Deskaheh's Legacy: Reclaiming the Cayuga Indian Nation's Land Rights at the Inter-American Commission on Human Rights," 35 *Syracuse Journal of International Law and Commerce* 341 (2008).

[47] Joane Nagel, "American Indian Ethnic Renewal: Politics and the Resurgence of Identity," 60 *American Social Review* 947 (1995), 947.

[48] The number of self-identified American Indians increased in the census of 1990 to 1,878,285, a rise attributed to the combined effect of "federal Indian policy, American ethnic politics, and American Indian political activism." Ibid.

[49] See generally Rachel A. Bonney, "The Role of AIM Leaders in Indian Nationalism," 3 *American Indian Quarterly* 209 (1977).

[50] Ibid., at 216. For information on the initial 1890 battle at Wounded Knee, see Dee Brown, *Bury My Heart at Wounded Knee* (New York: Holt, Rinehart & Winston, 1970), 444–46.

indigenous peoples: Hernando Pizarro's 1536–37 siege of Cusco, resulting in the killing or maiming of all Indian inhabitants and the razing of this beautiful Inca city; the forced removal from the East Coast of the United States of the "Five Civilized Tribes" in the 1830s – the "Trail of Tears" with its countless deaths, trauma, and misery; and the widespread prohibition of the use of indigenous languages and the practicing of their religion around the globe. The American Indian Movement's international off-shoot, the International Indian Treaty Council,[51] was founded in 1974, followed by the World Council of Indigenous Peoples,[52] allowing leaders to unite indigenous pursuits in the Western hemisphere, from Canada to Venezuela and beyond. The Fourth World had found its voice,[53] and it soon found entry into the institutions of the First World – in particular, the United Nations. Internationally bonded, the newly founded organizations created media attention for the plight of their members and ultimately gained a seat at the formal table of international decision-making, the United Nations.

In 1971, the UN Economic and Social Council appointed Mr. José Martínez Cobo to study patterns of discrimination against indigenous peoples. He submitted a landmark report.[54] In 1982, the UN Subcommission on the Prevention of Discrimination and the Protection of Minorities appointed a working group on indigenous

---

[51] The International Indian Treaty Council defines itself as "an organization of Indigenous Peoples from North, Central, South America and the Pacific working for the Sovereignty and Self Determination of Indigenous Peoples and the recognition and protection of Indigenous Rights, Treaties, Traditional Cultures and Sacred Lands." Official Website of the International Indian Treaty Council, www.treatycouncil.org/home.htm.

[52] The World Council of Indigenous Peoples (WCIP) was founded in 1975 as a powerful force for uniting dispossessed indigenous peoples across the globe. Douglas E. Sanders, "The Formation of the World Council of Indigenous Peoples" (International Working Group of Indigenous Affairs (IWGIA), Doc. 29, 1977). It formulated the basis for international indigenous claims with its 1977 Declaration on Human Rights and its 1984 Declaration of Principles. World Council of Indigenous Peoples, Declaration on Human Rights, September 24–27, 1977, available at www.cwis.org/fwdp/ International/wcip_dec.txt; World Council of Indigenous Peoples, Declaration of Principles, September 23–30, 1984, available at www.cwis.org/fwdp/Resolutions/ WCIP/wcip.txt. The WCIP was dissolved in 1996 due to internal conflict. Christian J. B. Hicks, "Stallo's Knife?: An Historical Analysis of the Saami/United Nations Relationship," in Northern Veche, Proceedings of the Second NRF Open Meeting, Veliky Novgorod, Russia, September 19–22, 2002, 116 (2004), 118, available at www.nrf.is/images/stories/pdf/reports/northern_veche/theme2.pdf.

[53] Cf. Wilmer, *supra* note 2. See generally Battiste, *supra* note 4.

[54] José Martínez Cobo, Special Rapporteur, *Study of the Problem of Discrimination against Indigenous Populations* (E/CN.4/Sub.2/1986/7/Add.4).

populations with the mandate to review pertinent national developments and to draft international standards concerning the rights of
indigenous peoples.

Driven by Dr. Erica-Irene Daes, the chairperson of the UN Working
Group on Indigenous Populations, established in 1982, indigenous
peoples found a forum in Geneva, where every community received
five minutes, and not one second more, to bring its complaints to the
attention of the world. The Working Group fielded these claims and
responded in 1993 with a Draft Declaration on the Rights of Indigenous
Peoples.[55]

In 1995, the Human Rights Commission appointed a new working
group, with predominantly government participation, charged with
elaborating a consensus on the draft declaration. As the Human Rights
Commission was transformed into the Human Rights Council, one of
its very first acts was to approve the draft declaration's final compromise
text as submitted by the chair.[56] Last changes were made over the course
of 2007, primarily to accommodate some of the demands of the African
states which had resulted in the deferral.[57]

The final version of the Declaration was adopted on September 13,
2007, by a landslide affirmative vote of 144 states in the UN General
Assembly.[58] Only four countries – the United States, Canada, Australia,
and New Zealand – voted against it, while Azerbaijan, Bangladesh,
Bhutan, Burundi, Colombia, Georgia, Kenya, Nigeria, Russia, Samoa,
and Ukraine abstained.[59]

Subsequently, Australia had a change of government and change of
heart: it endorsed the Declaration in April 2009. Similarly, on April
19, 2010, the government of New Zealand declared its support for the

---

[55] UN Economic and Social Council (ECOSOC), UN Commission on Human Rights,
Sub-commission on Prevention of Discrimination and Protection of Minorities,
Working Group on Indigenous Populations, *Report of the Working Group on Indigenous
Populations on its Eleventh Session*, 50–51, UN Doc. E/CN.4/Sub.2/1993/29 (1993) (here-
inafter Draft Declaration, repr. 9 *St. Thomas Law Review* 212 (1996).

[56] Human Rights Council, Working Group of the Commission on Human Rights to
Elaborate a Draft Declaration in Accordance with Paragraph 5 of the General Assembly
Resolution 49/214 of 23 December 1994, UN Doc. A/HRC/RES/1/2 (November 13, 2006),
available at http://ap.ohchr.org/documents/sdpage_e.aspx?b=10&se=2&t=11.

[57] For details see Siegfried Wiessner, "Indigenous Sovereignty: A Reassessment in Light of
the 2007 UN Declaration on the Rights of Indigenous Peoples," 41 *Vanderbilt Journal of
Transnational Law* 1141 (2008), 1159–62.

[58] United Nations Declaration on the Rights of Indigenous Peoples, *supra* note 1.

[59] Ibid.

Declaration.[60] On November 12, 2010, Canada formally endorsed this instrument.[61] Colombia and Samoa, originally abstaining countries, have now expressed their support for the Declaration.[62] Most importantly, on December 16, 2010, President Barack Obama endorsed the instrument on behalf of the United States of America.[63] We have thus arrived at a global consensus on the UN Declaration on the Rights of Indigenous Peoples.

The outcome of the Declaration process and the changes the global indigenous movement effectuated by consciously engaging the organized international community were nothing short of monumental. One important change was the delegitimization of the conceptual grounding of the Conquest in the notion of *terra nullius*, which European powers had used to justify the acquisition of overseas lands by simple conquest – not only disregarding the will of the conquered original inhabitants of the land, but treating them, in essence, as legally irrelevant, as Aristotelian "natural slaves," in the Spanish version of the Conquest.[64] The conquerors thoroughly believed in the superiority of European culture, as shown by France's promotion of its *"mission civilisatrice"*[65] and Spanish attempts to convert the "savages."[66]

Today, the international community generally accepts that the *terra nullius* concept in the acquisition of inhabited land is racist, as reflected in paragraph 4 of the Preamble of the 2007 UN Declaration on the Rights of Indigenous Peoples.[67] General international law discarded

---

[60] "National Government to Support UN Rights Declaration," press release, John Key, Prime Minister, New Zealand government (April 20, 2010), available at www.beehive. govt.nz/release/national+govt+support+un+rights+declaration.

[61] See "Canada's Statement of Support on the United Nations Declaration on the Rights of Indigenous Peoples," press release, Indian and Northern Affairs Canada (November 12, 2010), available at www.ainc-inac.gc.ca/ap/ia/dcl/stmt-eng.asp.

[62] UN Declaration on the Rights of Indigenous Peoples, *supra* note 1.

[63] Remarks by the President at the White House Tribal Nations Conference, December 16, 2010, available at www.whitehouse.gov/the-press-office/2010/12/16/remarks-president-white-house-tribal-nations-conference.

[64] UN Declaration on the Rights of Indigenous Peoples, *supra* note 1, Pt. I, Arts. 2–3 (delegitimizing the *terra nullius* notion by proclaiming that indigenous people are equal to all others and retain the right to self-determination).

[65] See generally Matthew Burrows, "'Mission Civilisatrice': French Cultural Policy in the Middle East, 1860–1914," 29 *Historical Journal* 109 (1986).

[66] See *Western Sahara*, Advisory Opinion, 1975 ICJ 12 (October 16).

[67] UN Declaration on the Rights of Indigenous Peoples, *supra* note 1, Preamble, 4 ("Affirming further that all doctrines, policies and practices based on or advocating superiority of peoples or individuals on the basis of national origin or racial, religious, ethnic or

terra nullius as a consequence of the 1975 *Western Sahara* Opinion of
the International Court of Justice (ICJ), which considered land agreements between indigenous peoples and states as "derivative roots of
title" rather than recognizing original title obtained by occupation of
terrae nullius.[68]

The 2007 UN Declaration is a milestone of indigenous empowerment.
Legally speaking, United Nations declarations, as almost any other resolution by the General Assembly, are, according to Article 12 of the UN
Charter, of a mere hortatory character: they are characterized as "recommendations" without legally binding character.[69] There have been
attempts to ascribe a higher degree of authority to General Assembly resolutions designated as "declarations." In 1962, the Office of Legal Affairs of
the United Nations, upon request by the Commission on Human Rights,
clarified, that "[i]n United Nations practice, a 'declaration' is a formal
and solemn instrument ... resorted to only in very rare cases relating to
matters of major and lasting importance where maximum compliance is
expected."[70]

Though not legally binding per se, a declaration may be or become
binding to the extent that its various provisions are backed up by con-
forming state practice and *opinio juris.*[71] This issue needs to be independently assessed – just like any other claim to the customary international
law character *vel non* of any purported new rule.[72] Thus, to the extent
that the Declaration reflects preexisting customary international law or
engenders any future such law, it is binding on states that do not qualify
as persistent objectors.[73]

Regarding the Declaration's legal effect, another new development has
to be taken into account: there may be standards of evaluation of state conduct applied by intergovernmental bodies that cannot be counted among

cultural differences are racist, scientifically false, legally invalid, morally condemnable
and socially unjust.").
[68] The Court found that agreements between colonizing states and local rulers could be
"regarded as derivative roots of title, and not original titles obtained by occupation of
terrae nullius." *Western Sahara, supra* note 67, at 39. It also entertained the concept of
"legal ties" based on non-European ideas of governance as being relevant under international law. W. Michael Reisman, "Protecting Indigenous Rights in International
Adjudication," 89 *American Journal of International Law* 350 (1995), 354–55.
[69] UN Charter, Articles 10, 11. The one formal exception, referring to budget allocations to
member states (Art. 17(2) UN Charter), does not apply here.
[70] Economic and Social Council, *Report of the Commission on Human Rights* (E/3616/
Rev. l), para. 105, 18th session, March 19–April 14, 1962.
[71] Ibid.   [72] Anaya and Wiessner, *supra* note 1.
[73] Ibid.

the traditional "sources" of international law enumerated in Article 38(1) of the ICJ Statute. The vanguard in this development is the process of "universal periodic review" instituted by the Human Rights Council. A standard of evaluation in this review, the Council announced, is, besides treaties to which the various countries are party, the Universal Declaration of Human Rights.[74] Similarly, in August 2008, Professor S. James Anaya, the United Nations Special Rapporteur on the rights of indigenous peoples, announced that he will measure state conduct vis-à-vis indigenous peoples by the yardstick of UNDRIP.[75] As a matter of policy direction, it has also been urged that the standards of UNDRIP be "mainstreamed" into the policies and programs of the UN, the International Labour Organization (ILO), and the United Nations Educational, Scientific and Cultural Organization (UNESCO).[76] Also, the concept of "soft law" has been offered to characterize the legal significance of UNDRIP.[77]

---

[74] Human Rights Council, Annex to Resolution 5/1, *United Nations Human Rights Council: Institution Building*, June 18, 2007, para. 1, available at ap.ohchr.org/documents/E/HRC/resolutions/A_HRC_RES_5_1.doc.

[75] According to UN Special Rapporteur S. James Anaya, UNDRIP represents "an authoritative common understanding, at the global level, of the minimum content of the rights of indigenous peoples, upon a foundation of various sources of international human rights law … The principles and rights affirmed in the Declaration constitute or add to the normative frameworks for the activities of United Nations human rights institutions, mechanisms and specialized agencies as they relate to indigenous peoples." Human Rights Council, *Report of the Special Rapporteur on the situation of human rights and fundamental freedoms of indigenous people, S. James Anaya* (A/HRC/9/9), August 11, 2008, paras. 85, 88, available at www2.ohchr.org/english/bodies/hrcouncil/docs/9session/A-HRC-9–9AEV.doc.

[76] Mr. Koïchiro Matsuura, UNESCO Director-General, highlighted his organization's participation in the "UN Task Team to elaborate the United Nations Development Group (UNDG) Guidelines on Indigenous People Issues, which will orient UN country teams in their efforts to mainstream the principles of the UN Declaration on the Rights of Indigenous Peoples in development programmes." He added, "[w]e believe that it is only through intercultural dialogue between generations, cultures and civilizations, as well as between indigenous peoples, societies and States at large that indigenous cultures can fully flourish." Message from Mr. Koïchiro Matsuura, Director-General of UNESCO, on the occasion of the International Day of the World's Indigenous People, August 9, 2008, available at portal.unesco.org/culture/en/ev.php-URL_ID=37756&URL_DO=DO_TOPIC&URL_SECTION=201.html.

[77] Mauro Barelli, "The Role of Soft Law in the International Legal System: The Case of the United Nations Declaration on the Rights of Indigenous Peoples," 58 *International and Comparative Law Quarterly* 957 (2009). The term "soft law" has been used to characterize emerging principles of international law of quite some generality that have not "hardened" yet into binding sources of law. It has often been applied in the field of international environmental law. For a view opposing its application in the field of indigenous peoples' rights, see Siegfried Wiessner, "Joining Control to Authority: The Hardened 'Indigenous Norm,'" 25 *Yale Journal of International Law* 301 (2000).

The Declaration, even back in its draft form, has also already formed the basis for legislation in individual countries, such as the Indigenous Peoples' Rights Act in the Philippines,[78] and it has inspired constitutional and statutory reforms in various states of Latin America.[79]

Substantively, the Preamble of the Declaration recognizes indigenous peoples' essential contribution to the "diversity and richness of civilization and cultures, which constitute the common heritage of mankind." Even though their situation "varies from region to region and from country to country," indigenous peoples and persons enjoy all human rights, and they are free and equal to all others. The essential novelty of this instrument is its recognition of "indispensable" collective rights. Indigenous peoples' distinctive demands are those for self-determination, the preservation and flourishing of their cultures, and the protection of their rights to their lands. They will be addressed seriatim.

3.1.   Self-determination

As far as the indigenous peoples' claim to self-determination is concerned, it is recognized in a rather broad fashion in Article 3 UNDRIP: "Indigenous peoples have the right to self-determination. By virtue of that right they freely determine their political status and freely pursue their economic, social and cultural development."

This formulation is, however, immediately followed in Article 4 by a restriction of this right to local and internal self-government: "Indigenous peoples, in exercising their right to self-determination, have the right to autonomy or self-government in matters relating to their internal and local affairs, as well as ways and means for financing their autonomous functions."

Also, in reaction to various states' articulated fears of the specter of secession, Article 46(1) clearly outlaws violations of the territorial

---

[78] An Act to Recognize, Protect and Promote the Rights of Indigenous Cultural Communities/Indigenous Peoples, Creating a National Commission on Indigenous Peoples, Establishing Implementing Mechanisms, Appropriating Funds Thereof, and for Other Purposes, Rep. Act No. 8371, § 2(a)–(f), (1997) (Phil.), available at www.grain.org/brl_files/philippines-ipra-1999-en.pdf.

[79] See Wiessner, *supra* note 23, at 74–89 (discussing the increase in government protection of the rights of indigenous peoples in Latin America). As the first country in the world to do so, Bolivia in November 2007 incorporated the 2007 Declaration, via National Law 3760, wholesale into its national law. UN Declaration on the Rights of Indigenous Peoples passed as law in Bolivia, December 2007, available at www.iwgia.org/sw18043.asp.

integrity of states that might be justified by an indigenous people's claim to self-determination:

> Nothing in this Declaration may be interpreted as implying for any State, people, group or person any right to engage in any activity or to perform any act contrary to the Charter of the United Nations or construed as authorizing or encouraging any action which would dismember or impair, totally or in part, the territorial integrity or political unity of sovereign and independent States.

In most cases, indigenous peoples are not aiming at becoming independent nation states with all their attributes of embassies and consulates, modern defense forces, and so on.[80] Therefore the issue of whether a claim to external self-determination, with the option of political independence – that is, secession – can be based on Article 3 UNDRIP appears to be moot. In any event, while Article 46(1) UNDRIP does not expressly banish the specter of secession by indigenous peoples – it could be argued that such remedy could be justified, in the words of the Canadian Supreme Court, if an indigenous people, like any other definable group, is "denied meaningful access to government"[81] – it severely restricts the argument that a right to secession or external self-determination is guaranteed by Article 3's broadly formulated right to self-determination.

The claim to indigenous sovereignty is founded upon the aspiration to preserve their inherited ways of life, to change those traditions as *they* see necessary, and to make their cultures flourish. That goal drives the claim for independent decision-making on the structures and functions of decision-making within the indigenous community. Internal autonomy thus asks of modern nation states to recognize formally "democratic" as well as formally "non-democratic" forms of indigenous government – as long as they are essential to the traditional ways of life. This would include the recognition of law-making and -applying powers by traditional leaders

---

[80] See International Forum on Globalization, *Draft Report Toward a Campaign in Support of the UN Declaration on the Rights of Indigenous Peoples*, August 2, 2007, at 17: "Indigenous peoples insist that they are not looking for the right of secession, but for other forms of self-determination." Available at www.ifg.org/pdf/ draft%20report%20UN%20Dec.pdf.

[81] The Canadian Supreme Court, in its *Québec* Opinion, concluded that:
[T]he international law right to self-determination only generates, at best, a right to external self-determination in situations of former colonies; where a people is oppressed, as for example under foreign military occupation; or where a definable group is denied meaningful access to government to pursue their political, economic, social and cultural development. *Re: Secession of Québec*, [1998] 2 SCR 217 (Can.), repr. 37 ILM 1340 (1998), 1373, para. 138.

in their various spheres of authority – peace chiefs, war chiefs, shamans, elders, and so on. An obligation to have indigenous peoples accede to modern formal processes of periodic election and change of leaders runs against the spirit of preservation of the innermost core of their culture – that is, decisions about how their decisions are made. It might complete, as previous policies of extermination and assimilation did, the circle of conquest. On the other hand, indigenous peoples themselves might want to change the way decisions have been made. But that decision should be theirs, and theirs alone, not forced upon them by the outside world. A good intellectual tool to analyze the parallel legal spheres established by such notions of self-government is the understanding of law as a process of authoritative and controlling decision within a community.[82] It focuses on messages of policy content – that is, decisions – sent by persons with authority within a certain community to members of that community, messages backed up by a threat of severe deprivation of values or a high expectation of indulgences or benefits.[83] Law is thus made in a variety of diverse communities,[84] including, but not limited to, the state. This is a key insight that predates, but essentially agrees with, modern legal pluralism,[85] as applied to indigenous peoples[86] or with the idea of parallel sovereignty.[87]

There are issues that remain: What is the substantive range of decision-making within autonomous indigenous communities? Are there any externally imposed limits? Such sources of limitation may be found in international law, particularly in the form of universally recognized human

---

[82] Myres S. McDougal, Harold D. Lasswell, and W. Michael Reisman, "The World Constitutive Process of Authoritative Decision," 19 *Journal of Legal Education* 253 (1967); W. Michael Reisman, "International Law-Making: A Process of Communication," 75 *Proceedings of the American Society of International Law* 101 (1981); Siegfried Wiessner, "International Law in the 21st Century: Decisionmaking in Institutionalized and Non-Institutionalized Settings, in International Justice," 26 *Thesaurus Acroasium* 129 (1997).

[83] W. Michael Reisman, Siegfried Wiessner, and Andrew R. Willard, "The New Haven School: A Brief Introduction," 32 *Yale Journal of International Law* 587 (2007), 588, 591–592.

[84] In the context of indigenous peoples, the concept of the relevant community obviates the need to draw controversial lines between territorial and personal communities.

[85] See, e.g., Paul Schiff Berman, "A Pluralist Approach to International Law," 32 *Yale Journal of International Law* 307 (2007); Brian Z. Tamanaha, "Understanding Global Legal Pluralism: Past to Present, Local to Global," 30 *Sydney Law Review* 375 (2007).

[86] Nicole Roughan, "The Association of State and Indigenous Law: A Case Study in 'Legal Association,'" (2009) 59 *University of Toronto Law Journal* 135 (2009).

[87] Cf. Federico Lenzerini, "Sovereignty Revisited: International Law and Parallel Sovereignty of Indigenous Peoples," 42 *Texas International Law Journal* 155 (2006), 189.

rights.[88] Consensus might be reached relatively easily on limiting certain outcomes of autonomous indigenous decision-making processes – such as the prohibition of ancient practices such as human sacrifice, however culturally embedded this practice may have been with some indigenous peoples. Other issues, such as the differential treatment of gender groups, present problems similar to those encountered in the debate over cultural relativism with respect to practices in certain religiously bounded states: where is the proper line to be drawn between the authority of a community to govern itself in light of its own values and the minimum requirements of the global value system of a world order of human dignity established in positive international law after World War II? Much of this has to be worked out in respectful dialogue between cultures.

3.2.   Culture

The effective protection of indigenous cultures is key to the understanding of the Declaration. In fact, the essential claims of indigenous peoples to their lands and self-government can only be properly understood by linking them to their *raison d'être* – that is, the survival and the flourishing of their ways of life and traditions – that is, their culture. Cultural rights in the broadest sense thus include not only rights to culture narrowly conceived, but also the culturally bounded right to property and the culturally grounded right to self-determination.[89]

The fundamental desire to safeguard their culture undergirds, in particular, the novel prohibition of forced assimilation of indigenous peoples or destruction of their culture (Article 8(1) – going beyond the prohibition of genocide against them, as enunciated in Article 7(2)), the prohibition of their forced removal and relocation (Article 10), their right to practice and revitalize their cultural traditions and customs, including the right to maintain, protect and develop past, present, and future manifestations

---

[88] See Art. 46(2) UNDRIP:

> In the exercise of the rights enunciated in the present Declaration, human rights and fundamental freedoms of all shall be respected. The exercise of the rights set forth in this Declaration shall be subject only to such limitations as are determined by law and in accordance with *international human rights obligations*. Any such limitations shall be non-discriminatory and strictly necessary solely for the purpose of securing due recognition and respect for the rights and freedoms of others and for meeting the just and most compelling requirements of a democratic society. (Emphasis added.)

[89] Siegfried Wiessner, "The Cultural Rights of Indigenous Peoples: Achievements and Continuing Challenges," 22 *European Journal of International Law* 121 (2011), 139.

of such cultures (Article 11), including the right to manifest, practice, develop, and teach their spiritual and religious traditions, customs and ceremonies, as well as the restitution and repatriation of ceremonial objects and human remains (Article 12). Article 13 guarantees indigenous peoples the right to "revitalize, use, develop and transmit to future generations their histories, languages, oral traditions, philosophies," and so on, and obligates states to "take effective measures to ensure that this right is protected." An indigenous people's language is central to its culture – an ever more important issue in view of the accelerating threat that those languages will vanish and the need for this alarming downward spiral to be brought to a halt.[90]

Article 14 articulates individual and collective rights to education, including the right of indigenous peoples to "establish and control their educational systems and institutions providing education in their own languages, in a manner appropriate to their cultural methods of teaching and learning," as well as the right of "indigenous individuals, particularly children," to "all levels and forms of education of the State without discrimination." Article 15 guarantees indigenous peoples the right to have "their cultures, traditions, histories and aspirations ... appropriately reflected in education and public information." This includes the state's duty to combat prejudice and discrimination and to develop tools that "promote tolerance, understanding and good relations among indigenous peoples and all other segments of society." Article 16 grants indigenous peoples the right to "establish their own media in their own languages," an important aspect of self-determination, and to have non-discriminatory access to all forms of non-indigenous media; also states have a "duty to ensure that State-owned media duly reflect indigenous cultural diversity," and they "should encourage privately-owned media to adequately reflect" such diversity.

The essential treaty provision supporting the Declaration's rights to culture is Article 27 of the International Covenant on Civil and Political Rights (ICCPR):

> In those States in which ethnic, religious or linguistic minorities exist, persons belonging to such minorities shall not be denied the right, in community with the other members of their group, to enjoy their own

---

[90] For a recent discussion of these serious issues, see Allison M. Dussias, "Indigenous Languages Under Siege: The Native American Experience," 3 *Intercultural Human Rights Law Review* 5 (2008); Douglas A. Kibbee, *Minority Language Rights: Historical and Comparative Perspectives*, 3 *Intercultural Human Rights Law Review* 79 (2008).

culture, to profess and practice their own religion, or to use their own language.[91]

Similarly, according to Article 15(1)(a) of the International Covenant on Economic and Social Rights (ICESCR), "the States Parties to the present Covenant recognize the right of everyone to take part in cultural life." These formulations reflect the desire of important nation states to protect culture through (individual) rights of members of the group rather than (collective) rights of the groups themselves.[92] The jurisprudence of the respective treaty-monitoring bodies has, however, moved ever more strongly in the direction of collectivizing these rights. The UN Committee for Economic, Social and Cultural Rights stated that minorities and indigenous peoples are guaranteed the freedom to practice and promote awareness of their culture,[93] defined in both individual and collective dimensions and as reflecting "the community's way of life and thought."[94] The Human Rights Committee's General Comment No. 23 on Article 27 ICCPR states that this provision protects "individual rights," but that the obligations owed by states are collective in nature.[95] In its jurisprudence it has consistently stated that the right to enjoyment of culture, practice of religion, or use of language can only be meaningfully exercised "in a community" – that is, as a group.[96]

One of the other legal issues has been whether Article 27 requires positive measures to be taken to protect a culture. In its General Comment No. 23, the Committee observed that "culture manifests itself in many forms, including a particular way of life associated with the use of land resources,

---

[91] International Covenant on Civil and Political Rights, *supra* note 29, Art. 27.

[92] Cf. Ana Vrdolyak, "Self-Determination and Cultural Rights," in Francesco Francioni and Martin Scheinin (eds.), *Cultural Human Rights* (Leiden and Boston, MA: Martinus Nijhoff, 2008), 41, at 59, with reference to Professors Tomuschat and Rodley, who share the opinion that a variety of individual guarantees make minority rights redundant. Christian Tomuschat, "Protection of Minorities under Article 27 of the International Covenant on Civil and Political Rights," in *Völkerrecht als Rechtsordnung – Internationale Gerichtsbarkeit – Menschenrechte, Festschrift für Hermann Mosler* (Berlin and New York: Springer, 1983), 952; and Nigel Rodley, "Conceptual Problems in the Protection of Minorities: International Legal Developments?," 17 *Human Rights Quarterly* 48 (1995), 54–59.

[93] General Discussion on the Right to Take Part in Cultural Life as recognized in Article 15 of the International Covenant on Economic, Social and Cultural Rights, UN Doc. E/1993/23, Chapter VII, para. 205, as cited by Vrdolyak, *supra* note 92, at 58.

[94] General Discussion, *supra* note 93, paras. 204, 209, 210 and 213.

[95] General Comment No. 23, UN Doc. HRI/GEN/1/Rev.1, 38 (1994), para. 6(2).

[96] Vrdolyak, *supra* note 92, at 61, with further reference to the *Kitok, Ominayak, Länsman*, and *Apriana Mahuika* cases.

especially in the case of indigenous peoples. That right may include such traditional activities as fishing or hunting and the right to live in reserves protected by law. The enjoyment of those rights may require positive legal measures of protection and measures to ensure the effective participation of members of minority communities in decisions which affect them."[97]

It has also been argued that the establishment and development of indigenous cultural institutions and systems (that is, indigenous cultural autonomy) is properly located within the concept of collective cultural rights addressed by provisions such as Article 27, and not within the sphere of self-determination addressed by Article 1 of the ICCPR, for example – a concept referred to as essentially belonging to the political, or power, domain.[98] The better argument is, probably, a fusion of both: an understanding of indigenous sovereignty, like that offered by famed Native American leader and scholar Vine Deloria Jr., as based on an essentially cultural foundation. He stated that indigenous sovereignty "consist[s] more of a continued cultural integrity than of political powers and to the degree that a nation loses its sense of cultural identity, to that degree it suffers a loss of sovereignty."[99]

Other issues to be explored in this context are those relating to the work of UNESCO on cultural diversity, cultural heritage, traditional know-ledge, and the emerging concept of *sui generis* intellectual property rights for indigenous peoples in the context of the World Intellectual Property Organization, the United Nations Conference on Trade and Development (UNCTAD), and the Convention on Biological Diversity.[100]

3.3.   Land

Key to the effective protection of indigenous peoples' cultures is the safe-guarding of their land. Being "indigenous" means to live within one's

---

[97] General Comment No. 23, *supra* note 95, para. 7.

[98] Alexandra Xanthaki, *Indigenous Rights and United Nations Standards: Self-Determination, Culture and Land* (Cambridge University Press, 2007), 251.

[99] Deloria, *supra* note 25. See also Wallace Coffey and Rebecca Tsosie, "Rethinking the Tribal Sovereignty Doctrine: Cultural Sovereignty and the Collective Future of Indian Nations," 12 *Stanford Law and Policy Review* 191 (2001).

[100] For a most recent discussion of pertinent issues, see Francioni and Scheinin, *supra* note 92, including, in particular, Federico Lenzerini, "Indigenous Peoples' Cultural Rights and the Controversy over Commercial Use of their Traditional Knowledge," ibid., at 119. See also Stephen M. McJohn and Lorie Graham, "Indigenous Peoples and Intellectual Property," 19 *Washington University Journal of Law and Policy* 313 (2006), and Siegfried Wiessner and Marie Battiste, "The 2000 Revision of the United Nations Draft Principles and Guidelines on the Protection of the Heritage of Indigenous People," 13 *St. Thomas Law Review* 383 (2000).

roots.[101] Indigenous peoples, in a popular definition, have thus "always been in the place where they are."[102] While this definition may not reflect empirical truth as, historically, a great many migrations of human communities have taken place, the collective consciousness of indigenous peoples, often expressed in creation stories or similar sacred tales of their origin, places them unequivocally and since time immemorial at the location of their physical existence. More importantly, their beliefs makes remaining at that place a compelling dictate of faith.

The struggle of indigenous peoples led to a treaty that recognized the rights of groups, particularly with respect to resources, as formulated in the 1989 ILO Convention No. 169.[103] This treaty has now been ratified by virtually all of the Latin American countries with significant indigenous populations. It ensures indigenous peoples' control over their legal status, internal structures, and environment, and it guarantees indigenous peoples' rights to ownership and possession of the total environment they occupy or use.[104] Article 25 of the 2007 UN Declaration emphasizes their "distinctive spiritual relationship" with their lands, and Article 26 affirms their "right to the lands, territories and resources which they have traditionally owned, occupied or otherwise used or acquired" (s. 1); and their "right to own, use, develop and control the lands, territories and resources that they possess by reason of traditional ownership or other traditional occupation or use, as well as those which they have otherwise acquired" (s. 2). It also mandates that "States shall give legal recognition and protection to these lands, territories and resources. Such recognition shall be conducted with due respect to the customs, traditions and land tenure systems of the indigenous peoples concerned."

In addition, global comparative research on state practice and *opinio juris* over a period of five years in the late 1990s reached certain conclusions about the content of newly formed customary international law regarding the rights and status of indigenous peoples. The worldwide indigenous renaissance had led to significant changes in constitutions, statutes, regulations, case law, and other authoritative and controlling statements and practices of states that had substantial indigenous

---

[101] Etymologically, the Latin word "*indigena*" is composed of two words, "*indi*," meaning "within" and "*gen*" or "*genere*" meaning "root." *Longman Dictionary of Contemporary English* 724 (3rd edition, 1995).

[102] Definition of "indigenous," *Longman Dictionary of Contemporary English Online*, available at www. ldoceonline.com/dictionary/indigenous.

[103] International Labour Organization (ILO), Convention Concerning Indigenous and Tribal Peoples in Independent Countries, June 27, 1989, 28 ILM 1382.

[104] Ibid., Arts. 1–19.

populations. These changes included the recognition of indigenous peoples' rights to preserve their distinct identity and dignity and to govern their own affairs – be they "tribal sovereigns" in the United States, the Sami in Lapland, the *resguardos* in Colombia, or Canada's Nunavut.[105] This move toward recognition of indigenous self-government was accompanied by an affirmation of native communities' title to the territories they traditionally used or occupied.

In many countries, domestic law now mandates a practice that would have been unthinkable only a few years ago: the demarcation and registration of First Nations' title to the lands of their ancestors. Indigenous people achieved this dramatic victory through several means: a peace treaty in Guatemala, constitutional and statutory changes in countries such as Brazil,[106] modifications of the common law in Australia, and the law of Taiwan and Malaysia, as well as landmark judgments in Botswana, South Africa, and Colombia.[107] Indigenous culture, language, and tradition, to the extent they have survived, are increasingly inculcated and celebrated. Treaties of the distant past are being honored, and agreements are fast becoming the preferred mode of interaction between indigenous communities and the descendants of the former conquering elites. This now very widespread state practice and *opinio juris* regarding the legal treatment of indigenous peoples allowed the following conclusion in 1999:

> First, indigenous peoples are entitled to maintain and develop their distinct cultural identity, their spirituality, their language, and their traditional ways of life. Second, they hold the right to political, economic and social self-determination, including a wide range of autonomy and the maintenance and strengthening of their own system of justice. Third, indigenous peoples have a right to demarcation, ownership, development, control and use of the lands they have traditionally owned or otherwise occupied and used. Fourth, governments are to honor and faithfully observe their treaty commitments to indigenous nations.[108]

---

[105] Wiessner, *supra* note 57, at 1156.

[106] For a recent reaffirmation of the Constitution's guarantee to indigenous peoples of their right to their traditional lands, see the March 19, 2009, decision of the Brazilian Supreme Court in the case of *Raposa Serra do Sol*, a vast indigenous area located in the Amazonian state of Roraima defended against the claims of invading rice farmers and senators of the state; "Supreme Court Upholds the Demarcation of Raposa Serra do Sol Land," available at www.braziljusticenet.org/606.html#Supreme.

[107] For an up-to-date survey of these decisions and other incidents of state practice, see Federico Lenzerini, "The Rights of Indigenous Peoples under Customary International Law," 2010 ILA Interim Report, *supra* note 1, at 43–52.

[108] Wiessner, *supra* note 23, at 128. See also S. James Anaya and Robert A. Williams, Jr., "The Protection of Indigenous Peoples' Rights over Lands and Natural Resources under the

The Inter-American Commission on Human Rights took the key step from the global research effort to a practical application of those conclusions to the international legal status of indigenous peoples. Referring to this study and the opinions of other international legal scholars to argue for a new principle of customary international law,[109] the Inter-American Commission submitted the case of an indigenous group in the rainforest of Nicaragua to the Inter-American Court of Human Rights. The tribunal, in its celebrated *Awas Tingni* judgment of August 31, 2001,[110] affirmed the existence of an indigenous people's collective right to its land. It stated:

> Through an evolutionary interpretation of international instruments for the protection of human rights, … it is the opinion of this Court that article 21 of the Convention protects the right to property in a sense which includes, among others, the rights of members of the indigenous communities within the framework of communal property.
>
> Given the characteristics of the instant case, some specifications are required on the concept of property in indigenous communities. Among indigenous peoples there is a communitarian tradition regarding a communal form of collective property of the land, in the sense that ownership of the land is not centered on an individual but rather on the group and its community. Indigenous groups, by the fact of their very existence, have the right to live freely in their own territory; the close ties of indigenous people with the land must be recognized and understood as the fundamental basis of their cultures, their spiritual life, their integrity, and their

Inter-American Human Rights System," 14 *Harvard Human Rights Journal* 33 (2001); S. James Anaya, *Indigenous Peoples in International Law*, 2nd edn (Oxford University Press, 2004), 49–72; Chidi Oguamanam, "Indigenous Peoples and International Law: The Making of a Regime," 30 *Queen's Law Journal* 348 (2004); Lenzerini, *supra* note 107. For a concurring analysis of indigenous land rights under customary international law and UNDRIP, see Sarah M. Stevenson, "Indigenous Land Rights and the Declaration on the Rights of Indigenous Peoples: Implications for Maori Land Claims in New Zealand," 32 *Fordham International Law Journal* 298 (2008). A recent monograph on the protection of groups in international law also concluded that "there is sufficient proof of State practice and *opinio juris* among States to suggest the existence of a right to autonomy for indigenous peoples in international law": Nicola Wenzel, *Das Spannungsverhältnis zwischen Gruppenschutz und Individualschutz im Völkerrecht* (Berlin: Springer, 2008), 508. *Accord* Marc Weller, "Settling Self-Determination Conflicts: Recent Developments," 20 *European Journal of International Law* 111 (2009), 116.

[109] "Final Written Arguments of the Inter-American Commission on Human Rights before the Inter-American Court of Human Rights in the Case of *Mayagna Indigenous Community of Awas Tingni v. Republic of Nicaragua*," 19 *Arizona Journal of International and Comparative Law* 327 (2002), 349.

[110] *Awas Tingni*, *supra* note 21. For details of this case see S. James Anaya and Claudio Grossman, "The Case of *Awas Tingni v. Nicaragua*: A New Step in the International Law of Indigenous Peoples," 19 *Arizona Journal of International and Comparative Law* 1 (2002).

economic survival. For indigenous communities, relations to the land are not merely a matter of possession and production but a material and spiritual element which they must fully enjoy, even to preserve their cultural legacy and transmit it to future generations.[111]

Other decisions in the same vein followed, including *Saramaka*, the recent decision involving Suriname.[112] The decisions of the Inter-American Court of Human Rights broke new ground as they radically reinterpreted Article 21 of the Inter-American Convention, the right to property – a provision, like all the other guarantees of the document, originally focused on the rights of individuals. Such a fundamental reinterpretation of the treaty can only be based on a significant shift in the normative expectations of the states. It is highly conceivable that the evidence for such a shift is found in the same material that has been adduced to prove customary international law: pertinent state practice and *opinio juris*.

The African Commission on Human and Peoples' Rights, in a most recent case, concerning the displacement from their traditional land of an indigenous community living in Kenya, the Endorois,[113] also found that the government's forced eviction of this indigenous people from their ancestral lands constituted a breach of their right to religious freedom,[114] of their right to property of their traditional land,[115] of their cultural rights,[116] of their right to dispose freely of their wealth and natural resources,[117] and of their right to development.[118]

It is no surprise that courts not bound by jurisdictional treaty restraints fully express their legal opinion. On October 18, 2007, Chief Justice

---

[111] *Awas Tingni, supra* note 21, paras. 148–149.

[112] *Saramaka People* v. *Suriname*, Inter-American Court of Human Rights, Preliminary Objections, Merits, Reparations, Costs, November 28, 2008, Ser. C, No. 172. See also *Moiwana Village* v. *Suriname*, Inter-American Court of Human Rights, June 15, 2005, Ser. C, No. 124; *Yakye Axa Indigenous Community* v. *Paraguay*, Inter-American Court of Human Rights, June 17, 2005, Ser. C, No. 125; *Sawhoyamaxa Indigenous Community* v. *Paraguay*, Inter-American Court of Human Rights, March 29, 2006, Ser. C, No. 146.

[113] *Centre for Minority Rights Development (Kenya) and Minority Rights Group International on behalf of Endorois Welfare Council* v. *Kenya*, Communication No. 276/2003, February 4, 2010, available at www.reliefweb.int/rw/RWFiles2010.nsf/FilesByRWDocUnidFilename/SMAR-82H3UE-full_report.pdf/$File/full_report.pdf. This ruling followed an earlier decision to the same effect in *The Social and Economic Rights Action Center for Economic and Social Rights* v. *Nigeria*, para. 63; and the South African Constitutional Court's restoration of indigenous lands in *Alexkor Limited* v. *The Richtersveld Community and Others*, 2003 (19) SA 48–51 (CC).

[114] Ibid., para. 173.

[115] Ibid., para. 238; see also para. 209 (defining the property right in detail).

[116] Ibid., para. 251.   [117] Ibid., para. 268.   [118] Ibid., para. 298.

A. O. Conteh of the Belize Supreme Court concluded: "Treaty obligations aside, it is my considered view that both customary international law and general international law would require that Belize respect the rights of its indigenous people to their lands and resources."[119]

Such a clear expression of *opinio juris* is now joined by other manifestations of a sense of being legally bound. Indigenous peoples' rights are being ever more "mainstreamed" on the international institutional level.[120] This is evidenced, for example, by the fact that the European Union has granted an exception to its ban on the importation of seal products to Inuit traders who kill seals in accordance with their traditional ways in contribution to their subsistence economy, based on a direct reference to the authority of the UN Declaration.[121] In addition, the obligation to be legally bound is also manifested in countries' general acceptance of the UN Special Rapporteur's usage of the Declaration as a yardstick for their compliance with indigenous peoples' rights.[122] The resulting "compliance

---

[119] *Aurelio Cal* v. *Attorney General of Belize*, Supreme Court of Belize, Judgment, October 18, 2007, para. 127, www.elaw.org/node/1620, 25 May 2009.

[120] See *supra*, note 77.

[121] Regulation (EC) No. 1007/2009 of the European Parliament and of the Council of 16 September 2009 on trade in seal products, *Official Journal of the European Union*, L 286/36, 31.10.2009, Article 3(1): "The placing on the market of seal products shall be allowed only where the seal products result from hunts traditionally conducted by Inuit and other indigenous communities and contribute to their subsistence." (L 286/38). The Preamble to that regulation explains:

> The fundamental economic and social interests of Inuit communities engaged in the hunting of seals as a means to ensure their subsistence should not be adversely affected. The hunt is an integral part of the culture and identity of the members of the Inuit society, and as such is recognized by the United Nations Declaration on the Rights of Indigenous Peoples. Therefore, the placing on the market of seal products which result from hunts traditionally conducted by Inuit and other indigenous communities and which contribute to their subsistence should be allowed. (L 286/37)

Certain Inuit communities have challenged this regulation before the European Court of Justice as "unduly limiting" their "subsistence possibilities ... relegating their economic activities to traditional hunting methods and subsistence." Action brought on 11 January 2010 – *Inuit Tapiriit Kanatami e.a.* v. *Parliament and Council* (Case T-18/10), (2010/C 100/64), *Official Journal of the European Union*, C 100/41, 17.4.2010. The key point here is, though, the reference to the UN Declaration as the motivating force for the exception for indigenous peoples from the general ban on trading in seal products.

[122] As evidenced by the inclusion of the UN Declaration on the Rights of Indigenous Peoples as the first instrument in the "normative framework" of the UN Special Rapporteur on the Rights of Indigenous Peoples, available at www2.ohchr.org/english/issues/indigenous/rapporteur/framework.htm (last accessed July 23, 2011). See also Anaya, *supra* note 75.

pull" will generate ever more state practice in support of the customary international law rule.

Appraisal and recommendation: toward a legal regime fostering the flourishing of indigenous peoples

Whatever legally has been achieved – on the hard ground of positive international law[123] – ought to be evaluated against the unyielding standard of a global order of human dignity that responds, to the maximum extent possible, to human needs and aspirations.[124] As law, in essence, ought to serve human beings,[125] any effort to design a better law should be conceived as a response to what humans need and value. Our quest thus should be redirected from the cataloguing of states' grants of power or tolerance of indigenous peoples' authorities toward the proper guiding light: the authentic claims and aspirations of the people involved.[126] In our context, this approach would lead to a framework of laws more narrowly tailored to the inner worlds of indigenous peoples. The "things humans value" vary from culture to culture, and they change over time. As Michael Reisman has explained, humans have a distinct need

> to create and ascribe meaning and value to immutable experiences of human existence: the trauma of birth, the discovery of the self as separate from others, the formation of gender or sexual identity, procreation, the death of loved ones, one's own death, indeed, the mystery of it all. Each culture … records these experiences in ways that provide meaning, guidance and codes of rectitude that serve as compasses for the individual as he or she navigates the vicissitudes of life.[127]

[123] Wiessner, *supra* note 77.

[124] Siegfried Wiessner, "Law as a Means to a Public Order of Human Dignity: The Jurisprudence of Michael Reisman," 34 *Yale Journal of International Law* 525 (2009), 528, 531. This intellectual framework of policy-oriented jurisprudence, also known as the New Haven School, allows for thorough interdisciplinary analysis and the finding of solutions to problems in the global common interest. For details see Reisman, Wiessner, and Willard, *supra* note 83; Siegfried Wiessner and Andrew R. Willard, "Policy-Oriented Jurisprudence," 44 *German Year Book of International Law* 96 (2001); Siegfried Wiessner and Andrew R. Willard, "Policy-Oriented Jurisprudence and Human Rights Abuses in Internal Conflict: Toward a World Public Order of Human Dignity," 93 *American Journal of International Law* 316 (1999).

[125] Siegfried Wiessner, "The New Haven School of Jurisprudence: A Universal Toolkit for Understanding and Shaping the Law," 18 *Asia Pacific Law Review* 45 (2010), 51.

[126] Robert B. Porter, "Pursuing the Path of Indigenization in the Era of Emergent International Law Governing the Rights of Indigenous Peoples," 5 *Yale Human Rights and Development Law Journal* 123 (2002) 133–35.

[127] W. Michael Reisman, "International Law and the Inner Worlds of Others," 9 *St. Thomas Law Review* 25 (1996), 25.

Thus from the need to make sense of one's individual and cultural experiences arise inner worlds, or each person's inner reality. The international human rights system, as Reisman sees it, is

> concerned with protecting, for those who wish to maintain them, the integrity of the unique visions of these inner worlds, from appraisal and policing in terms of the cultural values of others. This must be, for these inner world cosmovisions, or introcosms, are the central, vital part of the individuality of each of us. This is, to borrow Holmes' wonderful phrase, "where we live." Respect for the other requires, above all, respect for the other's inner world.[128]

The cultures of indigenous peoples have been under attack and are seriously endangered. One final step is the death of their language. As George Steiner wrote in 1975,

> Today entire families of language survive only in the halting remembrances of aged, individual informants ... or in the limbo of tape recordings. Almost at every moment in time, notably in the sphere of American Indian speech, some ancient and rich expression of articulate being is lapsing into irretrievable silence.[129]

Reisman concluded that political and economic self-determination in this context are important, "but it is the integrity of the inner worlds of peoples – their rectitude systems or their sense of spirituality – that is their distinctive humanity. Without an opportunity to determine, sustain, and develop that integrity, their humanity – and ours – is denied."[130]

Similarly, the late Vine Deloria, Jr., revered leader of the US indigenous revival, stated, as related above, that indigenous sovereignty "consist[s] more of a continued cultural integrity than of political powers."[131] "Sovereignty," explains another great Native American leader, Kirke Kickingbird, "cannot be separated from people or their culture."[132] In this vein, Taiaiake Alfred appeals for a process of "de-thinking" sovereignty. He states:

> Sovereignty ... is a social creation. It is not an objective or natural phenomenon, but the result of choices made by men and women, indicative

---

[128] Ibid., at 26.

[129] George Steiner, *After Babel: Aspects of Language and Translation* (Oxford University Press, 1992), 53. For a recent discussion, see Dussias, *supra* note 90; and Kibbee, *supra* note 9.

[130] Reisman, *supra* note 127, at 33.   [131] Deloria, *supra* note 25.

[132] Kirke Kickingbird et al., *Indian Sovereignty* (Washington DC: Institute for the Development of Indian Law, 1977), 2.

of a mindset located in, rather than a natural force creative of, a social and political order. The reification of sovereignty in politics today is the result of a triumph of a particular set of ideas over others – no more natural to the world than any other man-made object.

Indigenous perspectives offer alternatives, beginning with the restoration of a regime of respect. This ideal contrasts with the statist solution, still rooted in a classical notion of sovereignty that mandates a distributive rearrangement but with a basic maintenance of the superior posture of the state. True indigenous formulations are non-intrusive and build frameworks of respectful coexistence by acknowledging the integrity and autonomy of the various constituent elements of the relationship. They go far beyond even the most liberal Western conceptions of justice in promoting the achievement of peace, because they explicitly allow for difference while mandating the construction of sound relationships among autonomously powered elements.[133]

June McCue, director of First Nations Studies at the University of British Columbia and a member of the Neduten tribe, states:

> I can connect sovereignty and self-determination within the distinct context of my people by making an analogy to the trees on my Clan or house territory. The roots, trunk, and bark of the trees represent sovereignty to me. The special sap, food, medicines and seedlings that come from our trees are symbiotic with the life force or energy of my people and the land, united in a consciousness and connected through the web of life ...
>
> Indigenous conceptions of sovereignty are found in the respective traditions of Indigenous peoples and their relationships with their territories. The power to exercise sovereignty flows from their laws, customs, and governing systems and their interconnectedness with the Earth ...
>
> My people's power is sourced or rooted in our creation stories, our spirituality and our organic and peaceful institutions. Sovereignty requires the energy of the land and the people and is distinct about locality.[134]

Creation stories, in particular, are much more than accounts of the genesis of the Earth. They are essentially normative, as they portray

---

[133] Taiaiake Alfred, "Sovereignty," in Joanne Barker (ed.), *Sovereignty Matters: Locations of Contestation and Possibility in Indigenous Struggles for Self-Determination* (Lincoln, NE: University of Nebraska Press, 2005), 33, 46; see also Alfred, "'Sovereignty': An Inappropriate Concept," in Robert Odawi Porter (ed.), *Sovereignty, Colonialism and the Indigenous Nations: A Reader* (Durham, NC: Carolina Academic Press, 2005), 67, 67–71.

[134] June McCue, "New Modalities of Sovereignty: An Indigenous Perspective," 2 *Intercultural Human Rights Law Review* 19 (2007), 24–25.

appropriate, model behavior[135] – like the *hadith*, the traditions of the Prophet in Islam. As the Western Shoshone say, decisions are made by consensus; the whole community thus has ownership of the decision made.[136] Those decisions are ultimately based on natural laws that are not written by humans but imposed by the Creator, variously referred to as Mother Earth and Father Sky.[137] There is no separation between church and state. McCue explains:

> From an Indigenous perspective, sovereignty is not just human-centered and hierarchical; it is not solely born or sustained through brute force. Indigenous sovereignty must be birthed through a genuine effort to establish peace, respect, and balance in this world. Indigenous sovereignty is interconnected with self-determination. Non-Indigenous formulations of sovereignty treat states as artificial entities that hold sovereign rights such as territorial integrity or sovereign equality. Self-determination is severed as a right possessed by peoples which can limit state powers. Finally, Indigenous sovereignty is sacred and renewed with ceremonies that are rooted in the land.[138]

In detail, she puts this concept into context:

> In this sense, sovereignty can be seen as the frame that houses the life force or energy that can flow at high or low levels depending on how the people are living at any given particular moment in their territories. Such sovereign attributes are renewed each and every time we use our potlatch system and when clan members choose to fulfill their roles and responsibilities to each other and to their neighbors. These attributes are renewed when we act as stewards for our ecological spaces. These sovereign attributes do not negate the fact that my people also exercise attributes of sovereignty similar to those upon which Western societies found their state systems – such as protecting and defending territorial boundaries, and engaging in external foreign relations with trade and commerce. I would add peacemaking, possessing governing institutions for the people, a citizenry or permanent population with a language, and powers of wealth and resource redistribution amongst our clans. The comparative inquiry is rather one of the priorities and whether or

---

135 Peggy V. Beck et al., *The Sacred: Ways of Knowledge, Sources of Life* (Tsaile, AZ: Navajo Community College 1996), 102. Medicine men or shamans interpret the creation stories and determine how people "must live in order to keep the balance of relationships that order the world." Ibid.; see also Carole E. Goldberg, "Overextended Borrowing: Tribal Peacemaking Applied in Non-Indian Disputes," 72 *Washington Law Review* 1003 (1997), 1012–14.

136 Goldberg, *supra* note 135, at 1010.   137 Ibid., at 1009.

138 McCue, *supra* note 134, at 25–26.

not conduct or behaviors of the people are coordinate with our principles of living a good life and maintaining and securing peaceful good
relations.[139]

Taiaiake Alfred, even more focused on culture, has called for a physical
and spiritual self-renewal of indigenous communities, a radical "indigenous resurgence."[140]

Self-help and re-empowerment are thus key to the survival and the
flourishing of indigenous communities. These gains cannot be achieved,
however, if indigenous peoples and their cultures are crushed by the constant onslaught of modern society's influences. While it is impossible and
undesirable to imprison indigenous peoples in a living museum of their
culture, the world community at large ought to support their choice to
live according to the codes of their inner worlds.

What would an appropriate legal framework for the flourishing of
indigenous identity consist of?

1. First, *safe spaces* ought to be created. The Western concept of exclusive
   property should be used to legally shield the land indigenous peoples
   have traditionally held. No one has ever explained this need for connection with the land as eloquently as the Coordinator of the Indian
   Nations Union in the Amazon:

   > When the government took our land ... they wanted to give us another
   > place. ... But the State, the government, will never understand that we
   > do not have another place to go. The only possible place for [indigenous]
   > people to live and to re-establish our existence, to speak to our Gods, to
   > speak to our nature, to weave our lives, is where God created us ... We are
   > not idiots to believe that there is possibility of life for us outside of where
   > the origin of our life is. Respect our place of living, do not degrade our liv-
   > ing conditions, respect this life ... [T]he only thing we have is the right to
   > cry for our dignity and the need to live in our land.[141]

---

[139] Ibid.

[140] Taiaiake Alfred, *Wasáse – Indigenous Pathway of Action and Freedom* (Peterborough,
Ont.: Broadview Press, 2005), 198. While this book to an extent rejects alliances with
non-indigenous groups as a condition for the recapturing of the indigenous self,
others have cautioned against a resulting possible threat to the success of the indigenous movement. See Austen Parrish, "Changing Territoriality, Fading Sovereignty, and
the Development of Indigenous Rights," 31 *American Indian Law Review* 291 (2006),
312–13.

[141] Ailton Krenak, Co-ordinator of Indian Nations' Union, Remarks to the World
Commission on Environment and Development (WCED) Public Hearing, Sao Paulo
(October 28–29, 1985), quoted in World Commission on Environment and Development,
Our Common Future (Oxford University Press, 1987), 115.

Land rights are thus critical to indigenous peoples' survival,[142] and significant progress has been reached in the field of customary law regarding this claim.[143]

2. Within these lands, indigenous peoples should have the right to order their lives the way their traditions teach them. *Local and internal self-government*, or autonomy, as recognized in Article 4 of the UN Declaration,[144] is essential. To assuage the fears of existing states, secession or other threats to the territorial integrity of a state should generally be disallowed. An exception, as referred to by the Canadian Supreme Court in its advisory opinion on the secession of Québec, would apply, as with any other ethnic group, if an indigenous people were excluded from the political processes and suffered from wholesale discrimination.[145]

3. The third important claim, which ought to be heeded, is the indigenous peoples' cry for *free, prior, and informed consent* before the government takes any measure affecting them.[146] That includes

---

[142] Cf. Andrew Huff, *Indigenous Land Rights and the New Self-Determination*, 16 *Colorado Journal of International Environmental Law and Policy* 295 (2005), 295.

[143] See the description of pertinent customary international law, *supra*, section 3; see also Lindsey L. Wiersma, "Indigenous Lands as Cultural Property: A New Approach to Indigenous Land Claims," 54 *Duke Law Journal* 1061 (2004), 1077–78.

[144] United Nations Declaration on the Rights of Indigenous Peoples, *supra* note 1, Art. 4.

[145] Reference *Re: Secession of Québec, supra* note 82, at 1372–73; see also 2010 ILA Interim Report, *supra* note 1, at 10.

[146] Art. 19 of the Declaration enshrines this idea: "States shall consult and cooperate in good faith with the indigenous peoples concerned through their own representative institutions in order to obtain their free, prior and informed consent before adopting and implementing legislative or administrative measures that may affect them." Whether that includes, under the *lex lata*, a right to veto projects of the larger community in which they live is contested. The Inter-American Court of Human Rights in *Saramaka* appears to affirm it in the case of large-scale development projects with a major impact on indigenous land. *Saramaka People v. Suriname*, 2007 Inter-Am. Ct. H.R. (Ser. C) No. 172, ¶ 134. UN Special Rapporteur James Anaya cites this statement and adds, in conformity with UNDRIP Articles 10 and 29(2), a requirement of consent also in the case of relocation from traditional lands and the storage of toxic waste on those lands. UN Human Rights Council, *Report of the Special Rapporteur on the Situation of Human Rights and Fundamental Freedoms of Indigenous People*, para. 47, UN Doc. A/HRC/12/34 (July 15, 2009). He also sees a duty to consult arising whenever a state is contemplating any development or resource extraction projects on indigenous or tribal lands. Ibid., at para. 48. In addition, *Saramaka* also asks for environmental and social impact studies prior to the commencement of projects with impacts on indigenous communities. *Saramaka People v. Suriname*, Interpretation of the Judgment on Preliminary Objections, Merits, Reparations and Costs, August 12, 2008, 2008 Inter-American Court of Human Rights (Ser. C) No. 185, para. 41.

relocation[147] and other displacement, as well as significant impairment of their distinct heritage. The term "indigenous heritage" should be broadly construed and subject to the same standards and means of protection as traditional intellectual property rights.[148]

4. The right to self-government ought to be granted with the express dedication to the survival of *their culture, their cosmovision, and their respect for the Earth*, including all living and nonliving things. The fact that, for some groups, religion is the law should be respected. While certain indigenous codes of criminal law may be restorative rather than retributive, those should be upheld as well. An indigenous people should also be entitled to make determinations regarding its membership and its internal structure of decision-making.[149] Indigenous sovereigns, like any government, should, however, be bound by the minimum threshold of universal standards of human rights.[150]

5. Indigenous peoples have already attained international legal agency through their equal representation on the United Nations' Permanent Forum on Indigenous Issues. The *treaties* concluded with them in the past should be honored, and disputes regarding their validity, breach, or interpretation should be resolved by appropriate *international bodies*.

6. Finally, affirmative steps should be taken more effectively to protect, promote, and revitalize indigenous languages and manifestations of culture.

This array of measures would serve to maintain indigenous sovereignty in the sense indigenous peoples themselves define it. These measures may be less threatening than traditional autonomy models suggest, and may prove to contribute collectively to the survival of the planet as a site of cultural diversity and mutual respect. Still, indigenous and non-indigenous forces need to combine in order to realize all of these aspirations. Many interests may stand in the way of these goals, and some of them may have

---

[147] Xanthaki, *supra* note 98, at 255 (referring to, *inter alia*, Art. 16 of the International Labor Organization (ILO) Convention No. 169).

[148] Cf. ECOSOC, Sub-commission on the Promotion and Protection of Human Rights, *Report of the Seminar on the Draft Principles and Guidelines for the Protection of the Heritage of Indigenous People*, UN Doc. E/CN.4/Sub.2/2000/26, June 19, 2000, para. 13,.

[149] See *supra* note 24.

[150] Draft Principles, *supra* note 148, para. 11. Such standards would appear to include the customary international law of human rights and entitlements under the human rights treaties ratified by the state concerned.

to be accommodated. In any event, struggle is essential to life, especially the life of the law,[151] and this is a battle worth fighting.

Conclusion

Indigenous sovereignty, just like any claim to sovereignty, is not granted. It inheres in its bearer; it grows, or it dies, from within. The 2007 United Nations Declaration on the Rights of Indigenous Peoples is based on the universal recognition of their claim to self-determination on their lands, an aspiration that lies at the heart of the rising indigenous peoples' claims to re-empowerment. In important respects, particularly regarding their rights to their territories, their culture, and internal self-government, the Declaration reaffirms preexisting rules of customary international law and treaty law. The right to recapture their identity, to reinvigorate their ways of life, to reconnect with the Earth, to regain their traditional lands, to protect their heritage, to revitalize their languages and manifest their culture – all of these entitlements are as important to indigenous people as the right to make final decisions in their internal political, judicial, and economic settings.

The flame of self-determination, however, needs to burn from inside the indigenous community itself. International and domestic law can, and should, stand ready to kindle, protect, and grow this flame until it burns fiercely, illuminating the path toward the ultimate self-realization of indigenous peoples around the world.

---

[151] Compare Rudolf von Jhering's introduction to his lecture *Der Kampf um's Recht*:
  The life of the law is struggle, – a struggle of nations, of the state power, of classes of individuals. All the law in the world has been obtained by strife. Every principle of law which obtains had first to be wrung by force from those who denied it; and every legal right – the legal rights of a whole nation as well as those of individuals – supposes a continual readiness to assert it and defend it. The law is not mere theory, but living force. Rudolf von Jhering, *The Struggle for Law*, trans. John J. Lalor, 2nd edn (1915), 1–2.

2

Treaties, peoplehood, and self-determination: understanding the language of indigenous rights

ISABELLE SCHULTE-TENCKHOFF

In memoriam Miguel Alfonso Martínez (1935–2010), former Special Rapporteur of the UN study on treaties between indigenous peoples and states

The debate over indigenous peoples' rights is presently dominated by a twofold reductionism. This involves a growing tendency to collapse indigenous peoples and minorities and, by the same token, to limit collective rights to their least controversial aspect, namely human rights exercised by individuals in community with other members of their group, as opposed to group rights claimed by non-state groups as such. In this manner, the beneficiaries of the Declaration on the Rights of Persons Belonging to National or Ethnic, Linguistic and Religious Minorities,[1] drafted in the wake of Article 27 of the International Covenant on Civil and Political Rights,[2] are not minorities as such (yet to be defined in international law) but rather "persons belonging to minorities." Indigenous peoples' rights are increasingly cast in a similar fashion (e.g. Malanczuk 1997: 105–08). Here, the debate mainly hinges on what has come to be termed "internal self-determination," that is, "the right to effective, democratic governance within States, making it possible for the population as a whole to determine their political status and pursue their development" (Eide and Daes 2000: para. 14). One would assume nonetheless that the recognition of "indigeneity" entails recognition of peoples' rights rather than solely (individual) rights set out in multilateral human rights treaties. Such an

---

[1] UN General Assembly Resolution 47/135, December 18, 1992.
[2] "In those States in which ethnic, religious or linguistic minorities exist, persons belonging to such minorities shall not be denied the right, in community with the other members of their group, to enjoy their own culture, to profess and practice their own religion, or to use their own language"; see UN General Assembly Resolution 2220 A (XXI), December 16, 1966.

assumption can be made in light of the long-standing treaty relationship between indigenous peoples and state parties (whether colonial powers or their present-day territorial successors). The importance of treaties is not only underscored by indigenous peoples themselves, who see in it evidence of their nation-to-nation relationship with the states in which they now live. It is also confirmed in the constitutional law of countries such as Canada and New Zealand (Schulte-Tenckhoff 2004a; 2004b), and it has found its way into the UN Declaration on the Rights of Indigenous Peoples,[3] whose Article 37 reads:

1. Indigenous peoples have the right to the recognition, observance and enforcement of treaties, agreements and other constructive arrangements concluded with States or their successors and to have States honour and respect such treaties, agreements and other constructive arrangements.
2. Nothing in this Declaration may be interpreted as diminishing or eliminating the rights of indigenous peoples contained in treaties, agreements and other constructive arrangements.

State recognition of treaty rights serves one crucial purpose: for instance in Canada, treaties with indigenous peoples are invoked to argue the lawful acquisition of the territory. At the same time, para-doxically, indigenous peoples are being denied nowadays any status in international law. It is difficult to see how Canada can argue the lawful acquisition of sovereign rights unless it admits in some fashion the cap-acity of indigenous peoples to cede such rights. The "founding dilemma" of Canada and other neo-European states hinges on this paradox (Schulte-Tenckhoff 2009). At the international level, things are hardly clearer, for Article 37 of the Indigenous Peoples Declaration coexists with an array of provisions stipulating various, sometimes contradictory, rights that promote the twofold reductionism alluded to above. In the following, these contradictions are contextualized and analyzed, and their implica-tions are discussed with a focus on the issue of self-determination as a group right.

Treaties and treaty rights

In the late 1980s, the United Nations mandated Miguel Alfonso Martínez to conduct a study on the meaning and relevance of treaties for the estab-lishment of better relations between indigenous peoples and the states in

---

[3] UN General Assembly Resolution 61/295, September 13, 2007.

which they now live (Alfonso Martínez 1999). The study looked into the origins of treaty-making between indigenous peoples and states, focusing on state practice rather than doctrinal developments to avoid *ex post facto* reasoning that projects into the past the current configuration of international relations (see also Schulte-Tenckhoff 2008). It further explored the contemporary significance of treaties by addressing indigenous treaty discourse and practice on an equal footing with those of states to avoid a legalistic bias. Finally, it addressed the relevance of the treaty model for the future, especially as a mechanism for conflict resolution. At stake here has been the establishment of an international treaty tribunal to adjudicate treaties involving indigenous parties, for, at the domestic level, states have turned out to be judge and party with regard to the implementation and adjudication of treaty provisions – a situation that generally disfavors indigenous claimants.

Based on some thirty case studies, the UN Study on Treaties addressed three main juridical situations. The bulk of the cases concerned treaties as instruments of international law – that is, concluded between sovereign entities, no matter that these are qualified as "indigenous" nowadays. Another set of cases addressed "other constructive arrangements." These are domestic agreements, most prominently so-called modern treaties in Canada based on the federal comprehensive land claims settlement policy launched in the early 1970s.[4] (Indeed, Canada pushed for this extension of the Special Rapporteur's mandate, although the expression "other constructive arrangements" has no legal meaning.) In Canada, aboriginal title is regarded as a burden on the Crown's sovereignty, to be lifted through the conclusion of negotiated agreements. Such agreements, pursued entirely within the domestic framework, are designed to achieve "certainty" by defining unequivocally the rights pertaining to land use, land ownership, and jurisdiction. With the removal of any doubt on the matter of aboriginal rights and aboriginal title, non-indigenous parties are put in a position to use and appropriate indigenous lands and resources. Moreover, any rights likely to flow from aboriginal title are defined solely under the terms of the agreement itself (Canada 1986), with the result that indigenous parties are deprived of any further recourse through invoking the survival of aboriginal title either in common law or in international

---

[4] The comprehensive land claims settlement policy has been promoted as a direct extension of nineteenth-century British treaty policy: "Treaties – both historical and modern – and the relationship they represent provide a basis for developing a strengthened and forward-looking partnership with Aboriginal people" (Canada 1997: 10).

law. From the state perspective, then, "certainty" means not having to engage with one fundamental premise of the current debate over native title, namely that "Aboriginal peoples' rights to their traditional lands *are not* derived from the legal systems which the Europeans imposed upon them" (McNeil 1997: 135, 136; emphasis added). The conceptual distinction between international treaties and internal agreements thus hinges on what may be termed legal domestication: relations with indigenous peoples are no longer regarded as belonging in the realm of international law. By the same token, domestication has acquired meaning as a paradigm that also governs mainstream scholarship on indigenous rights (Schulte-Tenckhoff 1998).

Finally, the Special Rapporteur considered the situation of indigenous peoples not party to any treaty. At stake here is the following: in international law all peoples, including indigenous peoples, have the right of self-determination. While treaties bear witness to this right, they do not create it. Therefore indigenous peoples not party to international treaties have no less status as peoples, and the onus to prove otherwise falls on the party challenging that status. While mainstream legal discourse has gone to considerable lengths to qualify treaties involving indigenous peoples as *sui generis*, the UN Special Rapporteur found that the international status of such treaties persists "if only because the 'legitimisation' of their colonisation and trade interests made it imperative for European powers to recognise indigenous nations as sovereign entities" (Alfonso Martínez 1999: para. 111).

A crucial aspect of the paradox in question is the culturalization of indigenous rights, which stresses cultural identity and distinctiveness over historical and legal-political aspects, such as the effects of colonialism. Presently, the allegedly cultural foundation of indigeneity seems to have gained wide acceptance (e.g. Corntassel 2008; UN Department of Economic and Social Affairs 2009; Xanthaki 2007).[5] It is also highly problematic. Not only does the invocation of culture in a rights framework favor an essentialist understanding of culture; it is also a crucial element of a growing tendency to address indigenous rights as minority rights. In this manner, the recognition of cultural rights comes at the price of the right of self-determination understood as a group right.

---

[5] A different take is followed by anthropologists interested in human rights issues (e.g. Cowan 2006; Riles 2006). Also, more critical voices have started to be heard among legal scholars (e.g. Engle 2009; Fitzpatrick 2005).

Three categories of rights

The United Nations Declaration on the Rights of Indigenous Peoples stipulates all at once individual human rights of non-discrimination, such as in the fields of employment, health, and education, collective rights, such as the right to preserve and develop one's own identity and culture, and, finally, special rights to be claimed by indigenous peoples as such, for example the right to restitution of traditionally owned lands that have been confiscated, occupied, or damaged. The similarities and differences between these three categories of rights are mirrored in ongoing debates over the characteristics of minorities and indigenous peoples as the beneficiaries of special rights. Although indigenous peoples often represent numerical minorities in the states in which they now live, this does not mean that, in terms of international law standards, their situation ought to be collapsed with that of minorities. Various criteria support the need for a distinction such as those relating to lands and territories. Indeed, the qualifier "indigenous" carries a territorial reference that is more explicit in its Greek counterpart, "autochthonous" (and its French equivalent, "autochtone", "one sprung from the land itself"). According to José Martínez Cobo (1987: para. 373): "As regards the circumstance that gave rise to the notion of indigenous population, it must be said that the special position of indigenous populations within the society of nation-States existing today derives from their historical rights to their lands, as well as from their right to be different, and to be considered as different." Moreover, the preservation of their traditional lands and territories is generally regarded as the *sine qua non* for the survival of indigenous peoples as distinct entities in light of the negative effects resulting from industrial development including the extraction of non-renewable resources.

Minorities or indigenous peoples?[6]

Viewed broadly, the term "minority" can be applied to a large variety of groups, as is apparent from the number of qualifiers attached to it: "national minority," "ethnic minority," "linguistic minority," "religious minority," "cultural minority," "indigenous minority," and so forth. In this connection, two points need to be underscored. First, minorities do not exist as such, they exist in relation to other collective entities and,

---

[6] Parts of this and the following section have previously appeared in other languages (Schulte-Tenckhoff 2000; 2011).

moreover, in constellations of specific power relations. Second, the multiplicity of qualifiers mentioned above, while an indication of the considerable geographic and historical diversity of minorities, illustrates the difficulty (at once legal, conceptual, and political) of pinpointing the specific characteristics of minorities – if these indeed exist – in comparison with other non-state groups claiming special rights, such as migrant workers or so-called new minorities resulting from immigration.

Similarly, at least at first glance, it is difficult to distinguish between minorities and indigenous peoples. Both often experience similar living conditions and voice comparable grievances, whereas their claims, as well as their legal situation, may differ considerably. In former European settler states, a relatively clear distinction seems to prevail between immigrant groups and indigenous peoples. Such a distinction is mirrored – and has partly been fostered by – the double-track approach of the United Nations, leading to two declaration of rights, with the corresponding institutional setup until the 2007 reform of the UN human rights system.[7]

While there is no definition of the term "minority," there exists a working definition of the expression "indigenous peoples" (or populations). Going back to a UN study carried out in the 1970s and 1980s, it involves four criteria that must exist in conjunction for one to speak of an indigenous people as a specific legal-political entity. By and large, then, indigenous peoples are non-dominant in economic, political, and sociocultural – albeit not necessarily numerical – terms; they are the descendants of the original inhabitants of a given territory; they have been victims of genocide, conquest, and colonization; and they seek to maintain their indigenous identity.[8] This definition clearly applies to the original peoples of the so-called New World and was quickly extended to other peoples, for

---

[7] This setup included the now defunct Working Groups on Indigenous Populations (1982–2007) and on Minorities (1995–2007). The former was replaced by the Expert Mechanism on the Rights of Indigenous Peoples (composed of five indigenous experts), the latter by the Forum on Minority Issues and an Independent Expert on Minorities.

[8] "Indigenous communities, peoples and nations are those which, having a historical continuity with pre-invasion and pre-colonial societies that developed on their territories, consider themselves distinct from other sectors of the societies now prevailing in those territories, or parts of them. They form at present non-dominant sectors of society and are determined to preserve, develop and transmit to future generations their ancestral territories, and their ethnic identity, as the basis of their continued existence as peoples, in accordance with their own cultural patterns, social institutions and legal systems … On an individual basis, an indigenous person is one who belongs to these indigenous populations through self-identification as indigenous (group consciousness) and is recognized and accepted by these populations as one of its members (acceptance by the group)." (Martínez Cobo 1987: para. 379).

instance the Samé of Fennoscandia, the Ainu of Japan and the (numeric-ally) Small Peoples of Russia. There is nonetheless a fundamental differ-ence between the former and the latter. The former comprise the original inhabitants of European settler colonies and raise yet again the issue of the so-called salt-water doctrine of colonization (a doctrine seemingly no longer prominent in current debates, however much it remains fundamen-tal to understanding the problematic of "indigeneity"). According to this doctrine, indigenous peoples must be viewed above all as the descendants of overseas peoples that came in contact with, and eventually were domi-nated by, European powers during the era of European expansion since the "age of discoveries," and that now form culturally separate as well as non-dominant groups in states having gained their independence via the exclusion of their original inhabitants. Canada, Australia, the United States, and New Zealand are cases in point. Interestingly, all four opposed the adoption of the Indigenous Peoples Declaration at the level of the UN General Assembly in 2007.[9] Conversely, Samé, Ainu, or Small Peoples of Russia are not overseas peoples in relation to the dominant majority and, from this viewpoint, rather seem to resemble minorities. Yet they are con-sidered to be indigenous, at least at the international level.

This can be partly explained by the growing tendency of subsuming under the qualifier "indigenous" socioeconomic life ways based on hunt-ing and gathering, trapping, or transhumance. Such life ways are now confined to the tropical or boreal rain forests and other frontiers located at the margins of modern industrialized society with its characteris-tic technologies and consumption patterns. Thus a number of pastoral and forest-dwelling peoples maintaining a mainly non-urban and non-industrial way of life in Africa and Asia for instance now self-identify as indigenous.[10] In this context, the relevance of the criterion of prior exist-ence in a given territory has been questioned, as in the famous contro-versy launched by Adam Kuper (2003)[11] which must be left aside here for reasons of space. Similarly, one can hardly find issue with people who use an identity label strategically to advance their cause or, for that matter,

---

[9] Since then, Australia, New Zealand, Canada and the United States – in that order – have endorsed the Declaration.

[10] ILO Convention No. 169 uses the expression "tribal peoples" to refer to such situations. Tribal peoples are defined as groups in independent countries that distinguish them-selves from other sectors of society by their living conditions, traditional lifestyle, and, if applicable, by the fact of coming under special legislation (such as the so-called sched-uled tribes in India).

[11] For a discussion, see also Bowen (2000), Guenther (2006), Kenrick and Lewis (2004).

to gain access to specialized international forums that allow them to voice their grievances, but, again, the issue of strategic essentialism cannot be addressed here. The question remains nonetheless in what manner the promotion of indigenous cultural rights may jeopardize the recognition of other categories of rights of which indigenous peoples are likely to avail themselves.

Individual human rights: the principle of non-discrimination

General human rights are set out in the Universal Declaration of Human Rights of 1948 and subsequently elaborated in the six major legally binding international human rights treaties. They can be claimed by everyone, including members of minorities and indigenous peoples. General human rights are based on two fundamental principles stipulated in the Universal Declaration. One is freedom and equality in dignity and rights for all (Art. 1). The other is non-discrimination (a principle also contained in the UN Charter). Thus, by virtue of Article 2 of the Universal Declaration, all human beings are entitled to the rights and freedoms set forth in the Declaration "without distinction of any kind, such as race, colour, sex, language, religion, political or other opinion, national or social origin, property, birth or other status."

The principle of non-discrimination lies at the core of international human rights standards. The UN Declaration on the Rights of Ethnic or National, Linguistic and Religious Minorities, adopted in 1992, confirms it in Article 3, but it also affirms in Article 1 – and it is the first international instrument to do so – that the identity of minorities must be protected and promoted by states using appropriate legislative and other measures. In obliging states to protect the identity of minorities, the Minorities Declaration reaches beyond the implementation of the principle of non-discrimination. Article 4 thus provides for special measures to allow persons belonging to minorities to live and develop their cultural identity, to practice their religion, to learn and practice their language, to learn about their history and traditions. Nonetheless, this provision also contains an important limitation which one finds in many human rights instruments: that the practices to be protected must not be contrary to national law or international norms, and especially not jeopardize the territorial and political integrity of states.

States often hesitate to accord special rights to non-state groups, arguing that such rights would contradict the individual nature of human rights. But the manner in which minorities are conceived of in international legal instruments mainly reflects technical and political considerations. The drafters of the Minorities Declaration simply stayed within the limits within which minimal agreement between states members of the United Nations was possible at the time. However, does the effective enjoyment of human rights not presuppose that a given collective be in a position to avail itself of such rights? At the outset, nothing precludes such a broadening of the human rights concept.

While the Minorities Declaration does not set out any rights to land, territories, or natural resources, such rights are important elements of the Indigenous Peoples Declaration. As we saw, indigeneity is inextricably tied to the historical relationship that the original peoples of former European settler colonies have with the lands which they continue to claim, use, or occupy. Similarly, there has been a clear sense from the outset that conventional human rights standards have failed to solve the predicament of indigenous peoples, thus alluding to the tension that exists between rights deriving from the principle of non-discrimination and special rights claimed collectively by virtue of a common identity, a common history, or the quest for restorative justice. In this manner, recognition of indigeneity puts a new spin on the classic debate over the possible reconciliation of the idea of the individual as the ultimate bearer of rights as opposed to the idea that collective entities other than states must also be viewed as rights bearers.

Collective (minority) rights

To the extent that international legal instruments provide for special measures benefiting persons belonging to minorities, these are conceived as state obligations, for the collective entities concerned cannot usually avail themselves of any standing in international law that would allow them to further the implementation of such obligations. In this regard, the situation is not the same for indigenous peoples and minorities. As mentioned earlier, historically, the former were often recognized – or at least dealt with – as international entities, as is evidenced by the hundreds of treaties that European powers concluded with them between the sixteenth and the nineteenth centuries. Conversely, in the case of minorities, the question would rather be whether some form of legal personality should be sought and, if so, on the basis of which criteria. Possible avenues (e.g. plebiscites) have not yet been integrated into positive international law. This is not by accident, the main objective of international law being to safeguard the stability of states and inter-state relations.

Indigenous peoples often assert that provisions concerning the rights of "persons belonging to minorities" do not apply to them. When looking broadly at the diversity of situations in which indigenous peoples may find themselves, one notes a twofold problem. Some indigenous people experience de facto a minority situation, notably when they have been geographically dispersed or dispossessed of their land base. Others still occupy vast tracts of land on which they subsist without – as yet – major interference from the dominant society. Nonetheless, such situations become more and more rare under the impact of globalization and grow-ing competition for natural resources. In a manner of speaking, then, the elaboration of standards applicable to indigenous peoples has pushed the envelope with regard to special rights as opposed to rights of non-discrimination.

Special indigenous rights differ significantly from special rights stipu-lated for persons belonging to minorities. As A. Eide puts it, the Minorities Declaration aims at "ensuring a space for pluralism in togetherness" (Eide and Daes 2000: para. 8), emphasizing effective participation in the wider society. Conversely, many indigenous people continue to affirm their preference for a predominantly indigenous way of life linked to specific territories and resources. Moreover, the debate over indigenous rights has brought a number of states face to face with their colonial past and their often questionable acquisition of sovereignty over the national territory and its resources. States are therefore rather unwilling to grant indigenous peoples any group rights as these reach beyond the scope of collective (minority-type) rights as defined above. Indeed, these may entail standing in international law – the most far-reaching group right being the right of peoples to self-determination. In this sense, the UN Declaration on the Rights of Indigenous Peoples adds a new dimension to a well-worn debate, in that it provides for a complex – and somewhat unwieldy – juxtaposition of individual human rights, collective rights, and group rights. For instance, individual human rights of non-discrim-ination in the Declaration concern areas such as employment (Art. 17) and adequate health and housing standards (Art. 21). Collective rights include inter alia protection against forced relocation (Art. 10) and the right to maintain and develop one's own institutions while participating fully in the life of the state (Art. 5). Finally, special rights to be claimed by indigenous peoples as such are, for example, the right to traditionally owned lands that have been confiscated, occupied, or damaged and, if this turns out to be impossible, the right to just and fair compensation (Art. 28); or the right to environmental protection (Art. 29) and cultural property (Art. 31).[12]

Article 3 of the Indigenous Peoples Declaration proclaims the right of indigenous peoples to self-determination – that is, to determine freely their political status and their mode of economic, social, and cultural development. This provision is nonetheless qualified immediately in Article 4, which stipulates that indigenous self-determination amounts to self-government at the local and regional levels. While Article 4 can be read as one of several possible options, persistent controversy reigns over the type of collective entity to benefit from the right of self-determination. There is general agreement that it applies to the populations of non-self-governing territories and those living in occupied territories. It also applies to the population as a whole of sovereign states. However, legal opinion is divided over the applicability of the principle of self-determination to indigenous peoples.

Peoples' rights

The main challenge thus lies in determining the scope and substance of group rights, that is, of rights that non-state groups are likely to claim as such, as opposed to collective (human) rights understood as rights exercised by individuals in community with other members of their group. While the principle of non-discrimination is firmly anchored and monitored in positive international law, this is not the case of special measures to be taken in favor of indigenous peoples as collective entities. Moreover, the Indigenous Peoples Declaration creates neither a legal obligation nor a monitoring mechanism, nor accords indigenous peoples subjective rights or any form of legal personality. It is useful therefore to revisit some of the conceptual implications, especially with regard to the definition of "indigenous peoples" under international law (e.g. Lam 2000; Morris 1986[13]).

In purely formalist terms, "a people" only has a legal existence if it is a state; by the same token, a people can only claim rights if it has gained

---

[12] For a detailed treatment of the various provisions of the Declaration from various viewpoints see, e.g., Charters and Stavenhagen (2009). For comprehensive treatments of indigenous rights and the international indigenous movement see, e.g., Anaya (2004) and Thornberry (2002). For a recent critical assessment, see Engle (2011).

[13] See Tennant (1994) for a highly useful – and critical – discussion of the first wave of international legal literature on this topic.

such a legal existence. This introduces a paradox, namely that a people actually has no means of obtaining legal status since it is per se an extra-legal or pre-legal entity … This circular view ignores the problem of how states came into being; and to the extent it does consider the creation of new states through decolonization, it is informed by a Eurocentric conception of statehood and law, based on the idea that the more or less artificial divisions created by the colonial powers gave rise to new peoples.

Nonetheless, since conventional wisdom considers a people to have a legal existence only if it is a state, one may start by assessing peoplehood by the criteria of statehood, of which there are four: a permanent population, a defined territory, an effective government, and the capacity to enter into foreign relations. Undoubtedly, not every human group is a people. But it is equally clear from the historical and legal record that indigenous peoples fulfill all four criteria – most importantly the last of the list, for the long history of treaty-making between overseas ("indigenous") peoples and colonial powers introduce an element of customary international law, namely state practice.

Attempts to identify criteria of peoplehood at the international level have mainly invoked social criteria. This applies in particular to descriptions grounded in the assumption that peoples' rights are group rights (sometimes also called *corporate* rights) that ascribe moral standing to the group qua group (e.g. Jones 1999; 2008), contrary to collective rights that ascribe moral standing only to individuals who jointly hold the group right, as we have seen in connection with rights of persons belonging to minorities. Conversely, group rights especially raise the issue of how a group is to be identified to be able to lay a claim to such rights – notably as a people. On this basis, it must be possible to identify a people by criteria other than, and substantially different from, those associated with statehood. A classical United Nations study argued that the term "people" "denotes a social entity possessing a clear identity and its own characteristics"; that it implies a "relationship with a territory," and that it "should not be confused with ethnic, religious or linguistic minorities" (Cristescu 1981: para. 279).

Attempts have also been made to define indigenous peoples by combining both objective and subjective criteria which would be equally problematic when considered in isolation. The former focus on characteristics such as a common territory, ethnicity, language, history, or culture; the latter may include aspirations to maintain an indigenous identity, or self-identification. Both types of criterion can be found in the so-called working definition which has guided UN activities in the field of indigenous rights for three decades.[14] At stake here is not the idea of "a people," how-ever, but rather the qualifier "indigenous." This is especially relevant to the problem of identifying the potential beneficiaries of existing inter-national legal standards. Given the controversial nature of indigenous rights in the ongoing debates – both nationally and internationally – one is led to wonder whether the addition of the qualifier "indigenous" to the term "peoples" does not entail the risk of diminishing the rights of indi-genous peoples under international law. If indigenous peoples are peoples, why qualify them by calling them indigenous? If they are not peoples, why call them peoples, all the while endeavoring to distinguish them from minorities? Not only has the (re)emergence of indigenous peoples on the international scene and their endeavors to seek recognition as subjects rather than objects of international law put a new spin on the debate over self-determination. It has also refueled the controversy over decoloniza-tion. The resulting confinement of the right of self-determination to the human rights framework has conceptual implications: for in viewing self-determination as a human right, one defines it as a collective right rather than a group right.

Peoplehood and self-determination

The absence of a generally accepted definition of "a people" in inter-national law has not prevented the international community from elab-orating principles and standards with regard to the rights of peoples. Most importantly, it is generally held that peoples are groups able to claim the right of self-determination – that is, to control their own des-tiny. Peoplehood and self-determination are thus inextricably linked. As the world situation has changed, both concepts have taken on new meanings. As to self-determination in particular, it has evolved from a general legal principle of international action to that of a "right," whether understood as a right of peoples in the specific context of decol-onization, or as a human right.

On the basis of key resolutions adopted by the UN General Assembly in 1960 and 1970, the principle of self-determination became the driving force used by the United Nations as a legal justification for decoloniza-tion. Judging by the shrinking agenda of the Committee of 24, established to implement decolonization, this process is now regarded as nearly com-plete. Moreover, the Committee of 24 has made no attempt to concern

---

[14] See Martínez Cobo, quoted in note 8 above.

itself with the modern understanding of self-determination as a human right.

Despite the long-dominant UN focus on the decolonization of European overseas possessions, it is widely held that the right of self-determination belongs to all peoples, as established in the 1960 Declaration on the Granting of Independence to Colonial Countries and Peoples.[15] Subsequently, the 1970 Declaration on Friendly Relations and Co-operation among States[16] places on states the duty to promote the principle of equal rights and self-determination of peoples with the intent "to bring a speedy end to colonialism, having due regard to the freely expressed will of the peoples concerned." But it subjects these lofty goals to the preservation of existing states: "the territorial integrity and political independence of the State are inviolable." This is upon one condition, however: that states conduct themselves "in compliance with the principles of equal rights and self-determination" – that is, are possessed of a government that represents the entire people "without distinction as to race, creed or colour." Not all states meet this requirement, which goes to say that, depending on circumstances, a group or a people is justified in demanding its own government to ensure the protection of the human rights and fundamental freedoms of its citizenry (e.g. Tomuschat 1993). Some have gone so far as to consider self-determination as *jus cogens*, that is, a peremptory norm of international law: "all States are under the peremptory obligation: (1) not to forcibly subject alien peoples to a colonial-type domination; (2) not to keep alien peoples by forcible or deceitful means under a colonial-type domination; and (3) not to exploit the natural resources of those alien territories, which are under their colonial-type domination, to the serious detriment of the people of those territories" (Hannikainen 1988: 421).

Self-determination and decolonization

Since the relevant international texts fail to define a people other than by declaring that it is a group having the right of self-determination, various attempts have been made to give further substance to the debate by engaging with related concepts. One attempt consisted in exploring the meaning of colonialism and hence decolonization. Of particular significance in this context is the so-called Belgian thesis brought forth in

---

[15] UN General Assembly Resolution 1514 (XV), December 14, 1960.
[16] UN General Assembly Resolution 2625 (XXV), October 24, 1970.

the initial debate over the application of Chapter XI of the UN Charter, which deals with non-self-governing territories "whose peoples have not yet attained a full measure of self-government." In the early 1950s, the Belgian UN representatives made various submissions stating that many indigenous populations in the Americas, Africa, and Asia were actually excluded from invoking Chapter XI despite the fact that they were non-self-governing. Thus various states were administering within their borders territories with well-defined limits and inhabited by peoples differing in culture and language from the rest of the population, and largely excluded from national life.

As a radical version of the self-determination principle in its application to indigenous peoples and minorities, the Belgian thesis did not prevail. Significantly, it met with considerable resistance from the Latin American countries whose representatives argued that the problems of indigenous peoples were of an economic and not a colonial order. This reaction brought about the salt-water doctrine of colonialism, which limits the scope of the decolonization process to "a territory which is geographically separate and is distinct ethnically and/or culturally from the country administering it."[17]

Since Belgium was still a colonial power at the time (and was supported in its endeavor by countries in a similar position, such as France and the United Kingdom), the Belgian thesis undoubtedly fulfilled a strategic function and must be situated in its proper political context. It is worth recalling, however, that no substantial debate took place at the time to determine why exactly indigenous peoples living in so-called metropolitan territories had to be excluded from the terms of Chapter XI and were considered unfit to apply to the international community to benefit from the decolonization process. With growing awareness of the persisting conditions of (internal) colonialism experienced by indigenous peoples even in liberal and pluralist Western countries, the moment may have come to reconsider the issue, especially since a number of indigenous peoples can still be identified on a territorial basis.

Self-determination as a human right

While self-determination was never limited to colonial peoples identified on the basis of the salt-water doctrine, the focus on decolonization with regard to Asia and Africa dominated UN reality until the end of the Cold

---

[17] UN General Assembly Resolution 1541 (XV), Principle IV, December 15, 1960.

War. Only subsequently has the right of self-determination been increasingly invoked by ethnic groups and indigenous peoples – that is, within and against established states. With the widespread ratification of the two International Human Rights Covenants, self-determination has come to be seen as a right from which all other human rights flow, and which is not limited merely to political aspects. Thus, Article 1 common to both instruments stipulates that

1. All peoples have the right of self-determination. By virtue of that right they freely determine their political status and freely pursue their economic, social and cultural development.
2. All peoples may, for their own ends, freely dispose of their natural wealth and resources without prejudice to any obligations arising out of international economic co-operation, based upon the principle of mutual benefit, and international law. In no case may a people be deprived of its own means of subsistence.
3. The States Parties to the present Covenant, including those having responsibility for the administration of Non-Self-Governing and Trust Territories, shall promote the realisation of the right of self-determination, and shall respect that right, in conformity with the provisions of the Charter of the United Nations.[18]

According to the Human Rights Committee, which monitors the implementation of the ICCPR, "the right of self-determination is of particular importance because its realization is an essential condition for the effective guarantee and observance of individual human rights and for the promotion and strengthening of those rights." The Committee adds: "It is for that reason that States set forth the right of self-determination in a provision of positive law in both Covenants and placed this provision as article 1 apart from and before all of the other rights in the two Covenants."[19] Moreover, self-determination is now viewed as creating legal obligations on states. In this context, self-determination claims may range over a variety of political rights, from secession to self-government within existing state structures.

Viewing the right of self-determination as a human right raises certain ambiguities, however. On the positive side, it challenges the preconception that human rights only concern individuals. In this

---

[18] International Covenant on Civil and Political Rights and International Covenant on Economic, Social and Cultural Rights, UN General Assembly Resolution 2200A (XXI), December 16, 1966.
[19] Human Rights Committee, General Comment No. 12: The Right to Self-determination of Peoples (Art. 1), 13 March 1983, para. 1.

manner, the exercise of the right of self-determination is meant to enable groups to transmit their culture and to participate collectively in the political, economic, and social processes. For such participation to be effective, however, groups must be free from the constraints of the international institutional – that is, statist – framework to be able to make their own choices. In an evolving international system, the rationalist liberal view of formally equal individuals united in states each governed by domestic law and constituting in turn the legal community governed by international law is open to scrutiny. By and large, it is uncertain whether states do indeed represent in a neutral fashion all those that constitute its citizenry, including groups seeking to advance rights on the basis of a common history or identity. But states, especially Western ones, are uncomfortable with identifying institutions of government with particular groups or, for that matter, with indigenous claims when these exceed what they are willing to concede, namely individual human rights or, at most, collective rights as long as these do not reach beyond the scope of individual human rights exercised in community with others. On the negative side, then, the conception of self-determination as a human right, in fact, restricts the scope of self-determination by excluding group rights.

Self-determination for indigenous peoples

For indigenous peoples, self-determination appears first and foremost as a tool to seek redress for centuries of dispossession and injustice. With the consolidation of international human rights law allowing states to be challenged if they fail to comply with established human rights norms, the question is whether indigenous peoples have justified claims of self-determination vis-à-vis established states. In this context, attempts have been made to limit or qualify the right of self-determination in a manner quite different from the earlier international debate over the decolonization process. In other words, while the term "indigenous peoples" is gradually gaining acceptance in international parlance, its use seems to be mainly rhetorical, since limitations are brought to bear on self-determination as the crucial element of peoplehood. The stumbling block here is that the right of self-determination includes per se the right to secede. This is despite the fact that various UN texts declare that statehood is not the only possibility of realizing the right of self-determination, which can also be implemented through "free association or integration with an independent State or the emergence into any other political status freely determined by a people," as already set out in the 1970 Declaration on Friendly Relations.

With the (re)emergence of indigenous peoples on the international scene, there has been a dislocating or disjoining of the concepts of "a people" and of "self-determination." In this manner, the right of self-determination is increasingly regarded as a right whose substance varies according to the (cultural) identity of its beneficiary, thus shaping and confirming the definition of self-determination as a *human* right as opposed to a *people's* right. Indigenous peoples, because they are indigenous, have been declared incapable of self-determination. To all intents and purpose, then, the addition of the qualifier "indigenous" to the term "peoples" entails the risk of diminishing the rights of indigenous peoples under international law.

Negating indigenous peoplehood: a form of discrimination

Is it possible to assert that some groups or populations are actually peoples but do not have the right of self-determination, or can only lay claim to such a right in a limited form? Moreover, is it possible to argue in terms of either logic or law that, since independent statehood is but one of several avenues for exercising the right of self-determination, some groups can lay claim to limited or internal self-determination understood as "a human rights norm that broadly benefits human beings in relation to the constitution and functioning of the government structures under which they live" (Anaya 2009: 194)? Does this not amount to a negation of the right of self-determination as such, whose essential feature is, precisely, that it allows a people to choose freely their internal and international political status? Having a limited choice is not, precisely, an exercise in self-determination.

In international law, the idea of self-determination is contentious because it challenges key assumptions such as state sovereignty, territorial integrity, and domestic jurisdiction, while creating a tension between the democratic principle of majority rule and the disruptive potential of minority separatism. Moreover, the question whether self-determination is to be viewed as a universal group right or rather as a human right remains open to debate. It is therefore all the more important to underline the historical significance of the sovereign standing that indigenous peoples have had in international law, especially since many of the treaties concluded with them are still valid. By entering into formal international agreements with collective entities now qualified as "indigenous,"

European colonial powers and their successors obtained territorial and other sovereign rights, and organized matters normally regulated by international law, such as trade relations and relations of war and peace. Consequently, states are hardly in a position to negate the peoplehood and hence the right of self-determination of indigenous peoples while, at the same time, arguing the lawful acquisition of sovereign rights; for these same peoples could not have transferred these rights – if this was indeed their intention – had they not been self-determining. It is on this basis that indigenous peoples continue to claim self-determination. They do so by framing their claim as a group right rather than a human right. Consequently, and independently of the existence or not of treaty relations, should indigenous peoples claim for themselves the status of sovereign nations, "it must be presumed until proven otherwise that they continue to enjoy such status" (Alfonso Martínez 1999: para. 288). Since the right of self-determination belongs to all peoples, including indigenous peoples, the burden of proof falls on the party challenging that status. Moreover, "any contradiction that may arise between the exercise [of the right of self-determination] by indigenous peoples in present-day conditions and the recognized right and duty of the States in which they now live to protect their sovereignty and territorial integrity, should be resolved by peaceful means" (Alfonso Martínez 1999: para. 256). Denying indigenous peoples their peoplehood as a matter of principle because of their "indigeneity" amounts to a form of discrimination that perpetuates racist notions harking back to the era of European colonial expansion, such as the doctrine of *terra nullius*, all the while legitimizing unilateral (state) action aimed at appropriating indigenous lands, resources, and jurisdiction.

Perspective

Having followed closely, since its very beginning in the early 1980s, the process leading to the adoption of the Declaration on the Rights of Indigenous Peoples, I recall some crucial changes against which I cannot fail to set off the text adopted in 2007. One of these is best illustrated with reference to the French translation of the Declaration. The 1993 draft of the Working Group subsequently adopted by the now defunct Sub-commission on the Prevention of Discrimination and Protection of Minorities provided in Article 3 that indigenous peoples have *le droit de disposer d'eux-mêmes*. In this, Article 3 recalled the well-established expression *le droit des peuples à disposer d'eux-mêmes* (also used in Art. 1

of the Covenants), that is, self-determination understood as a right of peoples. Again, the French language allows greater precision than does English, the term "self-determination" being potentially applicable to individuals and groups. In the 2007 text, Article 3 refers to indigenous peoples having – more vaguely – le droit à l'autodétermination, thus confirming the tendency I set out to illustrate in this chapter.

Although international action and standard-setting with regard to indigenous rights have intensified over the last twenty-five years, indigenous peoples are still in no position to seek redress collectively for decades, if not centuries, of land and resource theft as well as economic, political, social, and cultural marginalization. Moreover, while the special situation of indigenous peoples with regard to their prior existence in the states in which they now live, as well as their historical relationship with the territory of those states, has started to find a measure of international recognition, indigenous peoples continue to be deprived of the possibility of claiming any form of legal standing as peoples under international law.

It remains to be seen to what extent international law, as a creation of the state system, is capable of accommodating claims that are likely to threaten the raison d'être of that same system. In this regard, the ongoing debate over self-determination understood as a collective human right rather than a group right points to the existence of two different avenues to be followed by indigenous peoples, depending on their choice: to seek recognition either of collective rights within existing state structures or of some form of international standing. However, the current international debates and much of the literature consistently favors the first over the second.

Indigenous peoples have the right of self-determination in the sense that they have the right freely to decide their own destiny; they must therefore be given a genuine choice (and possibly the benefit of the doubt with regard to secession[20]). They must have the opportunity of reviewing the issue of colonialism: it would be discriminating were indigenous peoples to be deprived of the right to decolonize – a right that many other peoples across the world have exercised. As to the qualifier "indigenous," it ought to be rejected if it implies diminished rights as peoples. In this sense, failing to acknowledge the status of indigenous peoples as parties to international treaties concluded with states is discriminating because it

---

[20] E.g. Daes (1993), Kymlicka and Norman (2000); for a different take influenced by a focus on the situation in Africa, see Titanji (2009).

similarly risks diminishing the legal status of indigenous peoples as collective entities and their inherent rights under international law.

References

Alfonso Martínez, Miguel, 1999, *Study on Treaties, Agreements and Other Constructive Arrangements Between States and Indigenous Populations. Final Report by Miguel Alfonso Martínez, Special Rapporteur.* UN Doc. E/CN.4/Sub.2/1999/20.

Anaya, James, 2004, *Indigenous Peoples in International Law.* 2nd edn. Oxford University Press.

    2009, "The right of indigenous peoples to self-determination," in Charters and Stavenhagen, pp. 184–98.

Bowen, John, 2000, "Should we have a universal concept of 'indigenous peoples' rights'? Ethnicity and essentialism in the twenty-first century." *Anthropology Today* 16(4): 12–16.

Canada, Department of Indian Affairs and Northern Development, 1986, *Comprehensive Land Claims Policy.* Ottawa: Supply and Services Canada.

    1997, *Gathering Strength: Canada's Aboriginal Action Plan.* Ottawa: Public Works and Government Services.

Charters, Claire and Stavenhagen, Rodolfo (eds.), 2009, *Making the Declaration Work: The United Nations Declaration on the Rights of Indigenous Peoples.* Copenhagen: International Work Group for Indigenous Affairs, Document No. 127.

Corntassel, Jeff, 2008, "Toward sustainable self-determination: rethinking the contemporary indigenous-rights discourse." *Alternatives* 33: 105–32.

Cowan, Jane, 2006, "Culture and rights after *Culture and Rights*." *American Anthropologist* 108(1): 9–24.

Cristescu, Aureliu, 1981, *The Right to Self-Determination: Historical and Current Developments on the Basis of United Nations Instruments.* New York: United Nations.

Daes, Erica-Irene, 1993, "Some considerations on the right of indigenous peoples to self-determination." *Transnational Law & Contemporary Problems* 3(1): 1–11.

Eide, Asbjorn and Daes, Erica-Irene, 2000, *Working Paper on the Relationship and Distinction between the Rights of Persons Belonging to Minorities and those of Indigenous Peoples.* UN document E/CN.4/Sub.2/2000/10.

Engle, Karen, 2009, "Indigenous rights claims in international law: self-determination, culture, and development," in D. Armstrong (ed.), *Routledge Handbook of International Law.* Oxford: Routledge, pp. 331–43.

    2011, "On fragile architecture: the UN Declaration on the Rights of Indigenous Peoples in the context of human rights." *European Journal of International Law* 22: 141–63.

Fitzpatrick, Peter, 2005, "The 'damned word': culture and its (in)compatibility with law." *Law, Culture and the Humanities* 1(1): 2–13.

Guenther, Mathias, 2006, "The concept of indigeneity." *Social Anthropology* 14(1): 17–32.

Hannikainen, Lauri, 1988, *Peremptory Norms* (jus cogens) *in International Law: Historical Development, Criteria, Present Status*. Helsinki: Lakimiesliiton Kustannus.

Jones, Peter, 1999, "Human rights, group rights and peoples' rights." *Human Rights Quarterly* 21: 80–107.

2008, "Group rights." Available at http://plato.stanford.edu/entries/rights-group/

Kenrick, Justin and Lewis, Jerome, 2004, "Indigenous peoples' rights and the politics of the term 'indigenous.'" *Anthropology Today* 20(2): 4–9.

Kuper, Adam, 2003, "The return of the native." *Current Anthropology* 44(3): 389–402.

Kymlicka, Will and Norman, Wayne (eds.), 2000, *Citizenship in Diverse Societies*. Oxford University Press.

Lam, Maivan C., 2000, *At the Edge of the State: Indigenous Peoples and Self-Determination*. Ardsley (NY): Transnational Publ.

Malanczuk, Peter, 1997, *Akehurst's Modern Introduction to International Law. 7th Revised Edition*. New York: Routledge.

McNeil, Kent, 1997, "The meaning of aboriginal title," in M. Asch (ed.), *Aboriginal and Treaty Rights in Canada*. Vancouver: UBC Press, pp. 135–54.

Martínez Cobo, José, 1987, *Study on the Problem of Discrimination against Indigenous Populations*. Vol. 5, "Conclusions, Proposals and Recommendations." New York: United Nations.

Morris, Glenn, 1986, "In support of the right of self-determination for indigenous peoples under international law." *German Yearbook of International Law* 29: 277–316.

Riles, Annelise, 2006, "Anthropology, human rights, and legal knowledge: culture in the iron cage." *American Anthropologist* 108(1): 52–65.

Schulte-Tenckhoff, Isabelle, 1998, "Reassessing the paradigm of domestication: the problematic of indigenous treaties." *Review of Constitutional Studies* 4: 239–89.

2000, "Les minorités en droit international," in A. Fenet, G. Koubi, and I. Schulte-Tenckhoff, *Le droit et les minorités: analyses et textes*. Brussels: Bruylant, pp. 17–113.

2004a, "*Te tino rangatiratanga*: substance ou apparence? Réflexion sur le dilemme constitutionnel de l'Etat néo-zélandais." *Politique et Société* 23(1): 89–114.

2004b, "Droits collectifs et autochtonie: que penser des 'traités modernes' au Canada?" in T. Berns (ed.), *Le droit saisi par le collectif*. Brussels: Bruylant, pp. 133–64.

2008, "L'Autre et le traité: pour une anthropologie des traités autochtones," in A.-S. Lamblin-Gourdin and E. Mondielli (eds.), *Un droit pour des hommes libres: Etudes en l'honneur du professeur Alain Fenet*. Paris: Litec, pp. 239–51.

2009, "Peuples autochtones: penser le dilemme fondateur de l'État néo-européen," in N. Gagné, T. Martin, and M. Salaün (eds.), *Autochtonies: vues de France et du Québec*. Sainte-Foy (Quebec): Presses de l'Université Laval, pp. 111–27.

2011, "Los derechos culturales de las minorías étnicas y los pueblos indígenas," in S. Cardús et al. (eds.), *Laberintos del Mundo: Respuestas desde la Educación*. Barcelona: Gedisa Editorial, pp. 112–39.

Tennant, Chris, 1994, "Indigenous peoples, international institutions and the international legal literature from 1945 to 1993." *Human Rights Quarterly* 16: 1–57.

Thornberry, Patrick, 2002, *Indigenous Peoples and Human Rights*. Manchester University Press.

Titanji, Ernest Duga, 2009, "The right of indigenous peoples to self-determination versus secession: one coin, two faces?" *African Human Rights Law Journal* 9: 52–75.

Tomuschat, Christian, 1993, "Self-determination in a post-colonial world," in Tomuschat (ed.), *Modern Law of Self-Determination*. Dordrecht: Martinus Nijhoff, pp. 1–20.

UN Department of Economic and Social Affairs, 2009, *State of the World's Indigenous Peoples*. New York: United Nations.

Xanthaki, Alexandra, 2007, *Indigenous Rights and United Nations Standards: Self-Determination, Culture and Land*. Cambridge University Press.

3

Talking up Indigenous Peoples' original intent in a space dominated by state interventions

IRENE WATSON AND SHARON VENNE

Introduction

The road behind is a space in which Aboriginal peoples know who we are; we know our countries, families and peoples. For many Aboriginal people the road back to country is long and filled with colonial encounters. Colonial encounters have caused and continue to cause conflict, and conflict interferes with our capacity to remain connected and to reconnect with country and family. Our Aboriginal selves in relationship to country can bring us home; the dispossessed Aboriginal self confronts a space in which the only direction free of blocks and obstacles is onward and ahead. The road behind becomes increasingly hard to access. Confronted with this, do we simply walk forward? If so, what might we be walking into? What of the road behind and the Aboriginal selves?

This chapter examines the future directions which have been proposed in international law and the promises to remove the colonial roadblocks that separate many of us from our lands and reduce our capacity to govern our lives which they contain. We argue that the UN Declaration on the Rights of Indigenous Peoples (hereafter Declaration) falls short, that the talk and theorizing of indigenous rights is part of an illusion constructed while the colonial project continues to absorb indigenous peoples into itself, through the assimilation agendas of various states. This chapter investigates how far international efforts at recognition enable or otherwise the truth of decolonization and the cessation of ongoing genocides of Aboriginal peoples across the world.

The Australian state has never explored the option of Aboriginal self-determination in any truthful way. The term 'self-determination' has been appropriated by the Australian federal government from the 1970s in the enactment of various initiatives, but a quick examination of each of those acts and policies reveals their continuing colonial nature and intent.[1] It is clear that simply to gain control of state institutions is not enough to enable decolonization and, as Taiaiake Alfred suggests, 'without a cultural grounding, self-government becomes a kind of Trojan horse for capitalism, consumerism, and selfish individualism'.[2] The simplistic project of gaining political space without indigenous content is as meaningless as replacing the white mission managers with our own mob, while the policies continue. The interpretation of decolonization as an act of populating white political space with Aboriginal people as managers of that white political space is not an act of decolonization. It is rather a turn in the colonial project which enables at best Aboriginal self-management of the colonial project.

It is our argument that this is what the Declaration has become, that it is not an act of decolonization and that it is instead an instrument which ensures the continuance of the colonial project and is intent upon the assimilation of Aboriginal peoples. For a real act of decolonization to occur we need to regain an Aboriginal centre – that is, an Aboriginal centre that engages in its own decolonization and repair from the effects of colonialism – and to enable that centre to occupy the spaces of political power, rather than let it become assimilated into colonial processes

---

[1] The Australian government established the Aboriginal and Torres Strait Islander Commission (ATSIC) and promoted it as an initiative in self-determination. For a while it did provide an element of independence, although this was more in the form of indigenous management of the colonial state's policies than real autonomy. As a statutory body of the Australian government, ATSIC was tied to its purse strings and was rendered ineffective due to the limited powers allowed to it. Further, its role and authority were progressively restricted by the conservative Howard government, which for more than a decade ignored numerous reports highlighting a neglect of essential services to Aboriginal communities and a growing crisis across Australia. The government allowed and fomented reporting of a series of scandals involving ATSIC leadership, and eventually dismantled it and cited it as a failure of an Aboriginal self-determination policy. More recently the National Congress of Australia's First People was established in 2010. The marketing of the Congress notes that it will provide a national indigenous voice: see National Congress of Australia's First People, 'Welcome to the Congress Site', (2010), available at http://natiotu.customers.ilisys.com.au/?page_id=132. Critics argue that the National Congress has a limited voice due to a membership of only 2,000. Of that number just under 600 voted for the new Congress chairpersons. There are more than 800,000 Aboriginal peoples of Australia; it could be said that the 2,000 members of the National Congress are unlikely to provide an authentic representation of Aboriginal Australia. While this new Congress has adopted a gender balance in the election of a male and female co-chairs, there is a lot further to travel in providing Aboriginal representation of the diversity of Aboriginal Australia and the diverse relationships we have to the country.

[2] Taiaiake Alfred, *Peace, Power, Righteousness: An Indigenous Manifesto*. Oxford University Press, 2009, p. 3.

of power-sharing. To decolonize, the process needs to assimilate the colonizer into Aboriginal processes of power-sharing. And it is plain that the Declaration is light years away from undertaking that turn in power-sharing arrangements.

The passing of the Declaration

This section outlines the limitations in the Declaration and points out its ongoing colonial nature. We argue that the futures of Indigenous Peoples will be disabled rather than strengthened by the continuing colonial relationship between the UN and its nation states.

The Declaration on the Rights of Indigenous Peoples, which was passed by the UN General Assembly in September 2007, was actually a shadow of the indigenous Declaration which had been initially developed by the UN Working Group in Geneva. In the final UN General Assembly Declaration a number of articles, essential to the recognition of self-determination, had been expunged. This chapter will offer a close comparative reading of some of the articles taken from both the 1993 Draft Declaration and the final 2007 version. This comparative reading will illustrate that the possibility for the recognition of the sovereignty of Indigenous Peoples has become further removed in the final Declaration.

It is our argument that Aboriginal peoples' rights to exercise their free, prior and informed consent was violated in 2007 when the UN voted on the passage of the Declaration. At that time Indigenous Peoples were given only three days' notice of the Declaration coming before the General Assembly for the final vote, and it was impossible in that time for their representatives to examine the document and to act to remedy any deficiencies or betrayals within it. It therefore should not be construed that Indigenous Peoples had constructive notice of the General Assembly's passage of the Declaration. We are curious as to how any of the UN member states might have responded if they were placed in a similar position.

As it happened, when the Declaration was adopted by the UN General Assembly of the United Nations in September 2007, 144 countries voted in its favour, 11 abstained and 4 voted against. Australia, Canada, New Zealand and the United States were the four countries that voted against the Declaration. However, on 3 April 2009, the Australian government changed its position and formally supported the Declaration.[3] Evidently

---

[3] Jenny Macklin, 'Statement on the United Nations Declaration on the Rights of Indigenous Peoples', speech delivered at Parliament House, Canberra, 3 April 2009, www.un.org/esa/socdev/unpfii/documents/Australia_official_statement_endorsement_UNDRIP.pdf.

the Australian government came to realize that the Declaration actually posed no threat or risk to the state's ongoing hegemony. The likelihood of the Declaration enabling the right of Indigenous Peoples to self-determination was nil, and by 2009 the Australian government had become confident enough that it provided no risk to its hegemonic position. It was clear that the colonial project would emerge intact, indeed virtually undisturbed, with the Declaration upheld as a major initiative in the recognition of indigenous rights.

History of the Declaration

The drafting of the Declaration was initiated by indigenous peoples, and at the beginning the drafting process was an indigenous business. In the beginning the process had no relationship to the UN system, but this was to change in 1985 when it was taken up by the UN and vested with the Working Group on Indigenous Populations (WGIP) in Geneva. Notably, the taking up by the UN WGIP took place without the consent of Indigenous Peoples. Nevertheless the Working Group went ahead with drafting the Declaration, a process which complied with their mandate to draft standards and also to review recent developments.

The drafting of the Declaration did fulfil these two objectives, and while the WGIP sessions during the early 1980s and 90s involved Indigenous Peoples in the drafting standards, these same sessions also included state governments, including those of Australia, Canada, New Zealand and the United States. Once it had become incorporated into the UN system, states began their own manipulations, lobbying indigenous groups to surrender our inherent right as peoples.

In 2006 the drafting of the Declaration shifted from Geneva to New York, where Indigenous Peoples working close to governments participated in its final drafting. It was at this stage that it was gutted of articles which referred to the UN Charter and rights to self-determination. The Declaration does refer to 'internal rights' to self-determination; these are rights which are determined by the various colonial states which occupy indigenous peoples' lands. References to international standards in the Declaration are now made redundant and the focus has shifted from the rights of peoples to self-determination under international law to Indigenous Peoples as human rights issues within their respective colonial states. Thus Indigenous Peoples are further encumbered: rather than retaining the rights of peoples as enshrined in the UN Charter, we have become objects of local human rights issues.

The UN Declaration which was passed by the General Assembly has been stripped back to a human rights instrument rather than an instrument which would provide a mechanism for advancing Indigenous Peoples' rights as nations and peoples. The Declaration enables recognition of a range of human rights but fails to progress in any meaningful manner the right of Indigenous Peoples to self-determination as recognized under the UN Charter.

Until the Declaration drafting was shifted from Geneva to New York, Indigenous Peoples held the line on the international law recognition of our status as peoples. However, with the dismantling of the Commission on Human Rights and the Inter-Sessional Working Group a new UN body – the Human Rights Council – decided to move the Declaration along to the UN General Assembly in New York. When the Declaration did move to the General Assembly, no presentation was made which described the historical process and how the Declaration had evolved. This was important; the historical context of the indigenous struggle for self-determination was not given the context it should have been. Instead, indigenes and others who participated in this final process appear to have looked at it as simply a process of getting the Declaration through. Rather, there should have been a further critical analysis of its final content with further submissions made by Indigenous Peoples as to its inadequacies or otherwise as a statement on Indigenous Peoples' rights in international law.

The following discussion refers to articles in the Geneva Declaration which were removed from the final UN Declaration accepted and passed by the General Assembly in 2007.

The Geneva Declaration: colonization

The Geneva Declaration referred to colonization, in reference to the Martínez Cobo definition of Indigenous Peoples; this had developed from Martínez Cobo's UN study on discrimination practised against the world's Indigenous Peoples. In his study Martínez Cobo had worked towards the development of a universal definition of 'indigenous peoples':

> Indigenous communities, peoples and nations are those which, having a historical continuity with pre-invasion and pre-colonial societies that developed on their territories, consider themselves distinct from other sectors of the societies now prevailing in those territories, or parts of them. They form at present non-dominant sectors of society and are determined to preserve, develop and transmit to future generations their

ancestral territories, and their ethnic identity, as the basis of their continued existence as peoples, in accordance with their own cultural patterns, social institutions and legal systems.[4]

Martínez Cobo discussed the process he adopted in coming to a definition of 'indigenous peoples':

(a) Indigenous peoples must be recognized according to their own perceptions and conception of themselves in relation to other groups co-existing with them in the fabric of the same society;

(b) There must be no attempt to define them according to the perception of others through the values of foreign societies or of the dominant sections in such societies;

(c) The right of indigenous peoples to define what and who is indigenous, and the correlative, the right to determine what and who is not, must be recognized;

(d) The power of indigenous peoples to determine who are their members must not be interfered with by the State concerned, through legislation, regulations or any other means; artificial, arbitrary or manipulatory definitions must be rejected. The special position of indigenous peoples within the society of nation-states existing today derives from their historical rights to their lands and from their right to be different and to be considered as different.[5]

The Martínez Cobo definition highlights that in many cases Indigenous Peoples have been dispossessed by the processes of colonization, and have not been able to decolonize due to political circumstances. This definition applied to Indigenous Peoples of the Americas, Australia, New Zealand and parts of the Pacific. It was very clear who was being embraced by the Declaration. There was a link between colonization, territories, lands and resources, but these references were removed from the final UN General Assembly Declaration in 2007. Moreover the Declaration broadens the concept of 'indigenous' and as a result it is no longer clear to whom it applies. This is particularly problematic for Indigenous Peoples who have not had the opportunity to deal with the key issues of colonialism and the power to develop decolonization processes.

---

[4] José Martínez Cobo, *Study of the Problem against Indigenous Populations Vol. 5 Conclusions, Proposals and Recommendations* UN Doc. E/CN 4/Sub 2/1986/7, 1986/7, Add. 4., paras. 379, 381.

[5] Ibid., pp. 50–51.

The New York Declaration and individual or collective rights of peoples

The UN Declaration added reference, in the preamble, to individuals; previously the Draft had referred to collective rights of Indigenous Peoples. This is from the Draft:

> *Recognizing and reaffirming* that indigenous *individuals* are entitled without discrimination to all human rights recognized in international law, and that indigenous peoples possess collective rights which are indispensable for their existence, well-being and integral development as peoples.[6]

This is from the Declaration; as well as the preamble, Article 1 was added:

> Indigenous peoples have the right to the full enjoyment, as a collective or as individuals, of all human rights and fundamental freedoms as recognized in the Charter of the United Nations, the Universal Declaration of Human Rights and international human rights law.[7]

It is difficult to imagine how the choice between being a member of a collective or an individual within a nation state might work. In the early days of drafting the declaration Indigenous Peoples were not thinking about individual human rights but rather the inherent rights of peoples to their lands and the right of the group to be self-determining. The tension between individual and collective rights is manifest in the 2007 Declaration, which, further, provides no guidance as to how collective rights might be attained and recognized by the state. What impact does this dual position then have on the idea of a collective right of Indigenous Peoples? For example, are you an individual of the state or a member of an indigenous nation, and does the individual identity position work to erode that of the collective?

---

[6] United Nations High Commissioner for Human Rights, Draft United Nations Declaration on the Rights of Indigenous Peoples, 1994/45, www.unhchr.ch/huridocda/huridoca. nsf/%28symbol%29/e.cn.4.sub.2.res.1994.45.en?opendocument (emphasis added). Subsequent references in this chapter will be to 'the Draft' or 'the indigenous Draft Declaration'.

[7] All the citations from the Declaration are from the online version available on the website of the United Nations Permanent Forum on Indigenous Issues (UNPFII), www.un.org/ esa/socdev/unpfii/documents/DRIPS_en.pdf. Subsequent references in this chapter will be to 'the Declaration'.

Rights of the child and state power

The UN Declaration includes a section in the preamble that subjects the Declaration to the Convention on the Rights of the Child, and the 'best interests of the child'. Historically this clause has empowered the state to interpret that which is in the best interest of the child. The Declaration retains this position and along with it the power of the state to continue to determine the removal of children from Indigenous Peoples. Both Australian and Canadian history are filled with stories of indigenous child-removal policies and state interventions. In Australia various states' Aborigines Acts provided for the removal of Aboriginal children into state institutions, along with prohibitions on children from speaking their language and having contact with their family and community. These policies of child removal provided for the forced removal of children and the attempted and ultimate assimilation. Canada has a similar history. These policies were deemed in the 'best interest of the child'.

The power of the state to determine the best interests of the child remains unchanged and is ensured by the following in the preamble to the Declaration:

> *Recognizing in particular* the right of indigenous families and communities to retain shared responsibility for the upbringing, training, education and well-being of their children, *consistent with the rights of the child.* (Emphasis added.)

In the preamble to the 1994 Draft Declaration, 'consistent with the rights of the child' was not included. With this additional phrase the Declaration leaves an opening for the state to determine what those rights are. In the past they have been read in support of state agendas, such as assimilation. Historically we have witnessed child-removal policies which were carried out under the auspices of being 'in the best interest of the child', and more recently this was one of the grounds for which the Northern Territory Intervention was legitimized. The commonwealth government of Australia enacted legislation[8] which enabled the Australian

---

[8] The National Emergency Response comprises the following legislation: Northern Territory National Emergency Response Act 2007 (Cth); Families, Community Services and Indigenous Affairs and Other Legislation Amendment (Northern Territory National Emergency Response and Other Measures) Act 2007 (Cth); Social Security and Other Legislation Amendment (Welfare Reform) Act 2007 (Cth). This legislation has affected the position of traditional owners with respect to the Aboriginal Land Rights Act 1975 (Cth). The emergency response legislation effected the suspension of the Racial Discrimination

army to enter Aboriginal communities across the Northern Territory; the commonwealth government argued that the intervention was necessary to stop the alleged rampant sexual abuse of young children.[9]

Exercising in conformity with international law

Indigenous Peoples began working on a declaration because international legal norms did not protect them. The work was supported by the Martínez Cobo Report which reported on the high levels of discrimination Indigenous Peoples experienced. However, instead of referring to international legal norms and guaranteeing the same standards to Indigenous Peoples, the 2007 UN Declaration ensured the internalization of legal processes:

> *Convinced* that the recognition of the rights of indigenous peoples in this Declaration will enhance harmonious and cooperative relations between the State and indigenous peoples, based on principles of justice, democracy, respect for human rights, non-discrimination and good faith.

So does that leave anything which might compel, for example, the Australian state to desist from further breaches of Aboriginal rights? Rhetoric concerning principles of justice, democracy, respect and good faith is unlikely to shift the genocidal process in Australia, or that suffered by any First Nations peoples.

When the Declaration drafting was initiated by Indigenous Peoples we were lobbying not for human rights but for recognition of our rights as peoples. Why would we develop a separate and distinct set of human rights standards? It is the recognition of the right to self-determination which was claimed, the logic being that if the right to self-determination was realized, so would basic human rights. The process of recognition should have been in reference to international legal norms as expressed in the UN Charter and intended to apply to all peoples.

Act 1975 (Cth), and impacts also on provisions in the Native Title Act 1993 (Cth) and the Northern Territory (Self-Government) Act 1978 (Cth).

[9] See Rex Wild and Patricia Anderson, *Ampe Akelyernemane Meke Mekale 'Little Children Are Sacred'*, Report of the Northern Territory Board of Inquiry into the Protection of Aboriginal Children from Sexual Abuse, 30 April 2007, www.inquirysaac.nt.gov.au/. This report recommended closer consultation and community development programmes across Aboriginal communities within the Northern Territory; instead, in a deliberate misreading of this report the findings were used to legitimize a military intervention in Aboriginal communities.

So what was the intent of developing a distinct standard of human rights for Indigenous Peoples, particularly when Indigenous Peoples live within democracies such as Australia, Canada, New Zealand and the United States which are deemed to uphold justice and human rights? The problem is that the human rights track record of these states, when it comes to recognition of Indigenous Peoples, is poor, and all of them have breached international norms regarding Aboriginal peoples. So how might they give recognition when the UN Declaration does not call on these states to comply with international legal norms when dealing with Indigenous Peoples?

Indigenous peoples lobbied for more than three decades at the UN for recognition as peoples and as members of the international community. Their quest was for recognition of our rights as peoples, not just human rights. In an important way, human rights diminish the collective rights of Indigenous Peoples because they concern individuals within the paradigm of the particular state. In just the same way we do not talk about the human rights of the state; we talk about the territory and the sovereignty of the state.

Human rights applied universally also have the capacity to negate the indigenous world view, in which we have both obligations as well as rights. The individual rights angle is a Western notion and has never been a good fit for Indigenous Peoples. The rights of the individual are often at odds with those of the collective and the collective relationship to the lands and territories, or the natural environment of each people.

Genocide and the Declaration

Article 6 of the original Draft Declaration read as follows:

> Indigenous peoples have the collective right to live in freedom, peace and security as distinct peoples and to full guarantees against genocide or any other act of violence including the removal of indigenous children from their families and communities under any pretext. In addition, they have the individual rights to life, physical and mental integrity, liberty and security of person.[10]

The above clause was removed from the Declaration; and its amendments are of particular concern especially when we are reminded that the

---

[10] Commission on Human Rights, 'Discrimination against Indigenous Peoples: Technical Review of the United Nations Draft Declaration on the Rights of Indigenous Peoples', UN Doc. E/CN 4/Sub. 2/1994/2Add. 120, April 1994.

prime reason for the Declaration was to provide minimum standards that would prevent the ongoing genocide of Indigenous Peoples. The clause was replaced with Article 7, which again elevates the rights of the individual over the collective:

Article 7 of the Declaration

1. Indigenous individuals have the right to life, physical and mental integrity, liberty and security of person.
2. Indigenous peoples have the collective right to live in freedom, peace and security as distinct peoples and shall not be subjected to any act of genocide or any other act of violence, including forcibly removing children of the group to another group.

The watering down of the reference to genocide is of particular concern, especially when we are reminded that the initial reason for working on the Declaration as conveyed in the Martínez Cobo report was to prevent the further genocide of Indigenous Peoples.

Self-determination

The possibility of addressing the power differentials which exist between Indigenous Peoples and states was seen to require the most significant intentions of the Draft Declaration. It was Article 3 which referenced the right to self-determination:

> Indigenous peoples have the right of self-determination. By virtue of this right, they freely determine their political status and freely pursue their economic, social and cultural development.[11]

More importantly Article 3 was reinforced by paragraph 14 in the preamble:

> Acknowledging that the Charter of the United Nations, the International Covenant on Economic, Social and Cultural Rights and the International Covenant on Civil and Political Rights affirm the fundamental importance of the right of self-determination of all peoples, by virtue of which they freely determine their political status and freely pursue their economic, social and cultural development.

Any reference or nexus to the UN Charter so as to affirm the significance or possibility of a core or solid recognition of self-determination

---

[11] Ibid.

was removed from the Declaration. However, the final version of the Declaration was reduced in its capacity and potential to provide for the recognition of the right to self-determination, and as a result Indigenous Peoples will remain captives of the colonial state, contained by its internal rights discourse or the 'domestic paradigm' which, Schulte-Tenckhoff argues, is the regime under which Indigenous Peoples continue to live.[12] Limiting the right to self-determination leaves the Declaration as having no external or international law meaning and without capacity to negotiate effectively a true Aboriginal space.

Article 5 of the Declaration does provide for a superficial recognition of self-determination; indigenous development will be enabled within the confines of the state:

> Indigenous peoples have the right to maintain and strengthen their distinct political, legal, economic, social and cultural institutions, while retaining their right to participate fully, if they so choose, in the political, economic, social and cultural life of the State.

But without the nexus or context with the UN Charter, Indigenous Peoples have again been reduced in their capacity to participate more fully in the UN system. It will continue to remain the position that whenever indigenous ways of knowing the world collide with the agendas of the state, the state will take over. For example, where Indigenous Peoples are opposed to development which is in conflict with their political, legal, social and cultural values but sanctioned by the state, there will remain no mechanism, in spite of the existence of the Declaration, which will assist in determining pathways to coexistence. Instead, the state perspective will overtake and determine the development, or otherwise. As we know, much of the history of colonial contact with Indigenous Peoples has been one of a long process of genocide. The Declaration will not perform against that historical and continuing trend.

The 2007 UN Declaration ensures that the principle of self-determination as it is applied to Indigenous Peoples is limited, and this is noted in its preamble in the following:

> *Solemnly proclaims* the following United Nations Declaration on the Rights of Indigenous Peoples as a standard of achievement to be pursued in a spirit of partnership and mutual respect.

---

[12] Isabelle Schulte-Tenckhoff, 'Re-assessing the Paradigm of Domestication: The Problematic of Indigenous Treaties', *Review of Constitutional Studies* 4 (1998): 239–89, at 239.

These are fine words, but the truth of respect and partnership can only be realized where the differentials of power are balanced, and this will not occur while the position of Indigenous Peoples is determined by the state. And it will not occur while international legal norms are disabled from being applied to the Declaration, and this is evident in the preamble which has no relevance to them. You cannot have a partnership where an imbalance of power works against the possibility of that partnership being realized. This position will not correct itself unless international legal remedies are able to compel states to comply. The state remains the final determiner of all things within the life of the state, including the lives of Indigenous Peoples. This has been the way since the advent of colonization, and nothing in this Declaration is likely to shift power imbalances which exist and which continue to determine the future of Indigenous Peoples.

Similarly Article 9 of the Declaration is rendered ineffective:

> Indigenous peoples and individuals have the right to belong to an indigenous community or nation, in accordance with the traditions and customs of the community or nation concerned. No discrimination of any kind may arise from the exercise of such a right.

Again, the above clause stands able to be interpreted by nation states as meaning the right to perform as communities or nations as might be determined or permitted by them. Therefore indigenous obligations to care for country or to regain stolen lands may be determined by the state. It is clear that the state will not permit the return of indigenous lands or prevent their development where any developments are in conflict with its agenda.

Indigenous life ways and the culture of colonialism

The UN Declaration speaks more to the culture of colonialism than it does to the possibility of recognizing Indigenous Peoples' life ways or cultures. Articles 12, 13, 14 and 15 have all been changed so as to limit the possibilities for ongoing sustainable indigenous cultures.

While Article 12 of the Draft Declaration read:

> Indigenous peoples have the right to practise and *revitalize* their cultural traditions and customs. This includes the right to maintain, protect and develop the *past, present and future* manifestations of their cultures, such as archaeological and historical sites, artefacts, designs, ceremonies, technologies and visual and performing arts and literature, as well as the right

to the restitution of cultural, intellectual, religious and spiritual property
*taken without their free and informed consent or in violation of their laws,
traditions and customs.* (Emphasis added)

Article 12 of the UN Declaration reads:

1. Indigenous peoples have the right to manifest, practice, develop and
   teach their spiritual and religious traditions, customs and ceremonies;
   the right to maintain, protect, and have access in privacy to their
   religious and cultural sites; the right to the use and control of their
   ceremonial objects; and the right to the repatriation of their human
   remains.
2. States shall seek to enable the access and/or repatriation of ceremonial
   objects and human remains in their possession through fair, transparent and effective mechanisms developed in conjunction with indigenous peoples concerned.

The indigenous Draft Declaration gave recognition to the need for the
revitalization of culture; it also focused on the need to protect the past,
present and future cultures of Indigenous Peoples and also to provide
restitution for cultural property that had been taken without the free
prior and informed consent of Indigenous Peoples. The UN Declaration
focuses only on the present, and there is no commitment to revitalizing
past practices or providing restitution for the stolen past. Without such
recognition indigenous communities that are engaged in rebuilding and
revitalization stand without a remedy which might otherwise support
their regeneration and their sustainable growth in the future.

The possibility for revitalizing Aboriginal culture is also limited by the
absence from Article 13 of the UN Declaration of any reference to land,
sites and material culture:

1. Indigenous peoples have the right to revitalize, use, develop and transmit to future generations their histories, languages, oral traditions,
   philosophies, writing systems and literatures, and to designate and
   retain their own names for communities, places and persons.
2. States shall take effective measures to ensure that this right is protected
   and also to ensure that indigenous peoples can understand and be
   understood in political, legal and administrative proceedings, where
   necessary through the provision of interpretation or by other appropriate means.

This Article purports to protect the culture of Indigenous Peoples'
histories, languages, oral traditions, philosophies, writing systems and
literature without any reference to the foundation which holds those indigenous knowledges – that is, the land. Without the recognition of the

indigenous connection to land there is no point to recognition of anything else. The lived, connected relationship to indigenous lands is fundamental to the future of indigenous culture, and that which is described
in Article 13 of the UN Declaration is a form of recognition that sits well
within a museum view of Aboriginal culture, one that can be divorced
from a living connection to indigenous lands. In that museum space there
is no recognition of a lived culture and one with a future.

In contrast, Article 13 of the indigenous Draft Declaration provided for
the possibility of a continuing, living connection to the land:

> Indigenous peoples have the right to manifest, practise, develop and
> teach their spiritual and religious traditions, customs and ceremonies;
> the right to maintain, protect, and have *access in privacy to their religious
> and cultural sites; the right to the use and control of ceremonial objects*; and
> the right to the repatriation of human remains. States shall take effect-
> ive measures, in conjunction with the indigenous peoples concerned, *to
> ensure that indigenous sacred places, including burial sites, be preserved,
> respected and protected*. (Emphasis added)

The UN Declaration provides no protection for indigenous places.
The destruction of indigenous lands is the greatest threat posed to the
ongoing future and cultures of Indigenous Peoples, and is the cause of
the greatest level of conflict between indigenous and non-indigenous
interests. Possibilities for negotiating for the protection of indigenous
places were limited by the passage of the UN Declaration and its failure
to deal with the ongoing relationships Indigenous Peoples have with the
land.

The cultural education of Indigenous Peoples is referred to in Article
14 of the UN Declaration and provides for a state-controlled framework
whereby Indigenous Peoples have opportunities, where deemed possible
by the state. This is the current position in Australia, where the Northern
Territory government has ruled against bi-lingual programs.

Article 14 of the indigenous Draft Declaration provided:

> Indigenous peoples have the right to *revitalize*, use, develop and transmit
> to future generations their histories, languages, oral traditions, philoso-
> phies, writing systems and literatures, and to designate and retain their
> own names for communities, places and persons. *States shall take effective
> measures*, whenever any right of indigenous peoples may be threatened,
> to ensure this right is protected and also to ensure that they can under-
> stand and be understood in political, legal and administrative proceed-
> ings, where necessary through the provision of interpretation or by other
> appropriate means. (Emphasis added)

Article 14 of the Declaration declared:

> 1. Indigenous peoples have the right to establish and control their educational systems and institutions providing education in their own languages, in a manner appropriate to their cultural methods of teaching and learning.
> 2. Indigenous individuals, particularly children, have the right to all levels and forms of education of the State without discrimination.
> 3. States shall, in conjunction with indigenous peoples, take effective measures, in order for indigenous individuals, particularly children, including those living outside their communities, to have access, *when possible*, to an education in their own culture and provided in their own language. (Emphasis added)

There is nothing in this article that would provide for shifts in the directions of states towards the embrace of Aboriginal culture.

The indigenous Draft Declaration is much stronger than the final version of Article 14. Obviously the state is more easily let off the hook by only having to provide a cultural education 'when possible', instead of being called upon to take effective measures whenever indigenous rights were threatened, and provide stronger support for the ongoing possibility of indigenous cultural life ways.

Similarly, Article 15 of the UN Declaration provides a token protection for indigenous cultural rights and reads more like a feel-good motherhood statement of good intentions rather than anything which directs or compels a state to take action:

> 1. Indigenous peoples have the right to the dignity and diversity of their cultures, traditions, histories and aspirations which shall be appropriately reflected in education and public information.
> 2. States shall take effective measures, in consultation and cooperation with the indigenous peoples concerned, to combat prejudice and eliminate discrimination and to promote tolerance, understanding and good relations among indigenous peoples and all other segments of society.

Not only does Article 15 of the indigenous Draft Declaration provide a much stronger statement, but it speaks of the right to establish and control educational systems and institutions and also to take effective measures to provide the resources to develop Aboriginal systems of education:

> Indigenous children have the right to all levels and forms of education of the State. All indigenous peoples also have this right and the right to establish and control their educational systems and institutions providing education in their own languages, in a manner appropriate to their

cultural methods of teaching and learning. Indigenous children living outside their communities have the right to be provided access to education in their own culture and language.

States shall take effective measures to provide appropriate resources for these purposes.

The territorial integrity of states is what matters

Perhaps the greatest discrepancy in the language of the UN Declaration in affirming the right of Indigenous Peoples to self-determination can be found in Article 46. The paramountcy of state sovereignty is guaranteed by Article 46(1), whereby the territorial integrity of the state is retained and guaranteed against all other claims including those of colonized and dispossessed Indigenous Peoples. The opportunity for the decolonization of indigenous territories or even a dialogue on coexistence between Indigenous Peoples and the colonial states is limited and will be determined by the clear intention of the UN to retain the territorial integrity of colonial states. The future political identities of all peoples will be guided by Article 46(2), and is a position that is likely to ensure the ongoing unequal and minority status of Indigenous Peoples, as it is unlikely to prove an opportunity for the development of Indigenous Peoples' governance initiatives, particularly where those initiatives are likely to be considered as repugnant or different to the majority rule.

The fears that the Australian, Canadian and other governments had of the Declaration – that it might have posed a threat to their hegemony – is without foundation. Article 46 makes it clear that the ongoing subjugation of Indigenous Peoples will continue and that this position will render impossible Indigenous Peoples being able to develop and articulate a decolonized Aboriginal space.

The indigenous Draft Declaration ended with Article 45:

> Nothing in this Declaration may be interpreted as implying for any State or group or person any right to engage in any act or activity or to perform any act contrary to the Charter of the United Nations.

The indigenous Draft Declaration provided the nexus to the Charter of the United Nations, and the intention was that it be interpreted in accordance with the legal norms of international law. However, the new Article 45 reads thus:

> Nothing in this Declaration may be constituted as diminishing or extinguishing the rights indigenous peoples have now or may acquire in the future.

The Declaration has entrenched Indigenous Peoples as objects of international law, and the possibility of the recognition of our status as peoples and nations in international law has been negated by the framing of this new Declaration. Indigenous peoples have been set apart from international legal standards and as Indigenous Peoples deemed to sit outside or perhaps inside international law, wherever the states determine our existence or otherwise, and its determinations are clearly to be seen by all – that is, we are deemed to reside inside the state and subject to state domestic laws. As a result of the further limitations that the UN Declaration places on the position of Indigenous Peoples our rights in international law have actually been diminished rather than affirmed. The link to the UN Charter was critical to the survival of Indigenous Peoples, whose very existence comes up against the genocidal practices of states, and without that link or possibility of international intervention or deemed status as independent sovereign peoples, the indigenous future remains a question as unresolved as it was when Indigenous Peoples were allowed to enter the UN in the early 1970s.

The Charter is supposed to uphold peoples' rights. It was really important to link the Declaration on Indigenous Peoples back to the Charter because of the reference to nations and peoples. The Charter says nothing about states having rights to self-determination. It refers to peoples and nations, and that is why the original indigenous Draft Declaration was linked to the Charter. The indigenous people who were involved in the final passage of the UN Declaration did not have the same historical background as those who had begun the process three decades earlier; they also had a limited knowledge of international law. Knowledge of international law was critical to the process of ensuring that Indigenous Peoples were favourably treated. Instead, we have ended up with a UN Declaration which is largely rhetorical and full of hollow statements without any power or remedy for Indigenous Peoples to enable and determine indigenous futures.

The rhetoric is not sufficiently strong to strengthen the position of Indigenous Peoples. We have ended up with a UN Declaration which is far less significant in the recognition of Indigenous Peoples than the Indigenous Declaration with which we began.

In examining shifts or some of the advantages of the UN Declaration we offer the following brief analysis of possibilities, although clearly the disadvantages can be seen to outweigh any perceived advantages.

Advantages

It is possible that the UN Declaration will be used as an international standard to negotiate domestic reform and frameworks for engagement with Indigenous Peoples. However, there is no mechanism to enforce any of those reform measures or frameworks for engagement. The Declaration resides purely in the realm of the goodwill of the state and the more powerful economic interests that limit or conflict with Indigenous Peoples' interests. A further advantage could be that the Declaration is used as a tool by the judiciary to assist in the interpretation of the terms used in human rights legislation.

Disadvantages

The biggest problem with the Declaration is that it is not clear to whom the Declaration applies. The Indigenous Declaration definition developed by Martínez Cobo clearly applied to Indigenous Peoples living in colonial states and territories, and also included indigenous resources controlled by the colonial state and Indigenous Peoples who did not have the opportunity to be listed and considered before the UN decolonization committee. This definition applied to the Indigenous Peoples of Australia, the Americas, parts of the Pacific and New Zealand.

The UN Declaration is broad in its definition of Indigenous Peoples, and as a result it is unlikely to assist Indigenous Peoples who were included in the Martínez Cobo definition of Indigenous Peoples.

Indigenous Peoples sought out UN forums in the 1970s to secure land rights, and self-determination. This aim remains unfinished business between states and Indigenous Peoples and is now further limited and marginalized by the UN Declaration. There are currently no effective UN mechanisms to promote Indigenous Peoples' concerns. The UN indigenous structures that do exist include the Indigenous Permanent Forum and the Indigenous Expert Mechanism; however, both of these forums are controlled by the states – that is, the state governments make decisions about what these mechanisms can or cannot do in the setting of their agendas. The Permanent Forum, for example, hears presentations from Indigenous Peoples, the body then reports on those sessions, and those reports are sent off to the UN Economic and Social Council (ECOSOC). The Permanent Forum is one of a number of bodies that feed into the ECOSOC agenda. It is unlikely that any of the presentations or reports will progress through the UN system, as there are no mechanisms to advance them further through it. The Permanent Forum cannot draft standards or hear complaints.

The previous standard-setting and complaints procedure that existed in the UN Working Group on Indigenous Populations (WGIP) no longer exists, and as a result the studies that were developed by the WGIP, such as the Free, Prior and Informed Consent Study, and the Treaty Study, remain in a state of limbo, shelved and growing dust. Without mechanisms that could bring those studies before UN bodies they are likely to disappear within the UN system. Similarly, Indigenous Peoples have nowhere to present general complaints and recent developments occurring on our territories. Under the now disbanded WGIP, Indigenous Peoples were able to participate in their forums and to provide information about recent developments. If a major event was occurring, then information about it could be moved up through the system, to the Sub-commission, and then to the Human Rights Commission. The event could also engage the Human Rights Centre and the possibility for the involvement of the High Commissioner for Human Rights. By contrast, the recently created UN Indigenous Expert mechanism agendas are set by the states. For example, the agenda set for 2008 was to discuss and meet for three days on indigenous education. In 2009 the agenda set by the states was to discuss housing issues. This forum commits each calendar year as a particular 'policy year' (where a 'special theme' is discussed), each odd calendar year being termed a 'review year' (where the implementation of the Forum's past recommendations on specific themes is reviewed).[13]

Since the disbanding of the UNWGIP there are no UN forums or mechanisms where Indigenous Peoples can raise general complaints affecting Indigenous Peoples; instead the Indigenous Expert Mechanism reports to the Human Rights Council, and this is considered in the context of all other priorities that come before the Human Rights Council. In the past those priorities have focused on Palestine, Darfur and Afghanistan. It is clear that, for example, a report on the lack of education of Indigenous Peoples would not be considered a priority.

In the past there has been support provided for Indigenous Peoples in the Human Rights Centre; this is no longer available, and the indigenous

---

[13] See, e.g., International Service for Human Rights, 'UN Permanent Forum on Indigenous issues: 7th Session: Climate Change: An Indigenous Call to Action', 2008, http://olddoc.ishr.ch/hrm/nymonitor/new_york_updates/permanent_forum/nyu_perm_forum_7session_climate_change.pdf.

experts who have been appointed are not engaged full-time, as with the Indigenous Rapporteur which is a voluntary unpaid appointment; therefore the capacity to act internationally has been substantially reduced as the resources are limited and those used in the past to bring the Declaration into existence now no longer exist in Geneva.

In the past, UN studies would be recommended by the Working Group and passed on to the Sub-commission, or the body of UN experts would approve or otherwise and make their recommendation to the Human Rights Commission. The Human Rights Commission would pass a resolution, which when passed would have attached to that resolution the financial implications of the resolution. Funding would be sourced for the study by the secretariat from the Human Rights Centre, which would also provide a warm body-technical support person to assist the study. This process ensured that there was institutional support for any studies that were proposed. However, the new Indigenous Expert Mechanism is not part of the new Human Rights Council Advisory Body of Experts, and as they have no relationship to the secretariat they cannot initiate studies.

Indigenous peoples are now more than ever under pressure to appeal to the UN and to better market the importance of our issues so as to compete effectively with the large number of priority issues that come before the Human Rights Council. This position brings into question the future of the UN Indigenous Permanent Forum and also the Indigenous Expert Mechanism and what might they be able to achieve within the current shifts and the illusory space created by the passage of the Declaration – that is, the illusion and recognition of indigenous rights. Further to this, the state governments have crafted the Indigenous Permanent Forum and the Indigenous Expert Mechanism to ensure they are unable to effectively draft standards and report and advance complaints that reflect the current position of Indigenous Peoples across the globe. For example, in 2008 a number of indigenous peoples attending the Expert Mechanism Forum came to speak on recent developments on their territories, one such development being the massacre of a number of Indigenous Peoples in South America. A widow who came to speak was shut down by the chairperson, and advised that unless she was to speak on the agenda item – at the time it was education – then she could not speak.

The current shifts and UN responses to Indigenous Peoples no longer enable a space for the complaints by Indigenous Peoples which address issues of survival and genocide to be heard. We argue that, following more than three decades of indigenous work within the UN system to develop humane standards for the states and the international community to engage and create coexistence, we have advanced no further than when the process first began. Our conclusions are that we must return to the main body of the UN if, as we are finding, the UN Indigenous Mechanisms are disabled from hearing these issues. The issue of colonialism has not been addressed, and colonialism remains alive and continues to threaten the survival of Indigenous Peoples. We need to ensure that Australia, Canada, New Zealand and the United States, and the states of South and Central America are not let off the hook for their continuing role as colonialist states and the possibility of decolonization. For those Indigenous Peoples whose lands and lives are controlled by those states we remain without any effective mechanism to deal with their being colonized peoples.

We argue that there is a need to return to the main game inside the UN forums and to be returned to those spaces from the side alleys and UN ghetto spaces into which we have been herded. We are peoples and we belong in the main game – that is, to humanize the world and its treatment of all peoples.

In reclaiming our space within the main game we also note that for Indigenous Peoples colonialism remains the main game in town, while the colonial states offer assimilation as the solution. The promise of strong international human rights standards and the Australian government's acceptance in 2009 of the Declaration is unlikely to shift the position of Indigenous Peoples. The assimilation agendas of states continue to illustrate the reductionist approach to indigenous rights and states seizing and setting agendas for indigenous survival and development.

We need to hold the line and our right to conceptualize the indigenous position and not hand over to the states our right to name who we are, at either a domestic or international level. The work continues, and we have an obligation not to trade off our inherent Aboriginal rights in the form of any agreement, compact or partnership that falls short of recognition in accord with the norms of international law and our right to determine the future of our lands and lives.

It is unlikely at this time in our history that the states will shift, so why the rush to negotiate? What are we negotiating towards other than the advancement of our own assimilation? If this position is correct, then we need to re-evaluate how we may work better towards securing the future of indigenous life on earth.

Works cited

Aboriginal Land Rights Act, 1975 (Cth).
Alfred, Taiaiake, *Peace, Power, Righteousness: An Indigenous Manifesto.* Oxford University Press, 2009.

Commission on Human Rights, 'Discrimination against Indigenous Peoples: Technical Review of the United Nations Draft Declaration on the Rights of Indigenous Peoples', 20 April 1994, UN Doc. E/CN 4/Sub. 2/1994/2 Add. 1.

Families, Community Services and Indigenous Affairs and Other Legislation Amendment (Northern Territory National Emergency Response and Other Measures) Act 2007 (Cth).

International Service for Human Rights. 'UN Permanent Forum on Indigenous Issues: 7th Session: Climate Change: An Indigenous Call to Action', 2008, http://olddoc.ishr.ch/hrm/nymonitor/new_york_updates/permanent_ forum/nyu_perm_forum_7session_climate_change.pdf.

Macklin, Jenny, 'Statement on the United Nations Declaration on the Rights of Indigenous Peoples', speech delivered at Parliament House, Canberra, 3 April 2009, www.un.org/esa/socdev/unpfii/documents/Australia_official_ statement_endorsement_UNDRIP.pdf.

Martínez Cobo, José, *Study of the Problem against Indigenous Populations Vol. 5 Conclusions, Proposals and Recommendations*, UN Doc. E/CN 4/Sub. 2/1986/7 Add. 4, 1986/7.

Native Title Act, 1993 (Cth).

Northern Territory National Emergency Response Act, 2007 (Cth) Social Security and Other Legislation Amendment (Welfare Reform) Act, 2007 (Cth).

Northern Territory (Self-Government) Act, 1978 (Cth).

Racial Discrimination Act, 1975 (Cth).

Schulte-Tenckhoff, Isabelle, 'Reassessing the Paradigm of Domestication: The Problematic of Indigenous Treaties', *Review of Constitutional Studies* 4 (1998): 239–89.

United Nations Declaration on the Rights of Indigenous Peoples, adopted by the General Assembly 13 September 2007, www.un.org/esa/socdev/unpfii/ documents/DRIPS_en.pdf.

United Nations High Commissioner for Human Rights, Draft United Nations Declaration on the Rights of Indigenous Peoples, 1994/45, www.unhchr. ch/huridocda/huridoca.nsf/%28symbol%29/e.cn.4.sub.2.res.1994.45. en?opendocument.

Wild, Rex and Patricia Anderson, *Ampe Akelyernemane Meke Mekale 'Little Children Are Sacred'*, Report of the Northern Territory Board of Inquiry into the Protection of Aboriginal Children from Sexual Abuse, 30 April 2007, www.inquirysaac.nt.gov.au/.

4

Australia's Northern Territory Intervention and indigenous rights on language, education and culture: an ethnocidal solution to Aboriginal 'dysfunction'?

SHEILA COLLINGWOOD-WHITTICK

The last region of the continent to be colonized, the territory with not only the highest ratio of indigenous inhabitants but also the greatest percentage of indigenous people living in often remote communities on Aboriginal lands owned under Western legal title, and the only part of the country where a majority of Aboriginal people continue both to speak their native languages and to practise their traditional customs, Northern Australia has long been represented in the nation's imaginary as the final remaining bastion of 'traditional' Aboriginal cultures.

When, therefore, on 21 June 2007, the Prime Minister, John Howard, and his Minister for Indigenous Affairs, Malcolm Brough, announced (with bipartisan support) the package of wide-ranging, draconian measures[1] that constituted the government's Northern Territory Emergency Response (NTER) to the 'evidence' of social dysfunction in remote indigenous communities presented in the *Ampe Akelyernemane Meke Mekarle 'Little Children Are Sacred'* (hereafter LCAS) report – there could be no mistaking the symbolism behind the punitive policy the two ministers presented to the press.[2] The problem the federal government had

---

[1] In the Request for Urgent Action (hereafter RUA) made under the Convention on the Elimination of All Forms of Racial Discrimination (CERD) by NT Aborigines on 28 January 2009, the authors point out that these measures apply only to 'prescribed areas'. An estimated 87 per cent of people living in prescribed areas are Aboriginal Australians. These areas 'encompass more than 500 Aboriginal communities' and 'cover an area of over 600,000 square kilometres' (Human Rights Law Reform Centre (hereafter HRLRC) January 2009: 14).

[2] A report by the Human Rights and Equal Opportunity Commission published in 2008 described NTER legislation as 'punitive and racist', stating that it 'contravenes a number of

set its sights on eradicating was clearly of much longer date and greater import for the country than the levels of child sexual abuse and alcoholism in Aboriginal communities in the Northern Territory (NT).[3]

The inquiry carried out by Rex Wild and Patricia Anderson (joint authors of LCAS) had been ordered by the government in mid 2006 following lurid rumours inflaming the national media 'of extreme levels of sexual abuse in Aboriginal communities [and] ... allegations of sexual slavery and sophisticated paedophile rings ... protected by community elders and cultural norms' (HRLRC January 2009: 57) – sensational allegations later declared to be unfounded by the Australian Crime Commission, a joint NT Police and Family and Community Services Taskforce and by Wild and Anderson themselves (ibid., 57).

What was particularly puzzling about the NTER was that the inquiry that, the government claimed, had triggered it was merely the most recent in a whole series of investigations into child sexual abuse (and other grave problems affecting indigenous communities) that had been conducted in a succession of Australian states during Howard's eleven years in office. Yet none of the previous reports had produced any response from the government that was remotely comparable to the declaration of a national emergency or to the drastic remedies that were announced on 21 June 2007.[4] As an indigenous specialist in trauma studies, Judy Atkinson, recounts,

> apart from numerous reports detailing the rising incidence of child abuse and neglect, the violence, suicides and suicide attempts, the juvenile offending and incarceration rates, the health statistics, the housing statistics, the unemployment rates, the lack of education achievement – all indicators of people in crisis – when I have spoken to Ministers of the

---

international human rights conventions and the Commonwealth Racial Discrimination Act' (Skelton 2008, n.p.).

[3] Three key points that need emphasizing at the outset are: 1. 'The Northern Territory Intervention legislation did not give effect to the recommendations contained in the Little Children Are Sacred Report. Indeed, '*the terms "children" or "sexual abuse" do not appear in any of the 480 pages of legislative instruments*' (HRLRC, January 2009: 3, emphasis added); 2. '[B]arely reported government statistics revealed that of the 7,433 Aboriginal children examined by doctors as part of the "national emergency" 39 had been referred to the authorities for suspected abuse. Of those, a maximum of just four possible cases of abuse were identified. Such were the "unthinkable numbers"' (Pilger 2008: n.p.); 3. Many Aboriginal communities in the NT had elected to become 'dry' well before the intervention took place.

[4] As the LCAS report indicated (5), these inquiries had produced the Gordon Report (Western Australia, 2002), the Protecting Children Inquiry (Queensland, 2004), the Report into Sex Offences by the Victorian Law Reform Commission (Victoria, 2004) and the Aboriginal Child Sexual Assault Taskforce (New South Wales, 2006).

Crown, I have been brushed aside. From Robert Tickner (1990): 'I know the problems – you tell me the solutions,' to Tony Abbot's office (2005): 'We know the problems – you don't have to keep describing them to me like this – can't your people just get over it?' (Atkinson 2007: 152).

Considering Australia's long history of indifference to the social and medical pathologies that have wiped out swathes of the Aboriginal population for generations, it is hardly surprising that certain political commentators should interpret the government's dramatic reaction to indigenous child abuse as a sign of 'Howard's desperate need for a lift' in the approaching federal elections (Rundle 2007: 37). Given the dubious relevance of some of the measures proposed, it is also understandable that some observers should read the NT intervention as mere political opportunism – the exploitation of Aboriginal community dysfunction for the purpose of allowing the federal government to 'impose its ideological agenda in relation to Aboriginal land', as David Ross, director of the Central Land Council put it (quoted in AAP 22 June 2007: n.p.).

Particularly worrying with regard to the latter hypothesis is Sinem Saban's assertion that 'a month after the legislation to seize the land was passed, Australia signed a uranium deal with China and Russia. Around 40% of the world's uranium is in Australia. Most of it is in the Northern Territory; a lot of it is on Aboriginal land' (Bruce-Lockhart 2007: n.p.). More worrying still is Australian scientist Helen Caldicott's claim that it is not only uranium mining that interests the government but that the NTER is also 'a ploy to allow the dumping of nuclear waste in the outback. ... The land grab from the Aborigines is actually about uranium and nuclear waste' (AAP 2 July 2007: n.p.).

Beyond the all-important question of whether the steps taken by the government were/are likely to be effective in curbing the alcoholism, violence and child sexual abuse that, most people agree, *do* blight certain indigenous communities, what can be affirmed with certainty is that while some actions were recognizably linked to the problems exposed by the LCAS report, several key measures just as obviously were not.

As Melinda Hinkson indicates, two anomalous aspects of the government's response were 'the refusal to take into account expert evidence or the views of Aboriginal people themselves,[5] and the severing of the

---

[5] There was no consultation whatsoever with Aboriginal communities or their leaders before the NTER was announced. As the RUA authors argue, this is 'one of the aspects of the NTER that has most profoundly disempowered Aboriginal people and their communities and led to a strongly articulated sense of helplessness. In particular, it has led to a perception of a reversion to a protectionist and paternalist era' (HRLRC January 2009: 44).

"crisis" from any consideration of past governmental action and neglect' (Hinkson 2007: 6). But perhaps the most aberrant feature of the intervention was the fact that, in order to be able to pass the 500 pages of emergency legislation it had assembled with indecent haste,[6] the Australian government had first to suspend the Racial Discrimination Act (RDA), 1975. Thanks to the suspension of this Act, 'Persons subject to the Northern Territory Intervention are prevented from challenging, on the basis of racial discrimination, its measures through existing domestic law and are prevented from seeking any remedy' (HRLRC January 2009: 57).

Since coming to power in November 2007, the Labor government has done little to repair this gross violation of indigenous rights. Even when, in March 2010, the government finally moved to repeal clauses in the NTER legislation that had suspended anti-discrimination laws, the new bills it proposed would not, Amnesty International immediately warned, 'reverse racially-discriminatory actions already initiated under the NTER and offer[ed] no redress for discrimination already suffered' (Amnesty International Australia 12 March 2010: n.p.). Moreover, to the dismay of human rights defenders, even this partial reinstatement of the RDA was not due to take effect before 31 December 2010. With the RDA suspended, there are, indigenous law professor Larissa Behrendt points out, 'few options for legal challenge' to the NTER's breaches of the international legislation underpinning UNDRIP.[7]

Not only has the present administration declined to relinquish the 'emergency' rights-denying measures adopted by Howard during his final months in office, it has even extended some of the policies initially prescribed exclusively for the NT – such as quarantining of welfare payments, which, as the Review Board Report noted, is 'unrelated to a person's capacity to meet family responsibilities' (quoted in HRLRC January 2009: 16) – to other parts of the country, and is aggressively pushing schemes designed to encourage the development of private home ownership. The current administration has also endorsed the controversial and symbolically crucial decision announced (again 'without warning or consultation with the affected communities') by the NT Education Minister,

[6] On 16 June 2008, Mal Brough, '[t]he architect of the federal intervention in the Northern Territory', admitted that 'it took 48 hours for the Howard government to formulate the policy to combat child sexual abuse in Aboriginal communities' (ABC News, 16 June 2008: n.p.). From 7 August 2007, when the 480 pages of legislation were first introduced to the Australian parliament, it took a mere ten days for the legislative process itself to be completed (Calma 2007: 210).

[7] Personal communication, 29 May 2010.

Marion Scrymgour, on 14 October 2008, to dismantle bilingual education in the last remaining remote NT schools where it had been maintained (Simpson and McConvell 2009: 15).

In many important respects, then, the so-called 'emergency' intervention constitutes an outright disavowal of the main principles enshrined in UNDRIP.[8] Not that there is anything unusual in an ex-white-settler colony like Australia adopting a refractory position on indigenous rights – the NTER could, after all, be regarded as an expression of the ambiguous, not to say overtly antagonistic, attitudes towards indigenous rights that persist in former settler societies. (It is no coincidence that the four countries that originally refused to sign UNDRIP in 2007 are former British settler colonies.[9]) As James Anaya acknowledged in a discussion on indigenous peoples in North America at a recent session of the Permanent Forum on Indigenous Issues, 'The violations of indigenous peoples are deep, systemic and widespread.' 'To ensure that appropriate institutions [are] in place' is, he admitted, 'not an easy task' (ECOSOC HR/5016 22 April 2010: n.p.). What *is* significant about the NTER, however, is the marked dissonance it reveals between what Australia is doing and saying at home and how it wishes to be perceived on the international scene.

In April 2009, seventeen months after taking office, Kevin Rudd overturned the Howard administration's decision not to sign UNDRIP. At the time of the UNDRIP signing, Australia's ambassador to the UN 'told the General Assembly that the Federal Government has long expressed its dissatisfaction with the references to self-determination, adding that the declaration also places customary law above national law' (ABC News 14 September 2007: n.p.). In her statement to the Australian parliament, however, Rudd's Minister for Indigenous Affairs, Jenny Macklin, declared that, in changing its position and endorsing UNDRIP,[10] the Australian

---

[8] For the details see Sabine Kacha's excellent and extremely well documented submission to James Anaya (the United Nations Special Rapporteur on the situation of human rights and fundamental freedoms of indigenous peoples), in which she reports that NTER legislation breaches 'a staggering 25 articles – more than half – of the … UNDRIP' and 'almost half of the 30 articles' of the Universal Declaration of Human Rights, 'which Australia endorsed decades ago'. http://stoptheintervention.orf/uploads/files_to_download/The_NT_Intervention-25_8_2009.pdf. I am indebted to Ms Kacha for the invaluable information with which she provided me during my research for this chapter. Further information on opposition to the intervention is available at http://stoptheintervention.org/facts/articles.

[9] Australia, Canada, New Zealand and the United States have since changed tack and indicated their support for UNDRIP.

[10] As Larissa Behrendt explains, 'Australia has *endorsed* the DRIP (you only have one chance to be an actual signatory – when it goes through the General Assembly – and

government was acting 'in the spirit of re-setting the relationship between Indigenous and non-Indigenous Australians and building trust' (Macklin 3 April 2009: 2). Nevertheless, seeking to counter the criticism of opposition legal affairs spokesman, George Brandis, that 'the UN document was deeply flawed, and supporting it would have unforeseen and far-reaching consequences for Australian law' (Drape 26 March 2009: n.p.), Macklin reassuringly pointed out that the declaration was 'non-binding and [did] not affect existing Australian law' (Macklin 3 April 2009: 3).

Significantly, it was the 'historic and aspirational' (ibid.) nature of the document on which Macklin chose to focus, describing it as setting 'important international principles for nations to *aspire to*' (ibid., emphasis added). Placing her main stress on Australia's commitment to 'closing the gap' between the hugely disadvantaged living conditions of Aboriginal people and those of mainstream Australia 'in the areas of education, employment, housing and health' (ibid., 5), she glossed over the full implications of the *rights* of indigenous peoples as defined by UNDRIP.

Although Indigenous Social Justice Commissioner Tom Calma hailed Australia's endorsement of UNDRIP as 'a watershed moment in Australia's relationship with Aboriginal and Torres Strait Islander peoples' (quoted by Australian Human Rights Commission, 3 April 2009: n.p.), and leading Aboriginal academic Mick Dodson congratulated the government for adding 'another piece in the jigsaw puzzle of reconciliation' (ibid.), most media coverage followed Macklin's cue in underlining the non-binding nature of that endorsement. Less optimistic than the Aboriginal leaders, certain commentators were cynically (though perhaps more realistically) suggesting that the government's decision was really 'aimed at garnering support for Australia's bid for a temporary seat on the UN Security Council' (Drape 2 April 2009: n.p.).

Notwithstanding the Rudd government's (belated) fulfilment of its election promise to support UNDRIP, and in spite of the highly publicized apology the Prime Minister made to the 'stolen generations' in February 2008, Aborigines' rights to their own land, language, culture and education and to self-determination are arguably under greater threat today than at any time in the last fifty years.[11] Opposition to the intervention is,

since Australia did not *sign* it then, it can only *endorse* it at a later date' (personal communication, emphasis added).

[11] According to Megan Davis, the NTER 'heralds the winding back of the few inherent Indigenous rights that exist in the Australian legal system, despite absolutely no evidence of a causal link between those rights and child sex abuse' (Davis 2007: 97–98).

nonetheless, gaining momentum, with demonstrations, protest marches and gatherings being regularly staged throughout Australia, and human rights activists increasingly denouncing the violation of international law that continuing NTER measures represent.[12]

In the discussion that follows, I shall both sketch in the historical context and examine the discourse of the so-called 'national emergency',[13] since it is in the conjunction of these two elements that we can best observe the continuity in the repressive, rights-denying behaviour that characterizes mainstream Australia's relationship with its indigenous peoples. I will also focus on the implications of the post-NTER decision to dismantle bilingual education in the NT (a clear violation of Arts. 14.1 and 15.1 of UNDRIP) because of the potentially devastating impact of that decision on Aboriginal cultures.

Decoding NTER discourse

By suggesting that child sexual abuse is the insidious legacy of a deviant pre-colonial culture, or that alcoholism is the result of Aborigines' disgraceful failure to handle alcohol responsibly, the intervention's apologists reduce problems that have complex, multilayered, multifactorial, but nonetheless predominantly socio-historical, determinants, to one-dimensional moral issues. In absolute contradiction both to the spirit and to the letter of UNDRIP, such discursive strategies are aimed at forging 'a new Australian story', one in which, '[c]ommunity dysfunction is … understood as the fault of the colonized and their persistent cultural practices, rather than as a result of violent dispossession, brutal colonization and authoritarian state intervention' (Dodson, P. 2009: n.p.).[14]

---

[12] In January 2009, Aboriginal people affected by the NTER lodged a complaint under the Convention on the Elimination of All Forms of Racial Discrimination (CERD), as a result of which Australia had, in August 2010, to answer to the UN's concerns at the 77th session of the CERD committee in Geneva (Marlene Hodder, member of the Intervention Roll Back Action Group, personal communication, 28 May 2010). Since this chapter was completed, a hard-hitting documentary, *Our Generation*, by Sinem Saban and Damien Curtis (2011) has been released, denouncing the intervention in the NT and its damaging impact on indigenous people's lives. Further information on *Our Generation* ('Best Campaign Film' at the London International Documentary Festival in May 2011), can be found at: www.ourgeneration.org.au.

[13] The Request for Urgent Action under the CERD affirms that '[t]he rhetoric justifying the implementation of the Northern Territory Intervention was sensationalist and has perpetrated prejudicial views of Aboriginal communities and culture' (HRLRC January 2009: 11).

[14] NB. The NTER Review Board's observation that 'there is a strong sense of injustice that Aboriginal people and their culture have been seen as exclusively responsible for

If John Howard was able to exploit the media-orchestrated 'cyclone of emotion' (Rundle 2007: 37) about child sexual abuse in indigenous communities in order to pass repressive, racially targeted laws, Labor prime ministers Kevin Rudd and his successor, Julia Gillard, have been able to count on increasingly voluble condemnations of Aboriginal community dysfunction to justify the government's maintenance of most of the NTER legislation. Driving non-indigenous indignation on indigenous affairs is 'the shame and horror that many mainstream suburban Australians feel at the continuing tales of social breakdown emerging from the north' (Rundle 2007: 38). This 'shame and horror', asserts Rundle, feeds directly into the 'hidden refrain' underlying much public comment on Aboriginal issues, namely: "'Why can't these damn people get their act together?'"(ibid., at 40). For, while many Anglo-Australians concede that Aborigines may once have suffered ill-treatment at the hands of settlers, opinion polls have shown that 'there is little recognition of the effect this may have had on present-day Aboriginal citizens' (Newspoll et al. 2000: 36). As anthropologist Gillian Cowlishaw observes, 'Historical injury is attributed to them, but not present pain' (Cowlishaw 2004: 164).

When non-indigenous Australians talk of indigenous peoples 'getting their act together', what they are voicing is the growing impatience and frustration mainstream society feels when confronted with ongoing signs of Aboriginal trauma. These are sentiments that were nurtured by the ethos of the Howard era, when the former Prime Minister stubbornly refused to acknowledge settler responsibility for the psychic injuries Australia's first peoples suffer as a result of colonization. By insistently emphasizing that 'genuine' reconciliation was a question, not of making symbolic gestures, but of taking concrete, practical steps to improve the material circumstances of indigenous Australians, Howard encouraged the settler tendency to deny the cataclysmic impact of the colonial past on the contemporary life experience of colonized peoples.

By 'shifting the focus from rights and justice to economic independence and equality in health, education and employment' (Bourke and Geldens 2007: 606), Howard's strategy thus successfully overturned the original priorities of the reconciliation agenda. Nowadays, while most contemporary Australians may express their readiness to be reconciled with the nation's first peoples, what they actually have in mind is 'the

problems within their communities that have arisen from decades of cumulative neglect by governments in failing to provide the most basic standards of health, housing, education and ancillary services enjoyed by the wider Australian community' (NTER Review Board 2008: 9).

reconciliation part without the truth of history upon which it must be based' (Phillips 2007: 149).

Reconciliation necessitates profound attitudinal change on the part of settler descendants, yet when questioning non-indigenous young-sters about their perceptions of reconciliation, sociologists Bourke and Geldens discovered that the discussion revolved principally around con-cepts of 'sameness and equity' and the need for Aborigines to conform to mainstream values. Seemingly oblivious of the structural inequalities, disadvantage and institutional racism that still determine Aboriginal experience of the world, and blind to the possibility that Aborigines might actually attach importance to their cultural traditions, the young respondents felt that, in order for reconciliation to take place, all that was required was for indigenous people to be and behave like everyone else (Bourke and Geldens 2007: 616–17).[15] According to anthropologist Barry Morris, many white Australians see *any* 'special treatment' of Aborigines as violating the sacrosanct principle of egalitarianism (Morris 1997: 162), widely held to be one of the founding values of the modern nation.

Thus, paradoxically, the current discourse of egalitarianism consti-tutes what Bourke and Geldens identify as a new 'more subtle and indir-ect form of racism' (Bourke and Geldens 2007: 617). For not only are the concepts of sameness and equity premised on the ethnocentric assump-tion that white culture is normative, they also preclude all possibility of a unique status, and therefore 'separate' rights, for Australia's indigenous peoples. Under the pretext that equality necessarily entails homogeneity, what Anglo-Australians demand is that Aborigines definitively renounce the markers of their cultural specificity and become, as Patrick Dodson says, 'like "us" in the Australian mainstream, living in urban concentra-tions, having a job, having debt and equity, and joining the market on these terms' (Dodson, P. 2007: 34). Indeed, as the authors of the Request for Urgent Action (RUA) point out, when the government introduced its NTER measures, '[i]ndigenous land tenure was described as working against "developing a real economy" and was to be transformed so that people can "own and control" their own houses and obtain loans to estab-lish small businesses' (HRLRC January 2009: 49 n. 243). Worried about this attack on their cultural identity 'as Aboriginal people with particular lifeways and cultural obligations',[16] Alice Springs Town Camp residents

---

[15] Research carried out in 1999–2000 revealed a similar mindset among non-indigenous Australians of all ages (Newspoll et al. 2000: 38).

[16] Which include being able to 'accommodate visiting family and friends, potentially in large numbers; fulfil obligations to young men after initiation into the law when they

issued legal proceedings to stop the current Indigenous Affairs Minister and the NT Housing Authority compulsorily acquiring forty-year leases of their land (HRLRC August 2009: 32). Interviewed on ABC News about her response to the Review Board's report on the NTER, Macklin revealed the ideological agenda behind the government's actions when claiming that she wanted to see the development of what she obliquely referred to as 'strong social norms' in Aboriginal communities (O'Brien 2008: n.p.).

It is the same ethnocentric outlook as that which informed the shock treatment the Liberal–National Coalition government prescribed for NT Aborigines with the promulgation of its emergency legislation. By sending in the police and the military to deal with the state of anomie into which certain indigenous communities have been inexorably driven, Howard signalled his rejection of pyscho-social analyses that explain this collective breakdown as stemming from the continuous accrual over generations of the grief, anger and hopelessness of Australia's First Nations. Rather than abandoning the Howard government's blinkered, disciplinarian approach to the ills of Aboriginal people, the current Labor government has, however, employed much the same neo-liberal, neo-*colonial* analysis to the profound *mal-être* that is poisoning their existence.

Fundamental to the policies now being implemented both in the NT and elsewhere in Australia is the idea that if Aborigines have developed pathological behaviour patterns it is because these wayward, morally and culturally deficient child-people have been left to run wild for too long. It is time, the new-old argument goes, to reassert control over chaotic native lives, to reimpose order and apply discipline there, where social anarchy has been allowed to reign unchecked. In this reading, the allegedly critical levels of child sexual abuse, spousal violence, gang rape, homicide and suicide are construed not as symptoms of the transgenerational traumas provoked by colonization but as indicators of a violence that has always been endemic in the Aboriginal world. As one prominent political journalist put it, current Aboriginal violence is 'part of a much wider pathology of violence which immemorially predated the arrival of Europeans' (Sheehan 2010: n.p.).

Such biased ethno-historical constructions of indigenous violence represent the latest version of the dystopian vision of Aboriginal culture that has held sway in Australia since colonial times (Anderson 2007: 134).

---

are "painted up"; howl and cry for sorry business and swap houses; cook kangaroo in the backyard; speak "language" and paint with friends in the front yard' (HRLRC August 2009: 6).

Judy Atkinson speaks of the outrage she felt over twenty years ago when 'the Department of Community Services provided substantial funding, under a court-stipulated consultancy, for anthropologists, social welfare and other "experts" to determine *whether it was traditional behaviour* for Aboriginal men and youth to sexually use five-, six- and eight-year-old children' (Atkinson 2002: 7, emphasis added).[17]

Predictably, the enormous media coverage devoted to allegations of entrenched violence in traditional Aboriginal culture has served to revive latent mainstream hostility to the kind of rights UNDRIP seeks to guarantee for indigenous peoples. Not only has the new orthodoxy diverted public attention away from the overwhelming evidence historians have assembled in recent years on the atrocities committed during colonization, it has also emboldened denialists to rubbish the very idea of colonization being an important causal factor in contemporary Aboriginal social and psychological distress. Indeed, it is becoming difficult even to speak of Aboriginal trauma today without being accused of indulging in what is now represented as the intellectually disreputable practice of 'victimology'. This despite the fact that the LCAS authors themselves, the government's own Review Board set up to assess the NTER one year after its commencement and the Australian Human Rights Commission have all 'situated the complex problem of child sexual assault in the context of Aboriginal disadvantage; past, current and continuing social problems; and decades of cumulative government neglect' (HRLRC January 2009: 8).

Having only recently endorsed UNDRIP, the government has immediately reverted to back-pedalling on indigenous rights, and the mainstream media are eagerly supporting this move by offering a platform to experts and pundits who stigmatize Aboriginal culture and its putatively ingrained deviance.[18] In the circumstances, it is, I think, both timely and salutary to look back over the contextual history of the behaviours the NTER is intent on punishing through the withdrawal of key indigenous rights.

---

[17] Behind Atkinson's anger is the knowledge that, within their extended family groups, Aboriginal children were traditionally treated with great gentleness and affection. To support her assertion she cites the observations of several non-indigenous anthropologists (Atkinson 2002: 37–8).

[18] To quote psychiatrist Ernest Hunter: 'There is often a naïve polarization of demonizing and romanticized representations presented (for instance by *The Australian*) which, under the guise of "balanced" reporting enables unfettered negative commentary' (Hunter 2010: 75).

Contextualizing sexual violence and alcoholism in indigenous communities

For a significant percentage of the 'almost womanless pioneer population' (Reynolds 1995: 70), raping Aboriginal females of any age was a routine solution to problems of sexual frustration. Taken by settlers 'in relations … of force, violence and rape', Aboriginal women were 'detained in the huts of the Europeans by being chained to the furniture' (Broome 1982: 56). At one pastoral station in Queensland in 1900, nine Aboriginal women were, for instance, 'confined by rabbit-proof fencing for the use of white station hands' (ibid., 97).

As the Reverend Threlkeld recalls of his time at Lake McQuarie mission, it was not just indigenous women who were the victims of European sexual abuse. The clergyman remembers being regularly disturbed at night by 'the shrieks of girls, about 8 or 9 years of age, taken by force by the vile men of Newcastle' (quoted in Broome 1982: 41).[19]

Scandalized by the settlers' widespread sexual predation on Aboriginal children, 'some as young as six', some '"adopted" females' (Kidd 1997: 50), Home Secretary Justin Foxton sought to change the law so that the onus of proving that an Aboriginal girl had attained the legal age of consent was placed on the offender. However, observes Kidd, parliamentarians opposed the proposed change, 'indignantly insist[ing] that a man could readily mistake the maturity of "native" girls of nine or ten because they "ripened so much earlier in tropical areas"' (ibid.).

Even when the scarcity of white women on the frontier diminished, the settlers' voracious appetite for transgressive interracial sex did not.[20] Adolescent Aboriginal girls, sent out from missions to work as servants on pastoral stations, could expect to be sent back pregnant after having been routinely sexually abused by their married white employers (Kidd 1997: 126). Once they had given birth, these young women were sent out to work again, whereupon the cycle of rape followed by pregnancy repeated itself – often many times.[21]

---

[19] Both past and present historical accounts and contemporary Australian historical fiction abound in such examples (see Atkinson 2002; George Augustus Robinson's diary quoted in Clendinnen 2002: 196; Reynolds 2005: 134–35; T. G. H. Strehlow's diary quoted in Greer 2008: 48; Flanagan's novel, *Wanting* 2008, etc.).

[20] The avowed predilection for 'black velvet' (the term used by white settlers to designate sex with Aboriginal women and girls) is widely reflected in Australian literature from the nineteenth century onwards.

[21] Discussion with the curator of the recently opened Cherbourg Museum (Queensland), 12 July 2009.

As recent inquiries have indicated, sexual assaults on Aboriginal children and women by European men have never ceased (Coorey 2001; Keel 2004; Wild and Anderson 2007). Today's predators – who include non-indigenous government employees and members of the clergy (Coorey 2001: 7) pursue their prey in Aboriginal territories, abusing their victims in the very communities that are stigmatized in the mainstream press as hotbeds (*sic*) of Aboriginal sexual deviance. Nevertheless, 'most literature referring to "sexual assault in indigenous communities" does not explore or state the race or cultural identity of the victims and perpetrators' (Keel 2004: 6).

The LCAS authors cite numerous examples of non-indigenous paedophiles having infiltrated remote Aboriginal communities and exploited their position of trust and authority in order to sexually abuse indigenous children (Wild and Anderson 2007: 61). Also cited in the inquiry's findings are instances of non-Aboriginal men offering alcohol, drugs, money or material goods both to pre-pubescent and adolescent girls (or to the latter's families) in exchange for sex (ibid., 63–65).

Tens of thousands of the mixed-descent children who resulted from the settler taste for 'black velvet' were forcibly removed from their indigenous families under the notorious assimilation policy Australia devised to deal with the 'shameful colonial secret' of 'miscegenation' (Moran 2005: 176). Many of them suffered horrific abuse – not just psychological, emotional and physical, but also, and to a very significant extent, sexual – at the hands of the white adults entrusted with their care.[22] Trapped within the infernal inter-generational cycle of abuse to which the traumatized victims of rape are so often condemned, some of these youngsters have become in their turn abusers of children.

As the *Bringing Them Home* report recounts, 'their removal as children and the abuse they experienced at the hands of the authorities or their delegates have permanently scarred their lives. The harm continues in later generations, affecting their children and grandchildren' (AHRC 1997: Part I, ch. 1, n.p.). It was not just the children who suffered, however; their distraught families 'literally never recovered from their loss … Whole communities were shown in the most brutal and explicit way that they were utterly powerless in the face of white authority' (Reynolds 2005: 222). To quote from the Australian Indigenous Doctors' Association (AIDA) report,

---

[22] According to the report *Bringing Them Home*: 'Children in every placement were vulnerable to sexual abuse and exploitation' (AHRC 1997: Part III, ch. 10, n.p.).

> The policies of assimilation, elimination, forced child removal, protection and segregation that were imposed after colonisation resulted in the huge disruption of traditional social institutions and kinship ties. The damage to the intricate kinship systems and community cohesion of Aboriginal people through the Stolen Generations *cannot be over-emphasised.* (AIDA 2010: 7, emphasis added)

When so much of the historical evidence incriminates colonization as the main cause of Aboriginal dysfunction, the disproportionate emphasis currently given to theories that explain contemporary forms of sexual violence as the result of atavistic cultural practices seems, to say the least, perverse. As does the discourse which spins Aboriginal alcohol abuse as a lack of moral responsibility.

According to neo-liberal opinion-formers and policy-makers, since the unrestricted access to grog allowed for by the granting of citizenship rights at the end of the 1960s, Aborigines have sunk inexorably into the irresponsible and degrading 'habit' of uncontrolled drinking. Not that there is any shortage of solid research evidence to support the exponential increase in excessive alcohol consumption in indigenous communities (Saggers and Gray 1997; Kidd 1997; Sutton 2001; McKnight 2002; Martin and Brady 2004), or any possible doubt about the link between drunkenness and violence (McKnight 2002; Keel 2004, Wild and Anderson 2007; Sutton 2008). Yet to explain Aboriginal binge-drinking solely – or even mainly – in terms of Aborigines having been granted the right to consume alcohol is an abusive over-simplification of a problem that is 'complexly over-determined' (Hunter 1992: n.p.).

Reflecting the popular wisdom that, due to an inherent lack of the moral qualities that enable civilized people to 'hold their grog', all Aborigines are potential drunks and should therefore never have been given the right to consume alcohol (Hunter 1992: n.p.), this reductive explanation combines conventional settler racism with the tendency in contemporary Western societies to regard problematic drinking 'as evidence of moral iniquity' (Room 2005: 152).

Ironically, if the problem of Aboriginal alcoholism *is* posed in moral terms, then the term 'moral iniquity' more appropriately describes the behaviour of those Europeans who consistently supplied alcohol to Aborigines than the self-destructive drinking in which many Aborigines subsequently indulged. For regular alcohol consumption by Aborigines only began as a result of settlers using grog 'to engage Aboriginal people in discourse, attract Aboriginal people into settlements, in barter for sexual favours from Aboriginal women, as payment for Aboriginal labour and to incite Aboriginal people to fight as street entertainment' (Langton 1993: 196).

One of the perverse effects of legislation, passed from 1838, deny-ing Aborigines the right to either buy or consume alcohol (McKnight 2002:195) was, Martin and Brady point out, '[t]he conflation of drinking rights with citizenship rights', which, in turn, 'led to the right to drink being viewed by some as a human prerogative' (Martin and Brady 2004: 1282).[23] Meanwhile, whatever the law said, nothing stopped the 'sly grog-gers'[24] supplying alcohol to indigenous people – a key factor frequently overlooked in mainstream discussions of Aboriginal alcoholism which, preferring to ignore the economic and political factors implied by such questions as 'who benefits from the distribution of alcohol to Aboriginal people?', tend to rely heavily on the 'evidence' of the drunken Abo stereo-type (Langton 1993: 199). Deriving significant revenue from taxation, licensing fees and excise duties, the Australian government has always treated the alcohol industry with indulgence. Like others before it, Brady explains, 'The present Federal Government ... collects $4 billion a year in alcohol revenue and likes to avoid antagonising the liquor industry' (Brady 2007: 190–91).[25]

Yet, in flagrant contradiction to the evidence of these historical factors and with sociological studies suggesting that indigenous alcohol addiction 'flows directly from people's experiences of colonisation' (Lyon quoted in Saggers and Gray 1997: 226), NTER discourse on Aboriginal alcoholism is characterized by '[its] focus on proximate risk factors, potentially con-trollable at the individual level' (Link and Phelan 1995: 80). Instead of acknowledging the crucial importance of socio-historical conditions in the development of substance addiction, regarded as a disease in most contemporary Western societies, NTER apologists 'emphasiz[e] both the ability of the individual to control his or her personal fate and the import-ance of doing so' (ibid.), thereby reducing the catastrophic problems of alcohol abuse in indigenous communities to a question of moral weak-ness. To quote the AIDA report, 'The alcohol measures in the NTER do

---

[23] See also Fink 1957; Broome 1982; McKnight 2002; and Cowlishaw 2004 on Aboriginal attitudes on the right to drink.

[24] Unscrupulous whites who peddled alcohol illegally to Aborigines.

[25] It is thanks to the government's attitude that non-indigenous suppliers of alcohol in Western Australia, for example, have felt able to resort to such unethical practices as 'sales to minors and intoxicated persons, credit sales, promotion of low-cost high-alcohol beverages, early trading, and reduction of costs by not providing appropriate levels of amenity on their premises' (Saggers and Gray 1997: 223).

not address the root causes of why people drink and therefore are ineffective in addressing alcohol misuse' (AIDA 2010: 42).

That many Aborigines initially used grog as an anaesthetic to deaden the traumatic shock of colonization is totally obfuscated by this focus on individual agency, as is indigenous Australians' use of alcohol as a means of coping with the no less traumatic phases of colonization that followed. The fact nevertheless remains that the state of absolute disempowerment to which white settlement has reduced Aborigines is one which 'underlie[s] many social conditions that put people at risk for elevated levels of psychological distress' (Link and Phelan 1995: 83), and there is little serious research on alcohol abuse today that questions the implication of psychological distress in the development of problematic drinking.

Exacerbating the profound psychological injuries inflicted by the different phases of colonization is the damage indigenous people repeatedly sustain in their encounters with white racism. Just how deep and corrosive the impact of settler hostility is on the mental (and physical) health of Aborigines can be inferred from a plethora of recent analyses of the effects of racial stigmatization on its victims (Kessler et al. 1999; Whitbeck et al. 2002; Paradies 2006; Richman et al. 2007; etc.). Using data from the MIDUS survey,[26] Kessler et al. suggest that 'discrimination is among the most important of all the stressful experiences that have been implicated as causes of mental health problems' (Kessler et al. 1999: 224). The AIDA report refers to the 'collective existential despair' (AIDA 2010: 8) felt by Aboriginal people as a result of ongoing mainstream intolerance and denigration of their culture, and there is strong evidence that the NTER has had the effect of intensifying that feeling by reinforcing the racist stereotypes that have always flourished in white Australia's popular imaginary. According to the NTER Review board,

> Experiences of racial discrimination and humiliation as a result of the NTER were told with such passion and such regularity that the Board felt compelled to advise the Minister for Indigenous Affairs during the course of the Review that such widespread Aboriginal hostility to the Australian Government's actions should be regarded as a matter for serious concern. (NTER Review Board 2008: 8)[27]

---

[26] The MacArthur Foundation Midlife Development in the United States survey, carried out in 1996 (Kessler et al. 1999: 210).

[27] One concrete example from Alice Springs: anti-intervention activist Lauren Mellor claims that not only have 'the last two years ... seen an alarming increase in white supremacy vigilantes harassing and abusing Aboriginal people', but the police have clearly felt more confident about targeting Aboriginal people, with the result that 'There have been

Research also shows that '[a] not uncommon reaction in those who have been touched by violent death is to repress grief, guilt or anger until these powerful emotions can be released by the disinhibiting effects of alcohol' (Shkilnyk quoted in Greer 2008: 33).[28] Yet the NTER's moralistic take on alcoholism excludes from consideration such crucial questions as: what link might there be between recent traumas like that of child removal and the epidemic rates of alcohol abuse recorded in Aboriginal communities today? Or, how does the experience of repeated bereavements (due to the high incidence of accidents, homicides and the extraordinarily frequent suicides of young people) impact on indigenous people's behaviour?

Attributing the aetiology of indigenous social dysfunction to the cumulative and collective psychic injuries provoked by successive phases of colonization obviously does not mean that *no* other causal elements are involved. There may indeed, as anthropologist Peter Sutton suggests, be aspects of behaviour resulting from the complex interaction between 'post-conquest, historical factors of external impact, with a substantial number of ancient, pre-existent social and cultural factors (Sutton 2001: 127). But simply nuancing previous blanket condemnations of Australia's colonization is not what NTER apologists aim to do. What their rhetoric conveys, either implicitly or explicitly, is the image of an Aboriginal culture that is both obsolete and morally pernicious.

As to the motivation behind such discursive strategies, it lies, I think, in the fact that white Australia has reached the limits of its limited patience with a population it has never ceased to regard as problematic. In the post-Apology era Anglo-Australians feel they have earned the right to 'turn the page' on the sins of their settler-ancestors. From that perspective, indigenous Australians with their seemingly irremediable negative social indicators are a ball and chain tethering the modern nation to a guilt-laden history it longs to escape. By positing cultural as opposed to socio-historical causes for Aboriginal dysfunction, NTER discourse provides the reasoning the government needs to justify its demolition of a society that has nagged the conscience of mainstream Australia for more than two hundred years. Once the last vestiges of Aboriginal culture have been swept away and 'Aboriginality' itself has been reduced to a historical phenomenon, indigenous peoples, it is insinuated, will simply melt into

---

at least four deaths in custody in Central Australia this year and a 10 per cent increase in Aboriginal incarceration rates since the Intervention began' (Mellor 2009: n.p.).

[28] Judy Atkinson similarly explains that indigenous peoples often react to their oppression with a rage that 'is not only turned inwards, but cascades down the generations, growing more complex over time' (Atkinson 2002: 80).

the multicultural mosaic of modern Australia, and the 'Aboriginal problem' will be no more. In the face of such discourse indigenous Australians
have every reason to be 'especially fearful of the impact of the Northern
Territory Intervention measures on Aboriginal cultural and social norms'
(HRLRC January 2009: 25).

Australia's long history of assimilationism

In many respects post-contact Australia's domestic history has been
dominated by the question of how to suppress the psychic irritant of an
indigenous presence judged incompatible with the values of a civilized
European society. After failing in the initial phases of colonization to physically exterminate the Aborigines, the default solution Anglo-Australians
have consistently fallen back on has been the 'absorption' (cultural and/
or biological) of the natives. As Patrick Dodson remarks, Australia is a
nation that is 'paralysed by [its] failure to imagine any relationship with
first peoples other than assimilation' (Dodson, P. 2009: n.p.).

Since homogeneity – both culturally speaking and in terms of the
national phenotype – was 'central to the settler nationalist dream' (Moran
2005: 170), the radically alien culture of the continent's Aboriginal
inhabitants was anathema to settler society. In the late nineteenth century, Anglo-Australia opted for the segregationist solution of banishing
Aborigines to remote locations outside the settlers' field of vision, where
they were destined to remain until their eventual and inevitable demise
(McGregor 1997). The alarming news of a dramatic increase in the 'half-
caste' population in the early twentieth century led, however, to more
drastic solutions (such as biological 'management' and the child-removal
policy) being adopted. But, with international opinion becoming hostile
towards racialist practices after the Second World War, white Australia
was gradually obliged to revise its treatment of Aborigines.

It is significant in the light of present government behaviour that,
although the United Nations Declaration of Human Rights (1948)
constituted 'an important statement of principle' (Chesterman 2001:
22) on the unacceptability of racially discriminatory practices, the
fact that it could not be legally enforced meant that it was largely disregarded in Australia. Until the late 1950s, historian John Chesterman
reminds us, there were 'so many laws that discriminated against indigenous people that it took pages simply to list them' (ibid., 23). From
the beginning of the 1960s, however, repeated criticism from overseas denouncing the country's racist behaviour towards its indigenous

peoples provoked 'growing concern about Australia's international reputation' (ibid., 34).

It was in response to the sting of international disapproval that, in the late 1950s, the government launched a sustained propaganda campaign aimed at breaking down the entrenched racial prejudices of white Australians. Most noteworthy about the series of pamphlets it subsequently published (showing Europeanized Aborigines visibly striving to integrate the lower levels of mainstream society) is the vision this literature reflected of assimilation as a way of 'protecting existing hierarchies and networks of power and privilege' (Haebich 2008: 65). That Aborigines were eager to adopt a white lifestyle was unquestioned. Neither 'the likelihood of Aboriginal resistance to the instruments and goals of assimilation' nor 'the seemingly insurmountable problems of institutionalized inequality' were envisaged (Haebich 2002: 64). 'The narrative of assimilation presented was of an imagined seamless, unproblematic and inevitable passage from a receding Aboriginal past to an assimilated present of modern suburban domestic life' (ibid., 63).

As T. G. H. Strehlow noted acerbically in 1964, the policy of assimilation was 'only a new name given to the old and discredited methods of forced culture change which have been employed in Australia for the last century and a half' (Strehlow 1964: 5). Familiar with the whites' ingrained sense of superiority, Aborigines, he asserted, saw right through statements assuring them that they were being prepared 'for association with the highest form of humanity – our own white selves' (ibid. 35). Consequently, the government's paternalistic warnings that if they were 'to survive and prosper, [they] must live and work and think as white Australians do' (Minister for Territories 1962: n.p.) left most Aborigines unimpressed.

Recognizing the ethnocidal subtext behind such exhortations and still seeing 'abiding value in their Aboriginal identities, despite all government attempts to break these down' (Moran 2005: 185), many Aborigines actively spurned attempts to assimilate them (Fink 1957: 103). When they were finally granted a limited form of self-management at the end of the 1960s, indigenous communities were generally relieved to escape, finally, from the relentless, culturally deforming pressure of white expectations. Since then, displaying their cultural difference in ways they know to be unacceptable to Anglo-Australian society has become, for many Aborigines, a sign of ideological resistance. 'There is', observes Gillian Cowlishaw, 'an apparent hunger among Indigenous people to assert a positive and unique identity, not as "equal citizens" but as Indigenous people in contrast to the settler, invader, or immigrant status of their fellow Australians' (Cowlishaw 2004: 173).

Saying 'no' to the assimilationist siren call of the society that systematically destroyed their cultural traditions is thus, for indigenous Australians, a way to exercise their right to 'Aboriginality'. The NTER seeks to deny them that right through policies whose common objective is to expunge all the cultural markers by means of which Aborigines have hitherto defiantly differentiated themselves from white Australia. Despite the humanitarian issues it claims to be addressing, what the Australian government is actually doing is 'promot[ing] the absorption of Indigenous communities into Anglo-dominant Australian society' (Dodson, P. 2007: 25). To that extent its maintenance of key NTER measures can be seen as fundamentally ethnocidal in intent.

Continuing violations of indigenous rights

Condemning NTER measures as 'racially discriminatory and oppressive', an intervention opponent, Barbara Shaw, asserts that 'under the camouflage of child abuse and alcohol abuse, the agenda of the intervention is a land grab' (quoted in Ravens 2009: n.p.). An Aboriginal leader and one of Arnhem Land's most senior custodians, Galarrwuy Yunupingu, having originally given qualified support to the intervention has now withdrawn it, claiming that 'It is discriminatory, it's a form of apartheid. It has never been any good to us' (quoted in Robinson 2009: n.p.).

The sending in of troops and non-indigenous business managers to take over the running of indigenous communities marked the triumph of the anti-indigenous-rights cohort in Australian politics. It was an action that drew its legitimacy from the bleak and bitter vision of degraded Aboriginal cultural traditions expressed several years earlier by Peter Sutton. In his angry essay, 'The Politics of Suffering', Sutton had lashed out at what he regarded as the rights-based progressivism of 'sympathetic Liberals' – contemptibly naive models of political correctness who, blinded by 'sad ignorance' and bourgeois romanticism, had, he sneered, erroneously 'assign[ed] all the causality of petrol sniffing to a history of colonial conquest' (Sutton 2001: 141).

Though Sutton's discussion of negative aspects of Aboriginal culture offers valid insights, the generally polemical, embittered and occasionally caricatural tenor of his observations results in precisely the lack of balance of which he is so contemptuous when attacking the discourse of his *bêtes noires* (the sympathetic Liberals). What is most troubling about his essay, however, is the injurious impact it has had. For it has given an intellectual imprimatur to mainstream convictions that blaming colonization for the ills of contemporary Aboriginal life no longer washes and that the main cause for the downward spiral in indigenous community life is 'progress in civil rights' (Sutton 2001: 131). In a later essay, published in 2008, Sutton expresses his satisfaction at having broken a taboo on speaking out about the seriously dysfunctional state of indigenous communities since, he asserts, 'an avalanche of evidence' (Sutton 2008: n.p.) subsequently emerged in support of his claims. It was this 'evidence' that provided the government with the ammunition it needed to launch its offensive against indigenous rights. Since it does not fall within the purview of the present chapter to examine the details of NTER legislation, I shall confine my remarks to the most salient issues with regard to UNDRIP.

The whole thrust of the emergency intervention was (still is) in total contradiction to Australia's ostensible support for indigenous peoples' right to self-determination. To the extent that land and the Aborigines' relationship with it are 'the source of [their] identity, social organisation, economy and spirituality; in essence, [their] life-force' (Turner and Watson 2007: 206), the suspension of the permit system, which confiscated in the most publicly humiliating way the power Aborigines had only recently regained over parts of their ancestral territories, constituted a major assault on Aboriginal culture. The compulsory acquisition of Aboriginal land and 'community living areas', combined with the encouragement of individual home ownership, aim unmistakably at subverting the traditional Aboriginal values of communal ownership and collective decision-making (Dodson, P. 2007: 22).[29] The removal of the future acts regime provided by the Native Title Act enables 'proponents of development' to act without any constraint of respecting Aboriginal rights and interests (HRLRC January 2009: 49).[30] All such measures incontestably breach indigenous peoples' right 'to own, use, develop and control the lands, territories and resources that they possess by reason of traditional

[29] The ideological underpinnings of the NTER are exposed by the RUA authors, who report that 'On the introduction of the Northern Territory Intervention, the Australian Government described the undermining of communal ownership as an explicit aim of the lease regime ... the Minister claimed that historic land rights decisions like *Mabo* and *Wik* had impoverished Aboriginal people and had not freed or empowered them. He stated the land rights decisions have locked people into collective tenure and that we "need to actually recognise that communism didn't work, collectivism didn't work"' (HRLRC January 2009: 49).

[30] This regime was 'specifically designed to protect native title rights and interests during the long process of resolution of a native title application' (ibid., 49).

ownership or other traditional occupation or use' (UNDRIP 2008: Art. 26(2)).

What I would like to signal for particular attention, however, is the fact that:

(i) in flagrant contravention of indigenous peoples' rights 'to establish and control their educational systems and institutions providing education in their own languages, in a manner appropriate to their cultural methods of teaching and learning' (ibid., Art. 14(1)) as well as 'to the dignity and diversity of their cultures, traditions, histories and aspirations which shall be appropriately reflected in education (Art. 15(1));

(ii) despite the alarm bell sounded by UNESCO warning that 100 languages in Australia are in imminent danger of extinction (ABC News 21 February 2009: n.p.); and

(iii) to the despair of linguists, language teaching specialists and many Aboriginal parents,

Australia has delivered what might well prove the *coup de grâce* to Aboriginal identity by backing the NT's decision to scrap bilingual education.[31]

The alleged reason for this last, profoundly retrograde step was the poor test results of indigenous schoolchildren in NT communities indicated in the Summary Report of the National Assessment Program – Literacy and Numeracy (NAPLAN). Yet, leaving aside

(i) the criticism that 'The testing itself relies heavily on knowledge of English so can be expected to bias results against people whose first language is not English' (McConvell 2008: n.p.); and

(ii) damning evidence that the report itself was based on 'a poorly selected sample, ... an incomplete data set and ... incorrect data' (Devlin 2009: 13),

there are many reasons other than bilingual education that could be adduced to explain the disappointing NAPLAN scores.

Chronic underfunding of indigenous schools, inadequately trained teachers, high teacher turnover, substandard and poorly maintained school buildings, lack of basic facilities/equipment/teaching

---

[31] The legality of this decision was challenged by indigenous residents of the Areyonga Community near Alice Springs, who lodged a complaint against the NT government with the Australian Human Rights Commission.

materials/technological resources, and the exceptionally high levels of otitis media,[32] with subsequent hearing loss among Aboriginal children, are among them. As, of course, are extreme socio-economic disadvantage, poor health and poor-quality parenting (often linked to a history of child removal leading to violence, sexual abuse, and alcohol and substance addiction) that are the background to some indigenous children's lives. On the other hand, bilingual education can, according to both linguists and the Australian Education Union, definitely be eliminated as a causal factor in poor performance at school (McConvell 2008; Devlin 2009; Simpson et al. 2009).

In 1958, Strehlow, urging that indigenous children be allowed to keep their own languages – 'those beautiful and expressive tongues, rich in true Australian imagery, charged with poetry and with love for all that is great, ancient and eternal in the continent' – bemoaned the fact that 'white Australians are among the few remaining civilized people who still think that knowledge of one language is the normal limit of linguistic achievement' (quoted in Dickson 2010: n.p.). More than fifty years later, that view remains unchanged. According to a recent discussion paper, although Australia is pluricultural, education curricula designers (from the essentially monolingual dominant culture), are woefully unaware of the mass of evidence – both Australian and international – showing that: 'Young children learn best when taught through their mother tongue [and] … that there are positive effects on children's cognitive development if they are encouraged to become strong bilinguals' (Simpson et al. 2009: 6). They are ignorant too, apparently, of research findings that emphasize the importance of bilingual education as a means of increasing children's pride in their culture and making them feel more at home in an educational environment permeated by the ethos of an alien society (ibid., 11).

If we accept Ngugi Wa Thiong'o's analysis of the symbiotic link between language and culture – 'Language as culture is the collective memory bank of a people's experience in history. Culture is almost indistinguishable from the language that makes possible its genesis, growth, banking, articulation and indeed its transmission from one generation to the next' (Wa Thiong'o 1991: 15) – it is clear that, without the maintenance of their languages, indigenous Australian cultures will have great difficulty in surviving. Mick Dodson was at pains to emphasize this point at the

---

[32] 'Hearing loss associated with OM [otitis media] has significant developmental, educational, social and vocational consequences for indigenous children and adults, and compounds the range of disadvantages they experience' (Burrow et al. 2009: n.p.).

UN Indigenous Forum when he described the 'right to education in the mother tongue' as 'fundamental to the growth of culture, identity and linguistic diversity' (ECOSOC HR/5014 20 April 2010: n.p.). Speaking of concern over the recent changes to bilingual education in the NT, Dodson warned that 'Dominant development paradigms meant that education was increasingly being seen through an economic lens.' In his view, decisions arrived at from that perspective 'risked extinguishing indigenous languages' (ibid.).

Decreeing that English will henceforth be the main medium of instruction for non-anglophone Aboriginal children living in the only part of Australia where indigenous languages still flourish amounts effectively to passing a death sentence on those languages. For that reason, it will, warns Yolŋu teacher Yalmay Yunupingu, 'only make the situation for our young people worse as they struggle to be proud Yolŋu in a world that is making them feel that their culture is bad, unimportant and irrelevant in the contemporary world' (quoted in Simpson et al. 2009: 29).

Conclusion

That many indigenous Australian communities are in a deplorable state today is beyond dispute. Community dysfunction is graphically chronicled in several recent anthropological and ethno-historical accounts (McKnight 2002; Sutton 2001, 2008; Kimm 2004; Jarrett 2009; etc.). Yet the behaviours the NTER identifies and seeks to punish as acts of moral turpitude are, as many sociologists and psychiatrists argue, responses to the transgenerational impact of the 'endlessly renewed catastrophe' of colonization (Greer 2008: 18). Sutton's contentious diagnosis notwithstanding, they stem from 'profound trauma, extreme powerlessness, denial of identity, marginalisation in society ... exclusion from mainstream institutions ... [and] ongoing intolerance and lack of understanding on the part of mainstream society of differences in knowledges and values' (AIDA 2010: 7–8).

If Australia's indigenous peoples are to recover the well-being that, according to their holistic concept of health, is composed of 'interrelating factors [that] can be categorised largely as spiritual, environmental, ideological, political, social, economic, mental and physical' (Swan and Raphaël 1995, quoted in AIDA 2010: 6), then they need above all to regain control of their land, of their cultures, in short, of their lives[33] – all

---

[33] Notable among the growing number of studies that demonstrate the healing power of pride in and control over cultural identity in peoples whose lives have been crippled

fundamental rights which are unambiguously spelled out under Articles 3, 4, 11–16, 25 and 26 of UNDRIP. Yet, as James Anaya has noted, the 'overtly interventionist architecture' of the NTER, contrives, through measures still in force today, to 'undermine indigenous self-determination, limit control over property, inhibit cultural integrity and restrict individual autonomy' (Anaya 2010: 4).

Anaya has unequivocally stated, moreover, that *all* the major UN treaty monitoring bodies are more or less agree in agreement that '[a]spects of the NTER as currently configured are racially discriminatory and incompatible with Australia's international human rights obligations' (ibid., paras. 11 and 12, 37). As a party to the International Covenant on Civil and Political Rights (ICCPR) and the International Covenant on Economic, Social and Cultural Rights (ICESCR) Australia 'must', he warns, 'respect the human rights protected by these treaties' (ibid., 7). In its defensive response[34] to Anaya's report the Australian government affirmed *inter alia* that 'since declaring its support for the Declaration on the Rights of Indigenous Peoples, it has acted consistently with the Declaration by consulting extensively with indigenous peoples on the future direction of the NTER' (ibid., 17). A claim the Special Rapporteur dismisses, sharply reminding the government of the reports he had received

> alleging that the consultations did not adequately accommodate to indigenous peoples' own leadership structures or decision-making procedures, that there often was an absence of interpreters or adequate explanation of NTER measures, and that the consultations were at times geared to specific predetermined outcomes. (Ibid., 11)

by the continuing aftershocks of colonization is Chandler and Lalonde's illuminating research on the incidence of suicide among young indigenous Canadians. The question the researchers posed at the outset was that since (as is well established) the risk of suicide is heightened by such factors as marital difficulties or job instability, then to what extent might the potential for self-destructive behavior be increased among people whose whole culture has been 'systematically root[ed] out' by 'explicitly conceived' government policies? (Chandler and Lalonde 1998: 208). Covering a period of almost twenty years, their research reveals that suicide rates in communities which had managed to 'preserve, rebuild or reconstruct their culture by wrenching its remnants out of the control of federal and provincial government agencies' (ibid., 208) are dramatically lower than in communities that had failed to do so. Consequently, the acts of epistemic violence to which colonizing societies resort with the aim of 'dragging some otherwise "stoneaged" peoples kicking and screaming into the "modern world"', can only, they conclude, 'guarantee the positional inferiority of indigenous people, further marginalize their voices, and undermine any possibility that they might be seen to know best how to manage their own affairs' (Chandler and Lalonde 2009: 245).

[34] A text that is too full of half-truths, spin, fallacious assertions and *mauvaise foi* to be adequately commented on in detail here.

The fact is that Australia is both extremely protective of its own parliamentary sovereignty and somewhat cavalier about its commitment to international legislation protecting human rights. Concerned for its reputation in the world scene, it has over the last fifty years become a party to numerous international treaties. Yet, as the Law Council of Australia (LCA) asserts, it has only ever partially incorporated them into its domestic legislation, and so only 'a limited range of its human rights obligations' have been given effect (LCA 2008: 19). As far as UNDRIP itself is concerned, 'the Australian government has never', emphasizes human rights lawyer George Newhouse, 'ratified the declaration or introduced it into Australian law. Australia is NOT legally bound by UNDRIP and the declaration's provisions are NOT legally enforceable in Australia.'[35]

Far from being an isolated incident in the history of Australia's relationship with its indigenous peoples, the flouting of international human rights legislation that has occurred under the NTER is part of a pattern that is described by the LCA in considerable detail. Indeed it is the LCA's view that Australia has an

> ambivalent and at times dismissive attitude towards the UN treaty body system and its authoritative role in determining whether States have adhered to their international human rights obligations … the Australian Government … prefer[s] its own view to that of various UN Committees when evaluating its performance of its international human rights obligations. (LCA 2008: 21)

The NTER is not just a matter of local importance. It offers crucial instruction on the difficulties of guaranteeing the implementation of indigenous rights in former white settler colonies. It also demonstrates the limited extent to which certain signatories to UNDRIP feel bound by their commitment to uphold those rights. At the recent Indigenous Forum, Anaya confessed to having been 'struck with fear' to hear a Youth Caucus representative refer to UNDRIP as a 'potentially empty instrument' (UNESC HR/5016 22 April 2010: n.p.). Nonetheless, as Tammy Solonec, representing the Indigenous Peoples' Organizations of Australia, observed, the Australian parliament 'had given little attention' to the concerns expressed by the Special Rapporteur in his report on the NTER. Worried by Australia's 'disregard of the issue', Ms Solonec recommended 'that the Forum urge States to commit to a process of responding to reports, and both develop and publicly promote a strategy

---

[35] Personal communication, 28 May 2010.

to implement a response to recommendations' (UNESC HR/5021 29 April 2010: n.p.).

For the moment, it remains to be seen whether the international legislation underpinning UNDRIP can be brought to bear on Australia, or whether the current government's endorsement of UNDRIP is indeed little more than an empty gesture designed to enhance the country's reputation in the eyes of the world.

Works cited

AAP, 'Aboriginal reforms arouse distrust', *The Age*, 22 June 2007, www.theage. com.au/news/National/Aboriginal-reforms-arouse-distrust/2007/06/ 22/1182019325305.html. Accessed: 13 February 2010.

'NT takeover is nuke dump ploy: Caldicott', *The Age*, 2 July 2007, www.theage. com.au/news/NATIONAL/NT-takeover-is-nuke-dump-ploy-Caldicott/ 2007/07/02/1183351107686.html. Accessed: 8 March 2010.

ABC News, 'Australia opposes UN rights declaration', 14 September 2007. www. abc.net.au/news/stories/2007/09/14/2032491.htm. Accessed: 13 May 2010.

'Intervention created in just 48 hours: Brough', 16 June 2008, www.abc.net.au/ news/stories/2008/06/16/2275863.htm. Accessed: 31 May 2010.

'Indigenous languages under threat, UN finds', 21 February 2009, www.abc. net.au/news/stories/2009/02/21/2497718.htm. Accessed: 13 May 2010.

AHRC (Australian Human Rights Commission), 'United we stand – Support for United Nations Indigenous Rights Declaration a watershed moment for Australia', Media Release, 3 April 2009, www.hreoc.gov.au/about/media/ media_releases/2009/21_09.html Accessed: 17 February 2010.

(Aboriginal and Torres Strait Islander Justice), *Bringing Them Home: Report of the National Inquiry into the Separation of Aboriginal and Torres Strait Islander Children from their Families*, 1997, www.hreoc.gov.au/pdf/social_ justice/bringing_them_home_report.pdf. Accessed: 8 March 2010.

AIDA (Australian Indigenous Doctors' Association) and Centre for Health Equity Training, Research and Evaluation, UNSW, *Health Impact Assessment of the Northern Territory Response* (Canberra: Australian Indigenous Doctors Association, 2010), www.aida.org.au/hia.aspx. Accessed: 30 March 2010.

Altman, J. and M. Hinkson (eds.), *Coercive Reconciliation: Stabilise, Normalise, Exit Aboriginal Australia* (Melbourne: Arena Publications, 2007).

Amnesty International Australia, 'Government misses opportunity to re-establish rights protection in the Northern Territory', *Home News*, 12 March 2010, www.amnesty.org.au/news/comments/22692/. Accessed: 30 March 2010.

Anaya, J., 'Observations on the Northern Territory Emergency Response in Australia: Advance Version', United Nations, February 2010, www.un.org.

au/files/files/United%20Nations%20Special%20Rapporteur%20-%20 Feb%202010.pdf. Accessed: 13 May 2010.

Anderson, I., 'Health policy for a crisis or a crisis in policy?', in Altman and Hinkson, *Coercive Reconciliation*, 133–45.

Atkinson, J., *Trauma Trails Recreating Songlines: The Transgenerational Effects of Trauma in Indigenous Australia* (Melbourne: Spinifex Press, 2002).

 'Indigenous Approaches to Child Abuse', in Altman and Hinkson, *Coercive Reconciliation*, 151–62.

Bourke L. and P. M. Geldens, 'Perceptions of reconciliation and related indigenous issues among young residents of Shepparton', *Australian Journal of Social Issues*, 42.4 (2007), 603–21.

Brady, M., 'Out from the Shadow of Prohibition', in Altman and Hinkson, *Coercive Reconciliation*, 184–95.

Broome, R., *Aboriginal Australians: Black Response to White Dominance 1788– 1980* (Sydney: Allen & Unwin, 1982).

Bruce-Lockhart, A., 'New dawn for the Aborigines?', *Guardian Weekly*, 3 December 2007, www.guardian.co.uk/world/2007/dec/03/australia-human-rights. Accessed: 8 March 2010.

Burrow, S., A. Galloway and N. Weissofner, 'Review of educational and other approaches to hearing loss among Indigenous people', *Australian Indigenous HealthInfoNet*, 2009, www.healthinfonet.ecu.edu.au/other-health-condi- tions/ear/reviews/our-review-education. Accessed: 24 April 2010.

Calma, T. (Aboriginal and Torres Strait Islander Social Justice Commissioner), *Social Justice Report 2007* (Sydney: Human Rights and Equal Opportunities Commission, 2007).

Chandler, M. J. and C. Lalonde, 'Cultural continuity as a hedge against suicide in Canada's First Nations', *Transcultural Psychiatry*, 35.2 (1998), 191–219.

 'Cultural continuity as a moderator of suicide risk among Canada's First Nations', in L. J. Kirmayer and G. G. Valaskakis (eds.), *Healing Traditions: The Mental Health of Aboriginal Peoples in Canada* (Vancouver: University of BC Press, 2009), 221–48.

Chesterman, J., 'Defending Australia's reputation: How indigenous Australians won civil rights part one', *Australian Historical Studies*, 116 (2001), 20–39.

Clendinnen, I., *Tiger's Eye: A Memoir* (London: Vintage, 2002).

Coorey, L., *Child Sexual Abuse in Rural and Remote Australian Indigenous Communities: A Preliminary Investigation* (Canberra: The Senate, 2001), www.aph.gov.au/SENATE/committee/indigenousaffairs_ctte/hearings/ lyla_coorey_report_march05.pdf. Accessed: 13 April 2010.

Cowlishaw, G., *Blackfellas, Whitefellas and the Hidden Injuries of Race* (Carlton, Vic.: Blackwell Publishing, 2004).

Davis, M., 'Arguing over indigenous rights: Australia and the United Nations' in Altman and Hinkson, *Coercive Reconciliation*, 97–107.

Devlin, B., 'A critique of recent government claims about the comparative performance of bilingual and non-bilingual schools in the Northern Territory',
paper presented to AIATSIS Research Symposium, Bilingual Education in
the Northern Territory: Principles, Policy and Practice, Canberra, 26 June
2009, www.abc.net.au/4corners/special_eds/20090914/language/docs/
Devlin_paper.pdf. Accessed: 24 April 2010.

Dickson, G., 'Teaching Indigenous Language', *The Greens*, 19 February 2010, www.
greens.org.au/node/5863. Accessed: 13 May 2010.

Dodson, M., 'Statement on Australian government announcement on the UN
Declaration on the Rights of Indigenous Peoples' (Canberra: Parliament
House, 3 April 2009), www.reconciliation.org.au/home/latest/mick-
dodson-statement-on-the-government-endorsement-of-un-declaration.
Accessed: 13 April 2010.

Dodson, P., 'Whatever happened to reconciliation?' in Altman and Hinkson,
Coercive Reconciliation, 21–29.

'Intervention turned our backs on reconciliation', *Sydney Morning Herald*, 20
August 2009, www.smh.com.au/opinion/contributors/intervention-turned-
our-backs-on-reconciliation-20090819-eqhv.html. Accessed: 20 February
2010.

Drape, J., 'Australia backs UN on indigenous rights', *The Age*, 26 March 2009,
news.theage.com.au/breaking-news-national/australia-backs-un-on-
indigenous-rights-20090326–9buw.html. Accessed: 8 March 2010.

'Charter won't elevate aboriginal law', *The Age*, 2 April 2009, news.theage.com.au/
breaking-news-national/charter-wont-elevate-aboriginal-law-20090402–9kn0.
html. Accessed: 8 March 2010.

ECOSOC (United Nations Economic and Social Council), 'Permanent Forum on
Indigenous Issues: Ninth Session', 3rd and 4th Meetings, HR/5014, 20 April
2010, www.un.org/News/Press/docs//2010/hr5014.doc.htm; 6th and 7th
Meetings, HR/5016, 22 April 2010, www.un.org/News/Press/docs//2010/
hr5016.doc.htm; 14th and 15th Meetings, HR/5021, 29 Apr. 2010, www.
un.org/News/Press/docs//2010/hr5021.doc.htm. All accessed: 31 May 2010.

Fink, R., 'The caste barrier – an obstacle to the assimilation of part-Aborigines in
north-west New South Wales', *Oceania*, 28.2 (1957), 100–10.

Flanagan, R., *Wanting* (Sydney: Random House, 2008).

Greer, G., *On Rage* (Carlton, Vic.: Melbourne University Press, 2008).

Haebich, A., *Spinning the Dream: Assimilation in Australia 1950–1970* (Fremantle
Press, 2008).

'Imagining Assimilation', *Australian Historical Studies*, 118 (2002), 61–70.

Hinkson, M., 'In the name of the child', (Introduction) in Altman and Hinkson,
Coercive Reconciliation, 1–12.

HRLRC (Human Rights Law Resource Centre), 'Request for urgent action under
the International Convention on the Elimination of All Forms of Racial

Discrimination', 28 January 2009, www.hrlrc.org.au/content/topics/equal-
ity/northern-territory-intervention-request-for-urgent-action-cerd/.
Accessed: 30 May 2010.

'Request for urgent action under the International Convention on the
Elimination of All Forms of Racial Discrimination: Update', 11 August 2009,
www.hrlrc.org.au/files/Update-to-CERD-11-August-2009.pdf. Accessed:
2 June 2010.

Hunter, E., 'Aboriginal alcohol use: a review of quantitative surveys', *Journal of
Drug Issues*, 22.3 (Summer 1992), 713–31. Accessed: 8 March 2010.

'Appendix 4: Mental Health Review', Australian Indigenous Doctors'
Association and Centre for Health Equity Training, Research and Evaluation,
UNSW, 74–78.

Jarrett, S. T., 'Violence: an inseparable part of traditional Aboriginal culture',
Occasional Paper for the Bennelong Society, 2009, n.p., www.bennelong.
com.au/occasional/stephFinal3.pdf. Accessed: 13 May 2010.

Kacha, S., 'The NT Intervention: Does the end justify the means?', *Aboriginal and
Social Justice Issues* (25 August 2009).

Keel, M., 'Family violence and sexual assault in indigenous communities:
"Walking the talk"', *Briefing*, 4 (Melbourne: Australian Institute of Family
Studies, 2004), www.aifs.gov.au/acssa/pubs/briefing/b4.html. Accessed: 13
February 2010.

Kessler, R. C., K. D. Mickelson and D. R. Williams, 'The prevalence, distribution,
and mental health correlates of perceived discrimination in the United
States', *Journal of Health and Social Behavior*, 40.3 (1999), 208–30.

Kidd, R., *The Way We Civilise* (St Lucia: University of Queensland Press, 1997).

Kimm, J., *A Fatal Conjunction: Two Laws and Two Cultures* (Sydney: Federation
Press, 2004).

Langton, M., 'Rum, seduction and death: "Aboriginality" and alcohol', *Oceania*,
63 (1993), 195–205.

Law Council of Australia, 'Shadow report to Australia's common core document',
(United Nations Human Rights Committee, 29 August 2008), www2.ohchr.org/
english/bodies/hrc/docs/ngos/LCA_Australia95.pdf. Accessed: 31 May 2010.

Link, B. G. and J. Phelan, 'Social conditions as fundamental causes of disease',
Journal of Health and Social Behavior, 35 (1995), 80–94.

McConvell, P. 'Call for a national indigenous languages policy', *Lingua Franca*
(ABC, 8 November 2008), www.abc.net.au/rn/linguafranca/stories/2008/
2410952.htm. Accessed: 1 May 2010.

McGregor, R., *Imagined Destinies: Aboriginal Australians and the Doomed Race
Theory, 1880–1939* (Carlton, Vic.: Melbourne University Press, 1997).

Macklin, J., 'Statement on the United Nations Declaration on the Rights of
Indigenous Peoples', 3 Apr. 2009, www.youmeunity.org.au/downloads/
c12b33eae46fa3b3760c.pdf. Accessed: 30 September 2011.

McKnight, D., *From Hunting to Drinking: The Devastating Effects of Alcohol on an Australian Aboriginal Community* (London and New York: Routledge, 2002).

Martin, D. and M. Brady, 'Human rights, drinking rights? Alcohol policy and Indigenous Australians', *Lancet*, 364 (2 October 2004), 1282–83.

Mellor, L., 'Intervention fuels racist violence in Alice Springs', Solidarity (October 2009),www.solidarity.net.au/18/intervention-fuels-racist-violence-in-alice-springs/. Accessed: 29 May 2010.

Minister for Territories, 'Our Aborigines' (Canberra: Commonwealth Government Printer: 1962).

Moran, A. 'White Australia, settler nationalism and Aboriginal assimilation', *Australian Journal of Politics and History*, 51.2 (2005), 168–93.

Morris, B., 'Racism, Egalitarianism and Aborigines', in G. Cowlishaw and B. Morris (eds.), *Race Matters: Indigenous Australians and Our Society* (Canberra: Aboriginal Studies Press, 1997), 161–76.

Newspoll, I. Saulwick, D. Muller and H. Mackay, 'Public opinion on reconciliation: snap shot, close focus, long lens', in M. Grattan (ed.), *Reconciliation: Essays on Australian Reconciliation* (Melbourne: Black, 2000), 33–52.

NGO Submission to the Human Rights Committee Australia: Addendum, 'Freedom, respect, equality dignity: action', March 2009, www2.ohchr.org/english/bodies/hrc/docs/ngos/HRLRC_Australia_HRC95.pdf. Accessed: 1 June 2010.

NTER Review Board, *Northern Territory Emergency Response: Report of the NTER Review Board Oct. 2008* (Canberra: Commonwealth of Australia, 2008), www.nterreview.gov.au/docs/report_nter_review.PDF. Accessed: 28 May 2010.

O'Brien, K., 'Govt responds to Northern Territory intervention review', ABC News (23 October 2008), www.abc.net.au/7.30/content/2008/s2399696.htm. Accessed: 30 May 2010.

Paradies, Y. C., 'Defining, conceptualizing and characterizing racism in health research', *Critical Public Health*, 16.2 (June 2006), 143–57.

Phillips, G., 'Healing and public policy', in Altman and Hinkson, *Coercive Reconciliation*, 141–50.

Pilger, J., 'Under cover of racist myth, a new land grab in Australia', *Guardian*, 24 October 2008, www.guardian.co.uk/commentisfree/2008/oct/24/australia-aborigine-howard-rudd. Accessed: 8 March 2010.

Ravens, T., 'Intervention critics write to Obama', *The Age*, 20 March 2009, news.theage.com.au/breaking-news-national/intervention-critics-write-to-obama-20090320–94ck.html. Accessed: 1 May 2010.

Reynolds, H., *The Other Side of the Frontier*, 2nd edn (Ringwood, Vic.: Penguin Books, 1995).

Nowhere People (Camberwell, Vic.: Penguin Books, 2005).

Richman, L. R. et al., 'Discrimination, dispositions, and cardiovascular responses to stress', *Health Psychology*, 26.6 (2007), 675–83.

Robinson, N., 'Yunupingu loses faith in intervention', *Australian*, 12 August 2009, www.theaustralian.com.au/news/nation/yunupingu-loses-faith-in-intervention/story-e6frg6nf-1225760427615. Accessed: 13 May 2010.

Room, R., 'Stigma, social inequality and alcohol and drug use', *Drug and Alcohol Review*, 24 (2005), 143–55.

Rundle, G., 'Military humanitarianism in Australia's north', in Altman and Hinkson, *Coercive Reconciliation*, 37–45.

Saggers, S. and D. Gray, 'Supplying and promoting "grog": the political economy of alcohol in Aboriginal Australia', *Australian Journal of Social Issues*, 32.3 (1997), 215–37.

Sheehan, P., 'A whitewash of criminal realities', *Sydney Morning Herald*, 8 January 2007. www.smh.com.au/news/opinion/a-whitewash-of-criminal-realities/2007/01/07/1168104864123.html. Accessed: 8 March 2010.

Simpson, J., J. Caffery and P. McConvell, *Gaps in Australia's Indigenous Language Policy: Dismantling bilingual education in the Northern Territory*, AIATSIS Discussion Paper Number 24 (Canberra: Australian Institute of Aboriginal and Torres Strait Islander Studies, 2009), www.aiatsis.gov.au/research/docs/dp/DP24.pdf. Accessed: 13 February 2010.

Skelton, R., 'Rights watchdog proposes overhaul of Howard's emergency intervention', *The Age*, 12 February 2008, www.theage.com.au/news/national/pressure-to-overhaul-intervention/2008/02/11/1202578694335.html. Accessed: 31 May 2010.

Strehlow, T. G. H., *Assimilation Problems: The Aboriginal Viewpoint* (Adelaide: Aborigines Advancement League Inc. of South Australia, 1964).

Sutton, P., 'The politics of suffering: indigenous policy in Australia since the 1970s', *Anthropological Forum*, 11.2 (2001), 125–73.

'After consensus', *Griffith Review: Hidden Queensland*, 21 (2008), www.griffithreview.com/edition-21/57-essay/611.html?start=1. Accessed: 13 May 2010.

Turner, P. and N. Watson, 'The Trojan horse', in Altman and Hinkson, *Coercive Reconciliation*, 205–12.

United Nations Declaration on the Rights of Indigenous Peoples. September 2007. www.un.org/esa/socdev/unpfii/documents/DRIPS_en.pdf. Accessed: 17 January 2010.

Wa Thiong'o, N., *Decolonising the Mind: The Politics of Language in African Literature* (Nairobi: Heinemann Kenya, 1991).

Whitbeck, L. B., B. J. McMorris, D. R. Hoyt, J. D. Stubben and Teresa LaFramboise, 'Perceived discrimination, traditional practices, and depressive symptoms among American Indians in the Upper Midwest', *Journal of Health and Social Behavior*, 43.4 (2002), 400–18.

Wild, R. (QC) and P. Anderson, *Ampe Akelyernemane Meke Mekarle: 'Little Children Are Sacred'*, Report of the Northern Territory Board of Inquiry into the Protection of Aboriginal Children from Sexual Abuse (Darwin: Northern Territory Government, 2007), www.inquirysaac.nt.gov.au/pdf/ bipacsa_final_report.pdf. Accessed: 26 February 2010.

5

Articulating indigenous statehood: Cherokee state formation and implications for the UN Declaration on the Rights of Indigenous Peoples

CLINT CARROLL

When I first heard the news of the adoption of the United Nations Declaration on the Rights of Indigenous Peoples, it evoked simultaneous feelings of pride and excitement, frustration and cynicism. As an indigenous citizen of the United States – one of the four settler-states that opposed the Declaration – perhaps this is not surprising. Yet, out of my cynicism came an acute realization that, as an international action, the Declaration had presented the global state community with a political litmus test that exposed (although simplistically) the unique relationships between indigenous peoples and the states into which they have found themselves subsumed. Thus, it is not shocking that the four settler-states, whose hegemony is most threatened by the existence of indigenous polities, originally voted it down.[1] In highlighting on a global stage the persistence of colonial relations between indigenous peoples and settler-states, it seems that the Declaration has already served an important purpose. Further, as an international act of recognition and an affirmation of indigenous rights to self-determination, the Declaration represents a significant political accomplishment.

The research for this chapter was generously funded in part by the US Environmental Protection Agency Science to Achieve Results (STAR) Fellowship program, the National Science Foundation Graduate Research Fellowship program, and a Morris K. and Stuart L. Udall Foundation Environmental Public Policy and Conflict Resolution Dissertation Fellowship. I would also like to acknowledge the help of the Indigenous Studies Writing Group at the University of Montana – especially Professors David Moore, Angelica Lawson, and Kathryn Shanley – for their perceptive comments and guidance in preparing this chapter. Any mistakes, of course, are my own.

[1] Australia, Canada, New Zealand, and the United States have all subsequently reversed their position on the Declaration, although in some cases with specific provisions.

Continuing in this frame of mind, I would like to offer a critical discussion of the Declaration while celebrating the momentous achievement
it represents. I am mainly concerned with how the Declaration speaks to
indigenous political formations and their international status, with a specific focus on American Indian nations in the United States. In my reading,
there are two articles in the Declaration that address this issue directly:

Article 5
Indigenous peoples have the right to maintain and strengthen their
distinct political, legal, economic, social and cultural institutions, while
retaining their right to participate fully, if they so choose, in the political,
economic, social and cultural life of the State.

Article 34
Indigenous peoples have the right to promote, develop and maintain
their institutional structures and their distinctive customs, spirituality,
traditions, procedures, practices and, in the cases where they exist, juridical systems or customs, in accordance with international human rights
standards.

These articles broadly touch on indigenous governance issues in terms
of *institutions*, noting their uniqueness and indigenous peoples' right to
"maintain and strengthen" them as such. The direct, but cautious, language of these articles points to important goals concerning indigenous governance and encourages indigenous peoples' pursuit of them.
Yet, despite their directness, the articles offer no promises to recognize
indigenous institutions within the structure of the UN itself, nor do they
possess any "teeth" for restructuring indigenous peoples' political relationships with "the States."

In a broader discursive analysis of the Declaration, it is clear that
the perceived place of indigenous nations continues to be below that of
the states in which they reside. This is evident in the repeated dichotomy between "indigenous peoples" and "the States" in the Declaration
itself, and it is made even more explicit in the United States' explanation of its vote against the Declaration. In an official response from
the US mission to the United Nations, Adviser Robert Hagen stated,
"We strongly support the full participation of indigenous peoples in
democratic decision-making processes, but cannot accept the notion
of a *sub-national* group having a 'veto' power over the legislative process" (Hagen 2007, emphasis added).[2] Indigenous nations in the United

[2] This statement is in response to Article 19 of the Declaration, which states that, "States
shall consult and cooperate in good faith with the indigenous peoples concerned through

States continue to be perceived through a paternal lens as "domestic dependent nations."[3]

Within the framework of federal Indian law, Chief Justice Marshall's phrase "domestic dependent nations" comprises a large part of the present definition of tribal sovereignty. As expressed by Wallace Coffey (Comanche) and Rebecca Tsosie (Yaqui), such qualifiers have historically framed the terms of the debate through unequal relations of power. They argue: "To the extent that we litigate our right to sovereignty within this legal framework, we have lost the true essence of our sovereignty" (2001: 196). Many Native nations identify the source of their sovereignty with their creation as a distinct people – a concept that, although rejected by the constructs of Western political traditions, is just as abstract and intangible (according to this paradigm) as the foundations of settler-state sovereignty today. Regardless of its source, tribal sovereignty has been upheld and defended largely by indigenous political structures that maintain and manage their relations with colonial settler-states. By engaging with colonial powers on these terms, American Indian nations have presented formidable political opposition to colonial policies and, in the process, have even changed the terms themselves. Such acts of resistance seem scantly represented in the Declaration, and certainly do not fit within Adviser Hagen's hierarchical framework.

Of course, the political status of indigenous peoples has been a contentious issue since the early deliberations on the Declaration (Barsh 1994). For example, the matter of whether or not to acknowledge the *collective* group rights of indigenous "peoples" (emphasizing multiple distinct and autonomous entities) versus the *individual* rights of indigenous "people" (lumping all indigenous persons together to form a subset of "minorities" within the global state system) was strongly debated (ibid.: 49–52), as was whether or not the definition of "self-determination" implied the "internal" or "external" exercise of the term (ibid.: 35–42). But while these debates have by and large been addressed through deliberation and clarification, the issue of geographical scale looms over the Declaration. As geographer Steven Silvern writes, the construction of geographical scale

their own representative institutions in order to obtain their free, prior and informed consent before adopting and implementing legislative or administrative measures that may affect them." Ironically, this article is not much different from US Executive Order 13175: "Consultation and Coordination with Indian Tribal Governments" (November 6, 2000), which establishes "regular and meaningful consultation and collaboration with tribal officials in the development of Federal policies that have tribal implications."

[3] *Cherokee Nation v. Georgia*, 30 US (5 Pet.) 1 (1831) at 27.

"operates as a framework, a set of normative assumptions about what constitutes the proper, preferred, 'natural,' and legitimate organization of political space and allocation of power between nested, hierarchically arranged geographical scales" (i.e., local, national, global, etc.) (Silvern 1999: 645).[4] The inability of the Declaration to recognize formally indigenous political institutions or to restructure indigenous peoples' political relationships with "the States" reinforces the established construction of geographical scale (and indigenous nations' place on this scale) in international law.

Reasons for this stem from what S. James Anaya has termed "state-centric" approaches to the acquisition of rights for indigenous peoples and the resulting UN member states' fear of indigenous secession (Anaya 2005).[5] Although Anaya notes that in most cases indigenous peoples do not wish to secede in order to form new independent states, he claims that a "state-centric" approach to indigenous rights – one that emphasizes the historical sovereignty of indigenous peoples – finds "little or no effective opening within the international system" (ibid.: 242). Indeed, it is logical to assume that "[b]ecause of legal, institutional, and political factors, the major international organizations necessarily favor the spheres of sovereignty asserted by their member states over any claim of competing sovereignty by a nonmember entity" (ibid.: 241). Conversely, Anaya notes that the UN has readily taken up claims that are grounded in the language of human rights "by virtue of the institutional energies that the United Nations and other international organizations have increasingly devoted to human rights matters and moral considerations over the last several decades" (ibid.: 242). As such, he argues that a human rights, or "realist," method for applying international law to indigenous claims is the most effective way of meeting the demands of indigenous peoples today.

While I agree that this method is effective to the extent that it is able to garner the most support from the UN and similar organizations (and therefore it can and has provided more immediate results, based on the *Awas Tingni*, *Maya*, and *Dann* cases he presents), Anaya's realist approach neglects the ongoing political struggles of indigenous peoples in terms of geographical scale. Anaya seems to imply that a human rights approach, as a path of least resistance, is preferable to complex and intense battles over sovereignty and state/nationhood. Perhaps this is so. I do not wish to undercut Anaya's long experience with such issues, nor his refreshing

---

[4] See also Smith (1992) and Swyngedouw (1997).
[5] See also Williams (1990) and Tullberg (1995).

optimism and faith in the institutions of international law. But while the UN Declaration can work as an instrument to hold the member states accountable for infringements of indigenous rights as outlined, it fails to work as a proper instrument for indigenous self-determination.

Although the Declaration was written in conjunction with indigenous representatives, it is a document that ultimately can only be approved (or rejected) by UN member states – many of which currently occupy indigenous territories. By this nature, and through the careful language throughout the document regarding indigenous governance institutions, it still upholds the overall interests of "the States" – namely, to maintain their hegemony as the only true sovereigns. The original opposition by the four settler-states further demonstrates the stern reluctance to acknowledge fully the colonial foundations of their own sovereignty – foundations that would not in the least live up to the current UN standards for human rights. Thus, while Anaya claims that international law has developed from a colonial institution to one that is able to support indigenous peoples' demands in terms of human rights violations (Anaya 2004: 4), the institution is far from recognizing the equal status of indigenous polities and the structures that continue to fight for this status.[6]

In this chapter I explore the makeup of an "indigenous state" in light of my ethnographic and historical research into the Cherokee Nation. In doing so, I argue that the tension surrounding the issue of indigenous "statehood" persists because of a lack of clarity on the subject on both sides of the divide (simplistically speaking, indigenous and non-indigenous). Reluctance by non-indigenous parties to recognize indigenous nations' sovereignty in its entirety stems from the perception that doing so would disastrously challenge the political and territorial integrity of the encompassing state. Yet, throughout the UN Declaration negotiations, it was repeatedly made clear that most indigenous nations have no intention of seceding from the states in which they now reside (Tullberg 1995). On the indigenous side (I refer mostly to North America), the increased development of indigenous state-like political structures evokes apprehension, which has tended to result in the renouncement of these forms of political organization (see, e.g., Alfred 1999). Yet indigenous peoples can form (and are forming) state-like governments that do not necessarily carry all the philosophical and ideological baggage of their imperial

---

[6] For a more in-depth discussion of the taken-for-granted character of settler-state sovereignty, see Tully (2000). Karena Shaw's (2008) work on the origins of sovereignty in political theory and the implications for indigenous politics is also especially salient.

counterparts. Using the Cherokee Nation as a springboard, I discuss the ability of indigenous state-like governments (hereafter shortened to "indigenous states") to confront external political pressures while maintaining culturally specific forms of governance, and how we might view these formations in light of current theoretical discussions and the growing presence of indigenous polities on the global scale. Here I should stress to the reader that my objective is not to *prescribe* indigenous state-building, but rather to *describe* a concrete instance of indigenous state formation (the Cherokee Nation) and offer a theoretical analysis of this phenomenon based on historical and ethnographic data.

Early Cherokee state formation and contemporary state-building

The beginnings of a Cherokee "state" first appeared in the late eighteenth century as adaptive mechanisms to Euro-American territorial and political encroachment (Gearing 1962; McLoughlin 1986). The process involved intense internal deliberation, as formerly autonomous Cherokee "towns" (villages) were asked to relinquish much of their autonomy in order to form a centralized national government that could stave off colonial forces. Although this proved a complicated and sometimes violent process, the Cherokees presented the US government with a formidable political body that mimicked the US tripartite constitutional structure. Further, the structure was able to maintain a sense of township autonomy (and therefore a somewhat traditional authority structure) through the bicameral legislature (Champagne 1992). A thirteen-member national "committee" oversaw day-to-day operations of the tribal government and dealt with mostly external measures. A much larger national "council" comprised town representatives (many of whom were influential elders), who guided the broad direction of the committee and the Nation during annual meetings, but who attended to mostly local affairs throughout the rest of the year. Still, despite this syncretic system, maintaining the centralized state involved constantly balancing tensions between the tribal government and Cherokee towns. In the case that leaders (both in the council and in the committee) moved too far away from a foundational body of beliefs and ethics, there were community sanctions that created dialog and led to reconciliation.[7]

---

[7] One such case was that of White Path, an old, respected chief who was expelled from the national council in 1825 for allegedly opposing too strenuously the rapid changes in

In the period between 1827 and 1906, the US government twice obliter-
ated Cherokee political institutions – once as a result of Removal and the
infamous Trail of Tears (1838–39) and again as a result of the assimila-
tory policy of Allotment (1887–1906).[8] The year 1907 dealt another blow
to Cherokee sovereignty by territorializing the former Indian Territory
in order to form the state of Oklahoma. Starting in 1907, the federal government proceeded to appoint Cherokee Nation principal chiefs, and the
tribal government was effectively under federal oversight for the next
sixty-five years. In the late 1940s, tribal leaders started to assert greater
control over their government, but it was not until 1971 that the Cherokee
Nation was able to hold its own elections and in 1975 a constitutional
convention, thus ending the overt and blatant federal control over tribal
affairs (Strickland and Strickland 1991).

Since this time there has been a slow progression towards modifying
the tribal governmental structure and wresting control of tribal institutions from the Bureau of Indian Affairs (BIA). The Cherokee Nation has
undergone a series of reforms, including another constitutional revision
in 1999, whereby the tribe held a convention free from BIA control and
drafted a new document for Cherokee citizens to ratify (Lemont 2006).
In 1990, the tribe established self-governance, eliminating BIA offices
in Tahlequah and assuming the responsibility for numerous tribal programs. In 2006, the tribe reclaimed the sovereign power to amend its constitution without the oversight or approval of the BIA, and on July 10 of
that year the first Secretary of State of the Cherokee Nation was sworn
into office. Yet, although much progress has been made, the Cherokee
Nation is still dealing with the legacy of federal control of tribal affairs. To
this day, there are few aspects of formal tribal institutions that resemble
the traditional sources of authority maintained by the earlier Cherokee
Nation governmental structure (before Removal and Allotment). The
constitution that was adopted in 1975 was a hasty attempt to build an

---

Cherokee politics. He was replaced by Elijah Hicks, a Christian. White Path reacted by
leading a counterrevolution against the Cherokee constitutional convention for the sake
of bolstering the old Cherokee way of life (McLoughlin 1986: 388–402). The movement
was nonviolent and was carried out by employing the traditional Cherokee method of
withdrawal to express disagreement and protestation. Its main concern was the limits
of assimilation, and many Cherokees, both traditionalists and sympathetic Christians,
mixed- and full-bloods, got behind White Path in order to raise important questions concerning the future of the Cherokee Nation.

[8] The Allotment Era technically lasted until 1934 with the passage of the Indian
Reorganization Act; however, much of the process of dividing up the tribal land base had
been accomplished by Oklahoma statehood in 1907.

institution that could quickly distribute funds and services to tribal citizens who were very much in need of them. It operates with a unicameral (single chamber) tribal council that is unable to accommodate the persistent makeup of Cherokee society: a network of autonomous communities (much like the former "towns"). This governmental structure continues to operate in the present day, despite the fact that it was never intended to serve as a functional government (Lemont 2006: 301).

Many Cherokee communities have consequently developed ambivalence toward the tribal government as it has become solely a central authority – *not* something that communities feel they can influence or change – which is precisely what Cherokee society resists. The Cherokee Nation government is responding to this through a significant repositioning of governance priorities, advocating the establishment of partnerships between Cherokee government and communities in an effort to recognize local authority and leadership. Principal Chief Chad "Corntassel" Smith's administration and political platform promotes "a new style of Cherokee politics, one that integrates traditional forms of Cherokee culture into their modern bureaucracy" (Sturm 2002: 104). While these efforts are not flawless, they speak to how Cherokee political leaders must respond to the constant tension between government and community mentioned above. I claim that this constant tension, rather than an annoyance or persistent flaw of the form, is actually a key aspect of an indigenous (Cherokee) method of state-building.

As a result of Chief Smith's platform of cultural revitalization (and a commitment of tribal funds toward this), a variety of cultural projects have been initiated within the tribal government. One such project, designed to focus on Cherokee ethnobotany, has proven to address much more than its stated objectives. In the summer of 2004, the Cherokee Nation Office of Environmental Programs sought to address the attrition of Cherokee traditional knowledge and the lack of such knowledge in departmental responsibilities by initiating a project to document ethnobotanical data for use in tribal environmental policy. I was hired as an environmental technician to conduct interviews with knowledgeable Cherokees and to develop a computer database. The project goal was to help perpetuate the knowledge through a concerted tribal effort to protect culturally significant ecosystems. Since then, the project has grown in scope and has been merged with the efforts of the Cherokee Nation Natural Resources Department (NRD). In conjunction with my graduate and post-doctoral research, I have continued to work on this project with NRD staff.

The story of the initiative's development highlights the key aspects of tribal governance that this chapter addresses. In the course of my interviews, every informant recognized that traditional medicinal knowledge of local flora was not being transmitted to future generations, and that it was important to do something to reverse this trend. But despite their enthusiasm for revitalizing this knowledge, many of them were hesitant to speak with me about it. The taboo of freely divulging Cherokee medicinal knowledge is widespread among Cherokee communities. This is mainly due to the large amount of sacred knowledge associated with it, and the long history of mistreatment and exploitation of traditional knowledge by outsiders. I had taken this important fact into account when designing the project, making sure to handle any knowledge with the proper respect and protocol, and only asking for basic information with regard to the cultural significance of individual species. Yet, despite these careful measures, something still seemed to inhibit the project's growth.

As a response to this conundrum, in October 2008 the NRD director and I decided to convene a small gathering at the grounds of a Cherokee community non-profit organization located in the woods of Sequoyah County. The purpose of the meeting was to bring together many of the elders and experts that I had consulted in the course of the project. We called together about ten women and men mostly over the age of 50, the majority of whom were fluent Cherokee speakers. We thought that if they all saw each other (rather than just me, an employee for the tribe and a university researcher), we might develop more confidence and trust in our initiative. The meeting was somewhat informal in nature, and took place outdoors and around a fire – not a typical meeting for a tribal governmental department. Comfortable with this setting, the elders (having free reign over the discussion) openly discussed the issues and strategies regarding the preservation of Cherokee plant knowledge. Significantly, they noted that their generation is possibly the last one that carries a substantial amount of this knowledge. The meeting closed that day with a unanimous decision by the group that the loss of this knowledge was not in the best interest of Cherokee people, and that measures to correct this problem should be undertaken immediately.

Meetings with this group have continued in the same manner, and they have resulted in the support and recognition of the project by highly respected practitioners of Cherokee medicine. Through our small meetings on Cherokee plant knowledge, as a group we have developed a productive collaboration between Cherokee community elders, a Cherokee community organization, and a Cherokee Nation governmental department towards the goal of preserving and maintaining knowledge and traditions that are rapidly disappearing. This type of partnership is uncommon, especially with reference to sensitive knowledge. It is significant that a meeting of this sort could not have been as successful in a stark conference room in Tahlequah (the Cherokee Nation capital). The alternative meeting style and setting illuminates issues of process – ways of making decisions and getting things done – and the contrast between bureaucratic methods and traditional ones. The meetings also call attention to changing perspectives on knowledge and authority – going out into the communities and valuing different forms of knowledge and different types of "experts" signifies a repositioning of priorities in the tribal government.[9]

Thus, whereas I believe one of the key aspects to indigenous (Cherokee) state-building is the tension between government and community, more importantly it is how this tension is addressed that determines the efficacy of the political form. In this case, redistributing authority and building relationships between the tribal government and communities are vital steps to ensuring the unique articulation of a Cherokee state. Regardless of the future of the group, its existence thus far speaks to the efforts on both sides of the government–community divide to bridge the gap created by state-building. It represents how Cherokee state-building is facilitated by diverging from standard bureaucratic procedure and bringing initiatives into the communities – thus providing a very different setting and recognizing a very different style and source of authority. The model of the group itself could serve as a prototype for similar institutions that coalesce around other pressing issues. Often these projects are not necessarily about the singular topic that they may use as a focal point. Rather, such projects, when carried out according to the appropriate social and cultural protocols, open up valuable channels of communication that connect community concerns and knowledge to tribal governmental policy. I assert that this process is a necessary aspect of indigenous state-building.

States in theory and practice

In the geopolitical sense, a state is "a centralized political system within international legal boundaries recognized by other states" (Nietschmann

---

[9] See Carroll (2011) for a more thorough discussion of the ethnobotany project, the elders group, and their implications for Cherokee Nation environmental governance.

1994: 227). While this definition applies to most analyses of states, scholars have taken numerous approaches to understanding the formation and workings of the modern state (see Migdal 1997). I present only a snapshot of such approaches in order to highlight the topics that pertain to my goal herein.

Political scientist James Scott argues that "seeing like a state" requires understanding the state's tendencies to simplify, make legible, and manipulate. Through an analysis of monoculture forestry, Scott details early European state simplification and manipulation of forests to conform to agendas of maximized economic gain (Scott 1998: 11–22). He traces how the term "natural resources" originated as a product of these policies to describe the state's commodification and systematic exploitation of forest products. Furthermore, Scott compares the state's domination over nature to its control of local populations by chronicling the state's manufacture of national citizenship (simplifying people through uniformity) and the origin of the cadastral map (making land tenure customs legible). To Scott, these are the measures that state officials take in order to create "a uniform, homogeneous, national administrative code" (ibid., 35).

Although many may take for granted the idea of a state as a monolithic, coherent body, sociologists Philip Corrigan and Derek Sayer (1985) focus on the ideological character of state authority, and provide an alternative to viewing the state as a singular entity. They observe that

> institutions of government are real enough. But "the" state is in large part an ideological construction, a fiction: the state is at most a message of domination – an ideological artifact attributing unity, structure, and independence to the disunited, structureless and dependent workings of the practice of government. (Corrigan and Sayer 1985: 7)

Corrigan and Sayer advocate the study of "state *formation* as cultural *revolution*" (ibid.: 199, emphasis in original). In other words, the state form of organization arises through the institutionalization of what they call "moral regulation" – previously considered the domain of the autonomous individual (ibid.: 4). Corrigan and Sayer's focus on moral qualities and values as instruments for social control shows how the state works *within* and *through* its subjects (ibid.: 199). Thus, in order to "see" the state, one must look at its manifestations in specific projects and practices. "Key questions," Corrigan later states, "then become NOT *who* rules, but *how* rule is accomplished" (Corrigan 1990: 264, emphasis in original).

In a similar vein, Michel Foucault's notion of governmentality emphasizes "the manufacture of subjects," and suggests viewing state formation
as a contingent process of forming "various types of agents with particular capacities and possibilities for action" (Dean 1999: 29). Further,
studies on governmentality have shown how economic neoliberalism
and other forces of globalization have contributed to the fading out of the
state as a concrete form, and how power increasingly works through more
indirect methods (Rose 1996, 1999; Dean 1999). Indeed, sovereignty in an
absolute sense over borders, culture, and economy is not possible today
for even the most powerful state (Clifford 2003: 83). Nevertheless, such
insights do not lead to the "end of states," but rather new understandings
of state forms and how they work.

These new understandings, as Hansen and Stepputat (2001) claim, are
advanced by looking at localized instances that emphasize historical specificity. They write:

> Instead of talking about the state as an entity that always/already consists
> of certain features, functions, and forms of governance, let us approach
> each actual state as a historically specific configuration of a range of lan-
> guages of stateness, some practical, others symbolic and performative,
> that have been disseminated, translated, interpreted, and combined
> in widely differing ways and sequences across the globe. (Hansen and
> Stepputat 2001: 7)

Such an "ethnography" of the state views it neither as a monolith nor
as a particular closed group of individuals, but as an ideological configuration, albeit with material presence and effects. Their ethnography is
an inquiry into how each unique formation is produced and reproduced,
imagined and reimagined by and through its subjects. This claim illuminates that *not all states are the same* and, furthermore, that not all state
projects are necessarily "bad." They elaborate: "Whereas certain forms
of state intervention may be loathed and resisted, other and more egali-
tarian forms of governance, or more benign forms of authority, may at
the same time be intensely desired and asked for" (ibid.: 9). Thus, while
some forms of state power have disastrous potential (as Scott 1998 demonstrates), there is also variation between states and differing degrees of
coercion among state projects – there are many paths to "stateness" (Li
2005). Viewing states and state formation as such offers some conceptual
space within which to discuss indigenous state formation as a creative
process through which indigenous nations can articulate unique expressions of "stateness."

Contextualizing indigenous states

Geographer Bernard Nietschmann notes that the distinction between many indigenous peoples and states is a matter of *nations* versus states. In his "Fourth World analysis," nations predate the creation of states, and, unlike states, nations are enduring systems of human organization: "States come and go – nations remain" (Nietschmann 1994: 242). Nietschmann writes, "A nation is a cultural territory made up of communities of individuals who see themselves as 'one people' on the basis of common ancestry, history, society, institutions, ideology, language, territory, and, often, religion" (ibid.: 226). States are "[i]mposed upon unconsenting nations," and they "attempt to erase the histories and geographies of the people they occupy" (ibid.: 227–28). Nietschmann notes that "two-thirds of the world's states use their armies against people they claim as citizens" (ibid.: 227). State-building in this sense is violent and oppressive.

But what does it mean when indigenous nations build states? Nietschmann only briefly mentions the "nation-state," a form that he claims is rare ("less than five percent of the world's states are nation-states"), although the term itself has been repeatedly misused to refer to most modern states (ibid.: 229). According to Nietschmann, a nation state comprises "A common people [self-defined and culturally/linguistically distinct] with a common identity, a common territory, and a government that is internationally recognized" (ibid.). He lists Iceland and Portugal as nation states. Significantly, most indigenous nations do not qualify under this last requirement, as they are not "internationally recognized" as states, nor do they have the same level of sovereignty within their reservation and/or territorial borders. The United Nations has instead recognized them as "stateless peoples" (Hanson 2004: 292). In the United States and other settler societies, indigenous nations are treated as "wards" of the state. Because indigenous nations "jeopardize state territorial claims" (Nietschmann 1994: 230), most states rely on this rhetoric to define their relationship to them.[10]

Central to understanding the dynamics of indigenous "stateness" is the fact that indigenous nations must operate within established systems of governmentality maintained by postcolonial or settler-states. In other words, in discussing indigenous states one must account for *two degrees* of

---

[10] Political scientist Walker Connor (1994) also provides a detailed discussion of nations, states, and nation states in the same vein as Nietschmann.

state dynamics – they are states within states. Although mainstream political theory would view this situation as an irresolvable conflict between "sovereigns," it is actually consistent with many indigenous views. Roger Maaka and Augie Fleras note that "Indigenous sovereignty rarely invokes a call for independence or non-interference" (2000: 93). Indigenous claims of "sovereignty without secession" (ibid.: 92), and "measured separatism" (Wilkinson 1987; Ranco and Suagee 2007) indicate a nuanced understanding of their historical relations with settler-states, and a firm conception of their contemporary political identity. The extent to which indigenous nations can successfully assert this unique view of sovereignty in part relies on their ability to fit this claim into the ideology of the settler polity.

In his work on postcolonial politics in the United States, Kevin Bruyneel (2007) suggests thinking in terms of a "third space of sovereignty" to visualize such claims. He describes how spatial and temporal boundaries created by American political discourse present American Indian nations with false choices constructed by imperial binaries – "assimilation or secession, inside or outside, modern or traditional" (ibid.: 217). Spatial boundaries demand that American Indians occupy a definitive political space: either sovereign (separate, self-sufficient), or citizen (dependent, with no "special rights"). Temporal boundaries prohibit American Indian sovereignty from being expressed in modern forms and from "[engaging] in practices commensurate with present-day American political life" (ibid.: xiv). Employing postcolonial theories, Bruyneel outlines how the refusal by American Indian nations to choose between these dualisms is an assertion of a political "third space" (Bhabha 1994; see also Johnson 2008). Thus a third space of sovereignty allows for "promising contradictions" (Tsing 2007: 57) in indigenous relations with settler-states: asserting difference and autonomy without implying secession, and holding the settler-state to its responsibilities toward indigenous nations without accepting its paternalism.[11]

Kanien'kehaka (Mohawk) political theorist Taiaiake Alfred (1999) offers a valuable alternative viewpoint on indigenous political aspirations. Alfred's work brings into question the philosophical foundations

---

[11] Anthropologist Anna Tsing writes: 'The global indigenous movement is alive with promising contradictions. Inverting national development standards, it promises unity based on plurality: diversity without assimilation. It endorses authenticity *and* invention, subsistence *and* wealth, traditional knowledge *and* new technologies, territory *and* diaspora. The excitement of indigenous rights claims draws from the creative possibilities of such juxtapositions' (2007: 33).

of the term "sovereignty." While many scholars and American Indian nations rely on sovereignty as a concept in order to frame discussions of American Indian political status, goals, and struggles, Alfred argues that indigenous nations should abandon sovereignty as a goal because of its philosophical roots in European notions of absolute rule, coercion, and domination. These notions run counter to his conception of indigenous political traditions: communal responsibility, individual autonomy, and respect for nature. Alfred writes,

> Sovereignty is an exclusionary concept rooted in an adversarial and coercive Western notion of power. Indigenous peoples can never match the awesome coercive force of the state; so long as sovereignty remains the goal of indigenous politics, therefore, Native communities will occupy a dependent and reactionary position relative to the state. (Ibid.: 59)

Alfred provides a similar critique of contemporary tribal governance institutions. He writes, "[T]he imposition of Western governance structures and the denial of indigenous ones continue to have profoundly harmful effects on indigenous people" (ibid.: 2). He questions the ability of imposed political structures to achieve any significant steps toward indigenous self-determination, on the grounds that they are foreign, destabilizing, and dysfunctional (ibid.: 28). Alfred's main point of contention is the reproduction of "statist" structures and ideologies in the development of political autonomy for Native nations. He argues that by accepting sovereignty and state formation as goals for tribal development, Native leaders are legitimating a dominant colonial framework and the subordinating political relations that it demands. This, Alfred claims, is a mistake, and it only further solidifies the "hegemonic myth" of the state and thus further clouds the significance of historical realities. In Alfred's opinion, it is better to undermine this hegemonic myth than to try to carve out spaces for the tribal polity within it. He states, "The problem is that the assertion of a sovereign right for indigenous peoples continues to structure the politics of decolonization, and the state uses the theoretical inconsistencies in that position to its own advantage" (ibid.: 57).

While I value Alfred's critical perspective, it is clear that my analysis diverges significantly from his. For one, his intellectual battle is constructed around monoliths: the state versus indigenous peoples. In the previous section, I discussed how such a construction obscures how state power works through ideology and the creation of subjects, rather than coherent policies and plans (Corrigan and Sayer 1985; Li 2005). As anthropologist Nicolas Thomas has argued, characterizing dominant discourses (e.g. colonialism, the state) in "unitary and essentialist terms" masks their internal contradictions and in turn *reproduces* their power and status (Thomas 1994: 3). Thomas writes, "Colonial discourse has, too frequently, been evoked as a global and transhistorical logic of denigration, that has remained impervious to active marking or reformulation by the 'Other'; it has figured above all as a coherent imposition, rather than a practically mediated relation" (ibid.). Not accounting for colonialism's inconsistencies overshadows indigenous resistances to, and alterations of, colonial/state projects.

Further, as Alfred's essay on sovereignty is part of a larger indigenous manifesto, his argument necessarily requires a certain amount of generalization and idealization of indigenous qualities and values. Of course, it is clear that Alfred employs a strategic essentialism – he states that certain broad assumptions about indigenous peoples must be made in order "to prepare the philosophical ground" (1999: xxiv). Yet some have interpreted this exercise as politically dangerous. As Barker (2005) and Moreton-Robinson (2007) have shown with regard to the use of the term "sovereignty" in localized indigenous struggles, theorizing on the abstracted grounds of the *Indigenous*, and then lending these theories to local struggles often overlooks crucial differences in the historical experiences and current political positioning of many indigenous nations. While I agree with Alfred that hegemonic constructions of power need to be interrogated, it is important to consider how each indigenous nation has experienced, reacted to, and impacted such constructions, and in turn, how indigenous people have appropriated these constructions in order to counteract ongoing injustices (see, e.g., Ranco 2007).[12]

Lastly, Alfred bypasses the new indigenous political formations that have resulted from the transformation of imposed structures. While he acknowledges the dynamic nature of traditions and culture (1999: xviii),

---

[12] In my view, Alfred's observations are most relevant when kept in a local (Kahnawake Mohawk) context. His earlier work (see, e.g., Alfred 1995) centers on Mohawk governance institutions and shows their transformation through a concrete and detailed study. Such a focus on tribal specificity and localized struggles highlights issues as they arise in particular contexts. These contexts can then be compared across indigenous nations. His later work gives less attention to tribal specificity, and often emphasizes the polarization of indigenous versus Western values and political forms. Both *Peace, Power, Righteousness* and *Wasáse* (2005) appear to struggle with whether to cast off all imposed structures or to renounce tradition altogether. He thus ends up with a zero-sum game of modernity for tradition, indigenous for Western (see, e.g., 1999: 20–30) – a predicament that I think can be circumvented when indigenous governance institutions are viewed as articulations (see my further discussion of this below).

he does not extend this perspective to conceptualize the same process for indigenous political structures. Conversely, I suggest that as much as the term "sovereignty" can be articulated to represent indigenous needs and political values (see Barker 2005), so can indigenous political institutions.

The question, rather than *should* indigenous states be forming, becomes: *how are* they forming? In illuminating the ideological character of "stateness," I ask: how have indigenous nations been able to envision this form for themselves? What attributes of this form are being addressed to account for various indigenous situations and values? What are the social and political obstacles to this process, both "externally" (in relations with their respective settler-states) and "internally" (regarding intra-tribal socio-political dynamics)? How might they occupy a third space in both national and global politics and, in doing so, "gain the fullest possible expression of political identity, agency, and autonomy" (Bruyneel 2007: 6)?

Yet some scholars in the liberal tradition have questioned the limits of this "fullest possible expression," warning that indigenous sovereignty should not lie beyond the reach of international human rights laws (e.g., Brown 2007). Liberalism's critique of collective indigenous rights interrogates the boundaries of sovereignty in any form, cautioning against the exploitation of internal minorities, and the "license to advance one people's goals at the expense of another's" (Brown 2007: 187). However, as anthropologist Ronald Niezen has illuminated (2003: 94–144), such liberal argumentation in the context of indigenous rights to self-determination falls victim to fallacy and paradox. For one, as Niezen writes, "How does one, in a tolerant and democratic way, impose tolerance and democracy? ... However much we agree with liberal values, liberal solutions to the challenge of universalizing the truth have been unsettling and ultimately self-defeating" (ibid.: 129–130). Furthermore, while the global community benefits from holding states accountable for human rights violations, unequal power relationships continue to structure indigenous relations with dominant societies. Until indigenous nations (and/or states) are recognized within the United Nations *as nations* (and/or states), relying on imperial oversight to determine what is best for indigenous peoples and their communities is a dangerous precedent.

Because indigenous nations have often been the victims of invader states, indigenous state formation is necessarily under different circumstances. Indigenous state-building does not require repressing or subsuming other nations, but rather articulating this form in ways that resonate with both their own citizenry and the postcolonial or settler-state. The concept of an "indigenous state" does not concern repeating the violence or mimicking the unethical behavior of "high-modern" states. Rather, like other indigenous versions of non-indigenous forms (e.g., indigenous mapping), it concerns the ability to display "commensurability with hegemonic configurations of power" (Bryan 2009: 27). Indigenous nations can use state structures – the bureaucratized and rationalized institutions of social control and regulation that result from the need to represent, govern, and provide services to a large population through a centralized government – without needing to replicate all of their philosophical and ideological assumptions.

Although it would be naïve to assume that indigenous nations are immune to any negative byproduct of the state form (e.g., oligarchy, nepotism, elitism, corruption, etc.), I have hoped to show through the Cherokee Nation case one example of how an indigenous nation reconciles the conflicting tendencies of state formation by balancing the constant tension between tribal government and the tribal community. Although there is never a perfect balance, the concept (or even the *ideal*) of maintaining equilibrium between the two entities is essential to a functional Cherokee state. Of course, this dynamic may be different for other indigenous nations (the discussion of indigenous statehood may not apply to some indigenous nations *at all*), but instead of discrediting tribal governments that employ state structures, attention should be paid to similar social dynamics that may exist to maintain such an equilibrium (and thus inhibit negative consequences of state-building, like those listed above).

Nevertheless, to assume that indigenous states will become exact replicas of high-modern states presupposes that all societies are on the same linear trajectory to a uniform modernity (often defined by Western European standards). But there are alternative modernities that are not necessarily synonymous with capitalist development. Indigenous peoples are creating their own versions of modernity, skirting the zero-sum game that has so often characterized non-indigenous notions of indigenous cultural change (Clifford 2001; 2003). The narratives of settler contact histories present such change as a trade-off: tradition for progress, Indigenous for Western. Marshall Sahlins illuminates this inclination and its fallacies:

> [A]rguments of dependency and capitalist hegemony [present] dim views of the historical capacities of indigenous peoples and the vitalities of their cultures. In too many narratives of Western domination, the indigenous victims appear as neo-historyless peoples: their own agency disappears,

> more or less with their culture, the moment Europeans irrupt on the scene … dependency is real but it is not the internal organization of [indigenous] existence … their experience of capitalism is mediated by the *habitus* of an indigenous form of life. (Sahlins 1999: ii, xvii, xvi)

Similarly, historian Colleen O'Neill states that American Indians have "transcended these rigid categories [traditional/modern] and created alternative pathways of economic and cultural change that [are] not merely static renditions of some timeless past or total acceptance of US capitalist culture" (O'Neill 2004: 3). Sahlins calls this "the indigenization of modernity" (1993: 21).

Thus, I view indigenous state-building as a counter-hegemonic strategy that is able to present non-hegemonic resistances to the ongoing forces of colonialism. This view offers an outlet to a key dilemma of indigenous governance studies: that of whether to cast off all imposed structures or to renounce traditional governance altogether. In the current light, the two choices are irrelevant. Indigenous nations can employ the "imposed" structures while revitalizing traditional ones – to the extent that they can modify both.

Scholars have proposed articulation theory as an alternative way of viewing indigenous identity politics and cultural change. One of the leading voices on this perspective, James Clifford, is worth quoting at length:

> Articulation offers a non-reductive way to think about cultural transformation and the apparent coming and going of "traditional" forms. All-or-nothing, fatal-impact notions of change tend to assume that cultures are living bodies with organic structures. So, for example, indigenous languages, traditional religions, or kinship arrangements, may appear to be critical organs, which if lost, transformed, or combined in novel structures should logically imply the organism's death. You can't live without a heart or lungs. But indigenous societies have persisted with few, or no, native-language speakers, as fervent Christians, and with "modern" family structures, involvement in capitalist economies, and new social roles for women and men. "Inner" elements have, historically, been connected with exterior forms, in processes of selective, syncretic transformation. (Clifford 2001: 478)

Clifford suggests that, as opposed to viewing social or cultural formation as an organism, "[a]n articulated ensemble is more like a political coalition or, in its ability to conjoin disparate elements, a cyborg" (ibid.). Thus, when indigenous peoples make political claims based on culture, instead of being false or invented, they are legitimate *articulations*. Such a view eliminates the need for essentialist claims of authenticity, and conversely, essentialist accusations of *inauthenticity*.

To be clear, articulation theory is not "anything goes" – it has constraints posed by the collective. Articulation is "actively produced and potentially challenged" (ibid.: 481). Like all social phenomena, articulation is mediated by the discursive boundaries set within a society at a particular time (Foucault 1972, 2003). A founding proponent of articulation theory, Stuart Hall, writes, "[A] theory of articulation is both a way of understanding how ideological elements come, under certain conditions, to cohere together *within a discourse*, and a way of asking how they do or do not become articulated, at specific conjunctures, to certain political subjects" (Hall 1986: 53, emphasis added). For indigenous peoples, the discursive boundaries are twofold: in order to make successful claims, they must meet the discursive conditions of both their own society and the dominant one. But while this seems limiting, an articulation is merely the shell – the outer appearance – of a set of political claims and/or cultural expressions. While the articulation must resonate with what others conceive as possible within "the order of things," its effects have the potential to change this order based on *how* the articulation is made. Thus, as I put forth, the ways indigenous peoples articulate indigenous states have the ability to contest the dominant order while operating within a mutually intelligible framework.

The UN Declaration and the politics of US–indigenous relations

While the UN Declaration has weaknesses with regard to recognizing the capacity of indigenous polities, it is significant that the world's four settler-states originally found the Declaration strong enough to reject it. The basis of this rejection warrants discussion. The United States' rejection was not with regard to the articles that I present above (5 and 34). Rather, it was concerned more with issues of land, territoriality, and resources – represented strongly in Articles 26, 28, and 32. These articles stress indigenous rights to "own, use, develop and control" traditional territories and their resources, and they call for redress in the form of restitution or compensation for expropriated lands.

Adviser Robert Hagen's response highlights the complications of such a stipulation for the United States: "Article 26 appears to require recognition of indigenous rights to lands without regard to other legal rights existing in land, either indigenous or non-indigenous." It is true that time has made neighbors and even family out of what was once a mostly adversarial relationship between indigenous peoples and settlers.

While tension does persist between groups, in many cases harmony is sought in lieu of conflict. Yet, with regard to non-indigenous property rights, the legality that Hagen references is debatable. The Allotment Era (1887–1934) created the current situation wherein most lands within most American Indian reservations are under non-Indian ownership. Whereas the Allotment Act itself was a suspicious piece of legislation, this period was also characterized by blatant instances of illegal land seizures by non-Indian settlers and the federal government (see Debo 1940). Hagen takes for granted the current land tenure system in the United States, which is a result of these illegal and unconstitutional acts. His failure to acknowledge this history illuminates how indigenous rights to land and resources within settler societies are discordant with a settler national consciousness. While Hagen's response is phrased in legalistic appeals to rights for all citizens, his viewpoint represents an unwillingness to deal with the aftermath of colonization. It raises the question: does the passage of time erase accountability for historical injustices? Disappointingly, Hagen prevents this conversation from occurring.

Maaka and Fleras' proposal for "constructive engagement" is a promising approach to settler-state indigenous politics, as it "goes beyond the legalistic (abstract rights) or restitutional (reparations), however important these concerns are" (2000: 98). They write,

> [A] constructive engagement policy is focused on advancing an ongoing relationship by taking into account shifting social realities … A dialectical mode of thinking is proposed under constructive engagement in which differences are not perceived as absolute or antagonistic, but as deeply interconnected in the sense of being held in tension within a larger framework. (Ibid.)

Constructive engagement requires that polities (indigenous and non-indigenous) within a settler-state paradigm act as partners "jointly exploring postcolonial possibilities" (ibid.: 109). While Maaka and Fleras note that a significant difference between their case (Aotearoa/New Zealand) and other settler-states is the existence of multiple indigenous nations as opposed to just one (Maori), their proposal is still salient. Whereas in Aotearoa/New Zealand constructive engagement involves "two consenting majorities," in the United States *multiple engagements* (from multiple American Indian nations) can simultaneously work to contest the federal "rule of law" and neocolonial forces, while participating as citizens (often American Indians are proud citizens) of the settler-state and working with common goals to build a better country (see Tully 2000: 53).

Written before the US endorsement of the Declaration, an article in *American Thinker* (Bom 2010) presents the Declaration as a threat to American politics. According to Professor Bom's calculations, endorsing the Declaration would allow American Indians to secure some sort of hold over the US political system and then infiltrate its legislative process. Similarly, Adviser Robert Hagen remarked that tribes should not possess "veto power" out of the fear that American Indians will veto any and everything that "may" pertain to them. A common assumption that runs though these two assertions is that people make decisions based on maximized personal gain. This assumption is couched in liberal economics and game theory, wherein predictions about the market economy are made in accordance with this tendency (see, e.g., Ostrom 1990: 1–28). "Third space" or "secessionless" sovereignty, as well as "constructive engagement" all account for completely different understandings of potential political relationships between settler societies and indigenous nations. These concepts allow for an indigenous "statehood" that recognizes the inherent sovereignty of American Indian nations instead of appealing to a neoliberal rights discourse wherein American Indian nations are interest groups requesting "special rights" over other citizens (much as Brown 2007 argues). The concepts also create a space for indigenous nations to assert *difference* based on this sovereignty while not sacrificing participation in the dominant society. Article 5 of the Declaration is commendable in that it attempts to articulate this concept.

Yet, in light of the finalizing disclaimer in Article 46, it is clear that the UN is very aware of how indigenous peoples threaten the territorial and political integrity of states. For the UN to maintain its own integrity with its member states, here it must reify them:

> *Article 46*
>   1. Nothing in this Declaration may be interpreted as implying for any State, people, group or person any right to engage in any activity or to perform any act contrary to the Charter of the United Nations or construed as authorizing or encouraging any action which would dismember or impair, totally or in part, the territorial integrity or political unity of sovereign and independent States.

With this rhetoric, indigenous nations are once again relegated to lesser political scales. The language inhibits possibilities for expressing indigenous statehood in the sense that indigenous nations can represent themselves as equal partners with the "sovereign and independent States." Article 46 exemplifies how, if indigenous nations are to make meaningful strides in global politics, they must eventually assert their own forms of political identity instead of relying on good faith in the international state community. Expanding Kevin Bruyneel's "third space of sovereignty" to the global scale, the question is how can indigenous nations carve out a political space from which to articulate difference while participating as equals with the global state community? Even the act of occupying a space within the UN is problematic, as this institution is dominated and controlled by Western states – many of which participated in the colonization of indigenous peoples. Where might we go from here?

The Organization of American States (OAS), although plagued with the same hierarchical dynamics as the UN, offers a valuable perspective in that it recognizes the sophisticated political formations of indigenous nations as something to address explicitly. In an interview on the Draft American Declaration on the Rights of Indigenous Peoples, Leonardo Crippa, an indigenous representative at the OAS, stated, "[A] big particularity is the existence of indigenous peoples with their own judicial system, with their own government, with their own legislative organizations which is something that is occurring here in the US" (quoted in Ove Varsi 2009). The extent to which these formations are recognized as entities worthy of inclusion in the OAS, rather than just vehicles for consultation, has yet to be seen. It is also noteworthy that Article 4 of the Draft American Declaration is identical to Article 46 of the UN Declaration, in which the "sovereign and independent States" are reified.

Of course, the situation is not entirely bleak, and President Barack Obama's recent endorsement of the Declaration on December 6, 2010, as well as his (seemingly) overall support of American Indian self-determination, is a promising step forward (State Department 2011).[13] Additionally, President Obama has made significant steps to hold federal agencies accountable to the "nation-to-nation" relationship with American Indian tribes, as outlined in former President Clinton's Executive Order 13175 (2000). Towards this goal, on November 5, 2009, the Obama administration held the largest tribal leader summit in US history, and as of January 2011, numerous federal agencies have detailed their commitment to implementing the Executive Order, including the Department of the Interior, the Department of Justice, and the Department of Agriculture (State Department 2011). It is also promising that citizens of American Indian nations continue to occupy important positions within the US

---

[13] But also see Newcomb's (2010) critical review of President Obama's announcement and the State Department's document detailing the US endorsement.

polity, namely Kimberly Teehee (Cherokee Nation) as the senior policy adviser for Native American affairs within the Domestic Policy Council, and Dr. Yvette Roubideaux (Rosebud Sioux) as the first American Indian to serve as the Director of the Indian Health Service. Indigenous involvement in the US political system, although it may be viewed by some as a compromising act (e.g., Porter 1999), serves as a clear example of Maaka and Fleras' "constructive engagement."

Conclusion

It is hard not to notice the proliferation of "nations" today throughout the media and pop culture – from the football team fan groups like the "Niners Nation" (San Francisco 49ers) and the "Tomahawk Nation" (Florida Seminoles), to Rupert Murdoch's "FOX Nation" and its satirical counterpart, Stephen Colbert's "Colbert Nation." With a simple Google search one sees scattered among these groups various official American Indian tribal nation websites, and wonders how best to describe the irony of it all. It seems that not only do we live in a world of states, where "[v]irtually every landmass on the globe is now the territory of some state" (Morris 1998: 1), but we are also living in a world of nations, where "nationhood" has become a matter of quick-and-easy group self-identification. Although on the surface this may appear as an issue of trivial trends in popular nomenclature, the widespread appropriation of the term "nation" carries with it the notion that nationhood can equate to simply membership in a group. It is not a far stretch to see how this mentality could reinforce hostile attempts by state legislators to "restructure the organization of geographical scale" (Silvern 1999: 640) and bolster anti-Indian organizations' perception of American Indian nations as interest groups that argue for "special rights."[14]

This chapter has proposed that indigenous political formations offer both difference from, and engagement with, dominant political systems. I have intended to show that "indigenous states" represent not merely replications of a flawed form, but new articulations that have the potential to transform how people think about international relations.[15] Of course, an

---

[14] For example, Oklahoma's 'One Nation United' (www.onenationunited.com). See also Silvern (2002) for a discussion of the 'equal footing' doctrine in the context of Anishinaabe fishing rights in Wisconsin.

[15] One question that remains is: should these formations still be called 'states,' given the negative connotations associated with the term? Perhaps better terminology exists, but the term 'indigenous state' itself seems to encapsulate my argument – that the articulation of this form by indigenous peoples necessitates its modification.

"indigenous state" is only one among many possibilities for indigenous political expression. As anthropologist Thomas Biolsi (2005) has shown, multiple "geographies" exist in which indigenous peoples can articulate political subjectivity. Furthermore, I do not wish to ignore the potential contributions of indigenous political formations that reject state forms. The vision of scholars such as Taiaiake Alfred are promising and relevant to some indigenous situations. But instead of dismissing indigenous governments that resemble the state form, it is important to study their internal deliberations, and in the process ask: how do they engage with their citizens and communities as these forms expand? And, further, what social and cultural mechanisms exist for tribal citizens and communities to hold such structures accountable to their needs and to their identity as a people? Indigenous nations might discover lasting solutions to crises in contemporary tribal governance as they address these questions in accordance with community protocols (one example being the elders' group meetings I described earlier). Additionally, the development and articulation of indigenous states could create new opportunities for indigenous nations to change the nature of global politics, offering different standards of governance that are not based in the philosophies of imperial states or centered on imperial control.

References

Alfred, Gerald R. (Taiaiake) 1995. *Heeding the Voices of our Ancestors: Kahnawake Mohawk Politics and the Rise of Native Nationalism.* Oxford University Press.

Alfred, Taiaiake 1999. *Peace, Power, Righteousness: An Indigenous Manifesto.* Oxford University Press.

2005. *Wasase: Indigenous Pathways of Action and Freedom.* Orchard Park, NY: Broadview Press.

Anaya, S. James 2004. *Indigenous Peoples in International Law.* 2nd edn. Oxford University Press.

2005. "Divergent Discourses about International Law, Indigenous Peoples, and Rights over Lands and Natural Resources: Toward a Realist Trend." *Colorado Journal of International Environmental Law and Policy* 16(2): 237–58.

Barker, Joanne 2005. "For Whom Sovereignty Matters," in Barker (ed.), *Sovereignty Matters: Locations of Contestation and Possibility in Indigenous Struggles for Self-Determination.* Lincoln: University of Nebraska Press, pp. 1–31.

Barsh, Russel Lawrence 1994. "Indigenous Peoples in the 1990s: From Object to Subject of International Law?" *Harvard Human Rights Journal* 7: 33–86.

Bhabha, Homi K. 1994. *The Location of Culture.* New York: Routledge.

Biolsi, Thomas 2005. "Imagined Geographies: Sovereignty, Indigenous Space, and American Indian Struggle." *American Ethnologist* 32(2): 239–59.

Bom, Philip C. 2010. "Obama and 'First Americans.'" *American Thinker* (online magazine), www.americanthinker.com/2010/02/obama_and_first_americans. html (posted February 13, accessed February 28, 2010).

Brown, Michael F. 2007. "Sovereignty's Betrayals," in Marisol de la Cadena and Orin Starn (eds.), *Indigenous Experience Today*. Oxford and New York: Berg Publishers, pp. 171–94.

Bruyneel, Kevin 2007. *The Third Space of Sovereignty: The Postcolonial Politics of U.S.-Indigenous Relations*. Minneapolis: University of Minnesota Press.

Bryan, Joe 2009. "Where Would We Be without Them? Knowledge, Space and Power in Indigenous Politics." *Futures* 41: 24–32.

Carroll, Clint R. 2011. "Re-imagining Community: Political Ecology and Indigenous State Formation in the Cherokee Nation," Ph.D. dissertation, Department of Environmental Science, Policy and Management, University of California-Berkeley.

Champagne, Duane 1992. *Social Order and Political Change: Constitutional Governments among the Cherokee, the Choctaw, the Chickasaw, and the Creek*. Palo Alto: Stanford University Press.

Clifford, James 2001. "Indigenous Articulations." *Contemporary Pacific* 13(2): 468–90.

    2003. *On the Edges of Anthropology (Interviews)*. Chicago: Prickly Paradigm Press.

Coffey, Wallace, and Rebecca Tsosie 2001. "Rethinking the Tribal Sovereignty Doctrine: Cultural Sovereignty and the Collective Future of Indian Nations." *Stanford Law and Policy Review* 12(2): 191–221.

Connor, Walker 1994. *Ethnonationalism: The Quest for Understanding*. Princeton University Press.

Corrigan, Philip 1990. *Social Forms/Human Capacities: Essays in Authority and Difference*. London and New York: Routledge.

Corrigan, Philip, and Derek Sayer 1985. *The Great Arch: English State Formation as Cultural Revolution*. Oxford: Basil Blackwell.

Dean, Mitchell 1999. *Governmentality: Power and Rule in Modern Society*. London and Thousand Oaks, CA: Sage Publications.

Debo, Angie 1940. *And Still the Waters Run: The Betrayal of the Five Civilized Tribes*. Princeton University Press.

Foucault, Michel 1972. *The Archaeology of Knowledge*. New York: Pantheon.

    2003. *Society Must Be Defended: Lectures at the Collège de France, 1975–76*. London and New York: Penguin.

Gearing, Fred O. 1962. "Priests and Warriors: Social Structures for Cherokee Politics in the 18th Century." *American Anthropological Association Memoir* 93 64(5), part 2.

Hagen, Robert 2007. "Explanation of Vote by Robert Hagen, US Adviser, on the Declaration on the Rights of Indigenous Peoples, to the UN General Assembly." US Mission to the United Nations, New York, September 13.

Hall, Stuart 1986. "On Postmodernism and Articulation: An Interview with Stuart Hall." *Journal of Communication Inquiry* 10(45): 45–60.

Hansen, Thomas Blom, and Finn Stepputat 2001. "Introduction," in Hansen and Stepputat (eds.), *States of Imagination: Ethnographic Explorations of the Postcolonial State*. Durham, NC: Duke University Press, pp. 1–38.

Hanson, Randel D. 2004. "Contemporary Globalization and Tribal Sovereignty," in Thomas Biolsi (ed.), *A Companion to the Anthropology of American Indians*. Malden, MA: Blackwell Publishing, pp. 284–303.

Johnson, Jay T. 2008. "Indigeneity's Challenges to the White Settler-State: Creating a Thirdspace for Dynamic Citizenship." *Alternatives* 23: 29–52.

Lemont, Eric 2006. "Overcoming the Politics of Reform: The Story of the Cherokee Nation of Oklahoma Constitutional Convention," in Eric Lemont (ed.), *American Indian Constitutional Reform and the Rebuilding of Native Nations*. Austin: University of Texas Press, pp. 287–322.

Li, Tania Murray 2005. "Beyond 'the State' and Failed Schemes." *American Anthropologist* 107(3): 383–94.

Maaka, Roger, and Augie Fleras 2000. "Engaging with Indigeneity: Tino Rangatiratanga in Aotearoa," in Duncan Ivison, Paul Patton and Will Sanders (eds.), *Political Theory and the Rights of Indigenous Peoples*. Cambridge University Press, pp. 89–109.

McLoughlin, William G. 1986. *Cherokee Renascence in the New Republic*. Princeton University Press.

Migdal, Joel S. 1997. "Studying the State," in Mark Irving Lichbach, and Alan S. Zuckerman (eds.), *Comparative Politics: Rationality, Culture, and Structure*. Cambridge University Press, pp. 208–38.

Moreton-Robinson, Aileen (ed.) 2007. *Sovereign Subjects: Indigenous Sovereignty Matters*. Crows Nest, NSW: Allen & Unwin.

Morris, Christopher W. 1998. *An Essay on the Modern State*. Cambridge University Press.

Newcomb, Steven 2010. "Has US Changed Position on Declaration? Not Really." *Indian Country Today* December 31.

Nietschmann, Bernard 1994. "The Fourth World: Nations Versus States," in G. Demko and W. Wood (eds.), *Reordering the World: Geopolitical Perspectives on the Twenty-First Century*. Boulder: Westview, pp. 225–42.

Niezen, Ronald 2003. *The Origins of Indigenism: Human Rights and the Politics of Identity*. Berkeley: University of California Press.

O'Neill, Colleen 2004. "Rethinking Modernity and the Discourse of Development in American Indian History, an Introduction," in Brian Hosmer and Colleen O'Neill (eds.), *Native Pathways: American Indian Culture and*

Economic Development in the Twentieth Century. Boulder: University Press of Colorado, pp. 1–24.

Ostrom, Elinor 1990. *Governing the Commons: The Evolution of Institutions for Collective Action.* Cambridge University Press.

Ove Varsi, Magne 2009. "Draft American Declaration on the Rights of Indigenous Peoples Moves Forward." Galdu (online resource), www.galdu.org (posted January 12, 2009, accessed February 28, 2010).

Porter, Robert B. 1999. "The Demise of the Ongwehoweh and the Rise of the Native Americans: Redressing the Genocidal Act of Forcing American Citizenship upon Indigenous Peoples." *Harvard BlackLetter Journal* 15: 107–83.

Ranco, Darren 2007. "The Indian Ecologist and the Politics of Representation: Critiquing *The Ecological Indian* in the Age of Ecocide," in Michael E. Harkin and David Rich Lewis (eds.), *Native Americans and the Environment: Perspectives on the Ecological Indian.* Lincoln: University of Nebraska Press, pp. 32–51.

Ranco, Darren, and Dean Suagee 2007. "Tribal Sovereignty and the Problem of Difference in Environmental Regulation: Observations on 'Measured Separatism' in Indian Country." *Antipode* 39(4): 691–707.

Rose, Nikolas 1996. *Foucault and Political Reason: Liberalism, Neo-liberalism and Rationalities of Government.* University of Chicago Press.

    1999. *Powers of Freedom: Reframing Political Thought.* Cambridge University Press.

Sahlins, Marshall 1993. "Goodbye to Triste Tropes: Ethnography in the Context of Modern World History." *Journal of Modern World History* 65: 1–25.

    1999. "What Is Anthropological Enlightenment? Some Lessons of the Twentieth Century." *Annual Review of Anthropology* 28: i–xiii.

Scott, James C. 1998. *Seeing Like a State: How Certain Schemes to Improve the Human Condition Have Failed.* New Haven: Yale University Press.

Shaw, Karena 2008. *Indigeneity and Political Theory: Sovereignty and the Limits of the Political.* New York: Routledge.

Silvern, Steven 1999. "Scales of Justice: Law, American Indian Treaty Rights and the Political Construction of Scale." *Political Geography* 18(6): 639–68.

    2002. "State Centrism, the Equal-Footing Doctrine, and the Historical-Legal Geographies of American Indian Treaty Rights." *Historical Geography* 30: 33–58.

Smith, Neil 1992. "Geography, Difference, and the Politics of Scale," in Joe Doherty, Elspeth Graham, and Mo Malek (eds.), *Postmodernism and the Social Sciences.* London: Macmillan, pp. 57–79.

State Department, United States 2011. "Announcement of US Support for the United Nations Declaration on the Rights of Indigenous Peoples." www.state.gov/s/srgia/154553.htm.

Strickland, Rennard, and William M. Strickland 1991. "Beyond the Trail of Tears: One Hundred Fifty Years of Cherokee Survival," in William Anderson (ed.),

Cherokee Removal: Before and After. Athens: University of Georgia Press, pp. 112–38.

Sturm, Circe 2002. *Blood Politics: Race, Culture, and Identity in the Cherokee Nation of Oklahoma.* Berkeley: University of California Press.

Swyngedouw, Erik 1997. "Neither Global nor Local: 'Glocalization' and the Politics of Scale," in Kevin R. Cox (ed.), *Spaces of Globalization.* New York: Guilford Press, pp. 137–66.

Thomas, Nicholas 1994. *Colonialism's Culture: Anthropology, Travel and Government.* Princeton University Press.

Tsing, Anna Lowenhaupt 2007. "Indigenous Voice," in Marisol de la Cadena and Orin Starn (eds.), *Indigenous Experience Today.* Oxford and New York: Berg, pp. 33–67.

Tullberg, Steven M. 1995. "Indigenous Peoples, Self-Determination and the Unfounded Fear of Secession." *Indigenous Affairs* Jan/Feb/Mar 1: 11–13.

Tully, James 2000. "The Struggles of Indigenous Peoples for and of Freedom," in Duncan Ivison, Paul Patton, and Will Sanders (eds.), *Political Theory and the Rights of Indigenous Peoples.* Cambridge University Press, pp. 36–59.

Wilkinson, Charles F. 1987. *American Indians, Time, and the Law.* New Haven: Yale University Press.

Williams, Robert A. Jr. 1990. "Encounters on the Frontiers of International Human Rights Law: Redefining the Terms of Indigenous Peoples' Survival in the World." *Duke Law Journal* 4: 660–704.

6

The freedom to pass and repass: can the UN Declaration on the Rights of Indigenous Peoples keep the US–Canadian border ten feet above our heads?

CARRIE E. GARROW

Introduction

Our Haudenosaunee[1] elders teach us that when the international border was drawn through our territories by the United States and Britain, the agreement was that the border was to be ten feet above our heads. It did not apply to the Haudenosaunee people. We were and are not citizens of the United States, Britain, or Canada. The border was not to entangle us as we moved between Haudenosaunee territories and exercised our right to engage in our political, social, and economic institutions. The Jay Treaty, entered into by the United States and Britain, acknowledged our right to freely pass and repass.

Over two hundred years later, the border entangles us more and more. We are required to provide more secure forms of identification to cross into the United States.[2] If you are a Haudenosaunee person in Canada, the identification cards come with the flag of Canada affixed to them, certifying that you are part of Canada. The right to bring goods duty-free across the border is no longer recognized as one of our rights. In summer 2009 Canada closed the border crossing through Akwesasne as the Mohawks refused to allow Canadian border patrols to carry guns within Mohawk

---

[1] The Haudenosaunee (People of the Longhouse) or Six Nations Confederacy are the Mohawk, Seneca, Oneida, Onondaga, Cayuga, and Tuscarora Nations.

[2] The Intelligence Reform and Terrorism Prevention Act of 2004 (IRTPA) changed the requirements for entry into the United States. The Act requires individuals to possess a passport to cross the border into the United States. PL 108–408, 118 Stat. 3638. See also Documents Required for Travel within the Western Hemisphere, 70 Fed. Reg. 52, 037 (Sept. 1, 2005) (to be codified at 8 CFR Chapter 1 and 22 CFR Chapter 1).

territory.[3] Now the border checkpoint has been moved off Mohawk territory, but Canada seizes the vehicles of Mohawks who refuse to travel outside their territory to report their entry into their own homelands.[4] On June 18, 2011, Canadian border officials confiscated the Haudenosaunee passport of Joyce King, the director of the Justice Department for the Mohawk Council of Akwesasne, as its status according to the Canadian government is a "fantasy document."[5]

The United Nations' adoption of the Declaration on the Rights of Indigenous Peoples "vindicates their international strategy and evidences the extent to which they have penetrated institutions that were previously reserved for States; in addition, it demonstrates their faith in the international legal project."[6] But the question remains, can the Declaration be used as a tool in the battle to defend our Jay Treaty rights to cross the US–Canadian border freely? This chapter examines a practical application of the Declaration and whether it can assist us in our battle to protect our rights to pass freely under a border ten feet above our heads. Section 2 briefly examines how the United States and Canada have interpreted our right to freely pass and repass over the border. Section 3 addresses what protection the UN Declaration on the Rights of Indigenous Peoples might provide. Section 4 concludes with our next steps in the battle to keep the border above our heads.

The Jay Treaty

In 1794 Britain and the United States entered into the Jay Treaty to avert another war.[7] Britain was maintaining posts south of the newly formed border to support its Indian allies and protect its access to trade routes

---

[3] Brian Mann, "Mohawk Protests Close US–Canada Border Crossing," NPR, June 11, 2009, www.npr.org/templates/story/story.php?storyId=105210542.

[4] Kevin Lajoie, "'Grace Period' for Natives," *Standard Freeholder,*www.standard-freeholder. com/ArticleDisplay.aspx?archive=true&e=1768726www.vancouversun.com/news/Mov ing+Canadian+border+post+still+option+union/2295248/story. l.

[5] ICTMN Staff, "Canadian Feds Still Holding Iroquois Passport," *Indian Country Today*, July 12, 2011, indiancountrytodaymedianetwork.com/2011/07/canadian-feds-still-holding-iroquois-passport/.

[6] Stephen Allen, "The UN Declaration on the Rights of Indigenous Peoples and the Limits of the International Legal Project in the Indigenous Context," in Stephen Allen and Alexandra Xanthaxi, eds., *Reflections on the United Nations Declaration on the Rights of Indigenous Peoples and International Law* (Oxford: Hart Publishing, 2011), electronic copy available at papers.ssrn.com/sol3/papers.cfm?abstract_id=1497946.

[7] Carl Benn, *The Iroquois in the War of 1812*, 22 (University of Toronto Press,1998).

and British lands, in violation of the Treaty of Paris.[8] During this time tensions between the Indian nations, particularly the Haudenosaunee, and the United States were also high as the United States continued to confiscate Indian lands and force Indians on to reservations.[9] The United States authorized John Jay in treaty negotiations to concede to Britain the formation of an Indian state.[10] But Britain, in another act of betrayal of its Indian allies, failed to push for the Indian state.[11] However, in addition to keeping the peace between the United States and Britain, the United States and Britain agreed in the Jay Treaty to recognize that

> Indians dwelling on either side of the said boundary line, freely to pass and repass by land or inland navigation, into the respective territories and countries of the two parties, on the continent of America ... and to navigate all the lakes, rivers and waters thereof, and freely to carry on trade and commerce with each other ... nor shall the Indians passing or repassing with their own proper goods and effects of whatever nature, pay for the same any impost or duty whatever. But goods in bales, or other large packages, unusual among Indians, shall not be considered as goods belonging bona fide to Indians.[12]

Subsequent treaties between the United States and Britain affirmed the Indian rights acknowledged in the Jay Treaty. The Treaty of 1796 acknowledged the right of Indians to freely pass, and carry on trade and commerce, and provided that stipulations in treaties with Indian nations could not be interpreted in such a way as to lessen the right to free intercourse and commerce.[13] In 1814 the Treaty of Ghent reaffirmed Indian rights recognized by the Jay Treaty by agreeing to restore all rights to nations which they enjoyed or were entitled to prior to the war of 1812.[14]

---

[8] Ibid., at 18. See also *McCandless* v. *US*, 25 F.2d 71, 72 (3rd Cir. 1928), where the Third Circuit Court of Appeals also acknowledged that the "Six Nations resented the establishment of any boundary line through their territory which would restrict intercourse and free passage to their people, and remonstrance was made to the assumption of sovereignty over what they regarded, and then occupied, as their own. See *Makers of Canada*, vol. 3, p. 256. The situation was met by the two countries inserting the article quoted (Article III) in the treaty."

[9] Benn, *supra* note 7, at 20.

[10] Paul Williams, "Treaty Making: The Legal Record," in G. Peter Jemison and Anna M. Schein, eds., *Treaty of Canandaigua 1794: 200 years of Treaty Relations between the Iroquois and the United States* (Santa Fe, NM: Clear Light Publishing, 2000), 37–38.

[11] Ibid.

[12] Treaty of Amity, Commerce and Navigation, Art. III, 1794.

[13] Treaty of 1796. See also *McCandless*, *supra* note 8, at 72.

[14] Paul Spruhan, "The Canadian Indian Free Passage Right: The Last Stronghold of Explicit Race Restrict in United States Immigration Law," 301 *North Dakota Law Review* 301 (2009), 304.

Although no Haudenosaunee nations or any other Indian nations were signatories to any of these treaties, they are critical affirmation of Indian rights by the United States and Britain. These treaties acknowledge that Indian nations existed across the North American continent prior to the formation of the British colonies. As a result, the residents of these lands, or indigenous peoples, have a right to cross the newly formed border to access their lands, families, and political, economic, and social institutions. Without recognition of the right to freely pass and engage in trade, the Indian nations, particularly the Haudenosaunee, may have been pushed closer to war in an effort to maintain their lands and economies.[15] By acknowledging our border-crossing rights, the United States and Britain recognized our rights as sovereign nations to freely access our territories, and thus placed the border ten feet above our heads.

US interpretation of the Jay Treaty

The Jay Treaty is still acknowledged by the United States as a treaty in effect.[16] However, the United States has altered its interpretation of our rights to pass freely across the border and engage in trade. The 1924 Immigration Act restricted the right to enter United States only to those who were eligible for naturalization[17] – essentially whites and those of African descent.[18] The end result was that Indian peoples were stopped at the US border, as they were not eligible for naturalization. This was challenged by Paul Diabo, a Mohawk ironworker born in Canada who made

---

[15] While the Jay Treaty was being negotiated, the Six Nations were negotiating the Treaty of Canandaigua with Timothy Pickering of the United States. The United States was nervous that the Six Nations were going to join the Indian nations in Ohio country who had gone to war against the United States. In 1791 in Ohio country, the United States lost half of its standing army. The Nations had gathered in Ohio and wanted a territory for all Indian nations and were making a stand to defend this land. See Williams, *supra* note 10, at 38. Thus, the United States was prepared to concede to an Indian state in the Jay Treaty negotiations, because they knew that if the Haudenosaunee were angry and joined the Indian war, the United States might not be able to win. Britain did not push for this independent state, but merely the recognition of border-crossing rights, in which the United States was happy to acquiesce.

[16] US Department of State, Treaties in Force, A list of Treaties and Other International Agreements of the United States in Force on January 1, 2011, p. 287, available at www.state.gov/documents/organization/169274.pdf.

[17] Immigration Act of 1924, ch. 190 s. 13(c), 43 Stat. 153, 162, repealed; Immigration and Nationality Act of 1952, Pul. L. 82–414 s. 403, 66 Stat. 163, 279. See also Spruhan, *supra* note 14, 306.

[18] Spruhan, *supra* note 14, 306.

trips into the United States to work. Although he had crossed the border numerous times prior to the adoption of the new law, he was now refused entry. Holding that the Jay Treaty was still in force and there was no justification for the arrest and deportation of Diabo, the court in *McCandless* noted that:

> Evidently that article [of the Jay Treaty] did not create the right of the Indian to pass over land actually in their possession, for, subject to the general dominant right of sovereignty claimed by all European nations based on discovery, the right of the Indian to possess the soil until he surrendered his right by sale or treaty has been recognized.[19]

Almost simultaneously Congress passed legislation exempting Indians from the 1924 Immigration Act.[20] In the process of exempting Indians from the 1924 Act, Congress also imposed the first limitation on our border-crossing rights by not including individuals whose Indian citizenship was due to adoption.[21] Congress amended the legislation in 1952 and imposed another limitation, requiring a 50 percent blood quantum to pass freely.[22]

Since the recognition by *McCandless* that the Jay Treaty did not create our border-crossing rights, the courts have become less receptive to these rights. They now question whether it is an inherent aboriginal right or treaty right, and claim our border-crossing right as a statutory right granted through Congressional legislation.[23] Some courts have found that the rights acknowledged in the Jay Treaty were terminated by the war of 1812 and that the Treaty of Ghent was not implemented by congressional

---

[19] *McCandless, supra* note 8.
[20] Act of April 2, 1928, ch. 308, 45 Stat. at 401.   [21] Ibid.
[22] 8 USC 1359. See also Spruhan, *supra* note 14, at 317 (discussing the US shift from a political definition of "Indian" to a racial definition of "Indian", as well as his discussion of how this is a difficult limitation to apply, as Canada does not measure blood quantum).
[23] See *McCandless* v. *United States, supra* note 8; *US* v. *Mrs. P. L. Garrow*, 88 F.2d 318 (US Court of Customs and Patent Appeals 1937); *US* v. *Karnuth*, 74 F. Supp. 660 (District Court Western New York 1914); *Akins* v. *United States*, 551 F.2d 1222 (US Court of Customs and Patent Appeals 1977); *US* v. *Curnew*, 788 F.2d 1335 (8th Cir. 1986). See also Bryan Nickels, "Native American Free Passage Rights Under the 1794 Jay Treaty: Survival under United States Statutory Law and Canadian Common Law," 24 *Boston College International and Comparative Law Review*, 313 (2001); Sharon O'Brien, "The Medicine Line: A Border Dividing Tribal Sovereignty, Economies and Families," 53 *Fordham Law Review* 315 (1984); Richard Osburn, "Problems and Solutions Regarding Indigenous Peoples Split by International Borders," 24 *American Indian Law Review* 471 (1999/2000); Marcia Yablon-Zug, "Gone but not Forgotten: The Strange Afterlife of the Jay Treaty's Indian Free Passage Right," 33 *Queen's Law Journal* 565 (2008).

legislation, thus these treaty rights are not recognized.[24] Moreover, courts have found that the right to cross is based upon race, not our political status or citizenship in an Indian nation.[25] Finally, courts have ruled that Congress has changed its policy regarding collection of duty and no longer recognizes the right to bring goods duty-free across the border or engage in trade.[26]

Canada's interpretation of the Jay Treaty

Canada, which succeeded to the treaty through its independence in 1912,[27] has been even less honorable in its recognition of the right of Indian peoples to freely cross the border and engage in trade.[28] Canada has not codified any recognition of the rights under the Jay Treaty, thus the Canadian legislature remains silent about Canada's obligations under the treaty.

As a result, Canadian courts claim that the Jay Treaty is not enforceable because it has not been implemented or sanctioned by Canadian legislation.[29] This results in a refusal to acknowledge border crossing as a treaty right, but rather as a limited form of aboriginal rights.[30] And to prove the existence of an aboriginal right, courts require Indian peoples to prove a historical and continuing nexus relationship to Canada and in the specific area within which they cross.[31] Canadian courts have also rejected the right to free passage of goods.[32] Moreover, in *Mitchell*, the Court stated that Mitchell did not prove his claim to an aboriginal right to bring goods across the border, because trade was not vital to the Mohawks' collective identity,[33] ignoring the fact that the right to trade was one of the reasons the Jay Treaty acknowledged border-crossing rights.

---

[24] *United States* v. *Garrow*, 88 F.3d 318, 418 (United States Court of Customs and Patent Appeals 1937).

[25] *United States* v. *Karnuth*, 74 Supp. 660, 663 (WDNY 1947).

[26] *US* v. *Garrow*, *supra* note 24; *Akins* v. *Saxbe*, 380 F. Supp. 1210 (D. Maine, 1974).

[27] See the following section on succession to treaties.

[28] See Nickels, *supra* note 23, 327–34.

[29] *Francis I*, [1956] SCR 618, 620; *Vincent*, 1993 TTR LEXIS 7, 11; See also Kerry Wilkins, "'Still Crazy After All These Years': Section 88 of the Indian Act at Fifty," 38 *Alberta Law Review* 458 (2000).

[30] *Francis I*, *supra* note 29, at 620.

[31] Nickels, *supra* note 23, at 315; *Watt* v. *Liebelt* (1998) [1999] 169 DLR (4th) 336 at 348.

[32] *Francis I*, *supra* note 29.

[33] *Mitchell* v. *MNR*, 2001 Can. Sup. Ct. Lexis 35; 2001 SCC 33 (2001).

The UN Declaration on the Rights of Indigenous Peoples and border-crossing rights

As illustrated by the case law noted above, indigenous peoples in the United States and Canada have continually sought out forums to protect their border-crossing rights. The UN Declaration may provide a valuable tool in our fight to protect these rights. The Declaration recognizes the urgent need to respect and promote the rights of indigenous peoples "affirmed in treaties, agreements and other constructive arrangement with states."[34] It also acknowledges our rights to access our political, economic, and social institutions, as well as the right to cross international borders cutting through our territories. In the discussion of what kind of tool the Declaration is to protect indigenous rights, many scholars quickly jump into the discussion of whether the Declaration is customary international law and binding upon the states.[35] We will leave that debate to those scholars and simply acknowledge that many scholars believe the Declaration is at best customary international law and at its least a standard nation states should strive to achieve.[36] More pertinent to our discussion is whether the Declaration *should* be used to defend the rights in question. Not all indigenous peoples, including the Haudenosaunee, ascribe to the Western understanding of human rights. Moreover, much of Western law fails to encompass indigenous notions of sovereignty and embraces only a limited definition. Thus an examination of whether the

---

[34] United Nations Declaration on the Rights of Indigenous Peoples (hereafter Declaration), Art. 37, at 17.

[35] S. James Anaya and Siegfried Wiessner, "The UN Declaration on the Rights of Indigenous Peoples: Towards Re-empowerment," *Jurist 2007*, http://jurist.law.pitt.edu/forumy/2007/10/un-declaration-on-rights-of-indigenous.php; Siegfried Wiessner, "Rights and Status of Indigenous Peoples: A Global Comparative and International Legal Analysis," 12 *Harvard Human Rights Journal* 57 (1999); S. James Anaya, *Indigenous Peoples in International Law*, 2nd edn (Oxford University Press, 2004); Stephen Allen, "The UN Declaration on the Rights of Indigenous Peoples: Towards a Global Legal Order on Indigenous Rights?," in A. Halpin and V. Roeben (eds.), *Theorising the Global Legal Order* (Oxford: Hart Publishing, 2009).

[36] Anaya and Wiessner, *supra* note 35, at 2; James (Sákéj) Youngblood Henderson, *Indigenous Diplomacy and the Rights of Peoples: Achieving UN Recognition* (Saskatoon: Purich Publishing Limited, 2008), 51; Permanent Forum on Indigenous Issues, Eighth Session, Item 7 of the provisional agenda, A Draft Guide on the Relevant Principles Contained in the United Nations Declaration on the Rights of Indigenous Peoples, International Labour Organization Convention No. 169 and International Labour Organization Convention No. 107 that Relate to Indigenous Land Tenure and Management Arrangements, 9; 61st Session of the UN General Assembly, 107th and 108th Plenary Meetings, GA/10612, September 13, 2007, 2; Allen, *supra* note 35, at 5.

Declaration supports the indigenous political philosophy and definition of indigenous rights and sovereignty is addressed first.

Indigenous political philosophy and the UN Declaration

International law was and is the foundation of colonization, as it "facilitated colonial patterns promoted by European states."[37] For many years, international law promulgated notions of Western, state-centered sovereignty, that Indian nations lacked sovereignty, and, as a result, indigenous peoples were barred from a seat at the League of Nations and the United Nations.[38] Today indigenous peoples have gained a limited voice and have contributed to the adoption of the ILO Convention on Indigenous and Tribal Peoples, Convention No. 69, and the UN Declaration.[39] However, international law, as well as most domestic law, is entrenched in Western political philosophy, which is often radically different from indigenous political philosophies and thus indigenous notions of rights and sovereignty. For example, Western political philosophy "define[s] man in terms of individualism, competition, and self-interest, [while] traditional Indian philosophies define man in terms of spiritual unity, consensus, co-operation, and self-denial. In short, the western-liberal tradition and Native American tribal philosophies represent two very different theories of the nature of mankind."[40] The beliefs focused on peace and fostered by consensus and cooperation lead to subordinating the individual to the community.[41] As a result, indigenous human rights often focus on the community, and the individual is the "repository of responsibilities rather than ... a claimant of rights. Rights can exist only in the measure to which each person fulfils his responsibilities toward others. That is, rights are an outgrowth of every person's performing his obligation in the cosmic order. In such a society there is no concept of inherent individual claims to inalienable rights."[42]

With regard to sovereignty, Canada and the United States illustrate Western states' move from an acknowledgment of full sovereignty

---

[37] Anaya, *Indigenous Peoples, supra* note 35, 15.

[38] Deskaheh, a Cayuga chief, petitioned the League of Nations for entry in 1923 but was denied. See Laurence M. Hauptman, *Seven Generations of Iroquois Leadership, The Six Nations Since 1800* (Syracuse University Press, 2008), 124–42.

[39] Anaya, *Indigenous Peoples in International Law, supra* note 35, 58–72.

[40] Menno Boldt and J. Anthony Long, "Tribal Philosophies and the Canadian Charter of Rights and Freedoms," in Boldt and Long (eds.), *The Quest for Justice: Aboriginal Peoples and Aboriginal Rights* (University of Toronto Press,1985), 167.

[41] Ibid., at 166.   [42] Ibid.

to Indian nations as "domestic dependents" that may only exercise limited sovereignty within their own boundaries and only over their own citizens.[43] Whereas Indian nations believe their sovereignty still exists, limits are continually placed on civil and criminal jurisdiction,[44] economic development,[45] adoption of laws,[46] and the alienation of lands without the consent of the United States and Canada.[47]

Haudenosaunee political philosophy illustrates the difference between Western and indigenous philosophies on rights and sovereignty. The Guswentah or Two Row Wampum made between the Haudenosaunee and the Dutch in 1677 acknowledges our sovereignty. The wampum belt contains two rows of purple wampum separated by three rows of white wampum. The purple wampum rows represent the Haudenosaunee's canoe and the Dutch ship side by side; neither path nor nation would cross or would try to interfere with or steer the other's vessel. The three rows of white wampum in between the purple rows represent peace, friendship, and respect.[48]

The Covenant Chain illustrates our political philosophy as well. The Covenant Chain was an alliance between the Haudenosaunee and British colonies. The first link in the three-link chain represents friendship and the second link peace, and the third link means that it will always be the same between the parties.[49] "All decisions were made by consultation and treaty, and all were implemented by each member individually."[50] Incorporating the Haudenosaunee principle of sovereignty and renewal, the allies agreed to respect each other's sovereignty and have their vessels side by side, but not interfere in one another's way of life.[51] The agreement

---

[43] *Cherokee Nation* v. *State of Georgia*, 30 US 1 (1831); *Worcester* v. *State of Georgia*, 31 US 515 (1832).

[44] See, e.g., *Oliphant* v. *Squamish Indian Tribe*, 435 US 191 (1978).

[45] See, e.g., the Indian Gaming Regulatory Act, 25 USCA, ss. 2701–2721.

[46] Canada continually refuses to acknowledge the right of First Nations to adopt their own laws. And in the United States the Indian Reorganization Act provides for the adoption of tribal constitutions that includes the requirement of the Secretary of Interior's consent.

[47] *R* v. *St. Catherine's Milling & Lumber Co.*, 79 DLR 4th, 415 (1885); *Johnson* v. *McIntosh*, 21 US 543 (1823). See also Robert Odawi Porter, "The Inapplicability of American Law to the Indian Nations," 89 *Iowa Law Review* 1595 (2004), for a discussion on how federal Indian law has arbitrarily rationalized an assumption of power over Indian nations.

[48] Chief Irving Powless Jr., "Treaty Making," in Jemison and Schein, *supra* note 10, 23.

[49] Oren R. Lyons, "The American Indian in the Past," in Lyons et al. (eds.), *Exiled in Land of Free, Democracy, Indian Nations and the US Constitution* (1992), 40–42.

[50] Francis Jennings, "Iroquois Alliances in Canada," in Jennings (ed.), *The History and Culture of Iroquois Diplomacy* (1985), 37, 38.

[51] Lyons, *supra* note 49, at 40–42.

is represented by a white gold chain, because it will not tarnish.[52] The parties agreed to come together in the future to sit together and renew the agreement, and "if there is any dust on the chain we will polish it anew."[53] The Haudenosaunee Confederacy and the British colonies met on numerous occasions as sovereign entities to polish the chain and agree to subsequent treaties.[54]

Even today, the Guswentah and the Covenant Chain are the basis of the Haudenosaunee political philosophy and our political relations. Oren Lyons, Onondaga Nation Faith Keeper, explains:

> The ideas and principles expressed in the Silver Covenant Chain and other traditions of the Haudenosaunee have been central to our relations with other nations and states, whether Indian, European, or American. In these traditions, there is recognition that peoples are distinct from each other. However, since the beginning of our memory this distinctiveness has been seen as a foundation for mutual respect; and we have therefore always honored the fundamental right of peoples and their societies to be different. This is a profoundly important principle, and one which, even in the twentieth century, humans continue to struggle to realize.[55]

Thus for the Haudenosaunee the analysis must begin by examining whether the Declaration embraces our political philosophy illustrated by the Guswentah and the Covenant Chain; otherwise it will not be an effective tool. Any defense of our rights that supports only a limited notion of sovereignty or a Western notion of rights forces our paths to cross and gives up control of our canoe, our freedom, and our right to govern ourselves.

Indigenous scholars have noted that prior human rights documents, such as the Universal Declaration of Human Rights, are "essentially a western capitalist ideology and [are] not relevant to societies with a non-western, non-capitalist cultural tradition."[56] However, a close examination of the Declaration reveals that it is a step forward from many other Western human rights documents. Although the Declaration may not fully encompass the Haudenosaunee political metaphors, it does acknowledge indigenous peoples' right to self-determination by stating: "Indigenous peoples have the right to self-determination. By virtue of that right they freely determine their political status and freely pursue their

---

[52] Ibid., at 42.   [53] Ibid., at 40.
[54] G. Peter Jemison, "Sovereignty and Treaty Rights – We Remember," in Jemison and Schein, *supra* note 10, 149, 161.
[55] Lyons, *supra* note 49, 42.
[56] Boldt and Long, *supra* note 40, at 167.

economic, social and cultural development."[57] It also acknowledges that indigenous peoples "possess collective rights which are indispensable for their existence, well-being and integral development as peoples."[58] With the acknowledgement of the right to self-determination and our collective rights, the Declaration is supportive of Haudenosaunee political philosophy. The Declaration provides room for our right to be distinct, on our own path, and free from interference, and provides that these rights are held collectively by our nations. With this understanding as a foundation, we can move forward to an examination of what type of protection the Declaration provides for our border-crossing rights.

The application of the Declaration

Article 37

Focusing first on the protection of treaty rights, Article 37 of the Declaration acknowledges the right of indigenous peoples to the "recognition, observance and enforcement of treaties, agreements and other constructive arrangements concluded with States or their successors and to have States honour and respect such treaties, agreements and other constructive arrangements."[59] There are two aspects of treaty law that are pertinent to our discussion: who may benefit from the rights in the Jay Treaty and what the parties intended when they signed the treaty.

Third-party rights The difficulty with the Jay Treaty is that it is not an Indian treaty such as we typically encounter. Entered into by two non-indigenous sovereigns, Britain and the United States, which acknowledged our bordering cross rights, no Indian nation was a signatory to it. This does not necessarily weaken the right acknowledged within, but it makes it more difficult to enforce the right, as Indian nations were only third-party benefactors, and some may question whether this is the type of treaty the Declaration encompasses. However, the Declaration did not create new rights, but simply provides for the application of current law to indigenous peoples, including the application of international treaty law.[60] And international law requires that states must recognize, observe, and enforce treaties.[61] This principle is acknowledged by Article 37 of the

---

[57] Declaration, Art. 3, at 17. [58] Declaration, at 16.
[59] The Declaration, Art. 37, at 35. [60] Henderson, *supra* note 36, at 41.
[61] T. O. Elias, *The Modern Law of Treaties* (Dobbs Ferry, NY: Oceana, 1974), 40–45.

Declaration which states that Indian nations, as third parties to the Jay Treaty, are entitled to the protection of treaty rights under international law. Thus, whether or not Indian nations are a signatory, if under international law they are entitled to rights acknowledged by the Jay Treaty, they are entitled to the protection of international law and the Declaration. Moreover, because it is a treaty recognizing indigenous rights by two non-Indian nations, it must be analyzed under international law, rather than federal Indian law or domestic law as normally occurs.

The international law governing treaties is the 1969 Vienna Convention. The Convention does not apply retroactively, but rather customary law applies to treaties entered into prior to 1969.[62] However, because the Convention codified customary law it is typically relied upon in analyzing treaties entered into prior to its coming into force.

> When law of treaties questions arise during negotiations, whether for a new treaty or about one concluded before the entry into force of the Convention, the rules set forth in the Convention are invariably relied upon, even when the states are not parties to it ... Whether a particular rule in the Convention represents customary international law is only likely to be an issue if the matter is litigated, and even then the court or tribunal will take the Convention as its starting – and normally also its finishing – point. This is certainly the approach taken by the International Court of Justice, as well as other courts and tribunals, international and national.[63]

As Indian nations did not sign the Jay Treaty, they are considered to be third parties. The general rule is that a third party cannot be bound by a treaty without its consent.[64] "Given the essential element of express and mutual consent, treaties cannot, at their inception, bind third states."[65] Because they are not signatories, the Indian nations did not concede any changes or limitations to border-crossing rights. Rather, the United States and Britain were merely acknowledging these rights as they were understood at the time. By not consenting to the treaty, the Haudenosaunee and other Indian nations did not concede anything and are not bound by any limitations posed by the Jay Treaty or its signatories.

---

[62] Vienna Convention on the Law of Treaties, Art. 4; Anthony Aust, *Modern Treaty Law and Practice* (Cambridge University Press, 2007), 10.

[63] Aust, *supra* note 62, at 12–13.

[64] D. P. O'Connell, *International Law Volume 1* (Dobbs Ferry, NY: Oceana, 1965), 266.

[65] Mark E. Villiger, *Customary International Law and Treaties*, 2nd edn (Leiden and Boston, MA: Martinus Nijhoff, 1997), 130; Vienna Convention on the Law of Treaties, Art. 34.

However, a treaty may have an effect on third parties, particularly when it stipulates benefits to a third State. "[T]he third State upon acceptance of the benefit acquires legal rights itself."[66] The Convention acknowledges that a treaty does not create obligations or rights for a third state without its consent, but a right can arise "from a provision of a treaty if the parties to it so intend and the third state assents."[67] Assent is presumed unless the contrary is indicated, unless the treaty provides otherwise.[68] Upon assent, the third state is required to comply with any conditions contained within the treaty or established in conformity with the treaty.[69]

The Jay Treaty did not create rights, as Indigenous peoples were already crossing through this area; it was merely an acknowledgement of these rights. There were no conditions contained in the treaty that limited these rights or required proof of assent by the Indian nations. Assent is presumed because Indigenous peoples continued to cross, unaffected by the border, until the United States and Canada began to impose limitations. When the third party has claimed and enjoyed the right, "it is only just that the third state's concurrence should be obtained where it was intended not to be subject to revocation or modification."[70] If the United States and Britain wanted Indian nations' border-crossing rights to be revocable, they could have so specified in the treaty,[71] but they failed to do so. Now, if an existing rule of law contained within the Treaty is to be changed, then the parties must include express terms.[72]

Critical to the indigenous rights recognized by the Jay Treaty, third-party treaty rights or benefits involving navigation of international waterways or transit through territory receive special consideration. Rights of this nature "should have a measure of solidarity and firmness. The parties may not therefore revoke or modify rights if it is established that they were intended not to be revocable, or subject to amendment, without the consent of the third state (Article 37(2)). If the parties wish to have such options, they can provide for this in the treaty, or by other means, when creating them. If they have not done so, and if the treaty creates a status or regime which is valid *erga omnes* [for all the world], there is a presumption that the right cannot be changed without the consent of third states."[73]

---

[66] O'Connell, *supra* note 64, at 266.   [67] Aust, *supra* note 62, at 257.

[68] Vienna Convention on the Law of Treaties, Art. 36(1).

[69] Ibid., Art. 36(2).

[70] L. N. Mathur, "Treaties and Third States," in S. K. Agrawala (ed.), *Essays on the Law of Treaties* (1971), 53.

[71] Ibid.   [72] Lord McNair, *The Law of Treaties* 463 (Oxford: Clarendon, 1961).

[73] Aust, *supra* note 62, at 259.

As the nations assented to recognition of these rights by continuing to cross, they became third parties. Within the Jay Treaty there are no express terms indicating a process to alter these third-party rights. Moreover, as rights that involve transit through territory, they cannot be revoked or modified without our consent. Our nations have never consented to any limitations or alterations. We have continually defended our rights as they existed at the time of the Jay Treaty. Thus any subsequent alterations are treaty violations by the signatories to the Treaty – the United States and now Canada.

The intended meaning of "freely pass and repass"   When interpreting treaties, it is understood that every treaty has its own history and surrounding circumstances and context.[74] To understand the meaning of treaties, the intention of the parties is important and "their intention as expressed in the words used by them in the light of the surrounding circumstances."[75] Often the "interpretation placed upon a treaty provision at the time of the conclusion"[76] is important. The Vienna Convention focuses on three main elements when interpreting treaties, "the text, its context and the object and purpose of the treaty,"[77] as well as the circumstances of a treaty's conclusion to confirm the "meaning established by the text, its context and the object and purpose."[78] Conduct may also assist with understanding the treaty. "[T]he relevant conduct of the contracting parties after the conclusion of the treaty (sometimes called 'practical construction') has a high probative value as to the intention of the parties at the time of its conclusion."[79]

A treaty's context is critical and a treaty cannot be understood "in the abstract, only in the *context* of the treaty and in the light of its *object and purpose.*"[80] Regarding indigenous rights, the context is critical in

---

[74] Siegfried Weissner, "American Indian Treaties and International Law," 7 *St. Thomas Law Review* 567 (1995), 580; Vienna Convention on the Law of Treaties, Art. 32. Although the Vienna Convention does not apply to the Jay Treaty because the Jay Treaty was entered into prior to the Convention, the Convention codified existing customary law and many of the provisions have the force of customary international law, which is applicable to the United States. See Evan Criddle, "The Vienna Convention on the Law of Treaties in US Treaty Interpretation," 44 *Virginia Journal of International Law*, 431 (2004), 443.

[75] McNair, *supra* note 72, at 365 (footnote omitted).

[76] Ibid., at 431.

[77] Aust, *supra* note 62, at 234; Vienna Convention on the Law of Treaties, Art. 31.

[78] Vienna Convention on the Law of Treaties, Art. 32.

[79] McNair, *supra* note 72, at 424 (footnote omitted).

[80] Aust, *supra* note 62, at 235 (emphasis in original).

understanding treaties in order not to project the current status of indigenous peoples into the past and reframe or reverse their political standing at the time of the treaty. "A critical historiography of international relations clearly shows the dangers of this particular kind of reasoning, which projects into the past the current domesticated status of indigenous peoples as it evolved from developments that took place mainly in the second half of the nineteenth century under the impact of legal positivism and other theories advocated by European colonial powers and their continuators."[81]

Thoroughly examining the context and the conduct at the time of the signing of the Jay Treaty illustrates that Indian nations were treated as sovereign, with all the rights of sovereign nations, which includes accessing our lands, and political, economic, and social institutions. In his study on treaties, the Special Rapporteur on Human Rights concludes: "the main finding that emerges from works relates to the widespread recognition of 'overseas peoples' – including indigenous peoples in the current sense of the term – as sovereign entities by European powers and their successors, at least during the era of the Law of Nations."[82] The context illustrates that Indian nations were treated as sovereigns and allowed to freely pass as recognition of their territories which lay on both sides of the border. Haudenosaunee were continually accessing lands by crossing the under the border. Moreover, treaties are to be interpreted and applied against the backdrop of the general principles of international law.[83] At the time of the treaty, European nations engaged with the Indian nations as just that – nations. Nations possess rights and thus cannot be stripped of them arbitrarily and without their consent.

The Haudenosaunee engaged in numerous treaties with European states and the newly formed United States, including the Two Row Wampum or Guswentah and the 1794 Treaty of Canandaigua. It is no coincidence that news of the signing of the Jay Treaty by Britain and the United States came during negotiations between the United States, represented by Timothy Pickering, and the Haudenosaunee over the Treaty of Canandaigua. And prior to the Revolutionary War, Britain had also entered into numerous treaties with the nations to maintain their alliance through the Covenant Chain, both illustrating that the United States and Britain not

---

[81] Miguel Alfonso Martínez, Special Rapporteur on the human rights of indigenous peoples, *Study on Treaties, Agreements and other Constructive Arrangements between States and Indigenous Populations, Final Report*, UN Doc. E/CN.4/Sub.2/1999/20, para. 102.
[82] Ibid., para. 104.   [83] McNair, *supra* note 72, 466.

only understood that the Indian nations were sovereign, but acted on this understanding by entering into treaties with the Haudenosaunee at the time the Jay Treaty was signed.

The United States came to this same conclusion an 1892 report. "The conclusion is irresistible that the Six Nations are nations by treaty and law, and have long since been recognized as such by the United States and the state of New York, and an enlightened public will surely hesitate before proceeding to divest these people of long-established rights without their consent – rights recognized and confirmed in some cases by the immortal [George] Washington and by more than a hundred years of precedents and legislation."[84]

It is important to note that, not just historically but also today, international law provides recognition of Indian nations as nation states, and thus affords them the rights of third parties as discussed earlier. International law entails four requirements in determining whether an entity is a nation state: "(a) a permanent population; (b) a defined territory; (c) government; and (d) capacity to enter into relations with other States."[85] There is no question that each of the Haudenosaunee nations currently has a permanent population and a defined territory. Each nation defines its own citizenship laws and the Haudenosaunee Grand Council even issues passports to its citizens. All nations possess a defined territory; even the Cayuga Nation, which lost all of its land through illegal maneuvers by New York, today holds land again and is moving its people to that territory. Each Haudenosaunee nation possesses its own governing structures that regulate the affairs of the individual nations. And, as discussed above, the nations entered into treaties in the past, and today continue to enter into agreements with the United States and Canada. Even if one wants to concede that Indian nations are under the authority of the United States and Canada, which the Haudenosaunee have never conceded, they are still considered sovereigns under international law. "[T]oday it is commonly accepted that a 'sovereign' entity may be under

---

[84] Thomas Donaldson, Henry B. Carrington, and Timothy W. Jackson, United States Department of Commerce, Bureau of the Census, *Extra Census Bulletin: Indians, The Six Nations of New York* (1982; repr., with new introduction by Robert W. Venables, Ithaca: Cornell University Press, 1995), 4, cited in Robert Venables, "Some Observations on the Treaty of Canandaigua," in Jemison and Schein, *supra* note 10, 85.

[85] Montevideo Convention of 1933, Art. I, December 26, 1933, Inter-American, 49 Stat. 3097, 3100 TS No. 881; see also John Howard Clinebell and Jim Thomson, "Sovereignty and Self-Determination: The Rights of Native Americans Under International Law," in S. James Anaya (ed.), *International Law and Indigenous Peoples* (Aldershot: Dartmouth, 2003), 669.

the authority (*de jure* or *de facto*) of another, greater sovereign without losing its own 'sovereignty.' The prerogatives recognized by customary international law in favour of indigenous peoples ... translate into an obligation of territorial states to recognize them a given degree of autonomy, which actually amounts to sovereignty in the modern sense of the term."[86] But, given that the Haudenosaunee nations meet the standards under international law of a nation state, it is not necessary to concede to the US law's definition of domestic dependent nations which seeks to limit indigenous sovereignty. Moreover, the political existence of a state exists independently of its recognition by other states, and the rights of each do not depend upon the power which it possesses to assure its exercise.[87] Thus, even if Indian nations have difficulty exercising some of their rights due to the failure of the United States and Canada to recognize their full sovereignty, under international law the inability to exercise their rights as sovereigns does not weaken their existence.

Returning to the interpretation of the Jay Treaty, it was also the custom at the time of the formation of the treaty to allow Indian nations to cross the newly formed border. At the time the treaty was entered into, both the United States and Britain dealt with Indian nations as nations, and they both strove to curry favor with them in order to keep them as allies, or neutrals at the very least. Both the United States and Britain entered into treaties with the nations and were aware of their land base and that it was the custom of nations to move back and forth throughout their territories in order to access their lands and political, economic, and social systems. This custom was then formalized by the Jay Treaty. A custom formalized by a treaty "does no more than create exceptional law for the parties, or evidence a customary rule which would be applicable even in the absence of the treaty."[88] Moreover, "[o]nce treaty provisions have become law even repudiation of the treaty will not disengage the parties from liability thereunder."[89] Thus the United States and Canada are bound by their interpretation of these rights at the time they signed the treaty.

The conduct of the parties after the treaty's conclusion also demonstrates that there was no intent to limit these rights. After the treaty was concluded and even after the war of 1812 and its subsequent treaty, there was still no regulation of Indians crossing the border. Legal regulation

---

[86] Federico Lenzerini, "The Status of Indigenous Peoples in International Law," in Lenzerini (ed.), *Reparations for Indigenous Peoples, International and Comparative Perspectives* (Oxford University Press, 2008), 102.

[87] Montevideo Convention of 1933, Arts. 3 and 4.

[88] O'Connell, *supra* note 64, 24.   [89] Ibid., at 25.

did not appear until 1924, and this was accidental since the legislation aimed towards dealing with Asian immigration.[90] Although subsequent legislation to effectuate a treaty may be evidence of the treaty's meaning,[91] legislation specifically regulating the crossings by indigenous peoples did not occur until well over a hundred years after the enactment of the treaty. It was not until 1924, when the first legislative limitation occurred, and then in 1937 that the courts adopted a limitation on bringing goods duty-free across the border. More importantly, the legislation did not take place until after a policy shift within both governments, and this legislation was adopted to rectify a court-imposed limitation.[92]

Context, conduct, and intent reveals that the United States, Britain, and subsequently Canada acknowledged our sovereign, unlimited right to pass freely under the border. The Jay Treaty was an acknowledgement of the fact that Indian nations were in these territories prior to the creation of the colonies that would later become the United States and Canada. It was an acknowledgement of our sovereign status, that as nations we had a right to live in our territories free from any entanglement with a foreign border that crossed through our lands. For the Haudenosaunee, it is an acknowledgment of the Guswentah or Two Row Wampum that our nations are separate from the colonist states, and live side by side, but we would not attempt to cross into the other's vessel and interfere in their nations and they would not interfere in our nations. At the time the United States and Britain were entering into treaties with Indian nations and used the same instrument to acknowledge our rights as sovereigns to cross the border and access our territories and political, economic, and social institutions. To keep this agreement and to continue to respect our sovereignty and avert war with our nations, they agreed to place the border ten feet above our heads.

But they have failed to uphold this binding contract, violating treaty law and our human rights under the Declaration. The United States failed to acknowledge that this is a permanent right despite the Treaty's failure to include a specific provision for ending the acknowledgement. At every point when the United States and Canada have limited our rights, they have failed to engage in any negotiation or obtain consent, which is required due to the fact that these rights involve navigation and

---

[90] Spruhan, *supra* note 14, 306.   [91] McNair, *supra* note 72, 426.

[92] The House of Representatives ended treaty making and Britain essentially removed itself from Indian affairs in 1871, and Canada subsequently succeeded to their obligations. It is important to note that Canada still enters into treaties with First Nations peoples.

movement across territories and no provision or procedure to change the acknowledgement of these rights was included in the treaty. The courts now see our border-crossing rights as statutory rights based in US legislation. Canada has whittled the rights down to a form of aboriginal rights defined as it sees fit. Despite the fact that for over one hundred years these treaty rights have been acknowledged and honored, now, by prohibiting individuals with less than 50 percent blood quantum, requiring an impossible nexus test, or closing the border, the United States and Canada are violating rights that have stood for over one hundred years.

Canadian and US defense of treaty violations   Before examining the Declaration further we need to address the US and Canadian defense of their treaty violations. Both Canada and the United States argue that they are not bound by the Jay Treaty, due to the fact that they did not enact implementing legislation – for the United States the Treaty of Ghent and Canada the Jay Treaty. However,

> a party may not invoke the provisions of its internal law as justification for its failure to perform a treaty. Thus, if a new law or modification to existing law is needed in order to carry out the obligations which will be laid upon it by the treaty, a negotiating state should ensure that this is done at least by the time the treaty enters into force for it. If this is not done, not only will the state risk being in breach of its treaty obligations, but also it will be liable in international law to another party if, as a result, that party, or its nationals, is later damaged.[93]

The Supreme Court of Chile, addressing Chile's failure to ratify a treaty, "held that the efficacy of the treaty as a source of international law was not detracted from by non-ratification, for the principles of international law are of general application and supplant the silence of the law in unforeseen situations; and among the several sources from which these principles emanate are agreements made by chancelleries."[94]

Canada also argues that it did not sign the treaty and is not bound by Britain's promises.[95] Canada's accession in 1931 with the passage of the Statute of Westminster included assuming some treaty obligations, particularly those involving boundary rights. The general principle is that newly established states have a clean slate with regard to treaty obligations, *except* "as regards the purely local or 'real' obligations of the State formerly exercising sovereignty over the territory of the new State."[96]

---

[93] Aust, *supra* note 62, 180–81.   [94] O'Connell, *supra* note 64, at 25.
[95] *Vincent, supra* note 29, 24–25.   [96] McNair, *supra* note 72, 601.

There have been two theories regarding former colonies and succession to treaties. "The first is the nineteenth-century theory of universal succession, which persisted up to the 1960s. According to this, a new state inherited all the treaty rights and obligations of the former power in so far as they had been applicable to the territory before independence."[97] It is important to note that the many former British colonies in Africa entered into devolution agreements and assumed any duties of the United Kingdom.[98] The second theory is the clean-slate doctrine, which was followed by the United States, which believed that it was free to choose to which treaties it succeeded. "However, even when the clean-slate doctrine is applied, treaties which concern territorial rights, such as boundary treaties and those granting rights of navigation or passage, will usually bind the new state."[99]

Neither argument, failure to implement legislation, nor succession applies to the Jay Treaty. Even if the war of 1812 ended the acknowledgment of our border rights, the Treaty of Ghent revived the acknowledgement, and failure to adopt implementing legislation is simply another treaty violation by the United States and Canada. The treaty, as it applies to Indian nations, involves the status of US/Canadian territory and boundaries of navigation; thus Canada succeeded to the responsibility for acknowledging these rights. Moreover, it is a historical fact that Indian people have crossed this border continually, without limitation, as citizens of Indian nations.[100] By summarily dismissing these rights as no longer treaty-based or narrowing them so that they are unusable, Canada and the United States are violating international treaty law.

Articles 20 and 36

In addition to protecting treaty rights, the Declaration's Article 20 acknowledges the right of indigenous peoples to maintain and develop our political, economic, and social systems, to be secure in the enjoyment of our own means of subsistence and development, and to engage freely in traditional and other economic activities. And, acknowledging that indigenous peoples have been divided by colonizing nations, Article 36 states: "Indigenous peoples, in particular those divided by international borders, have the right to maintain and develop contacts, relations and cooperation, including activities for spiritual, cultural, political, economic and

---

[97] Aust, *supra* note 62, 372.   [98] Ibid.
[99] Ibid.   [100] Ibid., at 370.

social purposes, with their own members as well as other peoples across borders."[101]

These articles encompass the Haudenosaunee philosophy that it is not simply the right of an individual to cross the border, but a right to exist as nations and as a confederacy, with our political, economic, and social systems intact, and with the foreign border ten feet above our heads. As sovereign nations with rights recognized by the Declaration we have a right to be a united Mohawk Nation and a Haudenosaunee Confederacy, with territories in the United States and Canada and with one governing political institution, recognized and respected by other states.

It is not only a right for an individual to cross but, as the Declaration recognizes, a right of peoples to cross the border to engage in our political, economic, and social institutions. This is what it means to have the border ten feet above our heads. Our political and economic institutions do not stop at the border. However, in violation of the Declaration, Canada and the United States believe that these rights do stop at the border. This is where the border fails to remain ten feet above our heads. With the United States and Canada entangling us more and more in the border, it has become difficult to maintain a united Mohawk Nation and Confederacy. Canada continues to interfere in this right by defining who is an Indian through the issuance of Indian status cards. The creation by the Canadian courts of a nexus test to exercise a limited "aboriginal" right to cross the border narrows this right to the extent that it is practically nonexistent. We are also forced to report to the government of Canada when simply returning home or visiting family, or risk confiscation of our vehicles. With three tribal governments[102] spanning two countries, two provinces, and one state, due to the refusal of Canada and the United States to acknowledge one united government spanning international borders, we will always be a splintered nation that is unable to function as a whole. Deprived of our collective rights to our political systems, we function as single "tribes" or "bands" or individuals when we cross the border, much less able to withstand the pressures of assimilation.

Our social institutions have survived and some individuals are able to travel back and forth for cultural events. However, this has become

---

[101] Declaration, Art. 36, at 35.

[102] In Akwesasne the St. Regis Mohawk Tribal government is the federally recognized government on the US side of the border, the Mohawk Council of Akwesasne is recognized by the Canadian government, and the Mohawk Nation Council is the traditional form of government. The Mohawk Nation Council is not recognized by the US and Canadian governments.

increasingly difficult with the new US requirements to have a passport to reenter, violating our rights acknowledged by the Declaration to cross the border and access our social, political, and economic institutions and maintain relations with our members.[103] This has been illustrated yet again by Canada's confiscation of a Haudenosaunee passport in July 2011. And Canada continues to violate these rights, as now Mohawk citizens risk confiscation of their vehicle if they fail to report to Canadian authorities, located outside the territory, that they have entered Mohawk territory. Moreover, due to treaty violations our economic institutions as nations have been crippled. First the Jay Treaty attempted without our consent to limit our economic activities to personal goods. Now a citizen is not able to bring across a washing machine for personal use,[104] much less engage in trade with our nations. Due to these violations of our rights, we cannot maintain economic institutions, engage in economic activities with other nations, or support our people without being labeled as criminals and smugglers.[105]

The next steps

The Declaration is a viable tool in the defense of our rights under the Jay Treaty. But what are the next steps in this defense? Our first step is to look back at where we've come from and follow the paths set by our elders and move forward, working to keep the border ten feet above our heads. By looking back we are able to develop a strategy that encompasses our political philosophy. The strategy must be based in indigenous political philosophy to lessen the risk of increasing the colonizers' hold over our nations. For the Haudenosaunee, any strategy must be based on the Guswentah and the Covenant Chain or maintaining our sovereignty and working side by side as nation states, not in a trust relationship and focusing on our rights as individual rights, into which the federal courts have turned our Jay Treaty rights.

---

[103] The Department of Homeland Security has acknowledged that Indian nations may use their own form of identification; however, it must meet the new security requirements which are cost-prohibitive.

[104] *Mitchell, supra* note 33.

[105] Michael Hill, "Mohawk Reservation a Soft Spot for Cigarette Smuggling," *News from Indian Country,* February 16, 2010, http://indiancountrynews.net/index.php?option=com_content&task=view&id=1968&Itemid=33; Audra Simpson, "Subjects of Sovereignty: Indigeneity, the Revenue Rule, and Juridics of Failed Consent," 71 *Law and Contemporary Problems* 191 (2008).

As illustrated by the current court decisions, resorting to domestic courts is not a viable option, nor are they a receptive forum to pursue the protection of the rights recognized by the Declaration. Professor James Sa'ke'j Youngblood Henderson, who was involved with the drafting of the Declaration, notes,

> The courts are not the answer to the realization of the human rights of Indigenous peoples. As our elders teach, the Declaration, like our Aboriginal and treaty rights, is but one wing of Indigenous diplomacy. The other wing is political action and strategy. As with eagles and condors, both wings are necessary for flight, and these two wings are necessary for us to move toward our dignity and responsibilities. The legal documents and the courts play a limited role, but the ultimate answer is political. The courts cannot do the political work of self-determining peoples ... We cannot wait for governments, political parties, or courts to act. We are self-determining peoples. We have the authority to act for the implementation of our rights in every venue.[106]

Moreover, domestic courts are not receptive to international law, much less indigenous rights as acknowledged and protected by international law. US courts rarely apply customary law "as a direct restraint against a government or a governmental interest. Of more than 2000 'international law' cases decided between 1789 and 1984, less than fifty involved the application of customary law when the executive branch had not expressed a position."[107] Moreover, courts do not apply customary international law to domestic officials, and they defer to domestic laws that violate customary international human rights law.[108] "And although there is widespread academic consensus that customary international human rights law should trump state law under the supremacy clause, US courts have never applied this law to the states, and show no inclination to do so."[109]

A more feasible option and one that fits more with Haudenosaunee philosophy is a political strategy, which will allow for "polishing the chain." This may also be a better option, as rights possess a political nature "that becomes glaringly apparent when rights conflict with each other. Such conflicts are not resolvable by reference to the rights in issue because their claimed absoluteness renders them incapable of mediation."[110] Our rights

---

[106] Henderson, *supra* note 36, 92–93.
[107] Phillip R. Trimble, "A Revisionist View of Customary International Law," 33 *UCLA Law Review* 665 (1986), 683.
[108] Jack Goldsmith, "International Human Rights Law and the United States Double Standard," 1 *Green Bag* 365 (1998), 369.
[109] Ibid.   [110] Allen, *supra* note 6, at 247.

are unconditional, not subject to moderation, and are not susceptible to being settled by legislative or adjudicative mediation or compromise.[111] The more appropriate forum is the political forum, where officials can meet to polish the chain, or renew our agreement to treat each other as sovereigns, using Haudenosaunee philosophy and the Declaration as foundations for our negotiations.

Negotiation is necessary to create a consensus about which rights are valid, and such a discourse gives participants the opportunity to justify claims and persuade others of their normative validity.[112] The role of law is then to give effect to the negotiated consensus.[113] As negotiations use the Declaration as a framework, it brings more validity to our border-crossing rights. The Declaration "offers a route to building genuine national consensus on indigenous issues. It can be used to engage political discourse on indigenous issues within national settings and can strengthen the political will needed not only to create paper rights but to ensure such rights are implemented properly as well."[114]

For the Haudenosaunee, we may consider a second step, as the Declaration requires states to take effective steps to facilitate the right to cross borders to maintain our right to political, economic, and social institutions.[115] Sharon O'Brien sets forth two possible options. The first is to use the International Joint Commission (IJC), whose purpose is to resolve boundary conflicts between the United States and Canada.[116] The difficulty with the IJC is that it is a quasi-judicial body which makes independent recommendations at the request of either Canada or the United States, not Indian nations.[117] Moreover, as a judicial body created by the United States and Canada, it will probably not embrace Haudenosaunee philosophy on sovereignty or use the Declaration as a framework to guide its decision.

Second, O'Brien suggests national comprehensive or piecemeal legislation.[118] This option presents a more feasible step, as it would be an opportunity for negotiations between the Haudenosaunee, the United States, and Canada using the Declaration as a framework. Moreover, this political process is supported by the Haudenosaunee philosophy of

---

[111] Ibid., at 247, quoting J. Gray, *Enlightenment's Wake: Politics and Culture at the Close of the Modern Age* (London: Routledge, 1995), 22.

[112] Allen, *supra* note 6, at 251.

[113] Ibid.   [114] Ibid., at 254.

[115] UN Declaration on the Rights of Indigenous Peoples, Art. 36(2).

[116] O'Brien, *supra* note 23, at 348.

[117] Ibid.   [118] Ibid.

polishing the chain. Using the Declaration as a framework, Haudenosaunee nations, as well as other Indian nations, can negotiate with the United States and Canada to adopt legislation that supports our border-crossing rights acknowledged originally by the Jay Treaty. It is imperative that these negotiations happen simultaneously with United States and Canada so that our people may "pass and repass" as the Jay Treaty acknowledged. For too long our people have been subject to differing and invalid inter-pretations of our border-crossing rights, which, as acknowledged by the Declaration, violate our rights as indigenous peoples.

This negotiation process would entail a step-by-step recognition of our rights that continually moves us back to the acknowledgment of our full border-crossing rights as nations. First is a repeal of the US 50 percent blood quantum restriction and then a restoration of Canada's acknow-ledgement of our inherent border-crossing rights. This must also include a process by which both the United States and Canada will recognize nation-issued identification cards, whether secure passports or tribal identification cards, as acceptable documentation to cross the border. This process must also include negotiations to facilitate an agreement by Canada that Canadian custom officers are not to carry weapons within Mohawk territory and that Mohawk citizens do not need to report to Canadian customs when they are only entering Mohawk territory. Finally, the negotiations must include legislation that recognizes the ability to exercise the right to economic systems between territories and member nations of the confederacy across the border. The ultimate goal is recognition through negotiation that it is not just our individuals who cross the border, but our nations and our political, economic, and social institutions, and that the border remains ten feet above our heads.

There is much work to be done. But if we follow the pathways our elders laid, progress will be made. It will be a slow progress, but we are used to that. At the time of the signing of the Jay Treaty, the Haudenosaunee Confederacy was a formidable friend and enemy, courted by Britain and the newly formed United States. Our territories expanded into both what is now considered the United States and Canada. The notion of separate territories was foreign to our ancestors as they lived the Great Law, which provided that each of the Haudenosaunee nations shared their territories – one spoon – so there was no fighting over land or game. We dealt with Britain and the United States as sovereigns, guided by the Guswentah and Covenant Chain. Our border-crossing rights were acknowledged in 1794 and again by the United Nations in 2007 with the adoption of the Declaration. The Declaration sets the framework for the recognition of our collective rights, which are entitled to the protection of international treaty law, and the right to cross international boundaries to maintain our political, economic, and social institutions. Moreover, the Declaration provides a framework for continuing to polish the chain and protect and strengthen these rights. As we press forward and fight to keep the border ten feet above our heads, our nations will be stronger. And perhaps one day we won't cross as individuals, but as nations with the border restored ten feet above our heads.

Traditional responsibility and spiritual relatives: protection of indigenous rights to land and sacred places

KATHLEEN J. MARTIN

This chapter examines issues, attitudes, and perspectives in relation to Articles 25 and 26 of the United Nations Declaration on the Rights of Indigenous Peoples,[1] and suggests possible reasons why the United States, with New Zealand, Australia, and Canada, originally voted against the Declaration.[2] Articles 25 and 26 are designed to protect indigenous homelands, particularly from conservation movements and national governments. However, as General Assembly President Sheikha Haya Rashed Al Kalifa warned, indigenous peoples will still be subject to "conflicts and land disputes that threaten their way of life and very survival."[3] This is due in part to significant cultural differences and assumptions about

---

[1] UN Declaration on the Rights of Indigenous Peoples, 7 September 2007.

    Article 25. Indigenous peoples have the right to maintain and strengthen their distinctive spiritual relationship with their traditionally owned or otherwise occupied and used lands, territories, waters and coastal seas and other resources and to uphold their responsibilities to future generations in this regard.

    Article 26. Indigenous peoples have the right to the lands, territories and resources, which they have traditionally owned, occupied or otherwise used or acquired; Indigenous peoples have the right to own, use, develop and control the lands, territories and resources that they possess by reason of traditional ownership or other traditional occupation or use, as well as those which they have otherwise acquired; States shall give legal recognition and protection to these lands, territories and resources. Such recognition shall be conducted with due respect to the customs, traditions and land tenure systems of the indigenous peoples concerned.

[2] The Rudd government of Australia formally endorsed the Declaration on April 3, 2009, and on April 21, 2010, New Zealand voted to approve it. In December 2010 President Obama announced the United States' support of the Declaration following Canada's endorsement the previous month. However, indigenous representatives have received US support for the Declaration with caution. See, e.g., Newcomb, "Has the US changed position?"

[3] United Nations press release.

the natural world, and the role and place of humans within it, as well as demands for natural resources. Presented in this chapter are the perspectives of Native peoples[4] in the United States through both literary studies and commentaries regarding traditional responsibility to and for the land, and interpretations that argue for their right to maintain reciprocal relationships. These rights and responsibilities incorporate notions of care, tending, and the continuation of traditional practices for future generations. Further, the perspectives are situated within a construct of moral and ethical behavior toward the earth and all her inhabitants. However, in the United States the general public holds a variety of attitudes regarding the natural world that are not mutually exclusive – conservation and leaving land untouched (or trammeled as sometimes posed) versus economic development and/or recreational uses designed for the benefit of humans. This disparity between Native and public perceptions provides little opportunity along the continuum for understanding, or for nature and human relations to interact in more complex and sophisticated ways.[5]

Although consideration of the importance of what has been termed "sacred lands" and the inherent sacredness of the environment continue to dominate discussions in environmental studies courses and by the general public in the United States, the conflict between Native and Western views regarding ownership, land use, and the incumbent rights and responsibilities inherent in ownership continue to exhibit cultural differences and conflict.[6] In addition, population growth, in combination with changes in Western attitudes regarding national parks and public lands, has stimulated an economy that is moving from resource extraction and ranching to a more service- and information-based tourism economy that increasingly attracts larger numbers of people.[7] Yet this shift in economics still suggests historical attitudes of "invasion and conquest," with rugged individuals seeking to partake in the panoramic beauty and expansiveness of the wilderness, a very different philosophy from that of Native peoples. Investigating the complexity of the mismatch between public perceptions in the United States, issues of land sovereignty, and Native rights and spiritual relations with places are key areas of discussion if

---

[4] In this chapter, the terms "Native" and "Native peoples" are used interchangeably and include peoples indigenous to the western hemisphere.

[5] Anderson, *Tending the Wild*, p. 339.

[6] For a detailed discussion of worldview difference and an analysis of the legacy of Columbus and what has been termed the "American Narrative," see Klein, "Heathens, infidels, and savages."

[7] McAvoy, "American Indians, place meanings and the old/new west," 384.

rights and responsibilities as articulated in Articles 25 and 26 are to have the suggested impact. In this chapter, differences in cultural worldviews regarding the meaning of rights to and responsibility for public lands are contrasted between Native views and those of university students studying issues of land and ethnicity.

Responsibility and relatives: Native peoples

Although briefly described here, Native interpretations and definitions of sacred places, spiritual relatives, access to sacred sites, and notions of wilderness contrasted with tending and care are based in philosophical principles of respect, responsibility, relevance, and reciprocity.[8] Native and indigenous peoples often explain, "many of our oral traditions tell of the place of the 'little brother' (the humans) in the larger Creation ... [and] the relationship of peoples to their sacred lands, to relatives with fins and hooves, to the plant and animal foods that anchor a way of life."[9] The sacred is in the relationships, and sacred places "reveal the ancestors and holy people, instructions and lessons for living, and stories of the animals"[10] who live in these places. Vine Deloria, Jr., noted with significant theoretical and social insight regarding land use in the United States, "You can go on the land to ski or strip a mountain and then leave cyanide pools, but you cannot go on public land to pray for her continued fertility."[11] Deloria's comments shed light on the differences in interpretation regarding the meaning of rights and responsibilities regarding sacred places and spiritual practices in the United States. They allude to differences in worldview that address a living animate world in which humans are not the most powerful, and one in which places have needs that humans can attend to and support. More significantly with relation to places, John Mohawk suggests that it is necessary for people to ask, "What is in the best interests of future generations of peoples of the world and of other species of the world?"[12] This question poses the crux of philosophical differences, and asks what is important for all the "relatives" for the next seven generations for maintaining sacred lands, caring for relatives, and accessing sacred sites.

---

[8] Kirkness and Barnhardt, 'First Nations and higher education."
[9] LaDuke, *Recovering the Sacred*, p. 12.
[10] Slick and Willeto, "The photographic vision of Delvin Slick," p. 184.
[11] *In the Light of Reverence.*
[12] Mohawk, "The Iroquois Confederacy," p. 58.

Sacred lands and places

Sacred places are "a particular geography that involves all people and animals of that area ... If you are taken off that land you become alienated; it becomes problematic. You cannot fulfill your responsibilities because you are not part of the land anymore."[13] Kaleikoa Kaʻeo, a professor of Hawaiian studies, explains:

> As the land is hurt, we are hurt as a people. If the land produces, we produce as a people. If we are kept off the land, we are kept away from who we really are. But as we return to the land, we return to who we really are as a people.[14]

This intimate relationship and connection to land supports the notion that when responsibilities are fulfilled, humans will be taken care of and thrive, and so will the land. Maintaining biological diversity and complex reciprocal relationships are key ideals. Balance and successful community relations are achieved through reciprocity to and responsibility for the land and her inhabitants.

The philosophy of community relations guides the collection of plants, natural materials, and relationships with other-than-human relatives. For example: sacred stone from the pipestone quarry in Minnesota; willow, beargrass, and sedges for weaving baskets and other items in California; the hunting of bison, elk, and deer in the Plains; and the fishing and maintenance of salmon and sturgeon throughout the rivers and lakes of the upper mid- and northwest regions. Humans are only one part of creation and as such have responsibility to and for particular places – geographies – or land that has been given to them specifically to care for and maintain as a relative in a community relationship. For instance, Australian Aborigines think of their land in terms of a "healthy country."

> By that they mean pretty much everything around them, including people, animals, plants, earth, minerals, water, and dreams; dreams that coalesce to create a multidimensional and spiritual relationship with the land. But foremost in the relationship that forms country, the Aborigines say, are people. "The country needs its people," they say ... Their entire existence is organized around a sophisticated awareness of biological functions that keep "country" in good health.[15]

The emphasis on relations and the maintenance of the health and well-being of the country and its inhabitants is significant. "Land is revered

---

[13] *In the Spirit of Crazy Horse.*   [14] *Hawaii: A Voice for Sovereignty.*
[15] Dowie, *Conservation Refugees*, p. 116.

and regarded as more than an economic resource, and nature is seen as the primary source of life, the center of the universe and the core of culture."[16] In this, the inherent sacredness of the land is affirmed and respected.

Many tribal histories record how and in what manner the peoples found their places and came to be on Mother Earth.

> They all knew their country was in exactly the right place … The peoples of the Plains learned from the cottonwood how to make tipis, and the tree became their sacred relative participating in the annual sun dance. It was not simply a task of living in their country as human beings. It was necessary to live as relatives.[17]

The Nuwuvi peoples (fourteen bands of the Southern Paiute) "describe a physical and spiritual landscape spanning ocean and desert, mountains and rivers, life and death" in the sacred Salt Songs,[18] and disagreements are put aside. Anishinaabeg demonstrate a complex environmental ethic based on the care of and responsibility to wild rice as a sacred food. "The wild rice harvest of the Anishinaabeg not only feeds the body, it feeds the soul, continuing a tradition that is generations old for these people of the lakes and rivers of the north."[19] In 1860, Kah-ge-ga-gah-bowh (also known as George Copway) was ending a long career of writing and described many of the places inhabited and favored by the Ojibway.

> I cannot but be convinced of the fact that in no other portion of the world can there be a territory more favored by Heaven. The waters are abundant and good; the air bracing and healthy; and the soil admiringly adapted for agricultural purposes. It is not much to be wondered at that in such a climate, such a strong, athletic and hardy race of men should exist, as the Ojibways.[20]

From Copway's interpretation we see the ways land and people work together in a mutual relationship to support each other and reflect the gifts and attributes available.

Spiritual relatives

Taking care of relatives in places for generations to come frames a Native epistemology of a way of life dedicated to concern and care for particular places. Over one hundred years ago, Melvin Gilmore, an ethnobotanist

---

[16] Ibid., p. 108.   [17] Deloria, *For This Land*, p. 237.
[18] Klasky, "The salt song trail map," pp. 8–9.
[19] LaDuke, *Recovering the Sacred*, p. 167.
[20] Copway, *Indian Life and Indian History*, p. 20.

fluent in a number of Plains Indian languages, found tribes the source of significant knowledge and awareness about the environment, and cognizant of coming changes. His text, *Prairie Smoke*, is revealing with regard to attitudes, oral narratives, and plant knowledge that he gained through extensive interviews and conversations with Native elders. He recounts:

> In the rituals of various tribes may be found numerous expressions of the love and reverence which the people had for Holy Mother Earth and for their own homeland in particular. In their thought of their homeland they did not regard it as a possession which they owned, but they regarded themselves as possessed by their homeland, their country, to which they owed love and service and reverence.[21]

This quote may seem overly romanticized if examined through Euro-American standards, yet it is indicative of Gilmore's careful interviewing of elders and tribal members regarding specific philosophies and knowledge of ethnobotany. Dakota philosophy reflects a belief centered on reciprocal community relations.

The Dakota people with whom Gilmore consulted also outlined the horrifying treatment of their homeland to come and the invasion of their territories by Westerners. They related to him the following story with immense sadness as seen in a vision by an elder many years before Gilmore's time:

> I saw a great incursion of human beings with a strange appearance … They move everywhere over the face of the land … and they will take our land from us … They have no holy reverence for our holy places, or for our holy Mother Earth. And they kill and destroy all things and make the land desolate. They have no ear for the voices of the trees and the flowers, and no pity for the birds and beasts of the field. And they deface and spoil the beauty of the land and befoul the watercourses.[22]

If we look back over the past one hundred years of life in the Plains, the Dakotas' prophetic words are sobering to say the least. The loss of approximately fifty million acres of land through treaties, the loss of approximately ninety million acres through the 1887 General Allotment or Dawes Act, homestead Acts and government policies in effect until 1934, evidence the "taking of land" in the Plains. Homesteaders and public works projects destroyed numerous generations of forbs and grasses, and natural habitat. This contributed to a number of environmental catastrophes in the Plains: the terrible dustbowl effect of the 1930s through the plowing of

---

[21] Gilmore, *Prairie Smoke*, p. 29.   [22] Ibid., p. 8–9.

land; the construction of five main-stem dams on the Missouri River by the Army Corps of Engineers in the 1950s to "alleviate flooding," which have fouled watercourses and destroyed cottonwood trees and bird habitat; the mining of uranium and gold in the Black Hills that has polluted the land and water; and more recently the large agriculture and farming projects, which now threaten the vast Ogallala Aquifer and the livelihoods of Lakota Peoples in South Dakota.[23] These are just a few of the ways this vision has been evidenced in recent times. Yet they are considered more to be errors in judgment that a technologically advanced society such as the United States can correct than the destruction of "our Holy Mother Earth" with horrifying consequences. Similar examples of this destruction are evident on Native lands throughout the United States.

Ethics, rights and preservation: US views

Cultural differences in interpretation between rights to and responsibility for sacred places and limited general public awareness of these rights as established in the US Constitution and treaties with Native peoples make obvious the mismatch in cultural worldviews. This section highlights three areas of mismatch and illustrates some of the differences in definition, interpretation, and worldview: (1) environmental ethics; (2) individual rights; and (3) preservation and management.

Environmental ethics

The first area of difference encompasses the relatively new field of environmental ethics, in which some scholars cite traditional Native worldviews for exhibiting a higher regard for nonhuman entities and the idea of nature as significant for life.[24] The growth of this field can be traced in part to the developing environmental crises of the 1960s and 1970s. Subsequent advertising campaigns were designed to raise awareness through the use of public service campaigns such as "the crying Indian" and the need for increased awareness of pollution and recycling efforts.[25] Campaigns such as these may have been spurred by the 1963 Leopold Report to the National Park Service (NPS), the United States Wilderness Act of 1964, and the

---

[23] Ashworth, *Ogallala Blue*.

[24] For further discussion, see Callicott and Nelson, *American Indian Environmental Ethics*.

[25] See, e.g., "Iron Eyes Cody and anti-pollution," poetv.com/video.php?vid=4935 and youtube.com/watch?v=gkhdMwQQ1fQ (viewed 19 January 2010).

"idea of active management of public lands in the United States."[26] The combination of reports, government actions, and "active management" campaigns argue for better care and attention to state and federal parklands even though processes of how to do that were not well understood at the time. They also built upon historical and stereotypical misrepresentations of Native connections to the land and beliefs about "Mother Earth." Furthermore, the environmental and conservation movements' agenda of raising public awareness and concern, something not unjustified, certainly utilized misconstrued ideas about Native peoples.

The notion that it is important to "conserve places" and reserve them with no human or limited human interference, something emphasized by the conservation movement, is of concern to indigenous peoples throughout the world. During one of the draft meetings for the UN Declaration in Vancouver, for instance, "all two hundred delegates to the International Forum on Indigenous Mapping signed a declaration stating that 'conservation has become the number one threat to indigenous territories.'"[27] Conserving and reserving places have been tenets of the environmental, conservation and national park movements since John Muir's time and the founding of the Sierra Club in 1892.[28] However, Muir's experiences and awe of Yosemite Valley were largely a response to the active tending, gathering, burning, seed scattering, and harvesting of the area by Miwok, Paiute, and Yokut inhabitants.[29] In fact, current public opinion in general continues to rarify the wilderness and support concepts of "conserve" and "preserve," ideas that may reflect Bradley Klein's interpretation of the notion of "wonder" as a component of the "American Narrative" that "dazzles the mind and induces 'ideological forgetting,' allowing even the most grotesque excesses and glaring inconsistencies to be legitimated and interpreted as necessary."[30]

---

[26] Anderson, *Tending the Wild*, p. 335.

[27] For insightful discussion on these issues, see Dowie, *Conservation Refugees*.

[28] It is important to note that conservation and the benefit to public lands as promoted by John Muir, the Sierra Club, and others committed to the preservation of places such as national and state parks were sorely needed. The idea that economic or recreational use would be the only option is almost unthinkable given the destruction that could have occurred over the past 150 years without preservation as a significant goal. Thus a catch-22, if you will, since it is important and recognized as so by Native People, but it has been at the expense of Native stewardship of these areas.

[29] See more detailed discussion in Anderson, *Tending the Wild*; Dowie, *Conservation Refugees*, as well as historical documentation of Native interaction with the landscape such as Gilmore, *Prairie Smoke*; Menzies, *Traditional Ecological Knowledge*.

[30] Klein, "Heathens, infidels, and savages," 36.

John Muir's reactions to the undisputed magnificence of the Yosemite Valley, and his political actions to "preserve" these places for future generations, had considerable influence on President Theodore Roosevelt. The president's subsequent policies, executive orders, and actions set aside lands for public use as national treasures, something Roosevelt believed to be of considerable importance. In fact, in the last two days of his presidency in 1909, Roosevelt placed "2.5 million acres of reservation lands in the hands of the US Forest Service [and] the measure stripped Indian tribes of rich timber lands, which were later exploited by lumber companies."[31] A goal of both Roosevelt and Muir was to eliminate Native presence in the parks in order to keep them as "pristine" wilderness. The most recent example of this continuing ideological influence can be found in the Ken Burns (2009) film series, *The National Parks: America's Best Idea*, a series that includes little if any recognition of Native peoples in the United States whose significant land sessions through treaties, and care and tending of these areas contributed to the formation of these very same parks. The films revel in the founding of the parks and, as Burns notes, "Everyone in the United States is a co-owner of some of the most spectacular seafront property, of the highest free-flowing waterfall on the continent, of the greatest collection of geo-thermal features on the planet, and the grandest canyon on earth."[32] Yet the films do not tell the story of "the violent and forcible evictions of Native Americans who had been stewards of these lands for millennia."[33] Further, Western notions of ownership, as indicated in Burns' comment, suggest equality for all citizens while ignoring the rights of Native peoples to these lands that go beyond those of non-Natives. These nationalized ideas regarding ownership, the natural world, and human interaction continue to evidence "either/or" propositions of use, while at the same time ignoring Native treaty rights, traditional uses, spiritual relationships and occupations, and cultural interpretations of care, tending, and respect.

The field of environmental ethics poses a related area of discussion regarding the environmental crises of the 1960s and 1970s and the rise in anti-pollution movements. These ideas emerged "from a widespread

---

[31] Hirsch, "Theodore Roosevelt and American Indians," 34–37.
[32] Ken Burns has noted that the amount of material for this film series was daunting and some footage of Native peoples ended up on the cutting room floor, as quoted in an interview with Ken Burns. See Starmer, "Ken Burns shares his national parks experiences." Burns also notes, "I think people need to remember that it's a common wealth and you should visit your property now and then and make sure it's being taken care of."
[33] Klinger and Adamson, "The national parks: America's best idea?"

belief within Western culture that the nonhuman natural world was but a pool of resources existing only to satisfy human needs and wants."[34] In other words, the use of natural resources and the economic and recreational gain from places was ruining something critical to maintain as separate and valuable resources. Therefore, preservation and conservation of land meant the curtailing or elimination of human activity in these places. Here again, this idea was quite foreign to Native peoples, since mutual relationships with land through care and tending of places had been performed for centuries. As James Garrett notes, "It is true that most indigenous people believe their biological resources were placed on the earth for the good of all humans, but their understanding and conceptual beliefs almost always entail giving knowledge and natural resources proper respect and [that they] not be made into commodities."[35] Although the conservation movement agrees with the idea of respect, the philosophical underpinnings regarding ownership, ethical treatment of land, and the need for humans to satisfy their own desires are significantly different.

Numerous examples of differences in sentiment and the interpretation of conservation and economic or recreational use exist in the history of US–Native relations. These include water resources and timber management, traditional and spiritual practices, and rights of access for Native peoples, particularly in national forest areas. A few of the more notable examples include the relatively recent fight by the Winnemem Wintu to preserve areas in the Mount Shasta and McCloud River Watershed by limiting the addition of new ski resorts, water bottling, and dams and timber/forest practices;[36] the massive mining efforts of Peabody Coal at Hopi Black Mesa in the southwest begun with Bureau of Indian Affairs (BIA) negotiated lease agreements over thirty years ago;[37] "the infamous *Lyng* v. *Northwest Indian Cemetery Protection Association* case where a logging road was allowed to go through a sacred area in order to facilitate economic exploitation of the forests in Northern California";[38] the desecration of and battle to protect Western Shoshone Land for almost

---

[34] Callicott and Nelson, *American Indian Environmental Ethics*, p. 3.
[35] Garrett, "Indigenous ecological knowledge."
[36] Winnemem Wintu Tribe, "Long Trail to Justice."
[37] An attorney, whose papers admitted posthumously that he had been working for both Peabody Coal and the tribe at the same time, negotiated these lease agreements with the Bureau of Indian Affairs. See Black Mesa Indigenous Support, blackmesais.org (viewed January 19, 2010).
[38] Garrett, "Spiritual freedom," p. 39. See also Weaver, *Other Words*.

forty years,[39] and a plethora of other such cases in which Native peoples have continuously fought for multiple decades and generations. Yet with continuing irony, since both in the promotion of environmental ethics as well as the pursuit of human use for economic gain and recreation, Native understandings are routinely subjugated to Western notions of how, when, where, and by whom use of land should be determined both for conservation and recreational or economic use.[40] Westernized dualistic interpretations prevalent in the United States both frame usage that is complicated by a series of environmental laws, congressional acts, and government orders that affect and influence tribal rights to access and use in complicated and complex ways.[41] Often, this provides direct evidence of a belief system supported by public policy that privileges the rights of the individual, and deems Native use or access as detrimental to the lands if not secondary to the notion of individual rights.

Individual rights

A second area of mismatch that influences public perceptions in the United States is that the rights of the individual are paramount. The US legal system, supported by the social psychology of Americans in general, is built upon the rarified and idealized notion of the individual and individual rights. Native philosophies and epistemologies, however, are concerned with community rights and the incumbent responsibilities to that community. However, this ideological disparity is rarely a matter of conversation or thoughtful consideration. Rather Native peoples are often characterized as citizens of the United States with the same "rights to public land as every citizen," even though they were "conquered" by a stronger power. These misperceptions stem from past governmental actions against Native peoples, and are supported by an implicit assumption that they should have fewer rights since they "were given reservations." Or, as luck

---

[39] For further details see "Spiritual genocide at Mt. Tenabo," *Indian Country Today*, December 2008, www.indiancountrytoday.com/opinion/35873484.html (viewed July 8, 2010).

[40] David Tomblin argues that two newly emerging cultures within the environmental restoration movement incorporate both restoration and social justice. These two cultures include the Indigenous Peoples' Restoration (IPR) and the Environmental Justice Restoration (EJR) movements, and finding common goals will be the result. Tomblin, "Ecological restoration movement," 185–207.

[41] For an excellent discussion on the complex and conflicted relationships between laws, policies, practices, and government and tribes see Clow and Sutton, *Trusteeship in Change*.

would have it, "while governments [and by extension the general public] were apologizing and complaining, they were also convincing themselves that they had given these things to Native people out of the goodness of their hearts, that Native rights were something that had flowed from governmental largesse."[42]

For the most part, non-Native university students are not unlike the general public in their lack of knowledge of the United States constitution, treaties made with Native peoples, land use rights and responsibilities often deemed for all citizens in places such as state and national parks and range and forestlands, or in the definition of the term "responsibility" itself. In classes, a number of students often believe that Native peoples should not have "special privileges for use or control of the land" above and beyond the rights of anyone else, and "they should abide by the same rules that all the inhabitants of this country do."[43] Student and public opinions support these notions in comments such as: "my rights end where yours begin" and that except for reservation land where "they can live" or "desert lands given to them by the US government," Native rights are no different than those of any citizen.[44] Students often suggest reservation lands were "given" to Native peoples by the government on which to live and continue their cultures. On these lands specifically, they "have rights on their reservations" that include "the right to use the specified lands as they please,"[45] but this does not include public lands. Some students remark, "[It's] very sad that we forced them onto reservations, especially the quality of land that we gave them."[46] These ideas reflect a number of misconceptions about Native peoples and their relationship with the United States government in terms of sovereignty and citizen rights, and erroneous interpretations of the history of Native rights as set by the Constitution and nation-to-nation agreements with tribes.

Examining the opinions of students, misunderstandings of Native views regarding sacred places, rights to land use in traditional territories, and the responsibilities Native peoples have for these places are evident. From the in-class surveys, only four student responses out of fifty-two

---

[42] King, *Truth About Stories*, p. 137.

[43] The comments by students in this chapter were made in answer to a question from the in-class surveys conducted at the beginning of a course regarding personal conceptual understandings of land, January 4, 2010, and March 29, 2010.

[44] Data were gathered from surveys and in-class writing exercises on Indigenous land ethics involving largely third- and fourth-year university students in California from 2007 through 2010.

[45] Student survey comment.   [46] Student survey comment.

indicated at least some amount of accurate knowledge of US–Native treaty agreements that stipulate off-reservation rights. Most importantly, there is a significant misinterpretation of an indigenous interpretation of the meaning of "responsibility for places" and land based on Western notions of personal responsibility. These include the paying of taxes, upholding laws and rules, and leaving land as it is. Often, there is little indication that responsibility is directly related to a relationship with and for the land itself.

Student comments also reflect notions of conservation and recreational use tied to monetary responsibilities as citizens. Comments include the idea that citizens must "manage [the land] to the best of their ability for current and future generations" and that "forestlands are open to many different kinds of recreation."[47] Or, as succinctly summarized by one student in particular regarding rights and responsibility, "The right to actively participate in your community (vote, activism, volunteer); the right to use parks (botanical garden, beaches); have to pay taxes (to maintain them)." In comments such as these, we see Western interpretations of rights as defined by law and framed within current ideas of conservation and use, as well as responsibilities that are limited to paying taxes or following the law. There is little indication of knowledge regarding the constitutional and legal relationships between the United States and Native nations, or any discussion of the responsibilities and relationships humans have to the "other-than-human"[48] inhabitants of the land or to the earth herself. Most often, comments are based on the primacy of individual rights, and responsible behavior regarding care and maintenance, thus leading to the third area of concern, based on cultural interpretations and worldview differences.

Preservation and management

The idea that "rights" refers to an individual's right to pursue the "American dream" (whatever that is), and that "responsibility" is limited to paying for or preserving land has created conflicts over a range of public lands and places. In cases around the United States and throughout the world, Native and indigenous peoples have been forcibly evicted from their homelands. This is done under the notion of preservation and "responsible" management of places, and officially labeled by conservation

---

[47] Student survey comment.
[48] Callicott and Nelson, *American Indian Environmental Ethics*.

organizations and supporters as a human "threat to the biological diversity of a larger geographical area" (i.e., Yosemite Valley and other places in the United States, Botswana, Brazil, Kenya, Tanzania, and Thailand).[49]

In some cases, Native peoples have been removed due to the desire of states, corporations, and individuals for economic gain, access to natural resources, and the pursuit of recreational activities. Any number of examples exist, yet a few illustrate the severity of the problem in the United States: the extraction of gold from the Black Hills for almost 130 years;[50] recreational use of various public lands from snowmobiling in Yellowstone to skiing in California, Arizona, and New Mexico;[51] the long battle in Wisconsin, Washington, and the upper northwest United States between sport and commercial fishing interests on the one hand and traditional fishing rights on the other;[52] and the presence of military testing, mining, and superfund sites near or on Indian reservations that impact traditional lifeways.[53] In all of these instances, rights to sacred lands, waters, and natural resources and the practice of traditions are threatened.

The in-class student surveys revealed a general misperception and ignorance of the rights, responsibilities, and spiritual traditions of Native peoples in the United States specifically as indicated in Articles 25 and 26 of the UN Declaration.[54] Student responses to a question regarding what constitutes "sacred places" in the United States tended to be nuanced,

---

[49] Dowie, *Conservation Refugees*, p. xvi.

[50] See current US Forest Service policies, fs.fed.us/r2/blackhills/resources/fact_sheets/gold.shtml (viewed 30 January 2010).

[51] See, e.g., "On Closing Day at Spirit Mountain, Wisconsin, 14 year old 'Honor the Earth Princess,' Mariah Cooper (Ojibwe-Oneida), a Native American Olympic hopeful, led their first Snow Gratitude Ceremony ... expressing appreciation for one of America's best snow years ...

> 'Just like people, Mother Earth and Creator, respond favorably to appreciation', say Tribal Elders. The phenomena followed an international prayer on December 10, orchestrated by NVF, in partnership with the 13 tribes of Arizona plus California and Colorado, to inspire natural snow at all USA Ski Areas to safeguard America's water. Arizona Snow Bowl was blessed with six feet, which protected its sacred San Francisco Peaks and other drought-challenged ski areas from needing to use wastewater in snowmaking, with unfilterable pharmaceuticals." (send2press.com/newswire/2008–05–0502–004.shtml, viewed 21 January 2010)

[52] For issues regarding fishing in Wisconsin and Chippewa responses, as well as other pertinent issues, see Native Americans and the Environment (NCSE), ncseonline.org/nae/fishing.html (viewed January 23, 2010).

[53] See the Environmental Protection Agency (EPA) website for further information, epa.gov/superfund/community/relocation/policy.htm (viewed January 30, 2010).

[54] UN General Assembly Report, p. 8.

but still evidenced differences in worldview. Over half (twenty-eight) of the students responded that "sacred" would include places of historical and/or religious or spiritual significance to a surrounding community, Native or otherwise unidentified. Included in this response were historical places such as, "Pearl Harbor, WTC [World Trade Center], Trail of Tears"; "National and state parks"; "temples, burial grounds, churches"; "places constituted as 'sacred' by recognized religions"; or that "give life and identity to a place" and where "a person feels a spiritual and religious experience." One student's response is representative of an underlying ethic of individual rights and history. "'Sacred' is a matter of opinion. Native Peoples will choose important landmarks."[55] Only five responses touched on aspects that included ideas such as "untouched pristine places of natural habitat"; "unique or especially beautiful"; or "cultural and natural value and beauty." These comments suggest the value of historicizing places of victory, defeat, or conflict, as well as the influence of the conservation movement or ideas about the validity of religious practices.

Only eight students of the fifty-two surveyed commented on a question that asked students about their awareness of Native spiritual traditions and/or a relationship with sacred places; most students left the question blank. In general the students who responded indicated minimal knowledge and understanding. For example, "Hopi used kiva huts to practice reading the underworld"; "Outside my home town, the Indians consider the table tops sacred places"; and "Indian tribes/Mounds of Ohio." They did not illuminate differences in cultural interpretations and spiritual relations with land and places. The next section presents some of the conflicts encountered as Native peoples endeavor to exercise their rights as stated in the Articles.

Articles 25 and 26: United States and Native affairs

In the UN Declaration, Articles 25 and 26 pose inherent and fundamental components of the rights and responsibilities of indigenous peoples with regard to land, territories, and resources. Article 25 specifically identifies "the right to maintain and strengthen their distinct spiritual relationship" with traditionally owned and occupied "lands, territories, waters and coastal seas and other resources."[56] It also recognizes the right of indigenous peoples to uphold their spiritual relationships for future generations. Article 26 reaffirms these ideas and conditions, and specifies

---

[55] Student comment, spring 2010.   [56] UN General Assembly Report, p. 8.

that with regard to traditionally owned and occupied lands, territories, and resources possessed by reason of traditional ownership, occupation or use, "states shall give legal recognition and protection to these lands, territories and resources."[57] The Declaration further asserts the "urgent need to respect and promote the inherent rights" of Native peoples, particularly as they have been created, affirmed, and ratified through the signing of treaties, agreements, and other constructive arrangements.[58]

Treaties, courts and land

Although a largely uninformed public in the United States holds opinions significantly different than those of Native peoples, the existence of treaties, agreements and arrangements establishes precedents both powerful and troubling. On the one hand, treaties and agreements document Native rights and sovereignty in nation-to-nation agreements, yet most non-Natives consider treaties a thing of the past or irrelevant, and the United States Congress and courts have circumvented and disavowed treaty agreements as a matter of routine. In fact, tribal law is considered one of the most complicated in the field, and is largely misunderstood by members of Congress as well as the courts.[59] Senator Daniel Inouye of Hawaii reported while serving on the Select Committee on Indian Affairs that many of his colleagues were uninformed on the issues of Native rights and treaties, and that of over four hundred treaties ratified by the US Congress, none were fully upheld. However, Native peoples were held fully responsible for upholding *all* conditions in *all* treaties. This limited knowledge has contributed to and stimulated numerous public misperceptions and unjust court rulings, as well as protests and aggressive actions against Native communities when they attempt to act upon treaty rights.[60] Further, the lack of fiduciary responsibility by the Bureau of Indian Affairs (BIA) has provided tacit acknowledgement of injustice. And, in some cases, the BIA engaged in the lease, sale, and distribution of

[57] UN General Assembly Report. The language of the articles sets out the conditions, yet the difficulty addressed here surfaces in the general public's interpretation.

[58] UN General Assembly Report, p. 2.

[59] See, e.g., Williams, *Like a Loaded Weapon.*

[60] One such prominent example is of the Makah in their attempt to exercise their treaty rights and continue traditional lifeways regarding the hunting of whale off the northwest coast of Washington State. On May 17, 1999, the first successful hunt in seventy years was conducted, but the non-Native citizens and animal rights activists opposed the hunt. Bumper stickers reflective of the US genocide of Native peoples read, "Save a Whale, Kill a Makah." See further makah.com/whalingrecent.html (viewed January 19, 2010).

Native lands and natural resources with blatant disregard for this responsibility, based on political or economic advantages.

By way of acknowledgement, some issues are now receiving more attention and correction and will probably do so even more in the near future, and leadership by Native professionals in government appointments may bring better awareness and justice in the treatment of grievances. For example, the Senate confirmed the nomination of Dr. Yvette Roubideaux as director of the Indian Health Service (IHS) on 30 April 2009,[61] the first Native American woman to head the IHS in over two hundred years of government-to-government negotiated responsibility.[62] As well, the Senate nomination and confirmation of Mr. Larry J. EchoHawk as Assistant Secretary for Indian Affairs at the Department of the Interior on May 20, 2009, may signal a better opportunity for tribes to be heard and assert their rights and responsibilities to land as indicated by treaty or fiduciary responsibility. Furthermore, the return of land to Native peoples was accomplished under the Nixon administration in two specific cases: Blue Lake in New Mexico to the Taos Pueblo in 1970, and in 1972 the return of Mount Adams in Washington State to the Yakama Nation. More recently, a number of Indian land claims in Michigan and Maine, and the thirteen-year *Cobell et al.* v. *Ken Salazar, Secretary of the Interior, et al.* class action suit regarding leases of tribal lands have been settled in favor of tribes and litigants, albeit for significantly reduced amounts and with "tremendous social, legal, and economic implications."[63]

In California, some tribes interpret the Pacific Forest and Watershed Lands Stewardship Council settlement as positive for tribes. The Council will oversee the placement of approximately 140,000 acres of lands owned by the Pacific Gas and Electric (PG & E) company into protective management, of which "74,000 acres will be available for donation to public entities, tribes recognized by state or federal government,

---

[61] See US Senate Committee on Indian Affairs, indian.senate.gov/public/index. cfm?FuseAction=PressReleases.Detail&PressRelease_id=dc161eeb-379e-4c7c-9709-a76fe3c7ea1a&Month=5&Year=2009 (viewed May 23, 2009).

[62] Established in 1954 and based on Article 1(8) of the Constitution (1787), the IHS provides health care services for American Indians and Alaskan Natives.

[63] Scully, "Maine Indian Claims Settlement"; Michigan Indian Land Claims Settlement Act; *Cobell et al.* v. *Ken Salazar, Secretary of the Interior, et al.*; as well as others since 2005. Payment of the *Cobell et al.* settlement agreement is another matter, and the US Senate rejected payment in July 2010. See Capriccioso, "Cobell settlement stumbles in Senate." However, Congress authorized funds in December 2010; see *Cobell et al.*, Claims Settlement Agreement.

and non-profit conservation organizations."[64] It remains unclear if this will actually improve the ability of tribes to access the land, but following public concern the "eighteen-seat board has one permanent Native American representative, Larry Meyers."[65] Further, the Maidu Summit Consortium documented more than 17,000 acres of Indian allotments lost to hydroelectric development that could be made available, and partnerships with the Native American Land Conservancy and the Feather River Land Trust are developing.[66] However, these examples represent only a few significant appointments, successful decisions, and potential partnerships. As Richard Clow and Imre Sutton posit, "Tribes still have not fared well ... If some conservation measures have led to beneficial results, gains in one area do not compensate for losses in another whether the trustee or the tribes were in charge."[67]

Land issues and the opportunity to exercise treaty rights for non-federally as well as federally recognized tribes present copious examples of areas of less than positive outcomes in US courts.[68] The recent Supreme Court decision in *Carcieri* v. *Salazar* has been assessed as a significant defeat for the Narragansett Tribe, and perhaps for hundreds of other Indian tribes not federally recognized in 1934. It determined that the Secretary of the Interior was not authorized to acquire lands in trust status, and the Indian Affairs Committee will seek to determine the effect this ruling has on Indian tribes, and what action by Congress, if any, might be required.[69] In the struggle to regain the Black Hills and lands east of the Black Hills by the Lakota as agreed upon in the Fort Laramie Treaty of 1868, the Supreme Court ruled in July

[64] Middleton, "Let this all return to us," 5.   [65] Ibid., 6.

[66] The outcome for tribes remains to be seen, since the forty-seven planning units across twenty-two California counties and the Council have only just embarked on the negotiations that will continue until at least 2013, and, as Middleton notes, "tribal representatives have expressed frustration with the slow nature of the process," as well as the "lack of clarity in the council's requirements for tribes" (p. 6).

[67] Clow and Sutton, *Trusteeship in Change*, p. 315.

[68] For further information on a number of identified sacred sites in North America and around the world, see www.sacredland.org (viewed January 19, 2010).

[69] The Supreme Court's decision has been criticized. For instance, Sarah Washburn, in an article published in the *Washington Law Review*, specifies, "The purposes underlying the IRA, the criteria imposed by federal recognition procedures, and long-standing principles of federal Indian law suggest that tribes formally recognized after 1934 should be entitled to benefits stemming from the trust-land provisions of Section 5 of the IRA." See also details of the decision of February 24, 2009, regarding *Carcieri, Governor of Rhode Island, et al.* v. *Salazar, Secretary of the Interior, et al.* law.cornell.edu/supct/html/07–526. ZS.html (viewed January 21, 2010).

1980 that "a more ripe and rank case of dishonest dealings may never be found in our history."[70] However, the court lacks the power of redress and Congress offered money rather than the return of this sacred land. These examples are similar to many, if not all, instances of negotiations with the United States engaged in by tribes. As might be assumed from these few examples, justice in US courts often has been elusive, and informing and changing public opinion so that justice is a reality will never be straightforward. More often than not, change itself does not proceed beyond what is termed as first order[71] and seldom has the number of positive decisions or appointments led to significant change in public, congressional, or court attitudes, perceptions, or outcomes that are often driven by economics.

For the most part, the efforts in the 1960s and 1970s to raise public awareness and change attitudes in the United States about environmental issues have been successful, and the public thinks of parks and land in terms of conservation. They are something necessary to "save" for future generations through conservation and preservation as in John Muir's time, and a resource to be used for economic gain or recreational activities. These ideas combine with notions of individual and equal rights for all citizens and a complex range of stereotypical assumptions and limited knowledge about the cultural worldview of Native peoples. As this discussion suggests, some of the implicit reasons why the United States voted against the ratification of the UN Declaration may become apparent, such as public opinion, beliefs in individual rights and the popular vote, and legal maneuvering; economic and recreational concerns that side largely with corporations; and court opinions that support government intentions. However, in the explanation of the vote against the Declaration, Robert Hagen explicitly cites the lack of "opportunity to discuss it

---

[70] The US Supreme Court decreed that the Black Hills did belong to the Sioux, and on July 23, 1980, awarded them $105,994,430.52 for the Black Hills (Docket 74B) and $40,245,807.02 for lands taken east of the Black Hills (Docket 74A). The money remains in what some call a "supposedly" interest-bearing account, since it has not been satisfactorily verified, which now amounts to over $757 million in interest, but the Lakota still refuse to take the money. They believe that accepting the settlement would validate the US theft of their most sacred land. See Giago, "Black Hills."

[71] See Watzlawick, Weakland, and Fisch, *Change: Principles of Problem Formation*. The authors assert that first-order change evidences surface changes but the underlying constructions and meanings remain the same, while second-order change creates substantive differences. Thus, second-order change is difficult to achieve, particularly if there is the perception that change did occur. Most Native peoples in the US recognize the lack of substantive change, and thus continue to fight for corrections and resolutions to issues.

collectively," and states needed to "undertake further work to generate a consensus text." These reasons appear disingenuous at best. It also may be apparent why the general public would oppose the precepts in the articles even given collective discussion, since they are intimately tied to Western notions of land rights, natural resources, and the appropriation of land. A more significant understanding of the meaning of land underlies Native perceptions, one that emphasizes care, responsibility, and the importance of knowledge of places.

Accessing sacred sites on public lands

A wide array of disputes among Native peoples and between Native peoples and the general public, corporations, government agencies, and the US National Park Service (NPS) exists. A few prominent examples regarding public lands and sacred sites are illustrative: the creation of Bear Butte State Park in South Dakota, and the practice of climbing Mato Tipila (Bears Lodge or, as it is known by non-Indians, Devils Tower) in Wyoming, particularly during the month of June.

Mato Tipila is a place considered sacred by a number of Plains tribes and shared as such. The basic idea is one of respect. "People don't understand that it's not that Indian people should have exclusive rights there. It's *that* location is sacred enough it should have time of its own. Then, the people who know how to do ceremony should come and minister to it."[72] At the same time, it is a national monument "open for recreational, aesthetic, research, and commercial uses under management by the NPS, a unit of the Department of the Interior."[73] The wants, desires, and needs of competing users such as local non-Indian landholders, rock climbers, and the general public frequently conflict with Native views. And conflicts often stem from a lack of respect for Native spiritual traditions, limited knowledge about long-term historical use, and notions of what constitutes "real" religious practice. The NPS makes "accommodations" for Native peoples, requesting that climbers do not climb Mato Tipila during the month of June,[74] the result of litigation that required the NPS to keep the park open to the public. Between 1990 and 1994, the number of climbers choosing to respect the voluntary ban reflected an average

---

[72] Deloria's comments and interview are part of the special features in the film *In the Light of Reverence*.

[73] Freedman, "Protecting sacred sites," 2.

[74] Freedman, "Protecting Sacred Sites."

annual 79 percent decline during that month. "However, the voluntary compliance rate has been declining and reached a low of 69 percent in June 2004, according to NPS statistics; there were 163 climbers in June 2004, 55 percent of whom were guided."[75] As so often happens, although climbers and the public were supportive of the voluntary ban at its inception, support for policies such as this wane over time and there is a reversion to dominant perceptions and attitudes.

In another example, a recent mode of suppression of Native traditions is to take reservation lands, particularly sacred sites, and turn them into public parks. Bear Butte State Park in South Dakota was and is held sacred as an important fasting site for several Native peoples in the Plains, and some tribes have purchased land surrounding the butte to protect it.[76] Yet, as a public park, "tourists can follow trails to watch Native people vision-questing. Lip service is given in the park literature to respect tobacco and cloth offerings, yet their very mention encourages tourists to look for them and take them home as souvenirs."[77] Native practices and traditions are promoted as exotic tourist attractions for a curious non-Native public. However, depending on the aim or needs of the local economy, changes in policy can occur if more lucrative financial benefits trump "tourist attractions." As James Garrett notes,

> Despite a large protest over the proposed construction [of the largest saloon and biker bar], the town of Sturgis and the State of South Dakota decided that Indian beliefs about the holiness of the butte were of such insignificance that they allowed the construction to go forward. The local newspapers published editorials that referred to Indian communities as being physically dirty and therefore not worthy of holding anything sacred.[78]

Most disturbing are the degrading and racist comments that surface to justify changes in use, particularly when economics are at stake and ideas of what is sacred differ. Western designations tend to memorialize war or conflict, and buildings such as churches are viewed as "appropriate" places designed for religious practice, not land and places such as wilderness or park areas.

Wilderness considered

The idea of "wilderness" has always invoked conflicting notions of land and landscape from John O'Sullivan's coinage of the term "manifest

---

[75] Ibid., 2–3.   [76] Martin, *Indigenous Symbols*, p. 19.
[77] Paper, *Native North American Religious Traditions*, p. 47.
[78] Garrett, "Spiritual freedom," p. 51.

destiny,"[79] to Lewis and Clark's travels, through Frederick Jackson Turner's frontier thesis to the present day. For advocates of the Western idea of wilderness such as Theodore Roosevelt, "young, virile, American men needed to practice the 'savage' arts of war, hunting, and a raw masculinity … legitimizing war and hunting as ways to ensure the 'survival of the fittest.'"[80] This is what the wilderness was for, and it reflected stereotypical notions such as the "Indian savage with cunning prowess over nature."[81] Yet Native peoples "did not distinguish between managed land and wild land as we do today."[82] The idea of "wilderness" was applied to land that had not been taken care of by humans for a long time, where dense understory shrubbery or thickets of young trees block visibility and movement, and a hands-off approach to nature promoted feral landscapes inhospitable to life.[83] The ideal was more one of tending and managing, not one of significantly altering the land for purposes other than indicated by the land and/or the community in general. As Louis Owens interprets, humanity is "a 'natural' part of the landscape; … [and] this displacement of humanity from nature points to perhaps the most profound cause of humankind's destructive relationship with the environment."[84] We see evidence of this, for instance, in the increase of understory that is powerful fuel for massive firestorms and the more recent change in NPS policy toward managed burns.

Current iterations of Western interpretations of wilderness are evidenced in the "risk culture" in which man conquers nature through the practice of extreme sports. As Sarah Ray indicates, "myths of the individual, the genetically superior body, and the wilderness powerfully shape contemporary adventure culture in ways that are at odds with any vision of an inclusive environmental movement." It's "manly" for Tom Cruise or "very feminist" for Angelina Jolie to hang thousands of feet above a valley floor in films such as *Mission Impossible* or *Mr. and Mrs. Smith*. They are virile, strong conquerors of nature and wildness. By implication and association, those brave enough can do the same heli-skiing in British Columbia – "the epicenter of deep powder skiing";[85] rock climbing Yosemite's Half Dome, the "outlet for the energies of the world's most passionate and adventurous people";[86] or bungee jumping at the Grand

---

[79] See "John O'Sullivan coins the phrase 'manifest destiny' 1845," historytools.org/sources/manifest_destiny.pdf (viewed April 28, 2010).

[80] Ray, "Risking bodies in the wild," 266.

[81] Deloria, *Playing Indian*.   [82] Anderson, *Tending the Wild*, p. 3.

[83] Anderson, *Tending the Wild*.   [84] Owens, *Mixedblood Messages*, p. 224.

[85] CMN Heli-Skiing, blog.canadianmountainholidays.com (viewed February 4, 2010).

[86] Supertopo, supertopo.com/climbingareas/yosemite.html (viewed February 4, 2010).

Canyon. Native peoples, on the other hand, do not interpret wilderness in such a way that calls for humans to think of it as untouched and pristine, a resource to change and adapt, or something to satisfy a drive for human adventure designed for individual fulfillment.

Realizing the promise of Articles 25 and 26

Over the past fifty years in particular, the conservation movement in combination with the perceived need for increased recreational and economic use of public lands have gained in momentum. These uses reflect attitudes in the United States that are supported and reinforced through the ideals of individual rights and, by extension, corporate rights, environmental ethics, and the use of natural resources. This also reflects complicated and profound misunderstandings of Native and indigenous cultural worldviews in the definition of nature and wilderness, sacred and protected areas, land and resource management, and cultural and traditional preservation. As Winona LaDuke indicates, "We have a problem of two separate spiritual paradigms and one dominant culture – make that a dominant culture with an immense appetite for natural resources."[87] Furthermore, the differences in paradigms are challenged by a dominant culture whose dedication to individual rights is paramount. And, even in cases of well-intentioned actions to redress wrongs such as at Mato Tipila, the power of cultural prescriptive triumphs over change.

Another significant aspect of this discussion is the explicit conditions and implicit definitions in the UN articles. They may be problematic to some extent, since they emphasize rights over responsibilities. Explicitly they create conditions to address the wrongs of the past. Implicitly, they foster the idea that rights, once established and put into print, can alleviate misperceptions and bring about justice. Is it even possible to change a dominant public whose attitudes were formulated out of a "wilderness" they did not understand and inhabited by peoples they preferred to eliminate? Or, of more concern as individual rights continue to be aggressively asserted, will it be possible for Native peoples to care for and fulfill a responsibility to land and places based in notions of community, relatives, and reciprocity? To address these questions and others, Vine Deloria, Jr. suggested two imperatives that need to be implemented if changes are to be accomplished.

---

[87] LaDuke, *Recovering the Sacred*, p. 14.

First, corrective measures must be taken to eliminate scientific misconceptions about Indians, their culture and their past. Second, there needs to be a way Indian traditions can contribute to the understanding of scientific beliefs at enough specific points so that Indian traditions will be taken seriously as valid bodies of knowledge.[88]

However, attempts to incorporate these imperatives have largely been ignored or avoided by a public intent on its own definitions and entrenched in notions of power and superiority.

Raising awareness, in combination with efforts that reimagine notions of conservation and preservation, may be important areas for consideration and have shown some impact on perceptions and attitudes. More recent work in environmental science and natural resource management by non-Native scholars is encouraging, if not reflective of what Indigenous peoples have known for centuries. Mark Dowie suggests that practices of "exclusionary conservation" do not represent a true ecosystem because it excludes the efforts of Native peoples.[89] Gathering, collecting, hunting, and fishing are ecological processes that cull animal and plant populations, thus making them stronger.[90] Practicing notions of care and tending fulfills and encourages Native imperatives of respect and reciprocal relationships. Yet in a number of ways these notions become constrained and co-opted by Western organizations that demand collaboration. As David Tomblin cautions, "grassroots groups rely on collaborations with large bureaucratic institutions (i.e., National Park Service, Forest Service, Bureau of Indian Affairs, Nature Conservancy, universities, industry) for either financial support or technical assistance."[91] Thus Native participation and the implementation of Native worldviews in the process is complicated and potentially limited. The dilemma of public use is further complicated by significant political winds and public demands that rarely include notions of sacred responsibility to the land. Explicitly, changing language so that the general public understands, and, more importantly, interprets and applies, an indigenous epistemology that reflects a spiritual relationship with the land may be difficult to achieve. Further, any changes most certainly will encounter numerous oppositions both in theory and practice. Individual rights, economics, and for-profit enterprises, and an environmental ethic based on conservation and preservation are deeply held ideals.

[88] Deloria, *Red Earth, White Lies*, p. 60.
[89] Dowie, *Conservation Refugees*.
[90] James J. Garrett, personal communication with author, February 10, 2010.
[91] Tomblin, "Ecological Restoration Movement," 199.

Although the UN Declaration and Articles 25 and 26 are a step in the right direction, it remains to be seen what effect and influence they will have in the United States. Public attitudes and beliefs are persistent and highly influential, and the demand for greater recreational experiences and uses, coupled with the drive for natural resources by powerful corporations continues to be supported by US courts and a public driven by consumerism. Many in the United States will continue to argue for the ideal of individual rights, and "your rights end where mine begin."[92] Yet others, possibly the next generation of students, may make philosophical changes that support community relations and the responsibility of humans to protect places.

Throughout the university course discussed in this paper some non-Native student perceptions remained unchanged. They noted at the end of the class:

> Indians lost the war and were put on reservations ... that is how war is waged. And now America is established. There is no longer an Indian nation ... As far as their right to land goes, this land is America.[93]

Yet other students did evidence a change in their perceptions, and for some Native students it was an opportunity to better articulate their understanding. Discussions of US history, relations, and agreements, coupled with opportunities to hear Native interpretations of relatives and sacred responsibility, helped them to appreciate another worldview and make adjustments in their own. In particular one student was moved to comment:

> The US [is] a "rights" society wherein people feel and believe they have an inherent common privilege to things and materials, when instead the nation needs to become a "responsibility" society that takes responsibility for virtues it has set up for itself, but moreover to recognize past wrongdoing and to do something about it. So whether it was the Lakota people at the "Lodge of the Bear" later to be termed "Devil's Tower" by white society, or the Wintu saving their holy place from western modernization, the facts are known and the people have spoken, and the appropriate action resides in favor of the ancient ones, the American Indians. It is still their home, still their source of medicine, still their place of worship and blessing, all of which belongs to mother earth, the eternal giver of life who hopefully can sustain in enduring the struggles so that all can live on peacefully.[94]

[92] Student comment from in-class survey.
[93] Student comment from an assignment, February 8, 2007.
[94] Student comment from an assignment, February 8, 2007.

From the comments of these students, furthering the education of coming generations and providing direction to ensure the rights and responsibilities of indigenous peoples to care for the earth is critical. However, it will not be a clear and easy path since some will remain entrenched in their beliefs and argue forcefully for Western perspectives, particularly when monetary and economic gains are at issue.

Changes in public attitudes, however unthinkable one hundred years ago, have occurred, and the possibility for further change as indicated in Articles 25 and 26 may be realized in the future. The ratified UN Declaration identifies and supports important areas of concern and is evidence of a shift worldwide in the ways in which indigenous ethics are supported and upheld. It has led to efforts by Native and indigenous peoples to bring to reality the imperatives that Vine Deloria, Jr., suggests, and, "despite opposition, they are restoring their Original Instructions in a modern context."[95] Significantly, "Ecological restoration is inseparable from cultural and spiritual restoration … [and] indigenous spiritual values must be central to the vision of ecological restoration."[96] Groups such as the Indigenous Peoples' Restoration Network and others are posing hope for the future and gaining in political power. But, maybe in the United States it is still the same duck (or public attitude) that can change on a whim or economic benefit as has been evident in the past? Some will support indigenous ethics when it is politically correct, economically feasible, or expedient, but this support can be easily abandoned. I am reminded of the work of Thomas King and the story of the ducks: Coyote is still after the ducks' feathers and trying to hide them from the Human Beings.[97] The story has not really changed; Native peoples still have things that others want – land – resources – rights – traditional responsibilities – spiritual relatives. "Gnarly, difficult, tempting things that try the patience of governments, affront corporations, annoy the general public, and frighten the horses."[98] Indigenous peoples may still be like the ducks looking at their feathers and recognizing they are smaller and less brilliant than they once were, but no less important. And the fight to protect them must still go on. Throughout the world, indigenous peoples will continue to maintain relationships to sacred places and care for all the relatives.

---

[95] Nelson, "Mending the split-head society," 289.
[96] Indigenous Peoples Restoration Network, ser.org/iprn/default.asp (viewed 29 January 2010).
[97] King, *Truth about Stories*, p. 130.   [98] Ibid.

References

Anderson, M. Kat 2005. *Tending the Wild: Native American Knowledge and the Management of California's Natural Resources.* Berkeley: University of California Press.

Ashworth, William 2006. *Ogallala Blue: Water and Life on the High Plains.* New York: W. W. Norton.

Callicott, J. Baird and Nelson, Michael P. 2004. *American Indian Environmental Ethics: An Ojibwa Case Study.* Upper Saddle River, NJ: Pearson Education.

Capriccioso, Rob 2010. "Cobell settlement stumbles in Senate," *Indian Country Today.* July 2.

Clow, Richard L. and Sutton, Imre (eds.) 2001. *Trusteeship in Change: Toward Tribal Autonomy in Resources Management.* Boulder: University of Colorado Press.

Cobell, Eloise Pepion et al., plaintiffs vs. *Ken Salazar, Secretary of the Interior, et al. defendants*: United States District Court for the District of Columbia, Case No. 1:96CV01285-TFH, 14 October 2011.

Class Action Settlement Agreement. United States District Court for the District of Columbia, Case No. 1:96CV01285-JR, filed 10 December 2010.

Copway, George 1978 [1860]. *Indian Life and Indian History by an Indian Author.* University of Chicago.

Deloria, Philip 1998. *Playing Indian.* New Haven, CT: Yale University Press.

Deloria, Vine, Jr., 1995. *Red Earth, White Lies: Native Americans and the Myth of Scientific Fact.* New York: Scribner.

1999. *For This Land: Writings on Religion in America*, ed. and introduction by James Treat. New York: Routledge.

Dowie, Mark 2009. *Conservation Refugees: The Hundred Year Conflict between Global Conservation and Native Peoples.* Cambridge, MA: MIT Press.

Freedman, Eric 2007. "Protecting sacred sites on public land," *American Indian Quarterly* 31/1 Winter: 1–22.

Garrett, James J. 1996. "Indigenous ecological knowledge, intellectual property rights, and neo-colonization," unpublished ms., Humboldt State University.

2010. "Spiritual freedom, pious appropriation," in Martin, *Indigenous Symbols*, pp. 39–54.

Giago, Tim 2007. "The Black Hills: a case of dishonest dealings," *Huffington Report*, June 3, huffingtonpost.com/tim-giago/the-black-hills-a-case-o_b_50480.html (viewed January 29, 2010).

Gilmore, Melvin R. 1987 [1929]. *Prairie Smoke.* St. Paul: University of Minnesota Press.

Hawaii: A Voice for Sovereignty 2009. Film, produced, directed, and written by Catherine Bauknight. Othila Media.

Hirsch, Mark 2010. "Theodore Roosevelt and American Indians," *National Museum of the American Indian*, spring: 34–37.

In the Light of Reverence 2001. Film, produced and directed by Christopher McLeod. Independent Television Service and Native American Public Telecommunications.

In the Spirit of Crazy Horse 1992. Film, directed by James Locker, written by Milo Yellow Hair, produced by Michel Dubois and Kevin McKiernan. Parallax Productions and Access Productions in association with WGBH.

King, Thomas 2003. *The Truth About Stories: A Native Narrative*. St. Paul: University of Minnesota Press.

Kirkness, Verna J. and Barnhardt, Ray 2001. "First Nations and higher education: the four R's – respect, relevance, reciprocity, responsibility," in Hayoe and Pan, *Knowledge across Cultures: A Contribution to Dialogue Among Civilizations*, online resource, Comparative Education Research Centre, University of Hong Kong, eric.ed.gov/.

Klasky, Philip M. 2009/10. "The salt song trail map: the sacred landscape of the Nuwuvi People," *News from Native California*, winter: 8–9.

Klein, Bradley 2010. "Heathens, infidels, and savages: Columbus Day, the Western Shoshone, and the Christian foundations of American empire," *Journal of Race, Ethnicity, and Religion*, 1/4: 1–79, raceandreligion.com/JRER/Articles.html.

Klinger, Scott, and Rebecca Adamson 2009. "The national parks: America's best idea?" CommonDreams.org (viewed February 2, 2010), October 5.

LaDuke, Winona 2005. *Recovering the Sacred: The Power of Naming and Claiming* (Cambridge, MA: South End Press).

McAvoy, Leo 2002. "American Indians, place meanings and the old/new west," *Journal of Leisure Research* 34/4: 383–96.

Martin, Kathleen J. (ed.) 2010. *Indigenous Symbols and Practices in the Catholic Church: Visual Studies, Missionization and Appropriation*. Burlington, VT: Ashgate.

Menzies, Charles P. (ed.) 2006. *Traditional Ecological Knowledge and Natural Resource Management*. Lincoln: University of Nebraska Press.

Michigan Indian Land Claims Settlement Act, Public Law 105-143, 15 December 1997, www.gpo.gov/fdsys/pkg/PLAW-105publ143/pdf/PLAW-105publ143.pdf.

Middleton, Beth Rose 2009/10. "Let this all return to us: working to reclaim land through the pacific forest and watershed lands stewardship council," *News from Native California*, winter: multiple pages.

Mohawk, John 2008. "The Iroquois Confederacy," in Melissa K. Nelson (ed.), *Original Instructions: Indigenous Teachings for a Sustainable Future* (Rochester, VT: Bear & Co.), pp. 54–58.

Nelson, Melissa K. 2008. "Mending the split-head society with trickster consciousness," in Nelson (ed.), *Original Instructions: Indigenous Teachings for a Sustainable Future* (Rochester, VT: Bear & Co.), pp. 288–97.

Newcomb, Steven 2010. "Has the US changed position on the Declaration? Not really," *Indian Country Today*, December 31, indiancountrytodaymedia network.com/ict_sbc/has-us-changed-position-on-declaration-not-really (viewed July 18, 2011).

Owens, Louis 1998. *Mixedblood Messages: Literature, Film, Family, Place* (Norman: University of Oklahoma Press).

Paper, Jordan 2007. *Native North American Religious Traditions: Dancing for Life* (Westport: Praeger).

Ray, Sarah Jaquette 2009. "Risking bodies in the wild: the 'corporeal unconscious' of American adventure culture," *Journal of Sport and Social Issues* 33/3: 257–84.

Scully, Diana 14 February 1995. "Main Indian Claims Settlement," Maine Indian Tribal-State Commission (viewed 7 January 2012), www.mitsc.org/documents/21_Body.doc.pdf.

Slick, Delvin, and Willeto, Karen 2010. "The photographic vision of Delvin Slick," in Martin (ed.), *Indigenous Symbols*, pp. 175–84.

Starmer, Kate. "Ken Burns shares his national parks experiences," fodors.com/news/story_3625.html (viewed January 29, 2010).

The National Parks: America's Best Idea 2009. Film by Ken Burns, written by Dayton Duncan, produced by Dayton Duncan and Ken Burns. Florentine Films and WETA.

Tomblin, David 2009. "The Ecological Restoration Movement: diverse cultures of practice and place," *Organization and Environment* 22/2: 185–207.

United Nations, 13 September 2007. "United Nations Declaration on the Rights of Indigenous Peoples adopted by the General Assembly," press release, http://www.un.org/esa/socdev/unpfii/en/declaration.html (viewed 7 January 2012).

United Nations Declaration on the Rights of Indigenous Peoples, Adopted by the General Assembly September 13, 2007. www.un.org/esa/socdev/unpfii/documents/DRIPS_en.pdf.

United Nations Report to the General Assembly on the First Session of the Human Rights Council, 30 June 2006, UN Doc. A/HRC/1/L.10/Add.1 (2006).

Washburn, Sarah 2010. "Distinguishing *Carcieri v. Salazar*: Why the Supreme Court got it wrong and how Congress and Courts should respond to preserve Tribal and Federal interests in the IRA's trust-land provisions," *Washington Law Review* 85: 603–46.

Watzlawick, Paul, Weakland, John H., and Fisch, Richard 1974. *Change: Principles of Problem Formation and Problem Resolution*. New York: Norton.

Weaver, Jace 2001. *Other Words: American Indian Literature, Law, and Culture.* Norman: University of Oklahoma Press.

Williams, Jr., Robert A. 2005. *Like a Loaded Weapon: The Rehnquist Court, Indian Rights and the Legal History of Racism in America*. Minneapolis: University of Minnesota Press.

Winnemem Wintu Tribe, "Long trail to justice," winnememwintu.us (viewed January 19, 2010).

8

Seeking the corn mother: transnational indigenous organizing and food sovereignty in Native North American literature

JONI ADAMSON

The story of corn has been told in many literary works by Native North American writers. In *Pushing the Bear*, for example, Diane Glancy follows the Cherokee along the Trail of Tears, from the moment they are forcibly torn from their gardens in the 1830s, through the wrenching days of hunger they experience as they are driven to Oklahoma, mourning the loss of loved ones and lamenting the loss of their seed corn. When main character Maritole is removed from her farm by American soldiers, she remembers the place she was born and thinks, "The cornstalks were our grandmothers ... Their voices were the long tassels reading the air. Our spirits clung to them. Our roots entwined."[1] In *Fight Back*, Acoma Pueblo writer Simon Ortiz explains the fierce bond between indigenous North American peoples and "Grandmother Corn." Corn, writes Ortiz, cannot "be regarded as anything less than a sacred and holy and respected product of the creative forces of life, land, and the people's responsibilities and relationships to each other."[2] The earth regenerates the human body when people eat corn and, when they die, humans return to the earth and the cycle continues.

Other Native North American writers, however, point to the experiences of tribal groups whose relationships with the corn mother were interrupted or lost and who, as a consequence, disappeared as a culture and as a people. In *Gardens in the Dunes*, Laguna Pueblo novelist Leslie Marmon Silko tells the story of Sister Salt and Indigo, indigenous sisters living at the borders between Arizona and California at the turn of the nineteenth century. Throughout the novel, Indigo makes connections

---

[1] Diane Glancy, *Pushing the Bear* (New York: Harvest Books, 1996), 4.
[2] Simon Ortiz, "Fight Back: For the Sake of the People, For the Sake of the Land," in Ortiz, *Woven Stone* (Tucson: University of Arizona Press, 1992), 346.

between the foodways of her own tribe and those of other tribal peoples who value "Mother Corn."[3] Silko names the sisters' tribe the "Sand Lizards" and details how they have been hunted, rounded up, moved to reservations or shipped off to boarding schools. As a consequence of this dispersal and because of the construction of a dam that deprives them of the water for their subsistence gardens, the Sand Lizards can no longer sustain themselves and are disappearing from their traditional homelands. Silko bases the Sand Lizards on an actual band of the Tohono O'odham people known as the Hia C-ed O'odham or Sand People.[4] According to Gary Nabhan, the Sand People left their traditional lands in the 1920s, after engineers upstream from their village "damned and diverted [the river's] entire flow. There was suddenly not a drop available to flood-irrigate native crops as there had been for centuries. Without the ability to farm … nearly all the Sand [People] left the area."[5] Today this once-distinct band has faded into the larger group of O'odham people still living in the Sonoran Desert on both sides of the United States–Mexico border.

During her lifetime, another well-known North American writer, Gloria Anzaldúa, did not claim to be indigenous but did write about her family's relationship to corn. She clearly recognized that the struggles of indigenous peoples in the Lower Rio Grande Valley where she grew up cohered around agriculture and labor. In passages where Anzaldúa is discussing her family, she explains that members of indigenous groups in both Texas and neighboring Mexican state Tamaulipas were often forced to fade into agricultural fields or mining camps, where they "passed" as "Mexicans" in order to survive. In an interview with Inés Hernandez-Avila and Domino Perez foregrounding the indigenous intersections manifested in Chicana/o and Native American literatures, Anzaldúa states that she first came to recognize similarities between her own "dark skin" and "demeanor" when she looked into the "faces of the braceros that worked for my father. Los braceros were mostly indios from central Mexico who came to work in the fields of South Texas."[6] Even though her heritage made her "three-quarters Indian," she had grown up in Texas, a state where every "Indian group including the Mexican indigenous" had

[3] Leslie Marmon Silko, *Gardens in the Dunes* (New York: Simon & Schuster, 1999), 166.

[4] Gary Nabhan, *Gathering the Desert* (Tucson: University of Arizona Press, 1985), 52.

[5] Gary Nabhan, *Cultures of Habitat: On Nature, Culture and Story* (Washington DC: Counterpoint, 1997), 143.

[6] Inés Hernandez-Avila and Domino Perez, "Speaking across the Divide," *MELUS: Multi-Ethnic Literatures of the United States*, 15.3 and 15.4 (Fall 2003–Winter 2004): 7–21, 8.

been "decimated."[7] Having lost the specifics of her bloodlines, she was proud to call herself a Chicana.

Her most well-known book of poetry and prose, *Borderlands/La Frontera*, lovingly portrays her mixed indigenous background. She employs "Mother Corn" as a metaphor for addressing the issues that face impoverished, detribalized, and displaced peoples living in the United States–Mexico border region. In a discussion of her family's experiences, Anzaldúa laments the poverty and displacement that follow loss of tribal affiliation, agroecological knowledge, and long-cherished supplies of seed corn. Describing her life among migrant workers and the few indigenous small-scale farmers still hanging on to their lands in Texas, she envisions her own individual strength as a woman as rooted and husked. "Indigenous like corn, like corn, the *mestiza* is a product of crossbreeding, designed for preservation under a variety of conditions. Like an ear of corn – a female seed-bearing organ – the mestiza is tenacious, tightly wrapped in the husks of her culture … with thick stalks and strong brace roots, she holds tight to the earth – she will survive the crossroads."[8] She also connects corn to the struggles of her father, a sharecropper who lost his land to fraud, then was forced to work for one of the Anglo-owned agribusiness corporations that was buying up land in Texas in the 1930s for large-scale farming. At only 38 years of age, he died a tragically early death. As an indigenous person with no recognized legal or civil rights on either side of the border, he had no recourse after losing his land and became representative of indigenous peoples displaced by nationalistic and corporate rhetoric about economic development and progress.

What we see in the work of a number of Native North American poets and novelists, then, is an awareness of the critical relationship between indigenous peoples and the foods that are culturally and nutritionally necessary to their survival, a connection that is often referred to as "food sovereignty." A people's right to food, or the right of communities or nations to control their own first foods and food supply chains has been prominently supported by the United Nations Declaration on the Rights of Indigenous Peoples (UNDRIP). Although international laws such as UNDRIP are most often crafted, studied, and analyzed by politicians, economists, historians, and policy analysts, I would like to illustrate in this chapter how literature can enhance public understanding of why indigenous peoples around the world are advocating a rights- and

---

[7] Hernandez-Avila and Perez, "Speaking across the Divide," 12.
[8] Gloria Anzaldúa, *Borderlands/La Frontera* (San Francisco: Spinsters/*aunt lute*, 1987), 81.

culturally based approach to food. Novels, poetry, and creative non-fiction can often be read as "case studies" that offer insights into why issues such as food sovereignty matter not just to indigenous peoples but to all people of the world. It is important at the outset of any discussion or course focused on indigenous food sovereignty and literature, of course, to state clearly that traditional indigenous agroecological activities are not just a "symbol" or "metaphor" for political resistance and that political resistance is not always the focus of the farmers who are exercising their autonomy without feigning to inspire or lead an organized political movement, although some do become part of such movements. Moreover, it is unlikely that many indigenous farmers in the Americas are themselves necessarily familiar with the creative works of Native North American writers, although it is understood that poetry and novels can inspire organized acts of political-discursive resistance.

That said, if literature which portrays the human relationship to first foods is set within larger contexts that illuminate the current necessity for global and local indigenous campaigns for food sovereignty and the need for international documents such as UNDRIP, then literary analysis can be seen as a form of intellectual inquiry that complements and enhances legal, political, or policy discussions of these documents. Literary works also contribute importantly to understandings of the cultures and local and global contexts from which these campaigns emerge, and set issues surrounding the industrialization of food production and globalization within more accessible frameworks that illuminate their connections to past and present. In this chapter I shall focus on the work of Diane Glancy, Leslie Marmon Silko, and Gloria Anzaldúa, to illustrate how literature can contribute to better understanding of hemispheric American indigenous alliance-building focused on corn, seeds, patenting, and food sovereignty, as I work to illuminate the relationship – to use the words of UNDRIP Article 31 – between indigenous knowledge and indigenous "manifestations of ... sciences, technologies and cultures".[9] This will allow me to examine how UNDRIP, and other international documents and declarations, are providing a framework for an emerging food sovereignty movement that is linking indigenous and small-scale farmers with

---

[9] United Nations Declaration on the Rights of Indigenous Peoples, Adopted by the General Assembly 13 September 2007, www.un.org/esa/socdev/unpfii/documents/DRIPS_en.pdf (accessed June 1, 2009). See Art. 3 on self-determination, Art. 20 on subsistence and development, Art. 24 on traditional medicines and health, Art. 26 on territories and resources, Art. 29 on environmental protection, and Art. 31 on the right to maintain and conserve seeds and flora.

ethnobotanists, microbiologists, progressive food policy-makers, and plant genomics scientists, NGOs, and the United Nations Environmental Programme's Convention on Biological Diversity (CBD).

Food sovereignty

Descriptions of military-enforced displacement in *Pushing the Bear*, dam construction in *Gardens in the Dune*, and corporate agribusiness in *Borderland/La Frontera* illustrate an awareness among Native North American women writers of how nation-state or corporate-sponsored land appropriations and development projects affect a community's ability – or inability – to control their own food supplies and food-producing resources and how this can mean the difference between survival or death. The experiences of Maritole, the Sand Lizard sisters, and Anzaldúa herself, especially after they are dispossessed of their lands, offer richly drawn images that help readers acquire a deeper understanding of the stance being taken by contemporary indigenous farmers throughout the Americas who are organizing around a food sacred to indigenous peoples – corn – which is increasingly at the center of fierce debates about neoliberal development projects, trade liberalization, genetic engineering, intellectual property rights, and food sovereignty.

"Food sovereignty," or the notion that humans have a sovereign "right to food" has been affirmed in an array of international instruments created by international governmental and non-government alliances. These documents include the United Nations International Bill of Human Rights (1948) and the International Covenant on Economic, Social and Cultural Rights (1976).[10] "Food sovereignty" entered international policy debates when it was put forward at the 1996 World Food Summit.[11] It was defined at the First Indigenous Peoples' Global Consultation on the Right to Food and Food Sovereignty in 2002 by the International Indian Treaty Council (IITC), an organization of indigenous peoples from North, Central, and South America, the Caribbean, and the Pacific. The "Declaration of Atitlán" which emerged from this meeting affirmed that "Food sovereignty for indigenous peoples is a collective right based on rights to our lands, territories and natural resources, the practice of

---

[10] International Covenant on Economic, Social and Cultural Rights, Office of the United Nations High Commissioner for Human Rights, www2.ohchr.org/english/law/cescr. htm#art27 (accessed July 16, 2010).

[11] World Food Summit, Food and Agriculture Organization (FAO) of the United Nations, www.fao.org/wfs/index_en.htm (accessed July 19, 2010).

our cultures, languages and traditions, and is essential to our identity as Peoples."[12] This declaration emerged from over thirty years of previous work, in the form of meetings and summits held throughout the Americas, and increasingly focused on the concepts of "nutritional sovereignty" or "food sovereignty," which called attention to the ideologies and external forces that have been threatening indigenous food systems for hundreds of years.[13]

At the 2007 Third Continental Summit of the Indigenous Peoples and Nationalities of Abya Yala, held in Iximché, Guatemala, for example, food sovereignty was at the center of discussion.[14] Many of the delegates were corn farmers who spoke out against rising prices for basic foods, noting that the cost of their most valued staple food – corn – was rising dramatically as it was being diverted to an expanding market for feed for beef and to an alternative fuel market for increased production of ethanol. In the declaration written at the summit, Abya Yala delegates, representing indigenous groups from throughout the Americas, reaffirmed their "decision to defend the nutritional sovereignty and struggle against the transgenetic invasion, convoking all peoples of the world to join this struggle in order to guarantee our future."[15] This summit highlighted many of the same problems surrounding neoliberal trade policies that the famously masked Zapatista rebels, many of whom were corn farmers, called to the world's attention when they burst out of the Lancandón jungle in southern Mexico in 1994 on the day the North American Free Trade Agreement went into effect.[16]

The range of rights required for the full exercise of "food sovereignty" was affirmed in 2007 by UNDRIP, which pays particular attention to the connections between the right to cultural and economic self-determination and the right to maintain and protect seeds and medicines

---

[12] International Treaty Council, Declaration of Atitlán, www.treatycouncil.org/new_page_5241224.htm (accessed July 6, 2010).

[13] For a summary of this organizing, see Marc Becker, "Third Continental Summit of Indigenous Peoples and Nationalities of Abya Yala: From Resistance to Power," *Latin American and Caribbean Ethnic Studies* 3, 1 (2008): 85–107.

[14] "Abya Yala" means "continent of life" and refers to all three of North, Central, and South America.

[15] Declaration of Iximché: Final Statement from the III Continental Summit of Indigenous Nations and Pueblos of Abya Yala, Iximché, *Native Web*, www.nativeweb.org/papers/statements/state/Iximche.php (accessed May 10, 2007).

[16] The Zapatistas, or Ejercito Zapatista de Liberación Nacional, are an indigenous-led group that surprised the world as a guerrilla uprising in 1994 and took a stand against the implementation of the North American Free Trade Agreement (NAFTA).

anciently developed through traditional agroecological practices. In any discussion of Native North American literature focused on first foods or connections to UNDRIP articles focused on the "right to food" or "food sovereignty," it is important to point to both Global South organizing since the 1960s (covered by Becker, cited above), campaigns such as the Zapatista rebellion, and the Abya Yala Summit, *and* the persistent responses of indigenous North American communities to broken treaties between First Nations and the expansionist United States.

For example, in the fifty years after the Pacific Northwest territory of Washington became a state (1889–1939), non-indigenous commercial fishers caught salmon by the millions of tons in the Pacific Ocean and Puget Sound, but the state blamed declining fish runs on Indian netting and lawlessness. It was argued that Indian fishermen did not follow state-mandated seasons, did not get licenses or heed catch limits. Then, in 1974, after years of protests and indigenous-led "fish-ins," and a lawsuit against the state of Washington based in sovereign treaty rights, Federal Judge George H. Boldt issued one of the most sweeping rulings in the history of the Pacific Northwest, affirming the treaty rights of Northwest tribal fishermen and allocating to them 50 percent of the harvestable catch of salmon and steelhead. According to University of Colorado law professor Charles F. Wilkinson, the Boldt Decision is still among the two or three most significant decisions in the history of Indian law.[17] But beyond its importance to US Indian law, what is important to indigenous food sovereignty movements about this decision is that it calls attention to the ways in which struggles for fishing rights in the Northwest were about the defense of first foods, which are at the center of many tribal identities. This means that the struggle for fishing rights, which began even before Washington's statehood, must be seen as an earlier form of the struggle for food sovereignty couched in the language of tribal sovereignty and treaty rights, and now in the language of UNDRIP.

Mother corn in the open hand and the closed fist

To the botanist, corn is maize, or *Zea mays*, a plant that originated in Mexico, one of the world's "centers of biological diversity."[18] In *The Story*

---

[17] See Charles Wilkinson, *Messages from Frank's Landing: A Story of Salmon, Treaties, and the Indian Way* (University of Washington Press, 2006).

[18] Gary Nabhan, *Where Our Food Comes From: Retracing Nikolay Vavilov's Quest to End Famine* (Washington DC: Island Press, 2009), 20.

of Corn, Betty Fussell writes that corn provided indigenous American cultures from Mexico north to the Great Lakes in North America with a seed and a food through which they encoded knowledge of thousands of varieties of corn bred for every ecological niche.[19] The wild progenitor of corn, according to molecular biologists and ecologists, is "teosinte," which, in the Nahautl language, means "mother of corn." According to Gary Nabhan, this tall grass can still be found growing wild near Mexico City and at the edges of corn fields where indigenous farmers credit it with cross-pollinating and reinvigorating their seed.[20] Writing about the place of corn in indigenous communities today, Patricia Kleindienst observes that after the "mother of corn" migrated with humans from Mesoamerica into what is now North America, it evolved into hundreds of "ethnoecological adaptations" that were dependent not only on the place "where it was cultivated" but on "the people whose hands planted, tended and harvested it. Oaxaca Green, Hopi Blue, Pawnee Black Eagle, Cherokee White Eagle, Iroquois White."[21]

The migration of "mother corn" over the course of thousands of years as it passed from one culture to the next helps to explain why Article 31 of UNDRIP refers to agroecological knowledge, in the form of sophisticated understandings of seed cultivation and domestication, medicines, and the properties of flora and fauna, as "traditional cultural expressions." Article 31 reads as follows:

> Indigenous peoples have the right to maintain, control, protect and develop their cultural heritage, traditional knowledge and traditional cultural expressions, as well as the manifestations of their sciences, technologies and cultures, including human and genetic resources, seeds, medicines, knowledge of the properties of fauna and flora … They also have the right to maintain, control, protect and develop their intellectual property over such cultural heritage, traditional knowledge, and traditional cultural expressions.

The work of Glancy, Silko, and Anzaldúa clearly illustrates what is at stake when the relationship between indigenous peoples and the first foods they depend on are threatened and why agroecological knowledge as a form of cultural expression is so vigorously defended. Glancy poignantly

---

[19] Betty Fussell, *The Story of Corn* (Albuquerque: University of New Mexico Press, 1992), 15.

[20] Nabhan, *Where Our Food Comes From*, 143, 149.

[21] Patricia Kleindienst, *The Earth Knows My Name: Food, Culture and Sustainability in the Gardens of Ethnic Americans* (Boston, MA: Beacon Press, 2006), 228–29. See also Fussell, *Story of Corn*, 16.

presents the emotional links between human and plant and thus provides her readers with a better understanding of the concept of food sovereignty with the words she puts in the mouth of Maritole's dying father. Forced onto the Trail of Tears, and far away from his tight log cabin, fragrant peach trees, and thriving garden, he thinks longingly of the farm from which he has been torn, and fears for the future of his family if they cannot regain access to their sacred corn seed. He cries, "Corn! That's what we eat. We can't live without corn. It's our bodies. Our lives."[22]

In *Gardens in the Dunes*, Silko emphasizes the importance of the migration of seed corn and other plants. Indigo and Sister Salt are taught by their grandmother to feed themselves by planting corn, beans, and squash in the "old gardens." Grandmother Fleet plants seeds in sand dunes that might look unfertile to an outsider. However, she understands the patterns of the desert climate and the intricacies of the soil and knows where to plant each variety of seed in order to get the highest yield. For Grandmother Fleet, seeds and other culturally meaningful foods represent the experience, inventiveness, and hard work of her ancestors. They call attention to indigenous, agroecological knowledges that have collectively and accretionally evolved through generations in the Americas. Grandmother shares her ethnobotanical knowledge with her granddaughters and encourages them to be innovative by urging them to "collect as many seeds as they could carry home."[23] Silko emphasizes Grandmother Fleet's belief that the essence of agricultural innovation is seed collection and exchange. Seeds shared and sown in new places reproduce themselves freely and adapt to new climates and environments. Thus, when indigenous and migrating people open their hands to share seeds, they help to increase botanical biodiversity as they assist the plants in adapting to new environments.

In *Borderland/La Frontera*, Anzaldúa's discussion of her father's experiences as a corn farmer illustrate how corporate greed turns the open hand offering seeds as a gift into a clenched fist symbolizing the enclosure of common resources for private profit.[24] This discussion reveals the deeper meaning of her use of the corn metaphor and its significance for the focus of UNDRIP on collective and individual rights, seeds, biodiversity, and the role of corporations in the increasingly rapid loss of indigenous

---

[22] Glancy, *Pushing the Bear*, 79.   [23] Silko, *Gardens in the Dunes*, 83.

[24] The idea of an open hand sharing seeds, as opposed to the clenched fist of corporate seed breeders, is developed in Andrew Mushita and Carol B. Thompson, *Biopiracy of Biodiversity: Global Exchange as Enclosure* (Trenton NJ and Asmara, Eritrea: Africa World Press, 2007), 27.

cultural and agroecological knowledges. What is tightly wrapped in the husk of the corn metaphor is the loss of hundreds of indigenous varieties of corn throughout the Americas due to the activities of plant breeders and agribusiness corporations in the late nineteenth century and the first half of the twentieth century.

North of the United States–Mexico border, writes Betty Fussell, a growing group of Anglo-American seed breeders were discovering the diversity of indigenous varieties of corn, called "landraces," which evolved through thousands of years of both natural and human selection. North American seed breeders took seeds that had been domesticated first in Mexico and (promising their US customers unlimited yields and progress on an infinite scale) focused their research on only a few varieties they called "primitive cultivars." Later in the twentieth century, after hybridizing or crossing certain varieties of seed, plant breeders and scientists termed these seeds "advanced or elite" cultivars, then patented them as private property and sold them for profit. Vandana Shiva has called the patenting of elite cultivars "biopiracy" because corporations claim private ownership over domesticated seeds while hiding the "prior use, knowledge, and rights associated" with indigenous uses of primitive cultivars over the course of thousands of years.[25]

For example, writes Betty Fussell, in the first half of the twentieth century, Henry Wallace, founder of Hi-Bred Corn Company proudly advanced the theory that hybridized varieties proved that the white man had done more for corn, more quickly, than the indigenous domesticators of the seed. Later, however, he began expressing alarm over his own work as it dawned upon him that the vast diversity of corn landraces were disappearing. The threat posed by the cultivation of too narrow a selection of food crops and seed varieties was demonstrated, he allowed, by the Irish potato famine of the 1840s and 1850s. Man's "exploitation of corn," Wallace eventually realized, "had altered the plant irrevocably and, in evolutionary lingo, more 'catastrophically' than all the millennia over which it had evolved."[26] By 1956, Wallace was predicting impending disaster and warned researchers to think more carefully about the fist that was closing around seed corn as breeders fell into a headlong rush to increase yields and profits. The disaster occurred in 1970, writes Fussell, when genetic uniformity of commercial hybrid corn had made

---

[25] See Vandana Shiva, *Biopiracy: The Plunder of Nature and Knowledge* (Boston, MA: South End Press, 1997), 51, 55, 73.

[26] Fussell, *Story of Corn*, 86.

it "susceptible to a new mutant strain of southern corn-leaf blight that dramatized the dangers of sacrificing diversity to yield."[27] Of the US corn crop grown that year, 13 to 25 percent was lost.

The impact of this disaster and others on small-scale farmers is poignantly illustrated in the section of *Borderlands/LaFrontera* subtitled "El Retorno," in which Anzaldúa visits her brother who is a corn farmer in Texas. Her brother tells her, "It's been a bad year for corn ... Farming is in a bad way. ... Two to three thousand farmers went bankrupt in this country last year."[28] Read in the larger context of global economic forces that led directly to the drafting of sections of the Abya Yala Declaration and UNDRIP that pertain to farming, it becomes clear that the brother's statement has implications for the entire hemisphere. Anzaldúa's brother is referring to 1980s blights that disastrously impacted small-scale farmers who were monocropping hybridized seeds. Their situations were made worse by the fluctuating costs of oil, synthetic fertilizers and pesticides, and machinery. Anzaldúa's brother makes his statement in 1982, the same year that oil prices fell and price guarantees were withdrawn from farmers in Mexico. As María Josephina Saldaña-Portillo explains in *The Revolutionary Imagination in the Americas*, during the oil boom years of the 1970s and early 1980s, the Mexican government used oil profits to invest heavily in energy development projects that drew indigenous corn farmers out of the highlands to work at dam construction sites. However, the majority of these workers continued to return and farm their lands because the government was also using oil profits to guarantee prices for corn. Farmers were able to grow enough corn not only to support themselves, but to enter the export market and, for the first time, to become integrated into the national economy. After oil prices fell in 1982, and on the advice of the World Bank, which was preparing the way for the North American Free Trade Agreement (NAFTA), the Mexican government abruptly curtailed corn subsidies. Thousands of corn farmers were now unable to compete in the international market.

Later, Saldaña continues, in pre-NAFTA negotiations with the United States and Canada, Mexican President Carlos Salinas de Gotarí further ushered in the new frontier of the free market. Comparing Mexican agriculture to the seemingly endless fields of grain production in the central United States, he viewed Mexican farmers "as relics of another era, their production techniques backward and inefficient, their

---

[27] Ibid., 93.   [28] Anzaldúa, *Borderlands/La Frontera*, 90.

communally held lands wastefully under-utilized."[29] Under the terms of NAFTA, Mexican farmers would be expected to modernize, and price supports would be unavailable. Meanwhile, in the United States, American farmers were still enjoying government subsidies and producing hybridized varieties of corn so cheaply that US agribusiness firms were able to sell it below the cost of production. This drove many more Mexican farmers out of the market for corn,[30] which helps to explain why, from 1982 to the 1994 rebellion, Zapatista ranks swelled with displaced corn farmers. It also helps to explain why, in 2007, many of the delegates to the Iximché Summit, who were also corn farmers, committed themselves to building alliances "among our indigenous nations and the movements for social justice of the continent that would allow us to collectively confront the policies of neo-liberalism and all forms of oppression."[31]

Thus, when Gloria Anzaldúa's brother observes that 1982 was a bad year for corn, he is linking small-scale indigenous and non-indigenous corn farmers in the United States to other small-scale farmers throughout the hemisphere who are confronting the fist closing around seeds that are sold only for profit and farmed using techniques that favor large corporate agribusiness. In a section of the book subtitled "El Otro Mexico," Anzaldúa remembers witnessing the end of small-scale dry farming in the 1950s as corporate farmers scraped "the land clean" of the natural "brush, chaparral and cactus" in order to introduce vast spans of monocultural crops and the synthetic fertilizers, pesticides, and irrigation systems needed to grow them.[32] The Rio Grande Valley had been "cut up into thousands of neat rectangles and squares, constantly being irrigated."[33] What she was seeing was something that agroecological farmers the world over are also witnessing. They are watching the health of soils decline as they are compacted by heavy machinery and deadened by agrochemicals and, as a result, require more irrigation than do living soils rich in organic matter and microorganisms. Anzaldúa clearly connects the loss of indigenous cultures

---

[29] María Josephina Saldaña-Portillo, *The Revolutionary Imagination in the Americas and the Age of Development* (Durham, NC: Duke University Press, 2003), 218.

[30] Kathleen McAfee, "Corn Culture and Dangerous DNA: Real and Imagined Consequences of Maize Transgene Flow in Oaxaca," *Journal of Latin American Geography*, 2, 1 (2003): 29.

[31] Declaration of Iximché, www.nativeweb.org/papers/statements/state/Iximche.php (accessed May 10, 2007).

[32] Anzaldúa, *Borderlands/La Frontera*, 9.   [33] Ibid.

and knowledge about soils and water with the loss of land and healthy ecosystems.

What is revealed by the corn metaphor in *Borderlands/LaFrontera* are the links between colonization, imperialism, displaced farmers, lost indigenous landraces of corn, broken cultural bonds, and trade liberalization that favors large-scale corporate farming techniques. Article 5 of UNDRIP calls for measures that will protect against these losses and ensure the human and civil rights that will allow the cultivators and domesticators of one of the world's most important crops to maintain their landbases and protect their knowledge of seeds and small-scale farming techniques. In the era of NAFTA, as the Zapatistas reminded the world during negotiations with the Mexican government, the farmer has become expendable and Mexico – along with the rest of the world – is being ushered into an era of industrialized food products over which it has no control. The problem in Mexico, then, is not simply economic oppression or environmental degradation; it is that the corporations backed by the World Bank are being given the right to make determinations about the nation's and the world's food and seed supply.

By refusing to have their struggle reduced to ethnicity or race, or a set of economic indicators, the Zapatistas summoned not only indigenous Mexican groups, but all "citizens of the nation to the process of remaking [the nation]."[34] A stranglehold on seeds in Mexico would not be a problem for Mexico alone, they told the nation; it would be a problem for the entire world. Article 5 of UNDRIP calls for the right of indigenous peoples, as individuals and/or as collectives, to enter into negotiations with nation states, just as the Zapatistas did with their own national government, in order to "maintain and strengthen their distinct political, legal, economic, social and cultural institutions, while retaining their right to participate fully, if they so choose, in the political, economic, social and cultural life of the State" (UNDRIP, Art. 5). Thus Article 5 calls upon international and national communities to recognize the civil, human, and collective rights of indigenous peoples to "maintain, control, protect and develop their cultural heritage, traditional knowledge and traditional cultural expressions" (UNDRIP, Art. 31). Anzaldúa's father's tragic death stands as a stark reminder of why indigenous peoples around the world are organizing to protect both human and civil rights that will guarantee their right to food sovereignty.

---

[34] Saldaña, *Revolutionary Imagination*, 247.

Science, transgenes, and patents

Leslie Marmon Silko's *Almanac of the Dead*, published in 1991, is still being celebrated for being one of the first novels to represent the transnational indigenous organizing that was taking place throughout the Americas for several decades before the adoption of UNDRIP.[35] In the novel, Silko imagines a growing alliance headed by indigenous leaders that includes not only recognized indigenous groups but other detribalized groups who self-identify as native even though they may not be formally recognized by a nation state. Thus the novel anticipates the Preamble to UNDRIP, which recognizes that "the situation of indigenous peoples varies from region to region and from country to country" and that "the significance of national and regional particularities and various historical and cultural backgrounds should be taken into consideration". In the novel, the main alliance organizers, twin sisters Lecha and Zeta, self-identity as members of a US Yaqui Pueblo Indian group that falls outside the category of "sovereign, treaty-recognized nation."[36] Lecha and Zeta are living on a ranch near Tucson, Arizona, and organizing a trans-hemispheric indigenous-led movement. In the southern hemisphere, they are working with Angelita, one of the Mayan leaders of an "Army of Resistance and Retribution" that is marching north towards the United States–Mexico border.[37] In the northern hemisphere, they are working with the Barefoot Hopi whose grassroots group works primarily to ensure the human rights of people being held in prisons. He has also formed an alliance with a group of "ecowarriors," whose objective is to oppose large-scale state and corporate development projects, or, more particularly, dams and nuclear reactors.

In an interview with Ellen Arnold, Silko states that if *Almanac* is about the transnational organization it will take to change the political and ecological directions in which we are going, then her next novel, *Gardens*

---

[35] United Nations Permanent Forum on Indigenous Issues, "About UNPFII and a Brief History of Indigenous Peoples and the International System," www.un.org/esa/socdev/unpfii/en/history.html (accessed August 17, 2009).

[36] The Yaquis were not recognized by the United States until 1978. For an in-depth history of the historical contact between the Maya of the Yucatán peninsula and the Yaqui of Sonora, Mexico, and Yaqui pueblos of Arizona, see Joni Adamson, *American Indian Literature, Environmental Justice, and Ecocriticism: The Middle Place* (Tucson, AZ: University of Arizona Press, 2001), 142.

[37] For more on *Almanac of the Dead* as fictional representation of the Zapatistas, see Adamson, *American Indian Literature*, 131–36, 145.

in the Dunes, asks, "Where do we go from here?"[38] By writing about two young sisters who are learning agroecological farming methods from their grandmother, Silko implies that "where we go from here" must be addressing global challenges to food sovereignty. Indeed, Silko tells Arnold that in the course of writing *Gardens in the Dunes*, she discovered that growing food and "how you grow your food" is "the most political thing of all."[39]

In the novel, the younger sister, Indigo, travels to Europe and back with the rich American couple which adopts her. This journey provides readers with further illustration of how seed collection and sharing contributes to the well-being of communities and nations, while the profiteering and greed of biopiracy and patenting undermines the ability of many indigenous communities to survive. Early in the novel, after she escapes from a US Indian Boarding School, Indigo is adopted by Hattie and Edward, who take her on an extended trip through Europe to study botany. Edward, a landed gentleman and botanist who collects plant materials worldwide keeps detailed records of his travels and carefully writes the Latin names of the plants he collects on specimen envelopes he keeps together with his field guides, maps, and steamer trunks. While she is in England, Indigo visits the "kitchen garden" of Hattie's Aunt Bronwyn who shows her how many plants from the Americas are growing there. "Your people," Aunt Bronwyn tells Indigo, "gave the world so many vegetables, fruits, and flowers."[40] Here, Aunt Bronwyn alludes to plants that originated in Mesoamerica, which is recognized as one of the world's centers of biological diversity or regions which are known to be centers for the domestication of food and medicinal plants. Plants first domesticated in Mesoamerica include corn, beans, squash, peanuts, cacao, tomatoes, sweet potatoes, and avocados. When Indigo sees plants familiar to her in Aunt Bronwyn's "kitchen garden," her "eyes widened at the sight of food she knew" and she suddenly understands that "seeds must be among the greatest travelers of all."[41] Indigo's growing understanding of the global movement of seeds original to the Americas helps readers better understand the contribution of indigenous American peoples to the food sovereignty of people around the world.

---

[38] Ellen Arnold, "Listening to the Spirits: An Interview with Leslie Marmon Silko," *Studies in American Indian Literatures*, 10, 3 (1998): 21.

[39] Ibid., 3.

[40] Silko, *Gardens in the Dunes*, 244.

[41] Ibid., 240, 291.

The novel celebrates seed diversity that nourishes people, but it also interrogates the ethics of plant breeding, hybridization, and biotechnologies that enrich colonizing nation states and transnational corporations while impoverishing the communities from which seeds are taken and failing to compensate indigenous collectors and cultivators. Detailed information about Edward, who has secret dealings with the US Bureau of Plant Industry in Washington DC, and the Royal Botanic Gardens, Kew, in Britain, reveals that he is actually engaging in the theft and transport of biological materials from foreign countries for the profit of countries that are capital-rich but biodiversity-poor. Edward pursues orchids, citron, and seeds of all kinds, and these activities raise questions about the history and practice of biopiracy. Before the nineteenth century, when Europeans collected plants deemed valuable by the indigenous peoples they encountered and returned home with them to their own countries, this was usually not considered theft or piracy, since the original cultivators of the resources often held open their hands and freely gave the seed. Both Grandmother Fleet's and Aunt Bronwyn's gardens are examples of the open hand of seed sharing. In contrast, the field of "economic botany," which emerged in the nineteenth century, brought plant breeders and botanists together with countries and corporations to develop new strains of plants to be sold and grown for profit. During this period, British and American adventurers and botanists pirated many valuable plants, including rubber from the Amazon, and failed to recognize or remunerate the original cultivators of the plants they were stealing for profit.[42]

Edward's activities are a clear allusion to this subversive history and reveal why Silko sees food production as a highly political activity in an increasingly globalized world. Edward travels with a "list of plant materials desired by his private clients," who were "wealthy collectors in the east and in Europe," all the while thinking with admiration about the history of Henry Wickham, a (real-life) British citizen who had "smuggled seventy thousand rubber tree seeds past Brazilian customs officers" so that Britain could profit from "vast rubber plantations in Malaya and Ceylon."[43] Silko also describes the destructive ecological impact such collecting has on the biodiverse places from which rare plants are stolen. When Edward first traveled to Brazil, a splendid "profusion of wild orchid flowers could be seen along the riverbanks, and specimens were easily

---

[42] For more on nineteenth-century "economic botany," see Mushita and Thompson, *Biopiracy of Biodiversity*, 26.

[43] Silko, *Gardens in the Dunes*, 129.

gathered. But the orchid mania swept in, and ... over the years ... made
the plants increasingly scarce and difficult to find."[44] Edward's illicit work
illustrates how biopiracy turns the open hand offering seeds as a gift into
a clenched fist symbolizing the enclosure of common resources for private profit. This type of removal of plants and seeds, write Mushita and
Thompson, was not an "exchange or free trade, for the Europeans com-
pensated neither the national governments nor the traditional healers nor
cultivators, for their knowledge or plant resources."[45]

Together, *Gardens in the Dunes* and *Almanac of the Dead* offer insights
into why indigenous communities are organizing around food sovereignty and why UNDRIP pays particular attention to issues surrounding patenting and genetic engineering of culturally meaningful first
foods. The United States produces 66 percent of the world's genetically
engineered crops.[46] Most agriculture in the United States involves large
farms or groups of growers under standardized contract to big agribusi-
ness/biotechnology firms for the use of patented hybridized or genetically modified seeds and the fertilizers and pesticides required to grow
them. As Vandana Shiva has observed, proponents of this model tout
the remarkable efficiency of "science-based" agriculture and base their
claims primarily on the idea that seeds patented by the large agrochemical conglomerates produce higher yields (and thus feed more people,
thereby reducing hunger) while using fewer resources. Most small-scale
agroecologists and adherents of food sovereignty, on the other hand,
oppose genetic engineering. This position, writes Shiva in *Stolen Harvest*,
exposes its proponents to accusations that small farmers care little about
the environment and are inevitably at odds with science as they adhere to
a romanticized, pre-modern past.

Such an accusation, Shiva insists, is based on false comparisons. When
corporations describe the benefits of industrialized farming, they base
their arguments and data on large-scale US models and fail to assess other
agricultural models which are capable of producing high yields while simultaneously protecting biodiversity.[47] While it is often argued that patenting of seeds promotes innovation in agriculture and will "save the world
from hunger," indigenous farmers are arguing that patents are leading
to an erosion of biodiversity because fewer indigenous seed varieties are

[44] Ibid.
[45] Mushita and Thompson, *Biopiracy of Biodiversity*, 27.
[46] McAfee, "Corn Culture and Dangerous DNA," 25.
[47] Vandana Shiva, *Stolen Harvest: The Hijacking of the Global Food Supply* (Boston, MA:
South End Press, 2000), 97.

being planted in a world that is increasingly cultivating transgenic varieties of corn, rice, and soy. Loss of biodiversity, Shiva argues, "starts a chain reaction. The disappearance of one species is related to the extinction of innumerable other species, with which it is interrelated through food webs and food chains."[48]

This helps to explain why Article 31 of UNDRIP links cultural heritage, traditional knowledge, and traditional cultural expressions with indigenous sciences, technologies and cultures, especially as they are applied to genetic resources, seeds, medicines, and knowledge of the properties of fauna and flora. The delegates and farmers who gathered at the Iximché Summit took a strong stand against the "transgenic invasion," a position that has been criticized as "unscientific" not only by the biotechnology firms that produce transgenics but by the World Trade Organization, which would like to strengthen hemispheric trading rules and require that all "decisions to import or reject products must be 'sciences based.'"[49] The precedent for this rule finds its basis in the US Plant Patent Act of 1930, the first legislation in the world that treated living organisms as intellectual property, and the subsequent US Plant Variety Protection Act of 1994, which strengthened the original Plant Patent Act by restricting farmers and breeders "from selling any seeds from protected varieties and from breeding new varieties from protected seeds."[50] Through hemispheric trade liberalization, such as that proposed by the Free Trade Area of the Americas (FTAA), US negotiators hope to extend these laws throughout the hemisphere and, in particular, strengthen standards for intellectual property rights (IPR) enforcement, by requiring damage payments for IPR violations.[51]

Thus when the framers of UNDRIP and Article 31 claim their right to develop their intellectual property rights over their own seeds, medicines, and the properties of flora and fauna, they are not simply worried about food safety or the contamination of their original varieties of seeds; they are taking a stand against the patenting of life. They understand that primary cultivars or original landraces are often modified through natural or human selection and naturally occurring hybridization. Indigenous peoples have been engaged in these agroecological processes for millennia. On the other hand, transgenic organisms "are those that contain

---

[48] Shiva, *Biopiracy*, 66.
[49] McAfee, "Corn Culture and Dangerous DNA," 33.
[50] Jane S. Smith, *The Garden of Invention: Luther Burbank and the Business of Breeding Plants* (New York: Penguin Press, 2009), 313.
[51] McAfee, "Corn Culture and Dangerous DNA," 33.

genetic material synthesized from DNA obtained from other species," and this process can only happen in a laboratory.[52] Abya Yala farmers have called for a ban on transgenic organisms because of the risks of cross-pollination or contamination with traditional indigenous landraces. Corn is a wind-pollinated plant, and the genetic information of transgenic corn could potentially spread though open pollination and contaminate the natural viability of indigenous landraces. As Vandana Shiva points out, when patented transgenic organisms cross-pollinate with indigenous landraces, even accidentally, corporations can claim that farmers owe them royalties.[53]

As Kathleen MacAfee has written in an article on the real and imagined consequences of genetic engineering of corn, much of the concern over transgenics by indigenous farmers has cohered around a contested article published in *Nature* that claimed that traditional varieties of corn in Oaxaca, Mexico, had already been contaminated with the traits of transgenic corn. However, the corn at the center of the controversy is a single-trait variety, with a natural pesticide introduced into its DNA. It is not known if this transgenic organism will actually contribute to the loss of valuable maize traits. Moreover, consumption of transgenic corn, if dangerous at all, is "less so than the myriad health risks from contaminated water, pesticide exposure, and malnutrition already endured by many Mexican campesinos."[54]

The much more troubling issue for indigenous communities, McAfee observes, are the likely consequences – for local food sovereignty, cultural survival, and national economic sovereignty – of the private ownership of staple-crop genetic resources and of the influences on trade policy, agricultural research, seed and food markets, and farming-system options of a small number of powerful states and transnational firms.[55] Members of the international food sovereignty movement "oppose genetic engineering as a strategy for agriculture not because it affronts an idealized 'harmony with Nature' or the 'purity' of traditional crop landraces" but because it introduces the threat that living organisms can be patented.[56] They point out that, if approved, the FTAA could make individual nations liable for

---

[52] According to Kathleen McAfee, "An organism can also be engineered to alter the location, number, or expression of its own genetic material. It would then be genetically engineered, but not transgenic in the strict sense." McAfee, "Corn Culture and Dangerous DNA," 36 n. 4.

[53] Shiva, *Biopiracy*, 54.

[54] McAfee, "Corn Culture and Dangerous DNA," 19.

[55] Ibid.   [56] Ibid., 34–35.

"unfair trade practices" if they decline imports of seeds on the ground that they are genetically engineered. If approved, writes Canadian water and human rights activist Maude Barlow, the FTAA will set "enforceable global rules on patents, copyrights and trademark. It has gone far beyond its initial scope of protecting original inventions or cultural products and now permits the practice of patenting plants and animal forms as well as seeds. It promotes the private rights of corporations over local communities and their genetic heritage and traditional medicines."[57] Under the FTAA, US negotiators have also moved to require damage payments if patented transgenic crops are found growing in the fields of local farmers who did not purchase the seeds from biotechnology corporations.[58]

UNDRIP and food sovereignty

As Carrie Garrow argues in this volume in Chapter 6, UNDRIP should be recognized at best as customary international law that recognizes the collective rights of indigenous peoples. At the very least, it should be recognized as a standard that nation states should strive to achieve. She also points out that most domestic courts are not receptive to international laws. So it is still unclear how much power UNDRIP will have for advancing the cause of indigenous peoples when it comes to food sovereignty.

It is clear that indigenous peoples cannot rely on any one document to achieve their objectives. Garrow's description of the Haudenosaunee people's fight to have their treaty rights recognized is a case in point. Recognizing that nation states often ignore international law, the framers of both the Iximché Declaration and UNDRIP continue to work on many fronts for food sovereignty for all indigenous groups and nations. They are working not only with the UN Permanent Forum on Indigenous Issues but with the World Social Forum, the United Nations Environmental Programme's Convention on Biological Diversity (CBD), and diverse non-governmental organizations (NGOs) to create documents that, together, are providing indigenous groups *and* nation states with a basis in international law for maintaining, controlling, protecting, and developing "their intellectual property over such cultural

---

[57] Maude Barlow, Council of Canadians Acting for Social Justice, "The Free Trade Area of the Americas and the Threat to Social Programs, Environmental Sustainability and Social Justice in Canada and the Americas," February 2001, www.ratical.org/co-globalize/MBonFTAA.html (accessed March 14, 2010).

[58] McAfee, "Corn Culture and Dangerous DNA," 33.

heritage, traditional knowledge, and traditional cultural expressions"
(UNDRIP, Art. 31).

As the Zapatista negotiations with the Mexican government made
clear, even nation states are compromised by already enforced and proposed trade liberalization policies when it comes to control over transgenic organisms and food sovereignty. In October 2009, the Mexican
government gave in to WTO pressures and decided to allow cultivation
of genetically modified corn in the country, despite repeated calls by indigenous groups not to do so.[59] Therefore if indigenous groups and nations
hope to achieve greater local and regional control over food sources and
supplies, they cannot reject the power of the nation state or regional governments outright, since indigenous farmers and local people must often
work to strengthen state regulatory and rural development agencies and
hold them accountable if they hope to resist the power of corporations
and the World Bank.[60] Trade liberalization policies (such as the proposed FTAA) would give transnational corporations almost free rein to
prosecute countries that refuse to allow seeds patented by multinational
agrochemical conglomerates to be grown within their borders. These policies are designed to shrink the power of governments, cripple attempts to
regulate corporations, and undermine long-established national protections for social welfare and economic justice, environmental values, and
individual rights.[61] For this reason, transnational food sovereignty alliances are organizing strategic public performances of democracy based
on models put into practice by the Zapatistas, by members and groups
working with the World Social Forum, and by the delegates to the Iximché
Summit, among others. They are calling for and hosting "national and
international forums, conventions, and delegations on issues of social
justice, indigenous rights, environmental protection, and representative
democracy."[62] In the space of such forums, indigenous peoples are working with ethnobotonists, microbiologists, food policy-makers and plant
genomics scientists, NGOs, the United Nations Permanent Forum on
Indigenous Issues, the World Social Forum, the Americas Social Forum,

---

[59] Arthur Brice, "Greenpeace Protests Genetically Modified Corn in Mexico," CNN.com,
    October 10, 2009, www.cnn.com/2009/WORLD/americas/10/20/greenpeace.mexico/
    index.html (accessed October 10, 2009).
[60] McAfee, "Corn Culture and Dangerous DNA," 35.
[61] William Greider, "The Right and US Trade Law: Invalidating the 20th Century,"
    The Nation, October 15, 2001, www.thenation.com/doc/20011015/greider (accessed
    September 7, 2008).
[62] Saldaña, *Revolutionary Imagination*, 223.

and the CBD. Under the auspices of the CBD, for example, many indigenous groups have worked in support of the Cartagena Protocol, which calls upon nations and the international community to provide "countries with a basis in international law for choosing to reject or postpone the import of transgenic planting or breeding materials."[63] Adopted by sixty countries in January 2000, the Protocol is based on the precautionary principle, and seeks to protect biological diversity from the potential risks posed by living modified organisms resulting from modern biotechnology. This Protocol, along with both the Iximché Declaration and UNDRIP, stands as a potential counterweight to proposed FTAA provisions for prosecuting countries which cannot provide "sciences-based" evidence for the rejection of GMOs.

Since 2005, implementation of the FTAA has been stalled as more countries recognize that two decades of economic liberalization have brought few of the promised benefits of free trade. This may point to the possible influence of documents such as Iximché Declaration, UNDRIP, and the Cartagena Protocol, as indigenous groups and their allies work to facilitate the equitable democratic participation by indigenous, working class, minoritized, and economically disadvantaged peoples in regional, national, and global societies. The work of Native North American writers reflects these global and hemispheric organizing efforts around people and the plants and medicines that are nutritionally necessary and culturally meaningful. Through visual images and metaphors emphasizing the central importance in many indigenous cultures of "mother corn," Glancy, Silko, and Anzaldúa are calling our attention to discussions of corn and its uses (and abuses) which are at the center of deepening distrust of patented varieties of transgenic corn and food safety regulators, and animal welfare concerns. The politics of nutrition and food policy are coming to the fore as more and more people recognize that denying access to high-quality, fresh and/or culturally meaningful foods is leading to poor health and shortened lives. As these creative works illustrate, transnational indigenous alliances, supported by UNDRIP, are often less about traditional politics and more about opening a political–economic–cultural space for multiple alternative developments, locally imagined but internationally networked.

⸻

[63] McAfee, "Corn Culture and Dangerous DNA," 30.

9

"Use and control": issues of repatriation and redress in American Indian literature

LEE SCHWENINGER

Article 12 of the United Nations General Assembly's Declaration on the Rights of Indigenous Peoples (2007) includes the proposition that indigenous peoples have the "right to the use and control of their ceremonial objects" and that they have "the right to the repatriation of their human remains." And, further, the Declaration stipulates that "States shall seek to enable the access and/or repatriation of ceremonial objects and human remains in their possession." Even though the Declaration as a whole only belatedly (2010) received support from the United States,[1] the US Congress had passed a repatriation bill as early as 1990 anticipating the issues noted in Articles 11 and 12 of the Declaration: the Native American Graves Protection and Repatriation Act (NAGPRA). The repatriation sections of this 1990 US statute (as well as the revisions since its original passage)[2] are similar to Articles 11 and 12 of the Declaration, and both documents suggest significant and continuing steps forward in a political

[1] In April 2010 the United States announced that it would reconsider its position regarding the vote not to support the Declaration, and in December that year President Obama announced that the United States did indeed support the UN Resolution. See the homepage of the UN Permanent Forum on Indigenous Issues (UNPFII), www. un.org/esa/socdev/unpfii/en/declaration.html. See also US Department of State, "Announcement of US Support for the United Nations Declaration on the Rights of Indigenous Peoples," media note, December 16, 2010, www.state.gov/r/pa/prs/ps/2010/12/153027.htm; and Announcement of US Support for the United Nations Declaration on the Rights of Indigenous Peoples, December 16, 2010, www.state.gov/documents/organization/153223.pdf. David Forsythe implies that it should come as no surprise that the United States initially refused to vote in favor of the Declaration, when one considers that "if you establish a global rule of law to deal with the human rights violations of others, you will restrict your own freedom of maneuver and highlight your own defects." David Forsythe, *Human Rights in International Relations*, 2nd edn (New York: Cambridge University Press, 2006), 38.

[2] See, e.g., Rob Capriccioso, "Scientists Ponder NAGPRA Lawsuit," *Indian Country Today*, 13 April 2010, www.indiancountrytoday.com/national/90350684.html.

state's acknowledging the "rightful ownership" of material culture.[3] Similar to Articles 11 and 12 of the Declaration, that is, NAGPRA requires that museums receiving any federal funding do the following: identify American Indian human remains and ceremonial objects; notify specific tribes accordingly; and, as appropriate, repatriate the human remains or objects. The language of the Declaration is similar, and it offers that issues of repatriation shall be "developed in conjunction with indigenous peoples" (Art. 11(2)).

Despite praiseworthy intentions, such resolutions as those in the Declaration and NAGPRA do necessarily raise important questions, not the least of which have to do with the fact that both the Declaration and NAGPRA rely on mainstream Western ideologies and Western ways of understanding the notions of indigeneity, of ownership, of individuality, and of who is in a position to stipulate such rights and to whom, in the first place. Underlying all of these issues are questions of the differences between *human* rights (stipulated by the UN, for example, as early as 1948) and *indigenous* rights, not ratified until almost sixty years later. In the context of indigenous rights and universal human rights in general, one must ask whether or not it is possible to reconcile a massively generalized Western ontology (identifying specific "indigenous peoples" or specific individuals as spokespersons, for example) with the particularity of the cultural, intellectual, religious, and spiritual requirements of many

---

[3] United Nations Declaration on the Rights of Indigenous Peoples, GA Res. 61/295, Annex, UN Doc. A/RES/61/295, September 13, 2007, Arts. 11 and 12:

Article 11

1. Indigenous peoples have the right to practise and revitalize their cultural traditions and customs. This includes the right to maintain, protect and develop the past, present and future manifestations of their cultures, such as archaeological and historical sites, artifacts, designs, ceremonies, technologies and visual and performing arts and literature.

2. States shall provide redress through effective mechanisms, which may include restitution, developed in conjunction with indigenous peoples, with respect to their cultural, intellectual, religious and spiritual property taken without their free, prior and informed consent or in violation of their laws, traditions and customs.

Article 12

1. Indigenous peoples have the right to manifest, practice, develop and teach their spiritual and religious traditions, customs and ceremonies; the right to maintain, protect, and have access in privacy to their religious and cultural sites; the right to the use and control of their ceremonial objects; and the right to the repatriation of their human remains.

2. States shall seek to enable the access and/or repatriation of ceremonial objects and human remains in their possession through fair, transparent and effective mechanisms developed in conjunction with indigenous peoples concerned.

diverse indigenous peoples worldwide. There are, according to the United Nations Permanent Forum on Indigenous Issues, for example, "more than 370 million indigenous people in some 90 countries worldwide."[4]

In this chapter I look at some of the responses of Native American writers, in the contexts of political underpinnings and issues of repatriation as articulated in the Declaration and in NAGPRA. Several literary artists do indeed write about museum collections, the role of Western science and/ or collectors, and issues of repatriation. I argue that Native American literature and other writings by indigenous Americans can actually provide an arena through which contemporary American Indian writers are able to re-present and/or challenge the ideas of "ownership" as they demonstrate the connections between themselves and their ancestors, between past and present, and between museum-piece artifacts and human dignity. By so doing, they tend both to identify and to close the gaps between notions of international law and indigenous rights, whether or not they are writing in direct response to the Declaration or to NAGPRA.

In his essay "Human Rights in Literary Studies," James Dawes contends that, "After years spent interacting with human rights and humanitarian fieldworkers, I have come to believe that human rights work is, at its heart, a matter of storytelling ... One of the tenets of literary studies is that storytelling is essential to how we come to be who we are. We make sense of ourselves and our lives, individually and collectively, by telling stories."[5] In this context the reference to literature in Article 11 of the Declaration is significant: "Indigenous peoples have the right to practise and revitalize their cultural traditions and customs. This includes the right to maintain, protect and develop the past, present and future manifestations of their cultures, such as archaeological and historical sites, artifacts, designs, ceremonies, technologies and visual and performing arts and literature." Cherokee writer Jace Weaver would seem to agree with this contention when he writes that "Narrative is a means that colonized people employ to assert their own existence and identity. The struggle may be land and sovereignty, but it is often reflected, contested, and decided in narrative."[6]

---

[4] United Nations Permanent Forum on Indigenous Issues, "About UNPFII and a Brief History of Indigenous Peoples and the International System," www.un.org/esa/socdev/unpfii/en/history.html.

[5] James Dawes, "Human Rights in Literary Studies," *Human Rights Quarterly*, 31 (2009): 394, 395.

[6] Jace Weaver, *That the People Might Live: Native American Literatures and Native American Community.* New York: Oxford University Press, 1997), 41–42.

Cherokee author Thomas King maintains that the "truth about stories is that that's all we are." He refers to several Native writers who make the same point, including Jeannette Armstrong (Okanagan), Leslie Marmon Silko (Laguna Pueblo), Gerald Vizenor (Anishinaabe), and Diane Glancy (Cherokee). In *The Truth About Stories* (2003), King tells a story in which Coyote attempts to trick the ducks into giving away all their feathers; in lie after lie, he keeps getting more and more feathers from them. After narrating the story, King makes an analogy between what Coyote is doing and the nature of treaties between a colonizer government such as the United States or Canada and indigenous people, writing that "the first rule of treaties was that Indians had to give up most of their feathers in order to keep some of their feathers for themselves."[7] Although he is writing before the passage of the UN Declaration, his suspicion of the favors colonizer governments wish to bestow on indigenous peoples is generally applicable. In the United States, for example, the stipulations of the Declaration apply to federally recognized tribes only, and the federal government, of course, decides which peoples to recognize. Through storytelling, then, King questions, and asks his readers to question, fundamental principles and ideologies behind such "treaties" as made manifest in such documents as the Declaration.

Before turning to further examination of individual American Indian literary artists, I would like to set the Declaration and NAGPRA in context, especially because, even though some do indeed find the ideas expressed in these legislative Acts hopeful, the Declaration does have its detractors, both as human rights legislation in general and in the specific context of repatriation.

In an essay questioning rights-based ethics, for example, Fiona Robinson maintains that universal human rights are based on an assumption she finds untenable, that of "the universality of human nature," and she thus prefers an "ethics which takes social relations as its starting point." She argues that "An adequate approach to global ethics … must be, at least in part, a morality of attachment and connection."[8] Cindy Holder and Jeff Corntassel problematize the "fact" of the "Declaration," for example, by pointing out its inherent Western bias: "For many, the problem lies in the individualistic nature of existing human rights discourse. The concern

---

[7] Thomas King, *The Truth About Stories: A Native Narrative* (Minneapolis: University of Minnesota Press, 2003), 2, 129.

[8] Fiona Robinson, "The Limits of a Rights Based Approach to International Ethics," in Tony Evans, ed., *Human Rights Fifty Years On: A Reappraisal* (New York: Manchester University Press, 1998), 60–61.

is that existing instruments emphasize individual needs and entitlements in a way that inadequately compares the collective nature of groups with non-Western world-views and priorities."[9] In *The Riddle of Human Rights* (2005), Gary Teeple argues that potentially excluded are indigenous peoples, "who maintain non-capitalist modes of production, live in ways marginal to the relations of capital, or have been dispossessed of their means of production."[10] Each of these scholars thus makes an argument for the relativism, and thus the inapplicability, of, or at least the apparent problems facing, global or universal, one-size-fits-all human rights legislation.

In another context Norman Lewis argues that "the ascendancy of the human rights discourse today expresses a social process which is fundamentally eroding democratic rights and threatens to legitimize and institutionalize domestic and global inequalities." Lewis continues: "Protecting children, indeed women or racial minorities, now overrides the considerations of liberty expressed in the classical concept of right and formalized in law." On the international level, maintains Lewis, state sovereignty is threatened. Lewis prognosticates that such universal human rights discourse "holds out nothing but a future return to empires and colonies, to a world where paternalistic great powers exercise democratic rights on the behalf of their dependencies."[11] As suggested here, then, one must acknowledge that the language and very principles of such documents as the Declaration and NAGPRA are unavoidably ultimately framed within Western ontologies and ideologies, and notions of citizenship, and that one of the major issues confronting indigenous peoples therefore is that it forces them to negotiate the terrain between their own ontologies and Western conceptions of human rights, indigenous rights, and international law, and thus, in a sense, render the very people identified as indigenous dependent upon the state.

Despite these several reasons to challenge the ideology as well as the efficacy of a universal human rights document, several scholars do indeed duly note its merits. In *Indigenous Peoples in International Law* (1996), for example, S. James Anaya maintains that "international law, although once an instrument of colonialism, has developed and continues to develop, however grudgingly or imperfectly, to support

---

[9] Cindy Holder and Jeff J. Corntassel, "Indigenous Peoples and Multicultural Citizenship: Bridging Collective and Individual Rights," *Human Rights Quarterly*, 24 (2002): 126–27.

[10] Gary Teeple, *The Riddle of Human Rights* (Amherst, NY: Humanity Books, 2005), 29.

[11] Norman Lewis, "Human Rights, Law, and Democracy in an Unfree World," in Tony Evans, ed., *Human Rights Fifty Years On: A Reappraisal* (New York: Manchester University Press, 1998), 79, 97, 100.

indigenous peoples' demands." Anaya's book "stands at the intersection of international law, indigenous peoples, and concern over the circumstances that have placed them in non-dominant positions relative to other segments of humanity."[12] In "Indigenous Internationalism: Native Rights and the United Nations," the final chapter of *Public Native America*, Mary Lawlor contends that "although the United Nations has overtly (even if inadvertently) helped to sustain the inherited order of neglect of indigenous rights, it has also created openings in the dense fabric of international state politics, such that indigenous peoples have been able to assert their claims to human rights with increasing effectiveness."[13] Writing very specifically about the Declaration as it applies to indigenous rights, Russel Barsh draws clear lines concerning the options different nation states have in their responses to indigenous rights legislation. After noting that Japan and the United States "claimed that the text was too intrusive into national legal systems" and that the text included unfortunate challenging financial elements, he clarifies as follows:

> States have two options for avoiding the more controversial legal principles contained in the existing WGIP [Working Group on Indigenous Populations] draft Declaration. They can press for the deletion of controversial elements, or they can try to downgrade the legal status of the final instrument as a whole. However, states sometimes use the 'soft' legal status of an instrument to *defend* the inclusion of strong principles ... Other delegations argued that the Declaration must be drafted conservatively because it could eventually *become* binding, through state practice, as customary international law.[14]

Whereas Barsh writes about the delicate political and legal balance supporters of such a declaration must maintain in order to get anything accomplished, Jack Donnelly addresses the issue of cultural relativism when it comes to universal human rights, another important and controversial issue. He maintains that "Cultural relativity is a fact. Social institutions and values have varied, and continue to vary, with time and place. Nonetheless [he argues], contemporary international human

---

[12] S. James Anaya, *Indigenous Peoples in International Law* (New York: Oxford University Press, 1996), 4.

[13] Mary Lawlor, *Public Native America: Tribal Self-Representation in Museums, Powwows, and Casinos* (New Brunswick: Rutgers University Press, 2006), 164.

[14] Russel Lawrence Barsh, "Indigenous Peoples and the UN Commission on Human Rights: A Case of the Immovable Object and the Irresistible Force," *Human Rights Quarterly*, 18 (1996): 789.

rights norms have near universal applicability, requiring only relatively modest adjustments in the name of cultural diversity." Donnelly
defends a form of what he calls "weak cultural relativism." "It is difficult
to imagine defensible arguments in the contemporary world to deny
rights to life, liberty, security of the person, or protection against slavery,
arbitrary arrest, racial discrimination, and torture. The rights to food,
health care, work, and social insurance are equally basic to any plausible
conception of equal human dignity." Donnelly also offers the caveat that
the "possibility of justifiable modifications, however, must not obscure
the fundamental universality of international human rights norms."[15]
In short, both Donnelly and Barsh acknowledge the importance and
necessity of compromise and generalization in making the Declaration
a reality.

Less theoretical, Mary Lawlor takes the perspective that from a realist's point of view the simple fact of the matter is that "if power relations
in the world are to be changed to any degree at all in favor of indigenous
peoples, native agents will need to deal with institutions like the United
Nations that attempt to operate as brokers of that power."[16] Here, Lawlor
implies that indigenous peoples will have to conform to Western institutions and Western understandings of what constitutes indigenous rights,
whether or not American Indian nations have sovereignty or not. That is,
they must understand that sovereignty and practicing it depend to a large
extent, if not completely, on the cooperation of the US government. In the
larger context of the United Nations, it should be remembered that that
august body has repeatedly refused to acknowledge the "nationhood"
or statehood of American Indian nations (consider the Oglala Nation at
Wounded Knee in 1973, for example). In this context, the Declaration,
whatever its theoretical value ultimately has, some argue, little, if any,
legal value, especially when one considers that its articles are nonbinding.
As S. James Anaya and Siegfried Wiessner point out, for example, the
US delegation argued that the Declaration should be "solely an 'aspirational declaration with political and moral, rather than legal force.'"
Anaya and Wiessner contend, however, "that all new rules of customary international law ... still remain part of the global consensus," and
that the "domestic practice of the four states [initially opposed to] the
Declaration is not opposed to the principle of recognizing indigenous

[15] Jack Donnelly, *International Human Rights, Second Edition* (New York: Westview Press, 1998), 33, 34.
[16] Lawlor, *Public Native America*, 182.

peoples' right[s]."[17] As the reversal of even these governments demonstrates in this regard, national governments maintain that the Declaration is an important milestone on the way to reempowerment of indigenous peoples.

Even while they recognize shortcomings of the Declaration and other universal human rights initiatives, however, advocates of such indigenous rights legislation insist on the importance of its principles and the huge potential of its practical measures. The recognition and articulation of indigenous rights is definitely a starting point, they maintain, no matter how nonbinding or finally unenforceable its dictates. Despite a potential disconnect between a Western-based initiative and indigenous worldviews, Haunani-Kay Trask, as a Native Hawaiian, relies on and even tends to valorize the principles articulated in the Draft Declaration (1993) (somewhat different from the 2007 version)[18] in order to demand redress for, among other things, the illegitimacy of the United States' military and political takeover of Hawaii in the nineteenth century. In her study of colonialism and sovereignty in Hawaii, *From a Native Daughter*, Trask implies that she very much relies on the "Draft United Nations Declaration on the Rights of Indigenous Peoples" (1993) as she challenges the US government to respond to the demands for federal recognition of the "unique status [of Hawaiians] as Native people," of "loss of lands and sovereignty" as a result of occupation, and of "the necessity for reparation." According to Trask,

> the United States committed ... undeniable violations of the right of self-determination. Under international law, these violations include
>
> 1. an arbitrary deprivation of our nationality;
> 2. an arbitrary deprivation of our lands;
> 3. a denial of our rights to self-determination as a people, including aboriginal rights to our natural resources.

Thus, she continues, "These depravations, as a whole, comprise violations" of several articles in the "Draft Declaration." In the specific context of American Indians, as opposed to native Hawaiians, Trask writes that "This mercurial colonial legacy is longer and more detailed for American Indians than for Native Hawaiians. But the shape of our histories is

---

[17] S. James Anaya and Siegfried Wiessner, "The UN Declaration on the Rights of Indigenous Peoples: Towards Re-empowerment," *Jurist*, 3 (October 2007), http://jurist.law.pitt.edu/forumy/2007/10/un-declaration-on-rights-of-indigenous.php.

[18] See, for instance, the discussion by Watson and Venne in this volume (Chapter 3).

similar." As Trask relies heavily on the Universal Declaration of Human Rights in formulating her arguments, she insists that, as a whole, the depravations she speaks of "compromise violations" of articles in the Declaration.[19]

The ideology and methodology behind the kinds of violations of which Trask speaks are, of course, at the heart of the anthropological and archaeological endeavor to collect and study the human remains, funerary items, and other objects of the material cultures associated with Native American anthropology and archeology. Archeologists and anthropologists practiced and continue to practice what Orlan Svingen calls "conquest archeology."[20] Their concern, rightly or wrongly, is for what they consider to be the disinterested, objective – because scientific – study of human remains. Archaeologist Kurt Dongoske complains, for example, about "the permanent loss of future research materials" that results from the right of indigenous peoples to rebury their dead.[21]

One can make an argument that the same mindset which endorses the colonial takeover of lands and people also incorporates or necessitates a colonial attitude toward the indigenous peoples, their religious beliefs and practices, and their material culture. In this sense, it is no surprise that archeologists and museum apologists tend to disregard the cultural integrity and human rights of indigenous peoples as they argue that "sacred materials are essential to maintaining the integrity of their collections and that the remains of [the] dead are part of the national heritage."[22] The apologists' arguments fly in the face of one of the opening contentions of the Declaration: "practices based on or advocating superiority of peoples or individuals on the basis of national origin or racial, religious, ethnic or cultural differences are racist, scientifically false, legally invalid, morally condemnable and socially unjust." Yet, as many Native American writers argue, some archeologists and museum curators are guilty of just such practices. By studying or housing and displaying such objects, researchers

---

[19] Haunani-Kay Trask, *From a Native Daughter: Colonialism and Sovereignty in Hawai'i* (Honolulu: University of Hawai'i Press, Revised Edition, 1999, 26–28, *passim*.

[20] *Who Owns the Past?* Video documentary, director and producer N. Jed Riffe, Independent Producers Services, 1999.

[21] Kurt E. Dongoske, "NAGPRA: A New Beginning, Not the End, for Osteological Analysis – A Hopi Perspective," in Vevon A. Mihesuah, ed., *Repatriation Reader: Who Owns American Indian Remains?* (Lincoln: University of Nebraska Press, 2000), 282–93, 289.

[22] Rick Hill, "Repatriation Must Heal Old Wounds," in Roy L. Brooks, ed., *When Sorry Isn't Enough: The Controversy over Apologies and Reparations for Human Injustice* (New York: New York University Press, 1999), 285.

imply that the material culture of one particular group of people can be relegated to scientific-object or museum-piece status for the edification and/or education of another group. In such contexts, the stipulation of Article 2 of the Declaration is crucial: "Indigenous peoples and individuals are free and equal to all other peoples and individuals and have the right to be free from any kind of discrimination, in the exercise of their rights, in particular that based on their indigenous origin or identity." Certainly the study of Native American remains to the exclusion of non-Indian remains is a transgression of that stipulation.

What the attitudes and behaviors of many archeologists, anthropologists, and museum curators suggest is that there remains a firmly entrenched colonial attitude toward Native Americans, living and deceased. Describing what he calls "conquest archeology," as noted above, historian Orlan Svingen maintains that archeologists' insistence on the inherent right to study such finds "suggests a kind of value system that transcends Indian interest. And when you talk about conquest archeology, you're talking about an archeology that really in many ways isn't responsible to American Indians. It's responsible to itself and to science."[23] Similarly, according to Robert Williams, "as a first step toward the decolonization of the West's law respecting the American Indian, the Doctrine of Discovery must be rejected. It permits the West to accomplish by law and in good conscience what it accomplished by the sword in earlier eras: the physical and spiritual destruction of indigenous people." He continues this argument, writing that "The reconstruction of the West's Indian law so that it could be grounded in a vision rejecting the discourse of conquest contained in the Doctrine of Discovery could begin its search for foundations in New World soil."[24] Clearly NAGPRA and the Declaration are steps in the direction toward reconstructing law and attitude.

Despite resolutions by the United Nations concerning indigenous rights and despite NAGPRA, it should nevertheless come as no surprise that many archeologists find fault with some of the requirements of repatriation. They argue that, if acted upon, indigenous rights simply interfere with the free access to studying artifacts and human remains. In a *New York Times* article concerning repatriation of ancient human hair, for instance, archeologist Robson Bonnichsen, who had excavated what he identified as ancient human hairs, complained that despite the scientific potential of his find,

---

[23] *Who Owns the Past?*
[24] Robert A. Williams, Jr., *The American Indian in Western Legal Thought: The Discourses of Conquest* (New York: Oxford University Press, 1990), 326.

he had to wait for permission to perform chemical analysis. Bonnichsen responded that "Repatriation has taken on a life of its own and is about to put us out of business as a profession." In the same article, Douglas Owsley, a forensic anthropologist at the Smithsonian, is quoted to have said that because of repatriation laws, he was "seeing irreplaceable museum collections that can tell us so much about the prehistoric past lost and lost forever."[25] Anthropologist James Chatters – whose research on the human remains found in Kennewick, Washington, in 1996, was held up because of repatriation claims – complains in the context of repatriation and restitution in general that "There are those kinds of things throughout history in all cultures. But we can't change them simply by apologizing now. They will always be there and some generation in the future will come back and want an apology again for those events because they're still there. They're still part of history."[26] Kurt Dongoske argues that the challenge or "the problem for physical anthropologists and archaeologists is the collection of data before repatriation and reburial."[27] Dongoske's argument actually seems to miss the point in that it clearly objectifies and has the potential to violate the integrity of reclaimed human remains. In a certain sense, the very objectification is at the heart of the problem.

Suzan Shown Harjo (Cheyenne and Muscogee Creek) links the present controversy concerning a scientist's right to study the skeletons of indigenous peoples with the racist and disrespectful goings-on of the past:

> Grave robbing, burial site desecration, sacrilege of our sacred sites and objects, theft of our items of native national patrimony, use of our dead relatives as commodities of trade and commerce, exhibition of our dead relatives' skulls and destruction of their remains in federal and private places of learning and education, classification of Native people as federal property, and other related practices are part of that shameful past and all continue today.[28]

Dan Monroe makes much the same point linking past and present desecration when he writes that "violation of the graves of their ancestors is a deeply painful reminder of a vast catalog of injustices."[29] In other

---

[25] George Johnson, "Indian Tribes' Creationists Thwart Archeologists," *New York Times*, October 22, 1996, C13.

[26] *Who Owns the Past?*

[27] Dongoske, "NAGPRA: A New Beginning," 290.

[28] Suzan Shown Harjo, "Testimony before the Senate Select Committee on Indian Affairs," *Congressional Quarterly's Editorial Research Reports* 3 (May 14, 1990): 45.

[29] Dan Monroe, "The Politics of Reparation," in Dane Morrison, ed., *American Indian Studies: An Interdisciplinary Approach to Contemporary Issues* (New York: Peter Lang, 1997), 394.

words, as Harjo and Monroe point out, issues of repatriation cannot be isolated as simply a late twentieth- or early twenty-first-century issue. The issue of modern-day analysis, these writers argue, is inextricably an extension of over five hundred years of such exploitation and experimentation which Europeans and European Americans have contributed to. From *Other Words* (2001), in a chapter called "Indian presence with no Indians present: NAGPRA and its discontents," Jace Weaver defends NAGPRA against its detractors. He suggests how scientists might be responsible and maintains that "Rather than fighting tribes in the name of science and denouncing their legitimate demands as 'religious fundamentalism,' the lesson for archaeologists to draw from NAGPRA is the need to cultivate good relations with the Natives whom they study and on whose ancestral lands they work."[30]

As noted above with reference to Thomas King's story about Coyote and the duck feathers, these, then, are some of the issues that Native American authors seek to address both directly and indirectly through their writing, through their storytelling, as they consider museum collections and issues surrounding governmental legislation concerning repatriation. According to King, even legislation such as the well-meaning Indian Arts and Crafts Act, whose intent was to guarantee that "made by an Indian," indeed meant "made by an Indian." The problem, King points out, is that the law allows the US government to determine who is Indian. "Indian" people without federal recognition of their "Indianness" cannot legally sell their art, for instance, as "Indian." The result, King argues, is that the law "allows [primarily non-Indian] members of the public to feel secure in their purchases" of Indian art, at the same time as it excludes many Native artists:

> How many Shadow Indians does this law affect? Does the value of the law outweigh the problems it might cause for a few individuals?
>   Well, those really aren't the questions, are they?[31]

The question, King maintains, is about who gets to legislate "Indianness."

King's stories about legislation concerning indigenous North Americans are only generally applicable to issues raised by the Declaration generally and repatriation specifically. Gerald Vizenor offers a more explicit connection between storytelling and issues of repatriation: "Tribal narratives

---

[30] Jace Weaver, *Other Words: American Indian Literature, Law, and Culture* (Norman: University of Oklahoma Press, 2001), 172.
[31] King, *Truth about Stories*, 140, 141.

are located in stones, trees, birds, water, bears, and tribal bones."[32] As suggested by Vizenor's contention, one need not look far to find instances in which American Indian writers acknowledge the importance of storytelling and narrative as central to their cultures and sense of who they are. In the opening section of her novel *Ceremony* (1977), Laguna Pueblo writer Leslie Marmon Silko stresses, and in fact insists on, the centrality of story and storytelling:

> I will tell you something about stories,
> [he said]
> They aren't just entertainment.
> Don't be fooled.
> They are all we have, you see,
> all we have to fight off
> illness and death.
>
> You don't have anything
> if you don't have the stories.[33]

Although a certain amount of time needs to pass between the General Assembly's 2007 Declaration on the Rights of Indigenous Peoples and the creation of a body of literature in response, in the years between the Declaration and NAGPRA (1990), a body of literature did develop that deals sometimes directly, oftentimes indirectly, with the issues represented. The authors use storytelling as a means of responding to the very real world issues involved with museum collections and repatriation.

In *Keeping Slug Woman Alive*, Greg Sarris maintains that basket weaver Mabel McKay "cannot separate a discussion about the material aspects of her basketry from a discussion about dreams, doctoring, prophecy, and the ancient basket-weaving rules, since for Mabel these things cannot be talked about or understood separately." In emphasizing the importance of holistic approaches to American Indian texts, including Pomo basketry, Sarris tells a story, pointing out the irony inherent in museum collections. At the same time as they display objects, they "inhibit, or at best render incomplete, an understanding" of the text because they inevitably take the object or the text out of context, remove it from its history and culture.[34] In the specific instance Sarris recounts, a culture under glass

---

[32] Gerald Vizenor, *Crossbloods: Bone Courts, Bingo, and Other Reports* (Minneapolis: University of Minnesota Press, 1990), 65.

[33] Leslie Marmon Silko, *Ceremony* (New York: Viking/Penguin Signet, 1978), 2.

[34] Greg Sarris, *Keeping Slug Woman Alive: A Holistic Approach to American Indian Texts* (Berkeley: University of California Press, 1993), 51, 52.

is a culture robbed of its story. In this sense, then, Sarris is critiquing the collection of "museum pieces," but he is also making a statement about the integrity of a culture that reaches beyond the immediate issue of museum collections, and he is at the same time insisting on the importance of storytelling as a viable means of holding a culture together and challenging impositions on that culture. By extension, then, one can see that the ideas articulated in the Declaration do provide a measure for insuring just such integrity.

Inherent in the notion of "cultural integrity" is certainly the suggestion that sacred objects deserve to be in their associated context. As Sarris writes, "It is imperative to ask how a fuller sense of the Pomo basket as an integral part of Pomo culture and history has been lost and continues to be obfuscated despite the growing attention Pomo basketry has garnered both in the academy and in the world of popular culture." Sarris makes the point that because of objective interest in McKay's basketry "she has become a spectacle ... that is not only somewhat incongruous to her world but also diminishes it to mere artifacts and snippets of disconnected information, so that a basket specialist can talk about design as separate from the craft of basketry. And this inquiry never seems to include a consideration of the history that shapes and maintains a context in which a surviving member of an entire tribe has herself become an object of study."[35] As an epigraph to his biography of the basket maker, *Mabel McKay: Weaving the Dream* (1994), Sarris quotes her statement about offering an account of her life. After briefly recounting marriages and children and stating that she is Pomo, she asks this: "There, how's that? That's how I can tell my life for the white people's way. Is that what you want? It's more, my life. It's not only the one thing. It's many. You have to listen. You have to know me to know what I'm talking about."[36] And with that, Sarris begins to narrate and contextualize the story of her life.

Gerald Vizenor, it would seem, could be said to agree with James Dawes's contention that "human rights work is, at its heart, a matter of storytelling."[37] In *Fugitive Poses* (1998), for example, he maintains that "Native American Indians actuate the stories of this continent, and natives are the traces of natural reason, the aesthetic fugitives of the originary. Native stories are the canons of survivance: the tease of seasons,

[35] Sarris, *Keeping Slug Woman Alive*, 52.
[36] Greg Sarris, *Mabel McKay: Weaving the Dream* (Berkeley: University of California Press, 1994), n.p.
[37] Dawes, "Human Rights," 394.

scent of cedar, oneiric names, shamanic creases, and the sure transmo-
tion of sovereignty."[38] Writing about Vizenor's collection, Elvira Pulitano
argues that in a work like *Fugitive Poses* Vizenor challenges the anthropological approach to understanding Native Americans: "Unlike the language of social-scientific discourse, which fixes Indians, makes of them
static artifacts ... the language of trickster stories aims, [Vizenor] insists,
at liberation, at the disruption of such static definitions."[39] Like Sarris,
then, Vizenor can be said to maintain that the scientific or anthropological approach tends necessarily to reify the culture under study just
as a museum must necessarily take objects out of their larger contexts,
isolate them to some degree, and ultimately deny the larger "story" of
those objects. Indeed, scientific language itself can tend to reify, stultify,
objectify.

In contrast to anthropological or scientific writing, the language of
Native American storytelling revivifies. Vizenor liberates through language, and if not specifically responding to the Declaration or to NAGPRA
itself, he does address specifically issues of museum collections and repatriation in the context of human rights. He does this through storytelling
in several different genres (drama, screenplay and film, essay, and fiction), and he repeatedly calls into question museum collections. In one
chapter of his novel *Dead Voices*, for example, he juxtaposes the concept
of non-contextual study of the "indigenous" with the idea of the power of
storytelling. His metaphor in this chapter is the "mantis." One night, the
reader learns, under the direction of the blonde (read: non-indigenous)
teacher, "thousands of mantis were captured in bottles ... for indentured
research." The first person plural pronoun in the chapter refers to the
mantis themselves:

> The blonde visited the glass cages at night and the students studied our
> sex habits by day. The blond might have asked the mantis what she wanted
> to know, or she could have played the wanaki game, but that would have
> ended her scientific power. We would exist the way she discovered and
> studied praying mantis. We were no longer the mantis of our stories in the
> city, we were laboratory mantis. Our stories would die at the end of their
> studies, and we would end in the dead voices of the wordies.[40]

---

[38] Gerald Vizenor, *Fugitive Poses: Native American Scenes of Absence and Presence* (Lincoln:
University of Nebraska Press, 1998), 23.

[39] Elvira Pulitano, *Toward a Native American Critical Theory* (Lincoln: University of
Nebraska Press, 2003), 168.

[40] Gerald Vizenor, *Dead Voices: Natural Agonies in the New World* (Norman: University of
Oklahoma Press, 1992), 83.

In this one paragraph in a work of fiction, a novel, Vizenor is able to embody much of his philosophy: the anthropologists or teachers (or "blondes" as he often calls them) create or invent the subject outside or without regard to that subject's context (i.e., by abducting them, taking them from their eucalyptus leaves). As a result of the invention, the stories are threatened, or as Silko also suggests, even destroyed. In contrast to the mantis in this case, rather than stories or narratives, the anthropologists, or "wordies," have merely dead voices. Despite the odds against them, however, in this version the mantis are able to survive by escaping the observation room through a trickster act; that is, by "becoming fleas" the mantis captives are able to ride the blonde herself to freedom: "You must meditate, you must hear how to be that flea in your memories, that flea is in your blood forever."[41] Bagese, from whom the narrator gets the stories in the first place, offers this advice in the opening pages of the novel: "The secret ... was not to pretend, but to see and hear the real stories behind the words, the voices of the animals in me, not the definitions of the words alone."[42]

Vizenor also berates anthropologists in the screenplay and film *Harold of Orange* (1984). In a scene set in a university museum, the trickster figure Harold stands on top of a glass display case and calls out to the assembled group: members of a board of directors, students, anthropologists, and eventually police officers. "Those anthropologists invented us, and then they put our bones in these museum cases. We come to the cities from our tribal past and pace around ... like lost and lonesome animals."[43] Vizenor here exposes the one-sided nature of the relationship between science and Native American dignity. Through the character Harold, Vizenor articulates the adverse effects of the lack of respect toward the sanctity of Native American beliefs, material culture, and human remains.

In an essay entitled "Mister Ishi: analogies of exile, deliverance, and liberty" (2003), Vizenor addresses the issue of museum collections and repatriation by telling the story of Ishi, who spent the last several years of his life as a living museum exhibit and object of study. Ishi was further dishonored after his death. In an autopsy, the man's brain was removed for study. Vizenor points out that, in this context, Alfred Kroeber writes that he would be "glad to deposit [Ishi's brain] in the National Museum Collection." Vizenor juxtaposes the perversity of

---

[41] Ibid., 84.   [42] Ibid., 7.
[43] Gerald Vizenor, "Harold of Orange," screenplay, 1984, in Vizenor, *Shadow Distance: A Gerald Vizenor Reader* (Hanover: Wesleyan University Press, 1994), 322.

such inhuman and inhumane collecting with the notion of the power of storytelling. The passage is worth quoting in full in that with it Vizenor moves from a section called "Ishi by archives" to the section called "Ishi by exile":

> Kroeber was not sentimental enough, and anthropology was not ethical enough at the time, to consider the spiritual presence, the natural unity, and repatriation of his good friend, the Native humanist he had named Ishi.
>
> …
> Ishi by exile
> Ishi created a sense of natural presence in his stories, a Native presence that included others. He was a visionary, not a separatist, and his oral stories were scenes of liberty. This Native humanist was amused by the silence of scripture. He was a tricky storier in exile.[44]

Vizenor here contrasts the dead voices and insensitivity of the anthropologist with the playfulness of the captive. Even the level of diction changes between the two paragraphs: Kroeber's paragraph is straightforward prose, including words such as *anthropology, ethical, spiritual presence, repatriation*. Ishi's paragraph in contrast exhibits Vizenor's playful use of language with words like *visionary* and *storier*. In the play *Ishi and the Wood Ducks* (1995), Vizenor makes the point that museum collections lack stories in their display of material culture and artifacts, a lack which signifies an intrinsic shortcoming of museums. The character Boots asks, "who could start a museum without stories?" And the Ishi character replies: "Everybody does."[45]

Some literary responses to issues of museum collections and repatriation in addition to those by Vizenor predate NAGPRA and the United Nations declaration of indigenous rights, of course. In *Wind from an Enemy Sky* (published posthumously in 1978, but written and set much earlier), for instance, D'Arcy McNickle describes the tragic results of the taking of a medicine bundle for museum storage. The tribe's loss of the bundle results in a loss in the people's sense of self and their spiritual

---

[44] Gerald Vizenor, "Mister Ishi: Analogies of Exile, Deliverance, and Liberty," in Karl Kroeber and Clifton Kroeber, eds., *Ishi in Three Centuries* (Lincoln: University of Nebraska Press, 2003), 366. See also Vizenor, "Mister Ishi of California," in Vizenor, *Native Liberty: Natural Reason and Cultural Survivance* (Lincoln: University of Nebraska Press, 2009), 239–56, a reprinting, with very few minor changes, of the 2003 essay.

[45] Gerald Vizenor, "Ishi and the Wood Ducks: Postindian Trickster Comedies," in Vizenor, ed., *Native American Literature: A Brief Introduction and Anthology* (New York: Longman, 1995), 305.

well-being.[46] In her novel *Ghost Singer* (1988) Pawnee-Otoe writer Anna Lee Walters also challenges any justification for housing American Indian remains and funerary objects that ignores the human element. As Choctaw novelist and scholar Louis Owens writes, although "other Indian writers have dealt with the subject, Walters is the first novelist since McNickle to make the highly controversial appropriation of American Indian remains a central theme."[47] Walters does this in part by insisting that the cultures whose artifacts and whose ancestors' bones are in the Smithsonian museum are still very much alive and very much pained by the collection: "The cultures who created these items ain't dead simply because you're blind to them and deem them so! ... *The people* who created these things *exist* – they're still here."[48]

Ojibwa novelist Gordon Henry devotes much of his novel *The Light People* (1994) to a discussion of what it means when a museum can house and display human remains. Henry actually makes his point the more emphatic by making his example somewhat grotesque: a partial human leg in ceremonial leggings is displayed in a glass case. As in Walters's narrative, here, too, the well-being of the family and tribe is adversely affected by the fact of the leg's being on display in a museum. As Henry writes, "all the people of our tribe should be able to rest assured in knowing that one of our tribal people can be reconnected, in every way, with the ground that is his home."[49] A character in Susan Power's (Dakota) story "Museum Indians" (2002) has an equally adverse reaction to discovering a family artifact in a museum; this time the grandmother's dress is on display. As the narrator describes it, "we stand before this glass case as we would before a grave."[50]

Jim Northrup (Chippewa) uses humor to great effect in "Looking with Ben" (1993), a story about a Chippewa man's visit to the Smithsonian Museum of Natural History, before the American Indian collection was moved off site. At one moment, Ben actually stands in a diorama as a "Contemporary Chippewa," as a living artifact.[51] In *Truth and Brightwater*

[46] D'Arcy McNickle, *Wind from an Enemy Sky* (repr. Albuquerque: University of New Mexico Press, 1988 [1978]).
[47] Louis Owens, *Other Destinies: Understanding the American Indian Novel* (Norman: University of Oklahoma Press, 1992), 28.
[48] Anna Lee Walters, *Ghost Singer* (repr. Albuquerque: University of New Mexico Press, 1994 [1988]), 127 (emphasis in original).
[49] Gordon Henry, *The Light People* (Norman: University of Oklahoma Press, 1994), 138.
[50] Susan Power, *Roofwalker* (Minneapolis: Milkweed, 2002), 163.
[51] Jim Northrup, *Walking the Rez Road* (Stillwater, MN: Voyageur Press, 1993), 160.

(1999), Thomas King also uses humor (and the surreal) as he depicts Monroe Swimmer's taking upon himself the responsibility of repatriating human remains from several museums around the world. He explains the bones in his possession this way:

> I stole them from lots of museums. Toronto. New York. Paris. London. Berlin. You name the museum, I've probably been there.
>   … Children. I found them in drawers and boxes and stuck away on dusty shelves. Indian Children.
>   Happens all the time … Anthropologists and archaeologists dig the kids up, clean them off, and stick them in drawers.[52]

As is evident from brief mention of these few examples in addition to Vizenor's writing, responses to issues of museum collections and repatriation by American Indian writers are legion. As Vizenor and others demonstrate, in the act of telling their own stories which point out the injustice and in fact the absurdity of museum collections from a Native American point of view, they make manifest the importance of human and specifically indigenous rights in the contexts of museums and repatriation.[53]

Despite the obvious injustice of housing and studying the remains of Native Americans, Jace Weaver points out what might be considered an unforeseen complication of a declaration of indigenous rights that would guarantee both the right to have human remains and funerary objects repatriated and the right to the free exercise of religion. As it turns out in practice, that is, some Native Americans have been accused of using religious belief systems as an argument to justify repatriation of human remains. In his *New York Times* article about the unearthing of skeletal remains near Kennewick, Washington, in 1996, for example, George Johnson makes just such an accusation: "Since the repatriation act was passed in 1990, American Indian creationism, which rejects the theory of evolution and other scientific explanations of human origins in favor of the Indians' own religious beliefs, has been steadily gaining in political momentum." The reporter also writes that "American Indian creationists have been adamant in their opposition to modern science." Because of repatriation laws, continues the reporter, "All across the West, clues about North America's past are on the verge of being returned to the ground

---

[52] Thomas King, *Truth and Brightwater* (New York: Grove Press, 1999), 250–51.

[53] For an account of literary responses to museum collections and NAGPRA, see Lee Schweninger, "'Lost and Lonesome': Literary Reflections on Museums and the Roles of Relics," *American Indian Quarterly* 33.2 (2009): 169–99.

with little or no analysis." To support his argument, the reporter quotes Sebastian LeBeau, a repatriation officer for the Cheyenne River Sioux: "If non-Indians choose to believe they evolved from an ape, so be it. I have yet to come across five Lakotas who believe in science and in evolution."[54] Unfortunately even as eminent a scholar as Lakota writer Vine Deloria, Jr., contributes to the confusion. In *Red Earth, White Lies* (1995), for instance, Deloria challenges the validity of Western science, and he expresses his gratitude to NAGPRA laws as a means to avert study of human remains.

> The recent restrictions placed on anthropological research and the passage of the repatriation law have finally brought a reduction in the rate of exploitation of Indians by scholars but have by no means eliminated it.
> If cultural evolution has been unkind to non-Western human societies, physical evolution has been devastating because it is the framework within which cultural anthropology is *supposed* to make sense.[55]

It seems fair enough that Deloria would want to point out the irreverence of scientists and the many historical misuses to which scientists have put their science as regards Native Americans (especially in arguments concerning the how and when of the populating of North and South America), as well as point out the fact that there is much science does not answer. But to disregard and willfully misinterpret the theory of evolution and theories of geological history in the process and then to use such arguments as valid reasons for repatriation, as Deloria does, is indeed problematic and unfortunate. Such dismissive attitudes toward what science has accomplished in geologic history and evolution, for example, tend to diminish the value of the kinds of legalistic and theoretical arguments Walters and Vizenor present. Without dismissing science outright, they can argue that there continues to exist a spiritual essence that science fails to recognize and that to deny such an essence damages contemporary, living Native Americans.

Jace Weaver delves into the controversy, insisting that the *New York Times* makes obvious its pro-science bias in presenting the case. He also argues that N. Scott Momaday "repeated the fundamentalist characterization" of Native Americans concerning repatriation. I shall get back to

---

[54] George Johnson, "Indian Tribes' Creationists Thwart Archeologists," *New York Times*, October 22, 1996): A1, C13.

[55] Vine Deloria, Jr., *Red Earth, White Lies: Native American and the Myth of Scientific Fact*. New York: Scribner, 1995), 65 (emphasis in original). For a detailed and scathing response to Deloria's book, see H. David Brumble, "Vine Deloria, Jr., Creationism, and Ethnic Pseudoscience," *American Literary History* 10.2 (summer 1998): 335–46. See also Deloria's response, ibid., 347–49.

Momaday's argument in a moment, but, first, as regards Weaver's argument: "Although traditional creation myths are an important part of tribal identity and are often deeply held, they are not the prime factor in NAGPRA repatriation requests." Rather, maintains Weaver, "Native traditions prescribe respect for the remains of ancestors. The fear among many Natives about scientific testing is not that it will contradict or disprove sacred accounts concerning tribal origins but that it will further desecrate the remains."[56] Anticipating just such a controversy, it seems, Gerald Vizenor demonstrates an even less patient view when he insists that neither creation myths nor religion have a place in issues of repatriation. He writes that his "proposal to establish bone rights in a new court does not rest on primitivism, naïve religionism, or semantic binaries, engendered in the recent spiritual and institutional bone wars, but is based on secular, theoretical propositions, and legal philosophies."[57] Vizenor's argument suggests his disagreement with arguments presented by other Native Americans, such as Vine Deloria, Jr., who at times has indeed relied on religion and a rejection of Western science to make his argument against the methods of anthropology and archeology.

In another disagreement between Native writers, Jace Weaver calls Kiowa writer N. Scott Momaday a "long time believer in the Bering Strait theory and in the benefits of Western science," and accuses him of repeating "the fundamentalist characterization. Referring to the long history of poor relations between scientists and Natives, [Momaday] labeled Native actions in situations like that involving the Ancient One [Kennewick Man] as 'vengeance' for past depredations."[58] Momaday does, to be sure, use the word "vengeance" in his op-ed piece in the *New York Times*, but he prefaces that usage by noting that the unearthing of the human remains might rekindle the battle between evolutionists and creationists. Momaday writes that "because these remains were found on the sacred land of an Indian tribe, the Umatilla in nearby Oregon, it is not quite as simple as that. There is also history to consider, and vindication." Vindication is, after all, much different from vengeance. The rest of Momaday's op-ed piece, in fact, is much more about setting things to rights, vindicating, than it is about seeking revenge or achieving vengeance. Momaday notes the lack of respect and the lack of reverence that scientists have demonstrated for hundreds of years, and he reminds his readers that "violations of burial sites and the confiscation of human remains have been shameful

---

[56] Weaver, *Other Words*, 165.   [57] Vizenor, *Crossbloods*, 66.
[58] Weaver, *Other Words*, 165.

and unprofessional." He concludes with the following paragraph, worth quoting in full:

> To many Native Americans, the theft of what is sacred to their community stands as the greatest of all the crimes perpetrated upon them. Wounds to the spirit are considered eminently more serious than wounds to the body. Indians have endured massacres, alcoholism, disease, poverty. The dese-cration of spiritual life has been no less an assault. Because the scientific scrutiny of human remains once interred in sacred ground is indelibly associated with this painful history, Native Americans will resist. They feel they must. At stake is their identity, their dignity and their spirit."[59]

Momaday's statement hardly comes across as the language of one who has been enlisted as an apologist for the anti-NAGPRA archeologists as Weaver suggests. Rather, it is the language of justification, the language of one who clearly aligns himself with those, like Vizenor and even Weaver himself, who acknowledge the importance of repatriation rights for legit-imate practical and theoretical reasons. As Vizenor insists, "The rights of bones are abstract, secular, and substantive ... the rights of bones to be represented in court are neither religious nor doctrinal. The rights of bones in this proposal would not violate the constitutional amendment restricting the 'establishment of religion'" (*Crossbloods*, 70).

As Momaday, Vizenor, and Weaver make clear, the philosophical and political underpinnings of ideas of universal human and indigen-ous rights in the context of repatriation extend well beyond the literal issue itself. There is a link, for example, between issues of repatriation and those of sovereignty, as Creek writer and literary scholar Craig S. Womack implies. In *Red on Red* (1999), he points out an important con-nection or relationship between literary and political understandings of sovereignty: "While this literary aspect of sovereignty is not the same thing as the political status of Native nations, the two are, nonetheless, interdependent. A key component of nationhood is a people's idea of themselves, their imaginings of who they are. The ongoing expression of a tribal voice, through imagination, language, and literature, contributes to keeping sovereignty alive in the citizens of a nation and gives sover-eignty a meaning that is defined within the tribe rather than by external sources."[60] What Womack suggests here is similar to the point Momaday makes about respect, identity, and selfhood, for instance.

---

[59] N. Scott Momaday, "Disturbing the Spirits," *New York Times*, November 2, 1996, 23.
[60] Craig S. Womack, *Red on Red: Native American Literary Separatism* (Minneapolis: University of Minnesota Press, 1999), 14.

In her study *Inventing Human Rights*, Lynn Hunt concludes that "The human rights framework, with its international bodies, international courts, and international conventions, might be exasperating in its slowness to respond to repeated inability to achieve its ultimate goals, but there is no better structure available for confronting these issues."[61] Similarly, in his essay "Bone Courts: the natural rights of tribal bones," Gerald Vizenor maintains: "The Bone Court is the best place to begin, where tribal bones are the narrators, where tribal bones have the legal right to be represented."[62] In that it acknowledges and stipulates responses to the rights of indigenous peoples to their artifacts and to the remains of their ancestors, and to their histories, to literatures, the Declaration on the Rights of Indigenous Peoples sanctions and provides opportunities for Native Americans and indigenous peoples across the world to tell their own stories, to take history into their own hands. Providing for such opportunities is promising indeed.

Works Cited

Anaya, S. James. *Indigenous Peoples in International Law*. New York: Oxford University Press, 1996.

Anaya, S. James and Siegfried Wiessner. "The UN Declaration on the Rights of Indigenous Peoples: Towards Reimpowerment." *Jurist*, 3 (October 2007), http://jurist.law.pitt.edu/forumy/2007/10/un-declaration-on-rights-of-indigenous.php.

Barsh, Russel Lawrence. "Indigenous Peoples and the UN Commission on Human Rights: A Case of the Immovable Object and the Irresistible Force." *Human Rights Quarterly* 18 (1996): 781–807.

Brumble, H. David. "Vine Deloria, Jr., Creationism, and Ethnic Pseudoscience." *American Literary History* 10.2 (1998): 335–46.

Capriccioso, Rob. "Scientists Ponder NAGPRA Lawsuit." *Indian Country Today*, April 13, 2010, www.indiancountrytoday.com/national/90350684.html.

Dawes, James. "Human Rights in Literary Studies." *Human Rights Quarterly*, 31 (2009): 394–409.

Deloria, Vine, Jr. *Red Earth, White Lies: Native Americans and the Myth of Scientific Fact*. New York: Scribner, 1995.

Dongoske, Kurt E. "NAGPRA: A New Beginning, Not the End, for Osteological Analysis – A Hopi Perspective." In Devon A. Mihesuah, ed., *Repatriation*

---

[61] Lynn Hunt, *Inventing Human Rights* (New York: Norton, 2007), 213.
[62] Vizenor, *Crossbloods*, 78.

Reader: Who Owns American Indian Remains? Lincoln: University of Nebraska Press, 2000. 282–93.

Donnelly, Jack. *International Human Rights, Second Edition.* New York: Westview Press, 1998.

Forsythe, David. *Human Rights in International Relations*, 2nd edn. New York: Cambridge University Press, 2006.

Harjo, Suzan Shown. "Testimony before the Senate Select Committee on Indian Affairs." *Congressional Quarterly's Editorial Research Reports* 3 (May 14, 1990): 45.

Henry, Gordon. *The Light People.* Norman: University of Oklahoma Press, 1994.

Hill, Rick. "Repatriation Must Heal Old Wounds." In Roy L. Brooks, ed., *When Sorry Isn't Enough: The Controversy over Apologies and Reparations for Human Injustice.* New York University Press, 1999. 283–90.

Holder, Cindy and Jeff J. Corntassel. "Indigenous Peoples and Multicultural Citizenship: Bridging Collective and Individual Rights. *Human Rights Quarterly* 24 (2002): 126–51.

Hunt, Lynn. *Inventing Human Rights.* New York: Norton, 2007.

Johnson, George. "Indian Tribes' Creationists Thwart Archeologists." *New York Times*, October 22, 1996: A1, C13.

King, Thomas. *The Truth About Stories: A Native Narrative.* Minneapolis: University of Minnesota Press, 2003.

    Truth and Brightwater. New York: Grove Press, 1999.

Lawlor, Mary. *Public Native America: Tribal Self-Representation in Museums, Powwows, and Casinos.* New Brunswick: Rutgers University Press, 2006.

Lewis, Norman. "Human Rights, Law, and Democracy in an Unfree World." In Tony Evans, ed., *Human Rights Fifty Years On: A Reappraisal.* New York: Manchester University Press, 1998. 77–107.

McNickle, D'Arcy. *Wind from an Enemy Sky.* Repr. Albuquerque: University of New Mexico Press, 1988 [1978].

Momaday, N. Scott. "Disturbing the Spirits." *New York Times*, November 2, 1996: 23.

Monroe, Dan. "The Politics of Reparation." In Dane Morrison, ed., *American Indian Studies: An Interdisciplinary Approach to Contemporary Issues.* New York: Peter Lang, 1997. 391–434.

Native American Graves Protection and Repatriation Act (NAGPRA). (2000 version). US Code, title 25, chap. 32, sec. 3001.

Owens, Louis. *Other Destinies: Understanding the American Indian Novel.* Norman: University of Oklahoma Press, 1992.

Northrup, Jim. *Walking the Rez Road.* Stillwater, MN: Voyageur Press, 1993.

Power, Susan. *Roofwalker.* Minneapolis: Milkweed, 2002.

Pulitano, Elvira. *Toward a Native American Critical Theory.* Lincoln: University of Nebraska Press, 2003.

Robinson, Fiona. "The Limits of a Rights Based Approach to International Ethics." In Tony Evans ed., *Human Rights Fifty Years On: A Reappraisal.* New York: Manchester University Press, 1998. 58–76.

Sarris, Greg. *Keeping Slug Woman Alive: A Holistic Approach to American Indian Texts.* Berkeley: University of California Press, 1993.

Mabel McKay: Weaving the Dream. Berkeley: University of California Press, 1994.

Schweninger, Lee. "'Lost and Lonesome': Literary Reflections on Museums and the Roles of Relics." *American Indian Quarterly* 33.2 (2009): 169–99.

Silko, Leslie Marmon. *Ceremony.* New York: Viking/Penguin, 1977; Signet, 1978.

Teeple, Gary. *The Riddle of Human Rights.* Amherst, NY: Humanity Books, 2005.

Trask, Haunani-Kay. *From a Native Daughter: Colonialism and Sovereignty in Hawai'i,* rev. edn. Honolulu: University of Hawai'i Press, 1999.

United Nations Declaration on the Rights of Indigenous Peoples. GA Res. 61/295, Annex, UN Doc. A/RES/61/295, September 13, 2007, www.un.org/esa/socdev/unpfii/documents/DRIPS_en.pdf.

United Nations Permanent Forum on Indigenous Issues (UNPFII). "About UNPFII and a Brief History of Indigenous Peoples and the International System," www.un.org/esa/socdev/unpfii/en/history.html.

Vizenor, Gerald. *Crossbloods: Bone Courts, Bingo, and Other Reports.* Minneapolis: University of Minnesota Press, 1976, 1990.

Dead Voices: Natural Agonies in the New World. Norman: University of Oklahoma Press, 1992.

Fugitive Poses: Native American Scenes of Absence and Presence. Lincoln: University of Nebraska Press, 1998.

"Harold of Orange", screenplay (1984), in Vizenor, *Shadow Distance: A Gerald Vizenor Reader,* Wesleyan University Press, 1994. 297–333.

"Ishi and the Wood Ducks: Postindian Trickster Comedies," in Vizenor, ed., *Native American Literature: A Brief Introduction and Anthology.* New York: Longman, 1995. 299–336.

"Mister Ishi: Analogies of Exile, Deliverance, and Liberty." In Karl Kroeber and Clifton Kroeber, eds., *Ishi in Three Centuries.* Lincoln: University of Nebraska Press, 2003. 363–72.

"Mister Ishi in California." In Vizenor, *Native Liberty: Natural Reason and Cultural Survivance.* Lincoln: University of Nebraska Press, 2009. 239–55.

Walters, Anna Lee. *Ghost Singer.* Repr. Albuquerque: University of New Mexico Press, 1994 [1988].

Weaver, Jace. *Other Words: American Indian Literature, Law, Culture.* Norman: University of Oklahoma Press, 2001.

That the People Might Live: Native American Literatures and Native American Community. New York: Oxford University Press, 1997.

Who Owns the Past? Video documentary, director and producer N. Jed Riffe. Independent Producers Services, 1999.

Williams, Robert A., Jr. *The American Indian in Western Legal Thought: The Discourses of Conquest.* New York: Oxford University Press, 1990.

Womack, Craig S. *Red on Red: Native American Literary Separatism.* Minneapolis: University of Minnesota Press, 1999.

10

Contested ground: 'āina, identity, and nationhood in Hawaii

KU'UALOHA HO'OMANAWANUI

'Ōlelo Mua (Introduction)

On February 17, 2010, the Hawaii State Legislature House of Representatives Finance Committee heard testimony on House Bill 2737, which proposed to help balance the state's budget and ease the economic crisis by selling off state and ceded lands, including important sacred and cultural sites to Kanaka Maoli (Native Hawaiians[1]), such as Mauna Kea.[2] On the same day, a *Honolulu Advertiser* editorial praised the move; while recognizing that it might be seen as an affront to Native Hawaiian "groups," it feebly defended its stance by reminding its readers that "20 per cent of the revenues raised would go to OHA [Office of Hawaiian Affairs]."[3] While the bill was deferred (for now), it is doubtful that this is the last battle over ceded lands – just one issue of indigenous rights – Kanaka Maoli will face, and it is far from the first.

Like many indigenous people around the world, Kanaka Maoli identity and nationhood are based on our relationship with our 'āina (land). Perhaps unique to Kanaka Maoli is the enduring battle we have ceaselessly waged against the US government over the restoration of our kingdom, illegally overthrown in 1893 with US military support, and the illegal annexation of our country to the United States in 1898. Since that time,

---

[1] "Kanaka Maoli," "Kanaka 'Ōiwi," "'Ōiwi," "Native Hawaiian," and "Hawaiian" are used interchangeably throughout this chapter.
[2] "Ceded lands" refers to the nearly 2 million acres of crown lands "ceded" to the US federal government at the time of annexation, and later to the state of Hawai'i at the time of statehood in 1959. For more information, see www. stopsellingcededlands.com. Mauna Kea is one of our sacred mountains threatened with overdevelopment through the siting of telescopes on it. For more information, see www.kahea.org, or "Mauna Kea Testimonies," *'Ōiwi: A Native Hawaiian Journal*, vol. 3 (Honolulu: Kuleana 'Ōiwi Press, 2005), available online at www.ukukau.org.
[3] "Selling State Land a Sensible Way to Raise Cash."

like the indigenous peoples of North America and the Pacific, our lands and identities have been consumed by settler states such as the United States, Canada, and New Zealand, settler states that could not exist without such forced removal. Along with expulsion from land, settler colonialism insists upon disenfranchising indigenous people from our cultural practices – speaking our native languages and practicing our native religions, for example. It also seeks to erase indigenous identity with the aim of elimination or assimilation – elimination eradicates the "problem," while assimilation integrates the indigenous into the broader arc of the "feel good" immigrant narrative. Complicating the issue in Hawaii is the multicultural influx and settlement of numerous immigrant groups, many of whom arrived in the nineteenth century to work on haole (Amer-European[4])-owned sugar plantations; descendants of these many groups consider themselves "locals," not settlers. Moreover, there is no agreement within the Hawaiian community regarding our status and political identity as an indigenous people. Within this context, then, Hawaii is literally and figuratively contested ground. This chapter examines the current situation in Hawaii with regard to our struggle for nationhood and identity, both of which focus on our 'āina, and how the 2007 United Nations Declaration on the Rights of Indigenous Peoples factors into this struggle.

Once were Maoli – native Hawaiians in an indigenous context

Hawaii is a geographical place, a contested space, a state of mind. It is the homeland of Kanaka Maoli, the "first nation" indigenous people of the Hawaiian archipelago. In 1893, the US government supported the overthrow of the Hawaiian monarchy; in 1898 Hawaii was annexed to the United States, a move Kanaka Maoli have been fighting against ever since. When Europeans first stumbled upon the Pacific islands in the 1500s, they discovered populated islands with dynamic, vibrant cultures and highly developed societies. In 1778, the British sea captain James Cook and his men were the first Europeans to record their observations

---

[4] "Amer-European" is a term adopted from Native American literary scholar Jace Weaver to describe "white" Americans of European ancestry. While synonymous with "Euroamerican," a more well-known term, "'Amer-European' connotes something very different. They are Europeans who happen to live in America," and this term "reflects the difference in worldview between the two peoples, Native and non-Native. Born of and shaped by a different continent, Amer-Europeans … never truly belong here, no matter how many generations they may dwell here." Weaver, *That the People Might Live*, xiii–ix.

in English, describing Kanaka Maoli as a highly industrious people, having "brought their agriculture to an incredible degree of perfection," with a society where "the utmost attention to cleanliness prevails"; the chiefs were also described as "men of strong and well-proportioned bodies, and of countenances remarkably pleasing" who were "fair and honest in all their intercourse."[5]

The native population of Hawaii, as Cook and other early explorers, traders, and missionaries described them had, like all indigenous peoples, their own terms in their own language to describe themselves, terms we still utilize today. Within ʻōlelo Hawaiʻi (Hawaiian language), Kanaka Maoli is the most recognized term we use to identify ourselves. The term derives from the words "kanaka" (people) and "maoli," "native, indigenous, aborigine, genuine, true, real, actual; very, really, truly; Hawaiian native."[6] There are a number of synonymous terms – "Kanaka ʻŌiwi" or "ʻŌiwi (Hawaiian native; lit. "of the bones"), "ʻŌiwi Maoli" (lit. "true bones"), "Kanaka Hawaiʻi" or "Hawaiʻi" (lit. "Hawaiian person"), "kupa," a citizen or one native to a specific place, and "kamaʻāina" (lit. "land child"), one who is "native born [or] born of a place."[7] These terns are associated with ʻāina – "Hawaiʻi" is the name of our land, and of ourselves, an ancient association expressed in the opening lines of an ancient chant, "Eia Hawaiʻi, he moku, he kanaka, he kanaka nui o Hawaiʻi ē" – "Behold Hawaii, an island, a man, a great chief is Hawaii indeed!"[8] This sentiment is also reflected in the "ʻōlelo noʻeau" (proverb), "he aliʻi ka ʻāina, he kauā ke kanaka" – "the *land* is the chief, served by the people."[9] The close connection between terms defining and describing both ʻāina and kanaka is not surprising, given our traditional beliefs of origin, as described by Hawaiian historian Lilikalā Kameʻeleihiwa:

> According to ancient Hawaiian beliefs ... Kumulipo (Source of Darkness) mated with ... Pōʻele (the Deep Dark Night), and from these two were born all creatures of the world in genealogical sequence, from the coral polyp in the slime of the ocean floor, to the fish of the sea, to the creatures of the land and the birds of the sky. All aspects of the world became one of the 40,000 Hawaiian *Akua* (gods), and from these *Akua* were born the Hawaiian people. Hawaiian identity is, in fact, derived from the *Kumulipo*,

---

[5] "British remarks on Hawaiians," *An Act of War*, DVD (Honolulu: Nā Maka o ka ʻĀina, 1993).

[6] Pukui and Elbert, *Hawaiian Dictionary*, 240.

[7] Ibid., 124, 184.

[8] Fornander, *Account of the Polynesian Race*, 10 (my translation).

[9] Pukui, *ʻŌlelo Noʻeau*, 62 (emphasis added).

the great cosmogonic genealogy. Its essential lesson is that every aspect of the Hawaiian conception of the world is related by birth, and as such, all parts of the Hawaiian world are of one indivisible lineage.[10]

This connection is also reflected in contemporary expressions of identity, as in the songs "Kulāiwi" (meaning both "homeland" and "native") and "He Hawai'i Au" (I am Hawaiian).[11] Kumu hula (dance master) and scholar Pualani Kanaka'ole Kanahele emphasized this point, saying, "every day I am reminded that I am who I am because of my participation with others around me, whether seen or unseen. I have two convictions in life ... one ... is that I am Hawaiian. The other ... is that I am this land and this land is me. There is a correlation."[12]

Since the mid-nineteenth century, Hawaiian ethnic and political identity has been complicated by outside interference and through multinational and multicultural interaction in various ways. Kame'eleihiwa writes that "Before the coming of the [haole] ... to our islands, the idea of *Ea* – of having political independence and sovereignty – was firmly established and supported by the traditional 'Aikapu religion."[13] A Western-influenced form of government was but one of the many cultural, social, and economic upheavals Kanaka Maoli faced in the early part of the nineteenth century. In 1810, the Hawaiian political structure was transformed by Kamehameha I from a traditional system to a monarchy; upon his death in 1819, his son and successor, Kamehameha II (Liholiho), Liholiho's mother Keōpūolani, and the Kuhina Nui (Regent) Ka'ahumanu abolished the traditional 'Aikapu religious order. In this way, "The Hawaiian Kingdom was governed until 1838, without legal enactments, and was based upon a system of common law, which consisted partly of the ancient kapu (restrictions) and the practices of the celebrated Chiefs, that had been passed down by tradition since time immemorial. The Declaration of Rights, proposed and signed by His Majesty King Kamehameha III on June 7, 1839, was the first essential departure from the ancient ways."[14]

In 1840, Kamehameha III (Kauikeaouli) promulgated the first constitution, and in 1859 a Civil Code was established. The Civil Code addressed

[10] Kame'eleihiwa, "History of Hawaiian Culture," para. 1.
[11] The mele "Kulāiwi" by Larry Lindsey Kimura includes the line, "He Hawai'i au mau a mau." The title of the mele "He Hawai'i Au," by Ron Rocha, Peter Moon, and Alice Namakelua, is self-explanatory.
[12] Kanahele, "I Am This Land and This Land Is Me," 26.
[13] Kame'eleihiwa, "History of Hawaiian Culture," para. 12.
[14] [Sai], "Political History," para. 3.

the issues of a political identity for Kanaka Maoli and other residents, wherein "the native inhabitants of the Hawaiian Islands became subjects of the Kingdom as a consequence of the unification of the islands by His Majesty King Kamehameha I at the turn of the 19th century."[15] Since Hawaii became constitutionally governed, "foreigners were capable of becoming Hawaiian nationals either through naturalization or denization" which included entitlement "to all the rights, privileges and immunities of an Hawaiian subject."[16]

In 1866, the issue of citizenship or Hawaiian nationality was clarified by the Minister of the Interior for the Hawaiian Kingdom, which stated that "no one acquires citizenship in this Kingdom unless he is born here, or born abroad of Hawaiian parents … or unless having been the subject of another power, he becomes a subject of this kingdom by taking the oath of allegiance."[17] Long-time Hawaiian nationalist David Keanu Sai explains that, "The position of His Majesty's Government was founded upon Hawaiian statute. Section III, Art. I, Chap. V of an Act to Organize the Executive Departments, 1845 and 1846."[18] This statute provided that

> All persons born within the jurisdiction of this kingdom, whether of alien foreigners, of naturalized or of native parents, and all persons born abroad of a parent native of this kingdom, and afterwards coming to reside in this, shall be deemed to owe native allegiance to His Majesty. All such persons shall be amenable to the laws of this kingdom as native subjects. All persons born abroad of foreign parents, shall unless duly naturalized, as in this article prescribed, be deemed aliens, and treated as such, pursuant to the laws.[19]

Sai and other Hawaiian nationals insist that since the US occupation of Hawaii is illegal, "American citizens born in [the] Hawaiian territory after 1898 cannot be construed to benefit from the nationality laws, and therefore cannot claim to be Hawaiian subjects by birth, *jus soli*."[20] Using modern Estonia and Latvia as examples, Sai argues that

> Therefore, it can be stated as a matter of law and based on contemporary examples, that the Hawaiian citizenry of today is comprised of descendants of Hawaiian subjects and those foreigners who were born in the Hawaiian Islands prior to 1898. This exclusion of the Hawaiian citizenry is based upon precedence and law, but a restored Hawaiian government does have the authority to widen the scope of its citizenry and

[15] Ibid.   [16] Ibid.
[17] David Keanu Sai, "Hawaiian Nationality," 1.
[18] Ibid.   [19] Ibid.   [20] Ibid., 2.

adopt a more inclusive model in the aftermath of prolonged American occupation.[21]

Regardless of the fight Kanaka Maoli continue to wage against US occupation, the overthrow of our government and the annexation to the United States continue to have an effect on 'Ōiwi identity. Hawaiian national and Hawaiian Studies professor Haunani-Kay Trask writes,

> Because of the overthrow and annexation, Hawaiian control and Hawaiian citizenship were replaced with American control and American citizenship. We suffered a unilateral redefinition of our homeland and our people, a displacement and a dispossession in our own country … orphaned in our own land. Such brutal changes in a people's identity – their legal status, their government, their sense of belonging to a nation – are considered among the most serious human rights violations by the international community today.[22]

While haole[23] have always struggled with classifying hapa[24] (mixed race) Hawaiians under US occupation, new terms to define 'Ōiwi ethnic and political status have emerged in the colonial language (English) that have divided the Hawaiian community – "Native Hawaiian" and "(part) Hawaiian." "Native Hawaiian" is legally defined at the federal and state level, for "descendant[s] with at least one-half blood quantum of individuals inhabiting the Hawaiian Islands prior to 1778"; this definition originated in the 1921 Hawaiian Homes Commission Act.[25] However, federal laws are confusing, as in other statutes and contexts "the term 'Native Hawaiian' is used to cover all persons who are descended from the people who were in the Hawaiian islands as of 1778, when Captain James Cook [arrived]."[26] One example is the highly controversial and contested Native Hawaiian Government Reorganization Act of 2009, most commonly

---

[21] Ibid.   [22] Trask, *From a Native Daughter*, 21.

[23] "Haole" used to mean "foreigner," but now refers to Caucasians, particularly Americans and Europeans. Pukui and Elbert, *Hawaiian Dictionary*, 58.

[24] "Hapa" is the Hawaiianization of the English word "half" (Pukui and Elbert, *Hawaiian Dictionary*, 58). It denotative meaning is, "portion, fragment, part, fraction, installment; to be partial, less; of mixed blood, person of mixed blood" (ibid.). Initially, it meant one who was half Hawaiian, and half haole (hapa haole). As Kanaka Maoli continued having children with people of multiple ethnicities, the word took on a larger meaning of one with mixed blood, heritage, or ancestry; one who is bi- or multiracial. Originating within a Kanaka Maoli cultural context, what has always been understood within this context is that part of that ancestry is Kanaka Maoli.

[25] Kauanui, *Hawaiian Blood*, 2.

[26] Van Dyke and MacKenzie, "Introduction to the Rights of the Native Hawaiian People," 65 n. 4.

referred to as the "Akaka Bill," which defines Native Hawaiians as "the native people of the Hawaiian archipelago that is now part of the United States, [who] are one of the indigenous, native peoples of the United States."[27] "Hawaiian" has been used in both contexts, and as an ethnic, political, and geographic identity by both Kanaka Maoli and non-Hawaiian residents of Hawai'i.[28]

Such blood racialization is heavily criticized throughout the Hawaiian community, in part because it "undercuts indigenous Hawaiian epistemologies that define identity on the basis of one's kinship and genealogy."[29] The contention over determining Kanaka Maoli ethnic and political identity has real-world ramifications, particularly in regard to claims to land and self-determination. Hawaiian national and American Studies professor J. Kehaulani Kauanui points out that the "historical division" between native Hawaiians with a 50 percent or higher blood quantum and other ethnic Hawaiians "is still at play in the contemporary sovereignty movement and is manifest in the current federal legislation before the US Congress [the Akaka Bill] threatening to transform the Hawaiian national independence claim to that of a domestic dependent nation under US federal policy on Native Americans."[30] Thus this "legal construction of Hawaiian indigeneity" has serious "implications for historical claims to land and sovereignty."[31]

As the sovereignty movement has progressed, a focus on ethnic and racial distinctions rather than nationality has clouded the issue, as opponents to Hawaiian sovereignty have accused Hawaiian nationals of being anti-haole, anti-American, and racist. Kanaka Maoli playwright and artist Alani Apio writes,

> America has defined us as a race seeking nation status, thus providing the groundwork for calling the Hawaiian sovereignty movement racist. America continues to recognize us solely by race because if it recognizes our Hawaiian nationality then they have to admit that the whole

---

[27] Native Hawaiian Government Reorganization Act of 2009, 111th Cong., S 1011, sec. 2, para. 2.

[28] For example, in her autobiography, Queen Lili'uokalani noted that "When I speak ... of the Hawaiian people, I refer to the children of the soil – the native inhabitants of the Hawaiian Islands and their descendants" – an "aboriginal people" with a "birthright" (Lili'uokalani, *Hawai'i's Story*, 325). On the other hand, some Hawaii residents who are not indigenous claim a geographic identity as "Hawaiians." Kauanui remarks on this when she writes, "the term 'Hawaiian' does not work as a residency marker in the way 'Californian' does" (Kauanui, *Hawaiian Blood*, xii).

[29] Kauanui, *Hawaiian Blood*, 3.

[30] Ibid.   [31] Ibid.

archipelago was stolen against its own and international laws at the time, and thus subject to the international laws of decolonization.[32]

It is important to emphasize that blood quantum distinctions are not rooted in Kanaka Maoli culture – prior to colonization, Kanaka Maoli did not discriminate against each other along the lines of blood quantum, a different construction of identity from cultural protocols regarding moʻokūʻauhau, or genealogical ancestry. Blood quantum is a weapon of settler colonialism that has been used against Kanaka Maoli to divide us; thus many reject the colonial terms altogether, in favor of Hawaiian-language ones. As Kauanui notes, "The emergence of these terms can be attributed to the contemporary indigenous nationalist struggle and the Hawaiian language recovery movement, both of which tend to advocate for genealogical forms of articulating identity."[33] Hawaiian history professor Jon Osorio summarizes Kanaka Maoli identity thus:

> [W]e choose to be Hawaiian. We choose to be nothing else. We don't want to be fragmented. We don't want to be part-Hawaiian. We don't want to be part of a country that is aiming for something very different and has very different values and very different understandings of its role in history. If we are to be true to the legacy of our … ancestors … we need to resurrect the nation. We need to be a country again … the longer we are in this movement, the surer we are of who we are …We're ready.[34]

Kanaka Maoli are not the "happy natives" settler colonialism and tourist industry propaganda imagine us to be. We are determined to regain our stolen kingdom, our right to self-determination and self-governance. Within this political context, then, what role does – or can – the Declaration play? Is there a place for the Declaration in such a lively political movement?

Kanaka Maoli and the Declaration

In 2007, the United Nations passed the Declaration on the Rights of Indigenous Peoples. Over two decades in the making, this important and groundbreaking document affirms many important areas of human culture and society that are equally applicable to indigenous peoples around the world. Yet the United States, one of the most powerful nations in the world, which itself is a colonizer, oppressor, and architect of genocidal

[32] Apio, "Kanaka Lament," para. 27.   [33] Kauanui, *Hawaiian Blood*, xi.
[34] Osorio, "On Being Hawaiian," 25.

campaigns against a number of indigenous peoples, including Kanaka Maoli, refused to sign it. Since 2007, the three other countries who initially refused to sign (Australia, Canada, and New Zealand) have all come around. Under Barack Obama's administration, the United States has reexamined its initial opposition, and in 2009, announced its support of the declaration.[35]

The document is important because, as Trask affirms, "When in conflict with colonizing powers ... Native peoples have increasingly come to argue in the language of indigenous human rights [as] individual civil rights – the kind common to modern constitutions – are inadequate to enunciate indigenous claims to land, language, self-government, and religious practices such as protection of sacred sites."[36] Thus a critical aspect of the document is that indigenous peoples are defined in terms of "collective aboriginal occupation prior to colonial settlement."[37] As such, indigenous peoples are acknowledged separately from minorities or ethnic minority groups.

No matter what course of action the United States ultimately decides to take, the UN Declaration is not legally binding on the United States or any other state that has signed it. In this regard, perhaps, the document is somewhat limited in what it can realistically accomplish for Kanaka Maoli or any other indigenous group. Moreover, Kanaka Maoli do not have a lot of faith in foreign governing entities such as the United States and the UN, as treaties, agreements, declarations, and other *palapala* (written documents) have been ignored in the past. Trask argues,

> In terms of international law, the American military invasion of our archipelago, overthrow of our Native government, imprisonment of our Queen, and immediate American diplomatic recognition of the hastily-constructed all-white, all-male Provisional Government, resulted in undeniable human rights violations, including our claim, as a Native nation and people, to self-determination. Under international law, these violations constitute: an arbitrary deprivation of our nationality, and of our citizenship in an independent country; an arbitrary deprivation of our national territory, including lands, waters, and other natural resources; a denial of our human right to self-government as both an indigenous people and as a formerly independent country.

---

[35] www.un.org/esa/socdev/unpfii/en/declaration.html. On June 4, 2010, the State Department posted a section on its website inviting comments. State Department, UN Declaration on the Rights of Indigenous People Review, www.state.gov/s/tribalconsultation/declaration/.
[36] Trask, "Restitution," para. 18.   [37] Ibid., para. 20.

These deprivations, as a whole, comprise violations of Articles 15, 17, and 21 of the Universal Declaration of Human Rights. In addition, they are also violations of the American Convention on Human Rights. The fact that the overthrow and annexation occurred before international covenants went into effect does not invalidate the Hawaiian case.[38]

In the meantime, Kanaka Maoli have not sat idle waiting for the UN or any other entity to right the injustices done to us on our behalf.

Originating with the overthrow of the Hawaiian government in 1893, the fight for indigenous Hawaiian rights was reinvigorated in the 1960s, influenced in part by the US campaigns for civil and equal rights. Keoni Kealoha Dudley and Michael Keoni Agard (1993) describe this period as the beginning of the modern sovereignty movement, when "the early 1970s brought a renewal of interest in traditional Hawaiian music, arts, and crafts ... The time was right ... It was okay to be Hawaiian again ... And Hawaiians began to be *proud* of being Hawaiian again."[39] The Hawaiian renaissance, as this period is often described, gave birth to the modern Hawaiian rights and sovereignty movement; Trask writes,

> Our human rights movement is now over three decades old. Beginning in the 1970s, our struggle evolved from anti-eviction actions and occupations of military reserves, including entire islands used as bombing targets, to civil and legal rights struggles, to the current demand for sovereignty ... Our focus has been on the injury our Native Hawaiian people continue to suffer at the hands of the American government. This injury began with those familiar American practices in the international arena: invasion, occupation, and takeover.[40]

For Kanaka Maoli, our struggle has always been about land and nationhood, essential foundations for the practice and perpetuation of all aspects of our culture – in essence, a fight for human rights – and it has always been difficult. For example, Trask (2002) argues that settler societies like the United States have had an easier time addressing the rights of immigrant/settler populations (such as Japanese Americans interned during World War II), as, "Ideologically as well as politically, it is far easier for the United States government to address, in a public and official manner, the forcible internment of one of the most successful settler groups in America than it is for the same government to render equal acknowledgement of mistreatment of an indigenous nation."[41] Moreover,

[38] Ibid., paras. 47–49.
[39] Dudley and Agard, *A Call for Hawaiian Sovereignty*, 107.
[40] Trask, "Restitution," paras. 36–37.
[41] Ibid., para. 12.

this is particularly egregious as "partially repairing injury to Japanese Americans reinscribes the American ideology of equality among settlers while recognition of harm done to indigenous peoples not only contradicts the dominant 'immigrant' paradigm but raises prior issues of responsibility for genocide against Native peoples."[42]

In reaction to the *Rice* v. *Cayetano* decision (2000), Hawaiʻi Senator Daniel Akaka introduced a bill to Congress "to establish a government-to-government relationship between the 'Native Hawaiian governing entity' and the United States. Using the context of federal Indian law, the 'Akaka Bill' is intended to recognize the Native Hawaiian peoples' right of self-determination within the United States" and to "create parity among Native peoples of the United States [with] ... Native Hawaiian peoples [having] increased authority over certain ancestral lands and control over the administration of trust assets."[43] Even if passed, however, it would "not settle the Native Hawaiian peoples' international claims against the United States."[44]

While some pro-sovereignty Kanaka Maoli organizations and representatives have been active in the domestic political arena, others have pursued claims at the international level. R. H. K. Lei Lindsey argues that "The international arena is an important forum for the Native Hawaiian peoples on two levels. One level involves standard-setting activities at the United Nations as an indigenous peoples. The other level involves claims to independence rooted in the United States' participation in the overthrow of the Hawaiian Kingdom and encompasses subsequent milestones in United States–Hawaiʻi relations."[45]

One example is the Hawaiian Kingdom government, represented by acting Regent David Keanu Sai. In 1999, Sai appeared before the World Court of Arbitration. In *Larson* v. *The Hawaiian Kingdom*, Sai argued that "when a nation, such as the United States, has a treaty with another nation, such as the Kingdom of Hawaiʻi, the United States cannot impose its own domestic laws."[46] While the World Court refused to rule in the case, the

---

[42] Ibid.
[43] Lindsey, "Akaka Bill," 693. In *Rice* v. *Cayatano*, haole Big Island rancher Harold "Freddy" Rice sought to overturn what he considered racial discrimination in voting for OHA based on the 14th Amendment of the US Constitution. The case was eventually heard by the US Supreme Court, which ruled in favor of the plaintiff. This was a landmark case because Kanaka Maoli indigeneity was not recognized by US law, hence Akaka's push for Federal recognition via the "Akaka Bill." A text of the US Supreme Court decision is found at www.law.cornell.edu/supct/html/98–818.ZS.html. Background for the case can be found at http://archives.starbulletin.com/1999/10/06/news/story1.html.
[44] Ibid.   [45] Ibid., 694.   [46] Kelly, "Kingdom Come," 11.

Hawaiian Kingdom government and similar organizations continue to pursue claims and redress at the international level. While Kanaka Maoli have yet to achieve victory in the international political arena, Kanaka Maoli stand firm upon our beliefs that justice will prevail.

What kind of influence the UN Declaration could have on such a powerful state as the United States is unknown. Amanda Mae Kāhealani Pacheco, JD, observes that,

> Realistically speaking, while the law may be on the side of the Hawaiian Kingdom, the United States is the most powerful government in the international arena, and as such, has decisive power on any debates surrounding the sovereignty of Hawaiʻi. If the Hawaiian Kingdom Government is adamant about achieving sovereignty, perhaps there needs to be a greater effort at engaging the United States itself in these debates, instead of relying on international law to force the US into compliance … [however,] the international arena has in fact taken notice and has listened to several of these cases. Sai considers this proof that sovereignty is possible.[47]

Sai himself does not see the Declaration as having any impact on the status of Hawaiian rights in the international arena, as he argues that Kanaka Maoli are not indigenous people, rendering the Declaration irrelevant to our political situation.[48] Sai's position stands apart from other pro-sovereignty advocates, who view Hawaiian claims for sovereignty as originating with, if not exclusively based on, our status as indigenous people.

In the meantime, the Declaration allows for the hopeful imagining of what is possible to further positive political and social transformation for Kanaka ʻŌiwi. Decades in the making, it is an important document meant to facilitate positive outcomes for a broad range of indigenous peoples around the world. Kanaka Maoli are skeptical but hopeful that our concerns and actions since the overthrow of our nation in 1893 will garner support and recognition at every level. We remain skeptical, as the United States has continued to ignore key points of history, legislation, and documentation from that time to this. From that perspective, the Declaration is just one more piece of paper. Yet the implementation of the Declaration also offers hope that such fundamental goals can help transform the planet into a more just world. At the very least, the Declaration offers support to social and political actions already in play, such as claims to reestablish and reinvigorate cultural practices, including control over

---

[47] Pacheco, "Past, Present, and Politics," 392–93.
[48] Personal communication, June 9, 2010.

indigenous intellectual property in fields such as the sciences (medicine, astronomy) and education. Simply put, Kanaka Maoli, as other indigenous peoples, have not sat idly by wringing our hands waiting for the UN (or anyone else) to do something. Over the years, we have continued to push to right the wrongs of the past, to practice our culture, to reclaim our lands, to establish schools in our language, and more. Looking at selected articles of the Declaration, just what more is possible with its implementation? Here I should like to comment on selected articles of the Declaration in the context of ongoing Kanaka Maoli advocacy for justice.

Self-determination, identity, reparations. A number of articles in the Declaration deal with issues of self-governance, political identity, and reparations. For example, Articles 3–5 address self-determination and identity, stating in part that "Indigenous peoples have the right to self-determination," to "determine their political status" and to "freely pursue their economic, social and cultural development."[49]

Moreover, Article 10 allows indigenous people "the right to belong to an indigenous community or nation, in accordance with the traditions and customs of the community or nation concerned. No discrimination of any kind may arise from the exercise of such a right," while Article 33 allows for the right "to determine their own identity or membership in accordance with their customs and traditions."[50] Thus, Kanaka Maoli would be free to identify as Kanaka Maoli, an identity based upon the cultural and ancestral practices of mo'okū'auhau. An important outcome for allowing such a practice would be the end of legalized fragmentation of Kanaka Maoli identity based on the false dichotomy of blood quantum. It could benefit Native Hawaiian health and well-being by ending the psychological anguish and internal discrimination Kanaka Maoli have enacted upon ourselves and each other, a significant consequence of blood quantum racialization.

Articles 8–10, along with Article 33 and Article 35, address nationhood and dispossession of land, including issues of identity and forced assimilation, and redress. In this regard, "States shall provide effective mechanisms for prevention of, and redress for …[a]ny action which has the aim or effect of dispossessing them of their lands, territories or resources."[51]

Article 28 addresses reparations and redress for "lands, territories and resources which they have traditionally owned or otherwise occupied or

---

[49] UN General Assembly, Declaration, 4.
[50] Ibid. 5, 10. [51] Ibid.

used, and which have been confiscated, taken, occupied, used or damaged without their free, prior and informed consent."[52] Moreover, such compensation "shall take the form of lands, territories and resources equal in quality, size and legal status or of monetary compensation or other appropriate redress." Such a statement could have positive outcomes at the state and federal level with regard to Hawaiian ceded lands, finally returning such trust lands to 'Ōiwi control. Aside from providing for natural resources and an economic base, it could greatly alleviate problems of homelessness, and could encourage (or enable) Kanaka Maoli who have moved away from Hawaii for economic reasons finally to return home.

In this regard Article 31 is helpful, in that it supports the right of indigenous people to "maintain, control, protect and develop their cultural heritage, traditional knowledge and traditional cultural expressions, as well as the manifestations of their sciences, technologies and cultures, including human and genetic resources, seeds, medicines, [and other] intellectual property."[53] Again, a lucrative economy could be developed from instituting such rights, allowing Kanaka Maoli greatly to increase our economic opportunities and cultural developing, contributing to Hawaiian economic, social, cultural, and psychological well-being in a myriad ways.

As such, Articles 26 and 29 address environmental issues, wherein indigenous peoples "have the right to the conservation and protection of the environment and the productive capacity of their lands or territories and resources. States shall establish and implement assistance programmes for indigenous peoples for such conservation and protection, without discrimination.[54] Mālama 'āina – caring for the land like family – is an essential Hawaiian value. Not only could such environmental protections, under Kanaka Maoli jurisdiction, protect our resources and allow for a more independent, sustainable future, but there are multiple social, cultural, and economic benefits as well. New job opportunities as forest rangers or marine biologists, for example, would provide more opportunities for 'Ōiwi, while maintaining the source of our medicinal and traditional plants for cultural activities such as hula would allow for the blossoming of these practices.

Treaties and agreements. Article 37 addresses the right to the "recognition, observance and enforcement of treaties, agreements and other

---

[52] Ibid., 9.   [53] Ibid., 9–10.   [54] Ibid., 8–9.

constructive arrangements concluded with States or their successors and to have States honour and respect such treaties, agreements and other constructive arrangements."[55] This is perhaps one of the most tantalizing articles in the Declaration, as Hawaiian sovereignty organizations could evoke this article in the international arena to force the United States to honor such treaties and agreements made with the Hawaiian government in the past; it is the contention of many sovereignty activists that, by ignoring such treaties, the United States has been in violation of international laws since its participation in the 1893 overthrow and the 1898 annexation of Hawaii to the United States, which itself was illegal.

Religion, repatriation, spirituality.   Articles 11–12 and 25 address issues of repatriation and religion, two areas of Hawaiian cultural practice which have suffered tremendously under the proselytizing influence of Christianity beginning with first Western contact. Aside from the right to "practice and revitalize" cultural traditions, a manner of redress "with respect to [indigenous] cultural, intellectual, religious and spiritual property taken without their free, prior and informed consent or in violation of their laws, traditions and customs" could be enacted.[56]

Article 12 states that "Indigenous peoples have the right to manifest, practice, develop and teach their spiritual and religious traditions, customs and ceremonies; the right to maintain, protect, and have access in privacy to their religious and cultural sites; the right to the use and control of their ceremonial objects; and the right to the repatriation of their human remains"; moreover, section 2 asserts that "States shall seek to enable the access and/or repatriation of ceremonial objects and human remains in their possession through fair, transparent and effective mechanisms developed in conjunction with indigenous peoples concerned."[57]

Article 25 in particular discusses spirituality and "the right to maintain and strengthen their distinctive spiritual relationship with their traditionally owned or otherwise occupied and used lands, territories, waters and coastal seas and other resources."[58] This article would be useful regarding a number of recent issues, such as repatriation of iwi kūpuna (ancestor remains) unearthed from new construction projects and recovered from museums worldwide, decision-making regarding the Forbes cave funerary objects, and even the reimplementation of traditional burial practices.[59]

---

[55] Ibid., 11.   [56] Ibid., 5–6, 8.   [57] Ibid., 5–6.   [58] Ibid., 8.
[59] Further information on these issues can be found at www.huimalama.tripod.com; www.archaeology.org/online/features/hawaii/index.html; and http://the.honoluluadvertiser.

Education.   Articles 13–14 address education, including the right to "revitalize, use, develop and transmit to future generations their histories, languages, oral traditions, philosophies, writing systems and literatures, and to designate and retain their own names for communities, places and persons."[60] While great strides in indigenous education have been made in Hawaii over the last decade, Kanaka Maoli have continued to struggle with the State Department of Education (DOE) and the Bush administration's federally mandated No Child Left Behind (NCLB) Act. Implementation of Article 13 within the DOE and private schools across the archipelago could have a dramatic, positive effect on Kanaka Maoli and other students who call Hawaii home. Indigenous knowledge with regard to environment is often superior to Western practices. As such, it could have a significant impact on global environmental issues. In Hawaii, the traditional 'Ōiwi practice of mālama 'āina could invigorate programs of environmental stewardship of the 'āina that could be beneficial not just to Kanaka Maoli, but to the planet.

Article 14 provides for the right to "establish and control their educational systems and institutions providing education in their own languages, in a manner appropriate to their cultural methods of teaching and learning"; moreover, that "States shall, in conjunction with indigenous peoples, take effective measures in order for indigenous individuals, particularly children, including those living outside their communities, to have access, when possible, to an education in their own culture and provided in their own language."[61] Public Hawaiian charter and private schools currently exist; Aha Pūnana Leo, a private preschool organization, and nā kula kaiāpuni, public (DOE) schools from grades K–12, are Hawaiian-language immersion schools. All of these schools, however, suffer from lack of financial and wider public support. Maoli students who attend Hawaiian immersion schools do not always feel comfortable with speaking Hawaiian outside their classes, as they do not hear or see Hawaiian utilized in any meaningful way in mainstream society or the mainstream media. Giving more credence to 'ōlelo Hawaii and providing more financial and social support could help students overcome their hesitation, and could help with general language revitalization.

---

com/article/2003/May/25/op/op07a.html. Traditional Hawaiian burial practices included the wrapping and safeguarding of bones, which is not an option for Kanaka Maoli today, as only Western practices of full body burial in a coffin and cremation are legal.

[60] UN General Assembly, Declaration, 6.   [61] Ibid.

Military. Article 30 is particularly relevant for Kanaka ʻŌiwi, as our lands have been coveted and possessed by US military forces since the 1800s. It states in part that "Military activities shall not take place in the lands or territories of indigenous peoples, unless justified by a significant threat to relevant public interest or otherwise freely agreed with or requested by the indigenous peoples concerned," and that "States shall undertake effective consultations with the indigenous peoples concerned, through appropriate procedures and in particular through their representative institutions, prior to using their lands or territories for military activities."[62] While it took decades of struggle, occupation, and loss of life, Kanaka Maoli were eventually victorious in reclaiming the island of Kahoʻolawe from US Navy jurisdiction, and we were able to stop the bombing and destruction of the island and its myriad significant cultural sites. Efforts to rehabilitate the island are ongoing; although much has been done, much remains to be done. An implementation of Article 30 could have an immediate and positive impact on other fights to reclaim Hawaiian lands being occupied and decimated by a continued US military presence. The return of army training facilities at Mākua valley on Oʻahu and Pōhakuloa on Hawaiʻi island, and military installations from Nōhili (Barking Sands) on Kauaʻi to Līhuʻe (Schofield) and Kāneʻohe on Oʻahu is another possibility. The Hawaiian Nation would decide whether to allow the United States continued use of Puʻuloa (Pearl Harbor).[63]

Achieving the goal. Article 38 urges states to consult and cooperate with indigenous peoples under their jurisdiction to "take the appropriate measures, including legislative measures, to achieve the ends of this Declaration."[64] This is an important position for the UN to take. One can only hope that the UN is able to utilize what influence it has for the Declaration to be effectively enacted.

Perhaps most important within the Declaration is Article 43, which states that all the rights outlined and addressed in the document "constitute the *minimum* standards for the survival, dignity and well-being of the indigenous peoples of the world."[65] That the document proclaims an understanding of such minimal standards for indigenous well-being

---

[62] Ibid., 9.
[63] Ann Keala Kelly's documentary, *Noho Hewa, the Wrongful Occupation of Hawaiʻi*, provides an excellent Kanaka Maoli perspective on the issue of military occupation of Hawaiian lands; see www.nohohewa.com for more information.
[64] UN General Assembly, Declaration, 11.
[65] Ibid. (emphasis added).

provides hope that such goals can be achieved for indigenous peoples around the globe, for the benefit of all peoples and our planet.

Haʻina ʻia mai ana ka puana (Conclusion)

Within the vast Kanaka ʻŌiwi community, differing and competing ideas about Hawaiian sovereignty and governance abound. For some, it is an issue of Hawaiian (indigenous) rights; for others it is an issue of nationhood, which has never been extinguished. Recognition of Hawaiʻi's independent nationhood and acknowledgement of the US occupation would include non-indigenous citizenry. In both cases, issues of mixed blood genealogies are inherent.

Regardless of which form Hawaiian recognition takes, indigenous rights and the UN Declaration as such are important to a healthy, vibrant Hawaiian future. Laenui, who participated in different phases of the drafting process of the document, is hopeful. "In all," he writes, "the Declaration is a tool that does not fit all peoples in all situations, but can be used by some folks in some situations. As a worldwide instrument, it is a major advancement for indigenous peoples."[66]

In a speech addressing Hawaiian identity and political choices, Hawaiian History professor Jon Osorio argues that it is our individual and collective choices as Kanaka Maoli that ultimately matter:

> The essential choices for Hawaiians today are ... Do we wish to live as Hawaiians, or don't we? And if that is the choice we must make, then federal recognition is irrelevant. What matters is not what the US Senate decides but how we will face the future together, whom we will entrust with leadership, and how far we are willing to commit ourselves to be Hawaiian. We've been hearing these conversations all around us, for the better part of a half century. Hawaiians must know their language, Hawaiians must know their history, Hawaiians must remain on the land, Hawaiians gotta stick together. The common thread to all of these imperatives is Hawaiian. Being Hawaiian. When I consider all the things American society possesses and promises, it almost surprises me that there are so many of us who insist on living our lives as Hawaiians. Especially since so few of us come well equipped for the task ... I might be a technically deficient Kanaka Maoli, but this I know: I am not an American ... It isn't just ancestry and it isn't just cultural proficiency; being Hawaiian is ultimately about not wishing to be anything else.[67]

[66] E-mail communication, February 19, 2010.
[67] Osorio, "On Being Hawaiian," 22–23.

While Osorio addressed the pending legislation of federal recognition, his statements are equally true of the UN Declaration – no piece of paper can ultimately determine our future, how we decide to live and chart our course for our collective and individual futures. Trask reminds us that

> As conquered nations, indigenous peoples were forced to become Americans. Our national status, then, is a result of subjugation, not choice. This indisputable history is critical because, as is universally acknowledged, citizenship must be freely chosen or it is meaningless in terms of representing the interests and binding the loyalty of citizens. And while our lands of origin have been collectively renamed the United States of America, indigenous peoples are now classified by the Federal American government as "Native Americans," a nonsensical category which tells worlds about our contradictory status.
>
> Given the primacy of homeland, of the place where Native people understand an ancestral sense of belonging, identification as "American" has no correspondence to any cultural, familial, or tribal origins ... my people, the Hawaiians, are Native to the Pacific archipelago of Hawaiʻi. We are not Native to a recent creation called the United States of America. Rather, we are aboriginal to a specific land base which defines us linguistically, geographically, and historically. As indigenous peoples and nations, our ancestral attachments are prior to colonial categorization as "Americans."[68]

Choosing to be Hawaiian and acting on that foundational belief in the face of such seemingly insurmountable odds exemplifies the Declaration in action, although such action has existed before and in spite of any UN proclamation. As assaults against Kanaka Maoli identity, culture, and lands continue, in the words of our kūpuna (ancestors), "he oia mau nō," – we continue to persevere.

In 1897, Kanaka Maoli representatives presented a petition to the US Congress requesting the restoration of the Hawaiian government; it was signed by over 38,000 people, at a time when the Hawaiian population was only 40,000 strong. Because of protests from the queen and her people, the US Senate failed to obtain the required two-thirds vote as mandated by the US Constitution to ratify the treaty. By March 1898, the treaty of annexation had died for lack of support. In response, senators introduced Joint Resolution 55, which was passed by a simple majority. The result has been a well-executed lie and illusion. Hawaiian national Kaui Goodhue writes,

> For the past 100 years, it was assumed that Joint Resolution [55] possessed the power and effect of a treaty. However, according to international law

---

[68] Trask, "Restitution," paras. 13–14.

and practice, it did not. Moreover, under US constitutional law, a joint resolution does not have the power to extend beyond the borders of the United States.

> Without a treaty of annexation, American sovereignty cannot exist in these islands. Nothing has legally transpired which can affect the lawful existence of the Hawaiian Kingdom and its subjects ... What took place on August 12, 1898, was nothing more than an illusion, an illusion that we went from being Hawaiian subjects to American citizens ... "hāweo" [refers] to a flow of light that makes things visible. It is in the light of knowledge that the darkness and confusion of the past 100 years are now being destroyed and the heroic deeds of our ancestors are being revealed. The responsibility is now ours to carry on where they left off. From resistance to affirmation, WE ARE WHO WE WERE.[69]

From 2010 forward, we continue to be who we were and will always be – Kanaka Maoli, the indigenous people of the Hawaiian archipelago. We continue to fight for our ʻāina, our identity, our culture, our well-being. We continue to contest the political status of our ʻāina as a US state and possession, standing as our ancestors over one hundred years ago, "kūpaʻa ma hope o ka ʻāina" – steadfast behind the land.[70]

On February 17, 2010, Kanaka Maoli, along with many other concerned citizens, presented lengthy testimony in opposition to House Bill 2737, which proposed to help balance the state's budget and ease the economic crisis by selling off state and ceded lands, including important native sacred and cultural sites, such as Mauna Kea. That same day, the Argentine president Cristina Fernández de Kirchner blasted the United Kingdom's move to drill for oil in waters off the Malvinas (Falkland Islands), waters controlled by Argentina. In part of her speech protesting Britain's proposed plan, Fernández de Kirchner said that the issue is about "international rights that have to do with the possibility of a world with rules other than force, war, [and] the imposition by those who are stronger."[71]

Indigenous peoples envision such a possibility. The UN Declaration affirms our rights, providing hope for such a future envisioned by Fernández de Kirchner, for the indigenous peoples of the world as well, who are often powerless against such governments as Argentina, the United Kingdom, the United States, and others who wield power over our

---

[69] Goodhue, "We Are Who We Were," 38–39.
[70] This sentiment is expressed in the Hawaiian Nationalist anthem, "Mele ʻAi Pōhaku" (Rock-eating song), composed by Ellen Kehoʻohiwaokalani Wright Prendergast after the 1893 overthrow. An article detailing the song and events is in ʻŌiwi: A Native Hawaiian Journal, vol. 4 (Kuleana ʻŌiwi Press 2009), www.hawaii.edu/oiwi.
[71] "Argentine Lawmakers Support President's Falklands Initiative."

lives, lands, and well-being. Trask reminds us that "For Native nations, the paramount issue is the return of Native people to their Native place. For us, as native people, the return of Native self-government is the only answer to total dispossession ... it is the repairing of damage, of harm, which must be attempted even if, as in the case of Native peoples, millions of Native human beings will never be restored to life. Nevertheless, return of some lands, entitlements, and other negotiated rights go a long way towards helping natives to survive as peoples and nations, not only as individuals."[72]

The UN Declaration on the Rights of Indigenous Peoples provides a template for beginning such negotiations of indigenous rights for Kanaka Maoli and other indigenous peoples worldwide. Regardless of the document or whether the United States decides to sign on or not, Kanaka Maoli will continue to seek "pono," justice and harmony for our people. The document, however, allows the United States a way to meaningfully address the wrongs of the past. It is a matter of "kuleana," responsibility at the national level. Addressing issues of reconciliation, Trask concludes that, "If we, as a community, and the United States as a country, are concerned about suffering, about citizenship, and about the larger context of international relations – including human [and indigenous] rights – then justice must be rendered before reconciliation can be considered. For it is justice, rather than specific amounts of money or carefully crafted apologies, which constitutes the first and primary obligation of nations and peoples."[73] Thus our quest for ʻāina, identity and nationhood continues.

Works cited

An Act of War. DVD, Honolulu: Nā Maka o ka ʻĀina Productions, 1993.

Apio, Alani. "Kanaka Lament." *Honolulu Advertiser.* March 25, 2001. http://the.honoluluadvertiser.com/article/2001/Mar/25/op/op05a.html.

"Argentine Lawmakers Support President's Falklands Initiative." CNN, February 17, 2010. www.cnn.com/2010/WORLD/americas/02/17/argentina.falklands/index.html.

Dudley, Michael Keoni and Keoni Kealoha Agard. *A Call for Hawaiian Sovereignty.* Honolulu: Nā Kāne o ka Malo Press, 1993.

Fornander, Abraham. *Account of the Polynesian Race.* Rutland: Charles E. Tuttle Co., 1989.

Goodhue, Kaui. "We Are Who We Were – From Resistance to Affirmation." *ʻŌiwi, a Native Hawaiian Journal* 1 (1998): 36–39.

---

[72] Trask, "Restitution," para. 17, 63.   [73] Ibid., para. 66.

Kameʻeleihiwa, Lilikalā. "History of Hawaiian Culture and Society Prior to Western Contact." *Holo Mai Pele, a Mythic Hawaiian Tale of Love and Revenge.* www.piccom.org/home/holomaipele/culture.html.

Kanahele, Pualani. "I Am This Land and This Land Is Me." *Hūlili: Multidisciplinary Research on Hawaiian Well-Being* 2 (2005): 21–50.

Kauanui, J. Kehaulani. *Hawaiian Blood, Colonialism and the Politics of Sovereignty and Indigeneity.* Durham, NC: Duke University Press, 2008.

Kelly, Ann Keala. "Kingdom Come," *Honolulu Weekly,* April 18–24, 2001. www.alohaquest.com/arbitration/news_honoluluweekly_010418.htm.

Noho Hewa, the Wrongful Occupation of Hawaiʻi, documentary film, 2008. www.nohohewa.com.

Liliʻuokalani. *Hawaiʻi's Story by Hawaiʻi's Queen.* Boston: Lee and Shephard, 1898. http://digital.library.upenn.edu/women/liliuokalani/hawaii/hawaii.html.

Lindsey, R. H. K. Lei. "Akaka Bill: Native Hawaiians, Legal Realities, and Politics as Usual." *University of Hawaii Law Review* 24 (2002): 693–737.

Native Hawaiian Government Reorganization Act of 2009. US Congress. Senate. S 1011. 111th Cong. (introduced May 7, 2009). www.govtrack.us/congress/billtext.xpd?bill=s111–1011.

Osorio, Jonathan. "On Being Hawaiian." *Hūlili: Multidisciplinary Research on Hawaiian Well-Being* 3 (2006): 19–26.

Pacheco, Amanda Mae Kāhelani. "Past, Present, and Politics: A Look at the Hawaiian Sovereignty Movement." *Intersections* 10 (2009): 359–405. https://depts.washington.edu/chid/intersections_Winter_2009/Amanda_Mae_Kahealani_Pacheco_The_Hawaiian_Sovereignty_Movement.pdf.

Pukui, Mary Kawena. *ʻŌlelo Noʻeau, Hawaiian Proverbs and Poetical Sayings.* Honolulu: Bishop Museum Press, 1986.

Pukui, Mary Kawena and Samuel H. Elbert. *Hawaiian Dictionary,* rev. edn. Honolulu: University of Hawaiʻi Press, 1986.

Sai, David Keanu. June 14, 2010. Personal communication.

"Hawaiian Nationality: Who Comprises the Hawaiian Citizenry?" unpublished essay (no date), available at http://hawaiiankingdom.org/info-nationals.shtml, 1.

[Sai] "Political History." www.hawaiiankingdom.org/political-history.shtml (no date).

"Selling State Land a Sensible Way to Raise Cash." Editorial, *Honolulu Advertiser,* February 17, 2010. www.honoluluadvertiser.com.

Trask, Haunani-Kay. *From a Native Daughter, Colonialism and Sovereignty in Hawaiʻi.* Monroe, MN: Common Courage Press, 1993.

"Restitution as a Precondition of Reconciliation: Native Hawaiians and Indigenous Human Rights." *Borderlands e-journal,* 1 (2002). www.borderlands.net.au/vol1no2_2002/trask_restitution.html.

UN General Assembly, 61st Session, Agenda Item 68, Report of the Human Rights Council, Declaration on the Rights of Indigenous Peoples, UN Doc. A/61/L.67 (2007).

Van Dyke, Jon and Melody MacKenzie. "An Introduction to the Rights of the Native Hawaiian People." *Hawaii Bar Journal* (July 2006): 63–69.

Weaver, Jace. *That the People Might Live, Native American Literatures and Native American Community* (New York: Oxford University Press, 1997), xiii–ix.

11

Kānāwai, international law, and the discourse of indigenous justice: some reflections on the Peoples' International Tribunal in Hawaii

ELVIRA PULITANO

All peoples possess the moral and legal right to defend themselves against substantial and consistent violation of their self-determination, essential human rights and freedoms and of other fundamental norms governing relations between peoples, nations, and states. In pursuit of this right, peoples are entitled to present their cases to the international community and to sit in judgment over the actions of those who have denied them their fundamental rights and freedoms.

Ka 'Olelo Mua O Na 'Olelo Ho'ahewa (Introduction to the Charges),
Presented by the Kanana Maoli Tribunal Komike, August 21, 1993

In August 1993, on the centennial anniversary of the overthrow of the sovereign Hawaiian government by a coup of plantation owners helped by US marines, a panel of nine distinguished international law experts and scholars convened in Hawaii to hear the history of dispossession and disempowerment of the Kanaka Maoli, the indigenous peoples of Hawaii.[1] Witnesses to the Peoples' International Tribunal included over a hundred scholars, activists, elders, and members of various grassroots organizations, all of whom presented informative and compelling evidence of the Hawaiian experience under US colonization. The Tribunal pressed nine

---

[1] Throughout this chapter I use the terms "Native Hawaiian" and "Kanaka Maoli" interchangeably to refer to the indigenous peoples of Hawaii and their intimate connection to the *aina* (land), without regard for the blood quantum rule. I occasionally use the term "Hawaiian" with the same connotation. I am aware, though, that the term "Native Hawaiian" often implies a much more specific legal meaning. See also ho'omanawanui's chapter in this volume.

A note on the Hawaiian language: The *Kahak ō* (macron), the Hawaiian diacritical mark used to stress vowels, has been omitted to facilitate printing. The *'okina*, or glottal stop indicating a brief break in words, has been occasionally used following usage in the primary sources.

charges against the United States including illegal annexation, imposition of statehood, illegal appropriation of the lands and resources of the Kanaka Maoli, environmental destruction, and acts of genocide and ecocide. The hearings were conducted over a twelve-day period, beginning on August 12, and involved site visits on five of the archipelago's major islands – Maui, Oʻhau, Molokaʻi, Kauaʻi, and Hawaiʻi – during which the Tribunal members reviewed written and oral documentation along with film and videotaped material. The Tribunal found the United States and the state of Hawaii guilty, and urged the United States, the United Nations, and the entire international community to appeal to their sense of justice and impart remedies to the Kanaka Maoli.[2]

Largely ignored in the US media, the Peoples' International Tribunal received a significant amount of press coverage in Hawaii.[3] A film documentary, *The Tribunal*, was produced in 1994 by Nā Maka o ka ʻĀina ("The Eyes of the Land"), an independent video production company that since 1982 has been documenting traditional and contemporary Hawaiian culture and history as well as the politics of independence and sovereignty (Nā Maka). From the arrival of the international judges on

---

[2] A complete set of the tribunal's findings and recommendations was submitted by Ka Lahui Hawaii (the nation of Hawaii) under the governorship of Mililani Trask to the United Nations Commission on Human Rights in the summer of 1996. According to Trask, the report seems to have mysteriously disappeared from the shelves of both New York and Geneva offices (personal interview). Among the remedies sought by the tribunal are recognition of the Kanaka Maoli's right to self-determination and sovereignty, reinscription of the Ka Paeʻaina (Hawaiian archipelago) on the UN list of non-self-governing territories, return of all Kanaka Maoli lands, and respect of the rights enunciated in the (at that time) UN Draft Declaration on the Rights of Indigenous Peoples (Churchill and Venne 332–33, 354–55).

[3] A quick review of the articles published in the *Honolulu Star-Bulletin* and the *Honolulu Advertiser* reveals the abundant coverage that the Tribunal received in Hawaii. See among others, "Hawaiians Putting US 'on Trial,'" *Honolulu Advertiser*, August 12, 1993, C6; "Voters to Decide Sovereignty," *Honolulu Star-Bulletin*, August 13, 1993, A-3; "Tribunal Weighs Crimes against Hawaii Natives," *Honolulu Star Bulletin*, August 13, 1993, A3; "Sovereignty Court Trying US," *Honolulu Advertiser*, August 13, 1993, A3; "Rally Kicks Off People's Tribunal," *Honolulu Advertiser*, August 13, 1993; "Tribunal Brings Out Litany of Ills Foisted on Hawaiians," *Honolulu Advertiser*, August 14, 1993, A5; "Tribunal Hears Waikiki History," *Honolulu Advertiser*, August 15, 1993, A3; "Peoples' Tribunal Greeted on Maui with Ceremony," *Honolulu Advertiser*, August 16, 1993, A5; "Tribunal Told of Injustices to Big Isle Hawaiians," *Honolulu Star-Bulletin*, August 19, 1993, A4; "Tribunal: Panel Finds Hawaiians oppressed,'" *Honolulu Advertiser*, August 21, 1992, A2; "Tribunal on Hawaiians Decries 'long litany of horror, illegality,'" *Honolulu Advertiser*, August 21, 1993 (front page); "Panel: US Stole Rights of Native Hawaiians," *Honolulu Star Bulletin*, August 21, 1993, A3; "For Sovereignty Groups, No State Celebration," *Honolulu Advertiser*, August 22, 1993 (front page).

the Hawaiian islands to the final verdict and recommendations, the documentary visually supplements the testimony of Native Hawaiians with graphics, political cartoons, archival photos, and contemporary footage of land occupations and ongoing struggles. Songs and hula dance were also part of the Tribunal's proceedings, offered as testimony by the hula dance group founded by John Kaimikaua from the island of Molokai. Joan Lander and Puhipau, the film's producers, describe the importance of music and dance at the international Tribunal:

> Music and dance at the Tribunal often carried more emotional and intellectual impact than spoken testimony. The traditional dances and chants performed at the Tribunal demonstrated to the international jurists that Kanaka Maoli culture is living and intact, showing not only the resilience of the Kanaka Maoli in preserving their culture despite a century of suppression, but their determination to transmit these cultural ways to future generations. The dances and chants also demonstrated a deep-seated relationship with the earth, serving to point up the fact that, when there is forcible alienation from the land and its resources, the result is literally genocide. Other songs of a more contemporary nature offered at the Tribunal expressed the reality of modern generations who simply want their country back. (Lander)

A contemporary form of archiving Kanaka Maoli history, *The Tribunal* functions as a powerful example of indigenous agency and self-expression. One of the primary commitments made by the Tribunal members was to make sure that the general public could access all the material presented at the hearings (both oral testimony and written texts). Two of the Tribunal's distinguished judges, Ward Churchill and Sharon Venne, undertook the onerous task of compiling such documentation in book form. The result was *Islands in Captivity: The Record of the International Tribunal on the Rights of Indigenous Hawaiians* (2004), an eight-hundred-page anthology that remains an unparalleled documentation of the history of the dispossession of the Hawaiian kingdom and its consequences for present-day struggles for sovereignty and self-determination.

This chapter discusses the Peoples' International Tribunal in the attempt to contribute to the debate fueled by UNDRIP on the importance of taking into account indigenous law when addressing indigenous issues in international forums. Throughout the hearings and all the way to the verdict, the Peoples' International Tribunal appealed to the principles of Kanaka Maoli law as valid instruments to attain justice for Native Hawaiians. According to Glenn Morris, one of the Tribunal's prosecutors, "Kanaka Maoli sovereignty and self-determination flows from the *maka 'āinana*, literally, 'the eyes of the land,' from the people. It can only be relinquished by the people voluntarily, which the Kānaka Maoli have never done" (*Tribunal: Transcript* 42). Through a close analysis of the film documentary and the transcript of the tribunal proceedings, as well as the more extensive compilation edited by Churchill and Venne,[4] I examine ways in which the Peoples' International Tribunal mediates concepts of indigenous law, human rights, and international law. Such mediations, I argue in my conclusions, can be taken as a teachable moment for future directions and the work ahead in the implementation of UNDRIP.

Ka Ho 'okolokolonui Kanaka Maoli:
the Peoples' International Tribunal Hawaii 1993

The Peoples' International Tribunal opened in Hawaii on August 12, 1993, with a rally for Hawaiian sovereignty. The tribunal was established as a people's court in the tradition of the Bertrand Russell-sponsored International War Crimes Tribunal convened in 1967, following the Vietnam War, which led to the establishment in 1979 of the Permanent Peoples' Tribunal (PPT) in Bologna and more recent tribunals in Puerto Rico and Iraq investigating human rights violations on the part of the United States.[5] The main goal of such popular tribunals is to raise awareness of atrocities committed by states against civilians and incite individuals throughout the world to fight for the liberation of oppressed peoples. From a strictly legal-juridical perspective, peoples' tribunals lack legal power. They are not trials in the strict sense of the term. They lack state authority and possess neither the power to condemn nor the power to acquit the defendants. Their power is located in the people rather than in

---

[4] Because Churchill and Venne's *Islands in Captivity* presents the most complete transcriptions of the testimonies offered at the tribunal, I often quote from this text when discussing the documentary production. Occasionally, I provide quotations from the film transcript as well (hereafter quoted as *The Tribunal: Transcript*). The transcript of the 86-minute documentary is available in PDF format through the Nā Maka o ka 'Āina website.

[5] In 1989 a Permanent Peoples' Tribunal convened in Barcelona, Spain, to investigate human rights violation on the part of the United States against Puerto Rico and Vieques (Ka Pakaukau, "International Tribunal"). The World Tribunal on Iraq (WTI) met in Istanbul on June 24–26, 2005, to investigate the legality of the war, the role of the United Nations, war crimes, and the role of the media, as well as the destruction of the cultural sites and the environment (World Tribunal). Popular tribunal hearings have also been used by women as a way to make visible gender-based abuses often perpetrated in the domestic sphere. See the Center for Women Global Leadership (CWGL) at Rutgers University ("Women Testify").

government institutions. Jean Paul Sartre, in his Inaugural Statement to the Russell Tribunal, elucidates the point:

> Certainly our tribunal is not an institution. But it does not claim to replace any established body; on the contrary, it emerged from a void, and in response to an appeal. We have not been recruited and invested with real power by governments ... We are powerless: it is the guarantee of our independence ... We will examine the facts "in our hearts and consciences" one might say or, if you prefer, openly and independently ... The Russell tribunal will have no other concern, in its investigations and in its conclusions, than to bring about a general recognition of the need for an international institution for which it has neither the means nor the ambition to be a substitute, whose essential role would be the resuscitation of the *jus contra bellum* ... the substitution of ethical and juridical rules for the law of the jungle. (43)

Given the political context in which the Peoples' International Tribunal in Hawaii was convened, what "ethical and juridical rules" did the Kanaka Maoli hope would right the US violation of both domestic and international law? And, most importantly perhaps, how could the principles of Kanaka Maoli law be taken into consideration throughout the tribunal's hearings? The panel of judges comprising the Tribunal included six attorneys – two of them specializing in international law, two in indigenous law, one in US constitutional law, and one in US law with a special focus on minority rights – a novelist, a theology professor, and a specialist in American Indian studies. Coming from countries that have experienced various forms of colonial subjugation, these judges were introduced as "individuals that have committed themselves over time to struggles for change in the world" (*Tribunal: Transcript* 6).[6] Having witnessed at first hand injustices and human rights violations in their own nations, these judges have been advocating the plight of indigenous peoples at the United Nations and other international venues. As Churchill and Venne

---

[6] The panel members comprised Professor Hyun Kyung Chung of South Korea; Ward Churchill, co-director of the American Indian Movement in Colorado; Milner Ball, professor of constitutional law at the University of Georgia; Professor Lennox Hinds of Rutgers University and a past director of the National Conference of Black Lawyers; Palestinian attorney Asma Khader; Te Moana Nui Jackson, director of the New Zealand Maori Legal Service; Japanese peace activist Makoto Oda; Cree attorney and human rights activist Sharon Venne; and Richard Falk, professor emeritus of international law at Princeton University. Heading the prosecution team was Glen Morris, of the Shawnee nation, professor at the University of Colorado, Boulder, Jose Morin (of the Puerto Rican nation), of the Center for Constitutional Rights in New York City, and Maivân Clech Lâm, professor of law at the City University of New York (*Tribunal: Transcript*). See also Churchill and Venne, 680–81.

point out, "the main qualification for the panel was knowledge and concern about human rights, especially in the setting of indigenous peoples and nations" (679).

The unique legal situation in which the indigenous peoples of Hawaii currently find themselves is a result of US policies that go back to the mid-1800s. The overthrow of the Kingdom of Hawaii (1893), the annexation of the islands through a joint resolution (1898) and the imposition of statehood (1959) through ambiguous legal means have often prompted a process of self-analysis on the part of the Kanaka Maoli in the context of human rights and international law, rather than within the specific frame of US constitutional and civil rights laws. Haunani-Kay Trask explains: "The US Constitution ... does not address the protection of native relationships to land, to language, to culture, to family, to self-government, indeed, to anything natives value ... As indigenous peoples we are all outside the Constitution, that settler document which declares ownership over indigenous lands and peoples" ("Hawaiians" 291–92). From a strictly constitutional framework, Trask goes on to clarify, the 1893 overthrow of the Hawaiian government and the ensuing forced annexation "were not unconstitutional acts"; they were, however, gross violations of human rights, specifically of Articles 15, 17 and 21 of the Universal Declaration of Human Rights, the articles that concern nationality (or forced deprivation thereof), property, and the right to take part in the government of one's country ("Hawaiians" 293–94).[7] In response to the legal question of whether or not these were customary rights at the time, Trask states: "Human rights scholars now agree that the idea of universal self-determination is a settled principle of peremptory international law, superseding customary rules and bilateral treaties. This means it is of sufficient importance to be applied retroactively to relationships among states and people before the adoption of the 1945 United Nations Charter" ("Hawaiians" 294). Even though the recognition of self-determination has evolved throughout the development of international law and the practice of states, the right always existed, Mililani Trask also contends ("Re: The Tribunal"). Similarly, James Anaya argues that "under international law, all peoples have the right to self-determination – and no less among them, the Native Hawaiian people" (20). Anaya thus situates the claims of Native Hawaiians within the evolving body of international norms

---

[7] Trask also points out that the act of depriving peoples of a nationality, lands, and natural resources constitutes a violation of both the International Covenant on Civil and Political Rights and the International Covenant on Economic, Social, and Cultural Rights, as well as of the American Convention on Human Rights ("Hawaiians" 293–94).

concerning indigenous peoples, norms that focus on the principles of self-determination and human rights.

The human rights agenda is certainly on the mind of the Tribunal judges as they prepare their final verdict. While acknowledging that at its onset international law often served as an instrument of colonial rule, in the past few decades, the Tribunal admits, international law, as a result of the decolonization movement worldwide, has increasingly become sympathetic to the plight of colonized peoples and nations who have tried to hold accountable their leaders and states. International law, however, was not the only understanding of law that guided the tribunal judges in their findings and recommendations. Elements of Kanaka Maoli law, the law of nations and peoples – as enunciated in some of the international peoples' tribunals which began at Nuremberg in 1945 – as well as "the inherent law of humanity" – all strongly influenced the judges' final decisions. The laws of the United States and the state of Hawaii were also taken into account (Churchill and Venne 682–83), but upon examining all the evidence presented, the Tribunal concluded that these laws "are not binding on the Kanaka Maoli inasmuch as neither the United States nor the state of Hawaii have valid jurisdiction over the Kanaka Maoli and their lands" (Churchill and Venne 683–84).

The Tribunal defined Kanaka Maoli law as law that "bears special relation to land and water, which are so essential to the identity, even survival of indigenous peoples and their nations" (Churchill and Venne 683). It also bears "special authority to elders (*Kupuna*) and to spiritual leaders in clarifying the essence of law" (Churchill and Venne 683). The Tribunal acknowledged the existence of a higher law, a law that establishes "the conditions of harmony between human activity and nature, drawing on ideas of stewardship that exist in many of the world's great cultural traditions" including, of course, indigenous peoples (Churchill and Venne 684). The Tribunal presented findings and recommendations for each of the main charges against the United States and the state of Hawaii based on these five "distinct but related and mutually reinforcing conceptions of law" (Churchill and Venne 682). The spirit guiding the tribunal reflected a distinctly Kanaka Maoli epistemology in that law is conceived of as a great river, a river "that draws on these five sources as tributary rivers" (Churchill and Venne 684).

At the beginning of the Nā Maka o ka ʻĀina video production, an anonymous narration indicates that the Hawaiian Tribunal "determined to redefine the ground rules of how tribunals are conducted" (*Tribunal: Transcript* 7). Unlike previous forms of people's courts, the Hawaiian

Tribunal set up a precedent in the sense that the hearings were held outside (rather than in the isolating environment of a closed room), among
the people who bear the pain of unjust legal provision on their daily lives.
As aptly noted by prosecutor Jose Morin, the Native Tribunal in Hawaii
brought the judges to the community, "to the grassroots" of the struggle
for self-determination (*Tribunal: Transcript* 41). The concept of *Kānāwai*
is invoked by Kekuni Blaisdell, the Tribunal convenor, following the introduction of the judges: "*Kānāwai* is our term for what westerners call law.
And *Kānāwai* contains that word '*wai*,' water, which has special *mana* to
us. And who controlled *wai* controlled the life of our people" (*Tribunal:
Transcript* 7). Traditional Hawaiian life was intimately tied to land and
water. The Polynesian ancestors of the Kanaka Maoli who settled in Hawaii
believed that the gods had created the land and the sea and all the living creatures. These resources were meant to be shared communally and
the concept of private ownership was alien within a traditional Hawaiian
culture (*Hearings* quoted in MacKenzie 3). "It is no wonder," Melody
Kapilialoha MacKenzie argues, that "the development of law relative to
Native Hawaiians reflects this relationship" (3). For Native Hawaiians, the
development of both water and land rights following European contact
reveals, MacKenzie explains, "the tension between this ancient concept of
use rights and the Western-imposed private-ownership system" (149). In
the Nā Maka o ka 'Aina documentary, the concept of *Kānāwai* is used by
Glenn Morris before the first charge is introduced, a reminder of the legal
importance of such a principle for Native Hawaiians. He states:

> Long before the United States was even a twinkle in James Madison's eye,
> there was Kanaka Maoli law and it existed in these islands. It's not enough
> to say what the United States has done in this land is a violation of US law.
> It's not enough to say it's a violation of international law over which we, as
> indigenous peoples, have had little to no input ... We must say it's a viola-
> tion of Kanaka Maoli law. (*Tribunal: Transcript* 8)

Equally important in the redefinition of the rules of how tribunals are
conducted was the inclusion in the Tribunal of song and dance, along
with the oral testimony of the people as undisputable forms of evidence.
As eloquently put by Trask, for people whose language was banned, contemporary music and traditional cultural practice such as the hula dance
are a powerful form of testimony because "they all testify to [Native
Hawaiians'] conditions, to [Native Hawaiians'] national life as a people"
(Franklin and Lyons).[8] For those engaged in "on-the-ground" struggle,

---

[8] For an excellent study uncovering a Hawaiian-language archive of Native resistance to
annexation, an archive containing songs, stories, poetry, and essays, see Noenoe Silva

Trask goes on to explain, it is very difficult to record history, unless of course, one considers history itself as a form of testimony, which is exactly what the Tribunal set out to do (Franklin and Lyons).

A strong and influential voice in the struggle of the Kanaka Maoli for sovereignty and self-determination, Haunani-Kay Trask has long acknowledged the arrogance of Western historians when it comes to establish what counts as evidence. In her provocative study *From a Native Daughter* (1993), she recounts the exchange she had with an American historian at a panel discussing the American overthrow of the Hawaiian nation. The American historian, Trask explains, refused to consider songs such as "Famous are the children of Hawaii" as evidence of the Kanaka Maoli's opposition to annexation. Addressed to the dethroned Queen Lili 'uokalani, the song captures Native Hawaiians' love for their land as well as their overall feelings against annexation to the United States. Trask notes: "Many Hawaiians in the audience were shocked at his [the Western historian's] remarks but, in hindsight, I think they were predictable. They are the standard response of the *haole* historian who has no respect for Native memory" (120). From an indigenous perspective, songs, chants, dances, stories, and various forms of cultural production are part of a long history of resistance to colonization since European contact. They are all part of that holistic approach to justice that values indigenous trad-itional values of reciprocity and equitable ceremonies rather than sub-stantive rules as a way to resolve conflicts.

In "Genocide Tribunals," Anishinaabe writer and critic Gerald Vizenor tells of Charles Aubid, a witness in a dispute with the federal government over the right to regulate wild rice on the Rice Lake National Wildlife Refuge in Minnesota.[9] Aubid, who at the beginning of the twentieth cen-tury testified in Anishinaabemowin through translators, told the judge that he was present when federal agents had promised Old John Squirrel that the Anishinaabe would have always had control over the wild rice harvest (132). The judge rejected Aubid's testimony, adding that "the court cannot hear as evidence what a dead man said, only the experience of the witness" (133). Annoyed by the judge's response, Aubid, Vizenor

---

(2004). The 1897 petition, which contained 95 percent of the native population's signatures and which caused the treaty of annexation to fail in the US Senate, represents a powerful testimony of the active resistance put up by the Native Hawaiians against oppression and colonization.

[9] Vizenor proposes establishing formal tribunals in states such as South Dakota (site of the *in*famous massacre at Wounded Knee) and across various US campuses to indict and prosecute alleged perpetrators, in absentia, of crimes against Native American Indians, according to international conventions and declarations.

humorously points out, promptly replied that the legal English books on the bench contained "the stories of dead white men" (133). Impatient to make his point, Aubid said: "Why should I believe what a white man says, when you don't believe John Squirrel?" (133). Amused by the analogy, Vizenor explains, the judge was "deferential" (133). Charles Aubid, Vizenor writes, "was a storier who created linguistic indirect evidence and a native sense of presence" (134). More important, "he declared by stories his *anishinaabe* human rights and sovereignty" (131). Vizenor writes that international criminal court tribunals recently have admitted "hearsay or indirect evidence" as relevant testimony (131).[10]

Hearsay and oral testimony have always been included in international peoples' tribunals. The Hawaiian Tribunal is no exception. Powerful narratives were presented by the witnesses at the various hearings. They were the evidence of "those who bear in their everyday lives the brunt of victimization, but also those who are often the most authentic custodians of Kanaka Maoli ways, including their all-pervasive sense of law" (Churchill and Venne 682). All the witnesses at the Tribunal were treated as "experts," and, out of reverence for Kānaka Maoli life and culture, the Tribunal sessions began and ended with sacred ceremonies and rituals.

International law recognizes the principle of *lex loci* – that is, the law of the place – although there is no substantive rule that says that it prevails. An old principle first found in Roman law, it still applies to disputes over contracts, private property, and family relations when the parties involved do not share the same national boundaries. The principle of *lex loci* becomes all the more significant in the relationship between states and indigenous peoples in that it acknowledges indigenous epistemologies. As explained by Erica-Irene Daes, former rapporteur for the UN Working Group on Indigenous Populations, "the principle of locality means that British Columbia cannot properly make laws controlling Tsimshian peoples' heritage – nor can Canada or the United Nations. Instead, British Columbia, Canada, and the United Nations should recognize, respect and reinforce Tsimshian law" (236). Unlike European law which can be carried around and applied to various places and peoples, the principle of locality within an indigenous context speaks to the fact that indigenous peoples think of their laws as inherently linked to their lands and territories.[11]

---

[10] On this specific issue see also Schabas.

[11] Daes also points out that the principle of locality has been adopted by the International Labour Organization, specifically in the Convention on Indigenous and Tribal Peoples,

In accordance with Kanaka Maoli natural law, the Peoples' Tribunal in Hawaii introduced individuals' experiences and ongoing stories of land dispossession as compelling evidence. When the Tribunal convened in the island of Hawaii, on August 18, one of the witnesses in the town of Hilo, Melissa Moniz, offered the following testimony:

> You've asked for evidence, videos, evidence of injustices, documents to back my statements. My evidence is all around you. It began from the moment when you arrived at the airport in Honolulu. The miles of cement highways that cover our 'Aina. The bustle of traffic and the hundreds of tourists, as you search the faces of the people wondering where are the Kānaka Maoli of this 'Aina.
>
> They are in jails. They are on the beaches, living in tents. They are the forgotten people. Our 'Aina, our lifeblood, has been stolen from us, the Kānaka Maoli. (Churchill and Venne 618–19)

By themselves, on paper the words do not convey the same kind of emotional response the audience experiences when watching *The Tribunal*. As viewers, we feel the pain in Ms. Moniz's gentle but determined voice; we feel the anger, frustration, and desperation at her feeling a stranger in her own homeland. More importantly, we feel the shame she honestly confesses to have felt during the years of brainwashing she experienced about her putatively inferior Kanaka Maoli culture. As viewers, we are brought to the Tribunal setting; we can see the judges' severe expression during Ms. Moniz's testimony and we are confronted with the deep wounds inflicted by colonialism. Through her testimony, Ms. Moniz created what Vizenor calls a "fourth person" (131), a sense of presence in stories that, though repudiated in common law and federal courts, becomes in peoples' tribunals, and in the Hawaiian Tribunal specifically, the most irrefutable evidence of Native survivance.

With 6.5 million tourists pouring into Hawaii in 2009, as reported by the Hawaii Tourism Authority, Native Hawaiians have suffered firsthand the devastating impact of the tourist industry on the environment and traditional lifestyle. While hotels and luxury resorts continue to be built with massive real estate speculation and devastating consequences for the native landscape, beaches are increasingly cordoned off and a profound divide has been created between Native Hawaiians and the mass-based corporately controlled tourist industry. Trask describes this system as "both vertically and horizontally integrated such that one multinational

1989 (No. 169), and is also included in the UN Convention on Biological Diversity (Daes 236).

corporation owns an airline and the tour buses that transport tourists to the corporation-owned hotel where they eat in a corporation-owned restaurant, play golf and 'experience' Hawai'i on corporation-owned recreation areas and eventually consider buying a second home built on corporation land" (*From a Native Daughter* 139). As in a Third World colony, none of the profits remains in Hawaiian hands but instead flow back to First World countries. These same countries – Australia, Canada, the United States, Japan, Hong Kong, Taiwan – in collaboration with the state of Hawaii, contribute, Trask adds, to perpetuate "the rape of Native land and people" (*From a Native Daughter* 139).

Charges of economic colonization and land dispossession

Addressing the "illegal appropriation of the lands, waters and natural resources of the Kanaka Maoli" as well as their "economic colonization and dispossession" (Churchill and Venne 347–50), the Tribunal, under charges 5 and 6, calls for a forceful revision of Hawaiian history. In the documentary, Ms. Marie Beltran from O'hau brings viewers to tears when she testifies about police posted eviction notices on her campsite. "It hurts me because they call us squatters on our own land, when they are the squatters. … But, like I tell my children, they walk in the path of their queen and king that walked this *'Aina*. And nobody has any right … telling my kids where they don't belong" (Churchill and Venne 485). Interspersed through her testimony are images of the "No Trespassing" signs that hinder the Kanaka Maoli's use of what is truly their land; we see people being arrested for refusing to relocate; we see bulldozers crashing into Kanaka Maoli houses, houses built on lands which had been granted by the government; we learn the difference between being "homeless" and being "houseless." "We are the people from this *'Aina*," Mr. Raymond Kamaka from O'hau says, "and nobody going to tell me I must get out of my own land" (Churchill and Venne 446).[12] Testimony after testimony by Native Hawaiians contest the absurd, racist, blood quantum and genealogy requirements imposed by the US Congress in order for the Kanaka Maoli to qualify for land claims.

In 1920, Congress passed the Hawaiian Homes Commission Act, making available approximately 200,000 acres of public land to a Hawaiian Homes program. These were lands that had been ceded by the Republic

---

[12] As Mr. Kamaka delivers his testimony, a text on the screen informs us that "Raymond Kamaka was sentenced to 2 years in federal prison for charging the government for the use of his land in his IRS tax returns" (*Tribunal: Transcript* 23).

of Hawaii to the United States at the time of annexation. Soon, however, the Native Hawaiians, Glen Morris points out, discovered that "the stated help of the United States became nothing less than a vicious and cruel joke" (*Tribunal: Transcript* 19). Not only were those lands, as acts in the congressional record clearly state, unusable for agriculture, but Congress designated a blood quantum restriction that would severely limit Kanaka Maoli's claims to those lands. Mililani Trask, who at the time of the Tribunal was serving in the role of Kia'aina (governor) of the Ka Lāhui Hawai'i Native initiative for sovereignty, explains that the blood quantum restriction was imposed to accommodate sugar planters' requests and that such a restriction was unprecedented (Churchill and Venne 437). Moreover, she contends, numerous federal laws such as the Native American Education Act, the Elderly Americans Act, and the Administration for Native Americans Act use a much more inclusive definition of Native Hawaiians, one that relies on genealogical descent of the people who inhabited the islands before Cook's arrival (Churchill and Venne 437).[13] When asked whether she considers the imposition of blood quantum a fundamental part of ethnocidal and genocidal policies orchestrated by the US government against Native Hawaiians, Trask replies: "I would have to say yes, because the effect of the imposition of a blood quantum was to limit, to the greatest extent possible, the ability of people to access land just for subsistence purposes. What possible reason could there have been for imposing blood quantum? What possible reason?" (*Tribunal: Transcript* 21).

On the island of Maui, Native Hawaiians are requested to meet a genealogical criterion going back to 1779 in order to make claims over the lands surrounding Hāna, a place which means "the breath of life." "Look, we all know who we are," Bernice Hokoana states at the Tribunal hearing. "The only problem is there is no document, for some of us, to prove who our 'ohana is. Without that proof, you lose your claim to your land" (Churchill and Venne 505). For Ms. Hokoana, the genealogical requirement is clearly part of an intentional policy to separate the Kanaka Maoli from their land. At the conclusion of Ms. Hokoana's testimony, Moana Jackson, one of the Tribunal judges, explains that in pre-contact time the genealogy of a person's family, a genealogy which tied that person to the

---

[13] The same more inclusive definition is used in the Apology Bill (also known as Public Law 103-150) issued by former president Bill Clinton on November 23, 1993. The term "Native Hawaiian," the resolution says, "means any individual who is a descendent of the aboriginal people who, prior to 1778, occupied and exercised sovereignty in the area that now constitutes the State of Hawaii" (United States Public Law).

land, was considered *kapu* (sacred), and that tie could not be broken. From the perspective of Kanaka Maoli law, "the state has no right to access that genealogy" (Churchill and Venne 506). Sharon Venne eloquently summarizes the point when she states that "the right to self-determination includes the rights of self-definition. If people can't define who they are, then it affects their relationship with the land" (Churchill and Venne 438).[14] Article 33 of the UN Declaration on the Rights of Indigenous Peoples states: "Indigenous peoples have the right to determine their own identity or membership in accordance with their customs and traditions" (UNDRIP). By imposing essentialist criteria founded on blood and genealogy, the United States and the state of Hawaii have violated both international and Kanaka Maoli law.

Charges of illegal annexation and imposition of statehood

Under charge 3, "Annexation of a sovereign people, their nation and territory without their free and informed consent," the Tribunal addresses the fundamental sovereignty of the Kanaka Maoli with respect to their inherent right to govern within the borders of their own nation. By invoking the principle of free, prior, and informed consent (FPIC), as it has been recognized by a number of intergovernmental organizations, international bodies, conventions, and international human rights law, the Tribunal recognizes the Kanaka Maoli's inherent and prior rights to their lands, territories and resources. Unlike Texas, which was allowed to vote on the joint resolution through a plebiscite, the Hawaiian people were denied the possibility of having their voice heard. Mililani Trask explains that Hawaii was brought to the Union by a joint resolution, otherwise known as the Newlands Resolution, since Congress could not get the two-thirds vote as mandated by the US Constitution to ratify a treaty of annexation.[15] A close analysis of the language of the resolution significantly questions the constitutionality of the annexation. With annexation, the Republic of Hawaii ceded the sovereignty of the islands to the United States. Paragraphs 1 and 2 of the Newlands Resolution address the absolute cession and ratification on the part of the United States. But paragraph 3

---

[14] For an excellent study on the racialization of Hawaii, see Kauanui.

[15] The legality of the Newlands Resolution has, to this date, been forcefully contested by Native Hawaiians. Noenoe Silva notes that Queen Lili'uokalani, appealing to the principles of international law, submitted formal protests to the treaty of annexation thus urging President McKinley to honor the treaties made by the United States with the legitimate sovereigns of the Kingdom of Hawaii (*Aloha Betrayed* 172–73).

states that "the existing laws of the United States relative to public lands shall not apply to such land in the Hawaiian Islands; but the Congress of the United States shall enact special laws for their management and disposition" (MacKenzie 15). Of utmost importance in this same paragraph is the part that guarantees that "all revenue from or proceeds of the same [lands] … *shall be used solely for the benefit of the inhabitants of the Hawaiian islands for educational purposes and other public purposes*" (MacKenzie 15, emphasis in original). The special laws mentioned in the joint resolution would later become the Organic Act (1900) in which, once again, it is underlined that the beneficial title to the ceded lands rests with the inhabitants of Hawaii. Clearly under US law there was no annexation. More importantly, perhaps, the question of beneficial title raised by the joint resolution confirms that the property rights of the Kanaka Maoli must be preserved.

One of the most critical points the Tribunal made during the annexation charge was to demonstrate that the Kanaka Maoli land dispossession as a result of Western laws does not invalidate the preceding Kanaka Maoli law. Like most indigenous peoples, the Kanaka Maoli consider themselves custodians of the land, a sacred responsibility they have been given by their gods, the *Akua*. "No act of a human institution can remove that responsibility or that right," Moana Jackson forcefully points out (Churchill and Venne 416). But it is Mililani Trask's testimony that clarifies to the tribunal judges the legal status of Kanaka Maoli title with regard to land. Within the doctrine of Western trust law, Trask explains, "title and ownership of land can be bifurcated … where the trustee has the legal title, but the equitable or beneficial title is said to vest with the beneficiary" (Churchill and Venne 428). Such a pattern, Trask maintains, has been perpetuated in Hawaiian history when, even under monarchical institutions, "the chiefs and the government had lands, but it was not for their personal property. Instead, it was held in common for the people. So, you have this idea of common, undivided title that is shared by the people" (Churchill and Venne 428). We find this bifurcation in the Constitution of Kamehameha II and, before that, in the Mahele.[16] Trask explains:

> Through annexation and into the period of the Organic Act … the federal government and the documents recite that the US government receives fee title. But there are clear exceptions, both in the documents of

[16] In 1848, the privatization of communal land (also known as Mahele) dispossessed Hawaiians and their descendants of lands that had been to this point held in common. See Kauanui (75–80).

annexation and the Organic Act, to underscore the fact that the beneficial equitable title – not just to the lands, but the proceeds and revenues therefrom – vest with the inhabitants. This is clarified and distinguished even further in 1959 when statehood is granted. In section 5f of the Statehood Act, there emerged two classes of beneficiaries: one, the public; the other, the Native Hawaiian. So, two things are demonstrated here: how various fundamental legal documents were utilized to allegedly transfer legal jurisdiction over lands into the hands of a trustee, but it is also very clear that equitable title is never extinguished. (Churchill and Venne 430–31)[17]

Unfortunately, Trask further states, the notion of "care for the people and the land," which was the primary obligation of the ali‘i (chiefs) in Hawaiian practice, becomes, in Western practice, a matter of jurisdiction over legal title, with the people having no rights unless they go to court (personal interview). Again, we see how fundamental incommensurable worldviews and epistemologies make it very difficult to reconcile Western and indigenous legal precepts. The case of the Hawaiian legal title over lands and resources cuts to the heart of the land rights debates fueled by the UN Declaration and offers us tangible evidence of the work ahead, when it comes to the question of implementation, in the relationships between indigenous peoples and states.

Writing about the dynamics of colonial oppression during the Algerian revolution, Frantz Fanon argued that "every manifestation of the French presence expressed a continuous rooting in time and in the Algerian future, and could always be read as a token of an indefinite oppression" (180). For the Kanaka Maoli, the US imposition of statehood is a perfect example of the token of indefinite oppression and dispossession set in motion in the nineteenth century. "Imposition of statehood on a people, their nation and their territory without their free and informed consent" is the fourth charge pressed by the Peoples' International Tribunal against the United States (Churchill and Venne 346).

In 1959, the islands of Hawaii were on the United Nations list of non-self-governing territories eligible for decolonization. With regard to non-self-governing territories, Article 73 of Chapter XI of the UN Charter states,

> Members of the United Nations ... accept as a sacred trust the obligation
> to promote to the utmost, within the system of international peace and

[17] As further evidence of the fact that native title remains, Trask notes that among all the states in the Union, Hawaii has the highest number of legal cases filed for title actions. Developers and home buyers cannot begin construction without filing a quiet title action in the attempt to extinguish the native title to their lands (Churchill and Venne 436).

security established by the present Charter, the well-being of the inhabitants of these territories, and, to this end ...

    b) to develop self-government, to take due account of the political
aspirations of the peoples, and to assist them in the progressive development of their free political institutions, according to the particular circumstances of each territory and its peoples and their varying stages of
advancement;

It was a primary responsibility on the part of the United States to assist
Hawaiians in the process leading to independence. Called to testify on
this specific issue, Trask explains that records seem to indicate that after
September 24, 1959 – the last date on which the United States filed a submission reassuring the UN that some measure of self-government had
been achieved in Hawaii – "the UN simply removed Hawai'i from the
list. There is no evidence at all that the United Nations inquired into the
validity of the documents submitted. Nor is there any kind of evidence
that the United Nations ever inquired into the status and conditions of
the native people" (Churchill and Venne 403). The result of the plebiscite, which took place on June 27, must have been a sufficient reason for
the UN not to ascertain the veracity of US claims about Hawaiian self-
determination. The plebiscite that was put together for Hawaiians contained only two options in the ballot: become a state or remain a territory.
But "was it informed consent?" Trask asks. "Did they know that under
international law that was applicable at the time, they had a right to have
a choice for independence, for commonwealth, a free associated status?"
(Churchill and Venne 402).[18] In the findings, the Tribunal sees the imposition of statehood on the Kanaka Maoli as "a repetition and extension of
the abuse of the fundamental law of the United States" as set forth in the
case of annexation (Churchill and Venne 700).

    All the more controversial is the way in which plebiscite procedures
overpowered the voices and sentiments of Native Hawaiians. According to
Anaya, international law practice outside Hawaii "has proscribed settler
participation in decolonizing plebiscites" for fear that such participation
could ultimately invalidate the indigenous vote (11). In the case of Hawaii,
the direct opposite occurred. In response to the requirements of Chapter

---

[18] Principle VI of General Assembly Resolution 1541 (XV) (1960), a resolution meant to
clarify what Resolution 1514 – otherwise known as the Declaration on the Granting of
Independence to Colonial Countries and Peoples – left unsaid, clearly states that full self-
government is manifested as follows: (a) emergence as a sovereign independent state; (b)
free association with an independent state; or (c) integration with an independent state
(UNGA Resolution 1541). See also Lâm, 114–22.

XI of the UN Charter and General Assembly Resolution 742 (VIII), Ka
Pakaukau, a coalition of Hawaiian sovereignty groups led by Kekuni
Blaisdell, notes that the United States "misconstrued" the term "people
of Hawaii" to indicate "the territory's settler population" ("Reinscription"
307). Under plebiscite rules, Anaya also observes, "all United States citizens who had been residents in Hawaii for one year were allowed an equal
vote" (11). Despite significant opposition to statehood among indigenous
Hawaiians, the lack of UN supervision allowed the United States to control
the plebiscite vote. According to Ka Pakaukau, "from this it is clear that
support for Statehood in Hawaii came not from indigenous Hawaiians
but from immigrant (settler) population" ("Reinscription" 307).[19]

After hearing the various testimonies, Moana Jackson proclaims
the Tribunal's findings: "The Kanaka Maoli nation is entitled to be
re-inscribed on the list of non-self-governing territories slated
for decolonization under the provisions of Article 73 of the United
Nations Charter" (*Tribunal: Transcript* 16). Ka Pakaukau argues that
the United Nations has a responsibility to Hawaii and that significant precedents exist for the General Assembly to investigate Hawaii's
incorporation into the union. With the establishment in 1961 of the
Special Committee on the Situation with Regard to Implementation
of the Declaration on the Granting of Independence to Colonial
Countries and Peoples (otherwise known as the Committee of Twenty-
Four) through Resolution 1654 (XVI), the United Nations took upon
itself the task of monitoring the processes of decolonization in non-
self-governing territories. The Special Committee has the power to
refuse, if necessary, "to endorse the results of elections" and recom-
mend, in special cases, that such countries be reinscribed on the list of
non-self-governing territories ("Reinscription" 317).[20] In light of the
fact that Native Hawaiians never had the choice to decide on their own
status, it would be appropriate, the Tribunal concluded, for the UN to
reinscribe the Hawaiian islands on the list and let the people decide
their future political status.

---

[19] Ka Pakaukau refers to the case of Niʻihau, the only electoral district in which Native
Hawaiians constituted the majority, whose vote was "solidly" against statehood. Anti-
statehood pamphlets also circulated among indigenous Hawaiians in the various islands
at the time ("Reinscription" 307).

[20] In 1967, for instance, French Somaliland's decision to remain French was not recognized
by the GA due to the fact that the plebiscite was held without a UN presence. And in 1993
Puerto Rico was given the opportunity to vote on its status, the majority of the population choosing the commonwealth option (Ka Pakaukau, "Reinscription," 317, 319).

Charges of genocide and ecocide

The most contentious charge that the International Peoples' Tribunal pressed against the United States was the charge of "acts of genocide and ethnocide against the Kanaka Maoli," conveyed through charge 7. A text on the Nā Maka o ka 'Āina video production announces that "by the year 2044 there will be no more pure Hawaiians" (*Tribunal: Transcript* 28). They will have become extinct. For the Kanaka Maoli, such predictions are the results of systematic acts of genocide and ethnocide committed by the invading forces. Over the years, Native Hawaiians have seen a tremendous decrease of the *lo'i kalo* (taro patches), the basis of their staple food, poi, from an estimated 36,000 acres in 1778 to 310 acres in 1991 (*Tribunal: Transcript* 29). Through the testimony of Hank Fegerstrom in Hawaii we hear about the devastating consequences of tourism development for the physical health of the Kanaka Maoli. Mr. Fegerstrom points out the high cost of poi when compared with other staple foods of the Hawaiian people. It takes a considerable amount of land to grow taro, he says, land that Kanaka Maoli no longer own, as well a considerable amount of water. Today Kanaka Maoli have to go to court to fight for water rights in order to grow their taro. Foreign investors, on the other hand, are granted water rights to irrigate the golf courses and the hotel resorts (Churchill and Venne 656). Once considered an exceptionally healthy people, today Native Hawaiians have the worst health record in the United States. "We are sick people," Bernice Hokoana from Maui states. Intentional acts leading to premeditated actual devastation of the sustainable way of living of the Kanaka Maoli have drastically contributed to the skyrocketing of diabetes, cancers, strokes, and the infant mortality rate. Rachel Tortolini, a local physician called to testify, provides appalling statistics with regard to the health of Native Hawaiians. She argues that "poor health is one of the tragedies suffered by a loss of Hawaiian sovereignty," adding that all these diseases are diseases of a lifestyle" (Churchill and Venne 543). As the Kanaka Maoli made the transition from a very healthy traditional Hawaiian diet – a diet made of taro root, seaweeds, greens, fresh fruit, and fish – to a diet comprised primarily of processed food rich in saturated fats and sugar, their health rapidly declined. Responding to Moana Jackson's question whether there is an implicit connection between the decline in health conditions and genocide, Dr. Tortolini concludes that the act of forcibly changing dietary habits "could be de facto genocide" (Churchill and Venne 544). Within this context the Tribunal anticipates major international gatherings such as the Iximché Summit to which Joni Adamson refers in her contribution to this volume, where nutritional sovereignty is being advocated as a way to protect people from policies that essentially result in slow genocide – diabetes, cancers, and so forth.

Today, as genetic engineering is forcing its way into indigenous peoples' views on land and land ethics, Native Hawaiians are fighting the battle against genetically modified organisms that are threatening local crops such as coffee, papaya, and the sacred taro. In Hawaii, Monsanto Corporation is credited with saving the Hawaiian papaya industry from a ringspot virus that threatened to devastate the crops. What is not well publicized, however, is the fact that the genetically modified papaya severely limited farm exports and heavily hit the local organic markets. Because all the genetic testing in Hawaii is conducted in open fields, GMO crops are contaminating the naturally grown crops. Once a natural crop is contaminated with GMO elements, it is impossible to reverse the process. Countries in Europe as well as Japan that have put a ban on GMO food and require, unlike the United States, that GMO food be labeled, have ended up boycotting products from Hawaii. A 2006 documentary produced by Earthjustice titled *Islands at Risk: Genetic Engineering in Hawaii* describes how the islands have become the open-air laboratories of chemical and biotech giants such as DuPont, Monsanto, Dow, Syngenta, and others for the testing of GM crops.[21] According to Mililani Trask, "Hawai'i has been targeted as national and international sacrifice area for biotech and genetic modification research" (*Islands at Risk*), and Native Hawaiians, I argue, have become the sacrificial victims to corporate policies of environmental racism. From a Kanaka Maoli perspective, genetic engineering undermines the sacredness of life and disrupts the balance of the natural order. Ethical and moral ramifications as well as valid health-related concerns surround the debates over genetic engineering in Hawaii. When the University of Hawaii launched its battle to "save" the sacred taro plant by genetically engineering disease resistance to it, Native Hawaiians in turn responded by launching a strong GMO-free Hawaii campaign. According to traditional Hawaiian belief, the taro is the first-born, the body form of the god Kane, the giver of life. It is more important than man. As Walter Ritte, a Native Hawaiian from Molokai, contends, "Haloha the taro is more important than Haloha the man. And Haloha the man's only job is to make sure that Haloha the taro

---

[21] According to Earthjustice, "over 4,000 field tests of genetically engineered crops have been conducted in Hawai'i, more than anywhere else in the world, including more than two dozen tests of biopharm crops" (Lawsuit Challenges).

survives forever, because Haloha the taro's job is to feed the man" (*Islands at Risk*). In response to the University of Hawaii's attempt to patent the taro, Hawaiians argue that "kalo as the 'elder brother' of the Hawaiian people should not be owned" (Essoyan).

Article 8 of the UNDRIP provides that "Indigenous peoples and individuals have the right not to be subjected to forced assimilation or destruction of their culture." It goes on to maintain that "States shall provide effective mechanisms for prevention of, and redress for," among others, "any action which has the aim or effect of dispossessing them of their lands, territories or resources." By targeting the local resources, transnational corporations, backed up by the US government and the state of Hawaii, have been undermining rights of Native Hawaiians, as indigenous peoples, not to be subject to the destruction of their culture. Even though the Declaration does not make explicit reference to cultural genocide, the question whether or not the systematic destruction of a culture can be considered a crime of genocide remains a highly contested issue among international law experts. All the more controversial on this issue is the position taken by indigenous peoples.[22]

"A group did not to have to be physically exterminated to suffer genocide. They could be stripped of all cultural traces of their identity," writes Samantha Power in *"A Problem from Hell"* (43). Even though the term "ethnocide" was omitted from the 1948 Genocide Convention, Raphael Lemkin, who coined the word "genocide" in 1944, had addressed the cultural dimension of genocide in his *Axis Rule in Occupied Europe*.[23] "It takes centuries and sometimes thousands of years to create a natural culture," Lemkin wrote, "but Genocide can destroy a culture instantly, like fire can destroy a building in an hour" (quoted in *"A Problem from Hell,"* 43). More than sixty years after the Genocide Convention, it might be time,

---

[22] Interestingly enough, the language of the Draft Declaration, agreed upon by the members of the Working Group on Indigenous Populations (WGIP) in Geneva in 1993, included the right "not to be subjected to ethnocide and cultural genocide" (Article 7). In the final draft the explicit reference to cultural genocide or ethnocide was left out. For further discussion, see Watson and Venne's contribution to this volume (Chapter 3).

[23] A Jewish-Polish attorney, Lemkin dedicated his entire life to having genocide recognized as a crime under international law. In December 1948, the UN Convention on Genocide was adopted as a result of Lemkin's tireless efforts. Genocide is defined as "any of the following acts committed with the intent to destroy, in whole or in part, a national, ethnical, racial, or religious group." These include: "a) Killing members of the group; b) Causing serious bodily or mental harm to members of the group; c) Deliberately inflicting on the group conditions of life calculated to bring about its physical destruction in whole or in part; d) Imposing measures intended to prevent births within the group; e) Forcibly transferring children of the group to another group" (Convention on Genocide).

David Nersessian suggests, for human rights jurisprudence to address the issue of cultural genocide through a new treaty. Cultural genocide, he writes, "is a unique wrong that should be recognized independently and that rises to the level of meriting individual criminal responsibility" ("Rethinking").[24]

At the Tribunal hearings, Maivân Lâm brings to the panel's attention the 1981 Declaration of San Jose as an additional instrument of international law in which the matter of cultural genocide is directly addressed. The declaration states:

> Ethnocide means that an ethnic group is denied the right to enjoy, develop, and transmit its own culture and its own language, whether collectively or individually. This involved an extreme form of massive violation of human rights and, in particular, the right of ethnic groups to respect for their cultural identity, as established by numerous declarations, covenants, and agreements of the United Nations and its Specialized Agencies ... We declare that ethnocide, that is cultural genocide, is a violation of international law equivalent to genocide, which was condemned by the United Nations Convention on the Prevention and Punishment of the Crime of Genocide in 1948. (UNESCO)

In light of the fact that neither the Genocide Convention nor UNDRIP includes any reference to cultural genocide, Lâm urges the Tribunal "to contest the colonial, exploitative interpretation of international law" (Churchill and Venne 465). Reminding the judges that law is, after all, a matter of interpretation, she calls on the tribunal to rethink the question of cultural genocide or ethnocide in a "progressive" and "liberating" manner.

Following the overthrow of the Kingdom of Hawaii and throughout all the period in which the islands remained a territory, Native Hawaiians experienced forced assimilation of US culture. In *The Tribunal*, oral testimonies on the devastating impact produced by forced assimilation are preceded by a text on the screen which reads, "In 1896, the newly formed Republic of Hawai'i made illegal the use of our language as a medium of instruction, severing the cord of language that attached the child to his own people, thereby completely destroying the life and sovereignty of the Hawaiian people" (*Tribunal: Transcript* 31). Woven through the testimonies presented at the hearings are stories by Hawaiians forced into cultural assimilation. We hear about the confusion in learning that one's

---

[24] For additional discussion on the necessity to re-think cultural genocide, see also Lâm, 26–32.

own culture is something to be ashamed of; we hear of physical punishment for speaking the Hawaiian language; of long years of brainwashing at school; of being admonished not to idolize false idols but to praise instead the Statue of Liberty; and we hear of forced eviction from sacred sites (Churchill and Venne 616–17, 619–20, 492–96). The Tribunal finds the United States and the State of Hawaii guilty of the charge of genocide and ethnocide. By engaging in such acts, the United States and the State of Hawaii have specifically transgressed Kanaka Maoli law, US domestic law, as expressed in the principles of liberty and justice of the Declaration of Independence and the Constitution, as well as several elements of international law including the 1948 Convention on Genocide and the Universal Declaration of Human Rights (Churchill and Venne 722–23).

The road ahead

Five days into the hearings, Glenn Morris reflects on the future of the Kanaka Maoli once the Tribunal judges leave the islands. He reflects on how the struggle of the Kanaka Maoli for self-determination will continue and that now more than ever the international community needs to act on the injustices committed against the Hawaiian people. When asked what exactly they expect from the Tribunal, Native Hawaiians reply that they would like the world to know the battles they are fighting. The more people know the more the strength of the Kanaka Maoli will rise.

The most ambitious aspiration of the tribunal, however, is to reformulate the existing international legal framework within the parameters of Kanaka Maoli law, or *Kānāwai*. In response to judge Makoto Oda, Mililani Trask presents the concept of justice in the Maoli language. She explains that there are two closely related concepts: *Lokahi*, "the relationship of the people to the Akua, to that which is sacred and to the land," a concept usually translated through the notion of balance and *pono*. "With justice in the Western sense, it's usually a question of human rights," she says, "but in the Hawaiian sense, justice is broader. If you strike the land, if you desecrate the land, you have violated something there" (Churchill and Venne 440). The second concept, *pono*, is roughly translated as righteousness, which becomes a way of life. "It's a posture that you assume, something you manifest with the gesture of your life more than a tenet or a treaty; you live righteously, you walk on the earth righteously. It's a question of how you perform and live your life" (Churchill and Venne 440). Whereas in Western justice individuals pursue righteousness in courts while at the same time often living in ways that are "hurtful to others and the earth," in Kanaka Maoli justice, Trask posits, people, land, and nation are significantly bound together by righteousness, an inextricable connection conveyed in the expression "Ua mau ke ea o ka ʻAina i ka pono" (Churchill and Venne 440).[25] For Trask and the Kanaka Maoli who took part in the Tribunal, Hawaiian law is very much alive, and they expect the international community to acknowledge such a vital aspect of indigenous cultures. The Tribunal's final verdict, in its "Findings and Recommendations," duly honors the Native Hawaiian request:

> We have found indigenous Hawaiian understanding of law to be an indispensable and powerful background for this verdict, and we believe that the experience and wisdom of indigenous peoples generally is helping the universal democratic movement to develop a more useful and equitable sense of law than has evolved exclusively under modern governments and states that sit in judgment of the world's peoples in existing organs of world order. (Churchill and Venne 684–85).

In the Nā Maka o ka ʻĀina video production, Moana Jackson authoritatively pronounces the findings and recommendations: "That the United States government and the world recognize the sovereignty and right to self-determination of the Kanaka Maoli people under the provisions of international law." And that "Kanaka Maoli lands, including all ceded lands ... should be returned to the control of the Kanaka Maoli people without delay" (*Tribunal: Transcript* 42). Earlier at the Tribunal hearings, Morris had reminded the Tribunal of a fundamental precept of Kanaka Maoli law when he stated: "Kanaka Maoli sovereignty and self-determination flows from the *maka ʻāinana*, literally 'the eyes of the land,' from the people. It can only be relinquished by the people voluntarily, which the Kānaka Maoli have never done" (*Tribunal: Transcript* 42). In the celebratory spirit of *aloha*, all the Tribunal convenors, along with Native Hawaiians, join in a choral voice of solidarity and mutual support. "Come home," are the last words we hear from one of the Kanaka Maoli participants (before the concluding prayer), a fitting expression to close the circle of voices that from the ʻAina of Hawaii in 1993 rose in front of the international community to fight for justice and self-determination.

---

[25] Often translated as "the life of the land is preserved in righteousness," this expression, which has become the motto of the state of Hawaii, conveys the quintessential notion of sovereignty that links Native Hawaiians to their lands. According to Mililani Trask, a more appropriate translation would be "our collective sovereignty over our lands is righteous behavior" (Personal interview).

Conclusion

It has been nineteen years since the People's International Tribunal in Hawaii convened, but justice for Native Hawaiians still seems a long time in coming. In February 2010, the US House of Representatives passed a new version of the Native Hawaiian Government Reorganization Act (commonly known as the Akaka Bill), a bill that would set in motion the process for federal recognition, but a bill strongly opposed by some in the Hawaiian sovereignty movement, including Ka Lahui. In the document issued by the State Department in December 2010, after President Obama announced the United States' support for UNDRIP, the Native Hawaiian Government Reorganization Act is welcomed as "a process for forming a Native Hawaiian governing entity that would be recognized by, and have a government-to-government relationship with, the United States" (Announcement).

It's hard to determine what the future holds for the Kanaka Maoli and to what extent the implementation of UNDRIP might further help their cause. There is no doubt, however, that the Tribunal and the excellent records that ensued allowed Native Hawaiians to organize themselves, to come forward in voicing their stories of past and present injustices and human rights violations in front of an international panel of judges. For Mililani Trask, the Tribunal was a strategic initiative that allowed her to advocate Native Hawaiian rights at the UN. "The best outcome of the Tribunal was to see the involvement and the impact on our people," she says, to be able to hear the various communities' stories and use them as concrete evidence of human rights violations against the Kanaka Maoli (personal interview). Though not a legal judicial institution, the Tribunal clearly demonstrated that in order for the international community to promote the economic, cultural, and social development of indigenous peoples, indigenous views and values must be taken into consideration. First and foremost among such values is a notion of justice originating from within an indigenous epistemology rather than from Eurocentric concepts of jurisprudence. The more the international community listens to the perspective of indigenous peoples the more the rights of indigenous peoples will be affirmed in compliance with the principles of both international and indigenous laws.

When considered within the context of UNDRIP, the 1993 Peoples' Tribunal of Hawaii seems almost prophetic in charting the journey that states will have to make in order to implement the provisions of the Declaration. In the Preamble to the Manila Declaration (2000), a document resulting from the International Conference on Conflict Resolution, Peacebuilding, Sustainable Development and Indigenous Peoples, the need for an international forum that addresses conflicts between indigenous peoples and states was clearly laid out:

> [Indigenous Peoples have the right] to create new systems and institutions of peace-making that are sourced in indigenous values and that co-exist with existing bodies such as the International Court of Justice and similar regional bodies.
>
> *Such institutions could include independent indigenous peoples' tribunals*; commissions of inquiry that are recognized as legitimate organs in any process of conflict resolution. (Manila Declaration, emphasis added)

Today, Mililani Trask posits, "the recommendations of the Manila Conference have not been implemented" ("Chapter VII"), but the need for an international forum where indigenous peoples can address conflicts and dispute resolutions with states has become crucial to affirm their inalienable rights. It is only with the full participation of indigenous peoples in the international legal system as equal partners, mutually recognized and mutually respected, that the international community will be able to claim to respect and promote the inherent rights of indigenous peoples as affirmed in the Declaration.

Works Cited

Anaya, James. "The Native Hawaiian People and International Human Rights Law: Toward a Remedy for Past and Continuing Wrongs." 28 *Georgia Law Review* 309 (Winter 1994). 1–39.

Announcement of US Support for the United Nations Declaration on the Rights of Indigenous Peoples, 16 December 2010. Web. Accessed June 27, 2011.

Churchill, Ward and Sharon Venne, eds. *Islands in Captivity: The International Tribunal on the Rights of Indigenous Hawaiians*. Cambridge, MA: South End Press, 2004. Print.

Convention on the Prevention and Punishment of the Crime of Genocide, Adopted by Resolution 260 (III) A of the United Nations General Assembly, December 9, 1948. Web. Accessed March 22, 2010. www.hrweb.org/legal/genocide.html.

Daes, Erica-Irene A. "Protecting Indigenous Knowledge – Traditional Resource Rights in the New Millennium: Defending Indigenous People's Heritage." In Wanda D. McCaslin, ed., *Justice as Healing: Indigenous Ways*. St Paul, MN: Living Justice Press, 2005. 231–39. Print.

Essoyan, Susan. "Activists Tear Up 3 UH Patents for Taro." *Star Bulletin*, 11, 172, June 21, 2006. Web. Accessed February 26, 2010. http://archives.starbulletin.com/2006/06/21/news/story03.html.

Fanon, Frantz. *A Dying Colonialism*. New York: Grove Press, 1965. Print.

Franklin, Cynthia and Laura E. Lyons. "Land, Leadership, and Nation: Haunani-Kay Trask on the Testimonial Uses of Life Writing in Hawai'i." *Biography* 27.1 (2004): 222–49. Web. Accessed January 26, 2007.

Islands at Risk: Genetic Engineering in Hawai'i. DVD. Produced and directed by Puhipau and Joan Lander. Nā Maka o ka 'Āina, 2006.

Kauanui, Kēhaulani. *Hawaiian Blood: Colonialism and the Politics of Sovereignty and Indigeneity*. Durham, NC: Duke University Press, 2008. Print.

Ka Pakaukau. "International Tribunal on Violation of Human Rights in Puerto Rico and Vieques by the United States of America." *Social Justice* 27.4 (2000): 143–53. Web. Accessed July 23, 2011.

"Reinscription: The Right of Hawaii to be Restored to the United Nations List of Non-Self-Governing Territories." In Churchill and Venne, 2004, 303–21.

Lâm, Maivân. *At the Edge of the State; Indigenous Peoples and Self-Determination*. New York: Transnational Publishers, 2000. Print.

Lander, Joan. "Re: The Tribunal." Message to the author. May 26, 2010. E-mail.

"Lawsuit Challenges Open-Air Testing of Genetically Engineered 'Biopharm Crops,'" November 12, 2003. Web. Earthjustice.org.

MacKenzie, Melody Kapilialoha, ed. *Native Hawaiian Rights Handbook*. Honolulu: Native Hawaiian Legal Corporation & Office of Hawaiian Affairs, 1991. Print.

Manila Declaration on Conflict Resolution, Philippines, December 6–8, 2000. Accessed 16 June 2010. Web. www.twnside.org.sg/title/manila.htm.

Nā Maka o ka 'Āina: Hawaiian Documentary and Educational Videos. Accessed July 23, 2011. Web. www.namaka.com/.

Native Hawaiians Study Commission: Hearings Before the Committee on Energy and Natural Resources, United States Senate, Ninety-Eighth Congress, Second Session, on the Report of the Native Hawaiians Study Commission. Washington: US GPO, 1985. Print.

Nersessian, David. "Rethinking Cultural Genocide Under International Law." *Human Rights Dialogue: Cultural Rights* (Spring 2005). Web. Accessed 27 June 2011. www.cceia.org/resources/publications/dialogue/2_12/section_1/5139.html.

Power, Samantha. *"A Problem from Hell": America and the Age of Genocide*. New York: Harper Perennial, 2002. Print.

Rampell, Ed. "America on Trial." *Pacific Islands Monthly*, October, 1993. 26–27.

Sartre, Jean Paul. "Inaugural Statement to the Tribunal." In John Duffett, ed., *Against the Crime of Silence: Proceedings of the Russell International War Crimes Tribunal*. New York: O'Hare Books, 1968. 40–45. Print.

Schabas, William. *An Introduction to the International Criminal Court*. Cambridge University Press, 2001. Print.

Silva, Noenoe. *Aloha Betrayed: Native Hawaiian Resistance to American Colonialism*. Durham, NC: Duke University Press, 2004. Print.

The Tribunal: Proceedings of Ka Hoʻokolokolonui Kanaka Maoli Peoples' International Tribunal, Hawaiʻi, 1993. Naʼalehu, Hawaiʼi: Na Māka o ka ʻAina, 1994. DVD.

The Tribunal. Transcript for 84-minute video documenting Ka Hoʻokolokolonui Kanaka Maoli Peoples' International Tribunal Hawaiʻi 1993. Naʼalehu, Hawaiʼi: Nā Maka o ka ʻĀina, 2005. Print.

Trask, Haunani-Kay. *From a Native Daughter: Colonialism and Resistance in Hawaiʻi.* Honolulu: University of Hawaiʻi Press, 1999. Print.

"Hawaiians and Human Rights. An Unfulfilled Promise of International Law." Churchill and Venne 291–301.

Trask, Mililani. "Chapter VII: Emerging Issues." In *State of the World's Indigenous Peoples.* February 17, 2010. Web. Accessed June 1, 2010. www.un.org/esa/ socdev/unpfii/documents/SOWIP_web.pdf.

"Re: The Tribunal." Message to the author. June 24, 2011. E-mail.

Personal interview. Honolulu, April 3, 2010.

UN Charter. June 26, 1945. Web. Accessed June 1, 2010. www.un.org/en/ documents/charter/.

UN Declaration on the Rights of Indigenous Peoples (UNDRIP). Adopted by the General Assembly, September 13, 2007. Web. Accessed September 29, 2011. www.un.org/esa/socdev/unpfii/documents/DRIPS_en.pdf.

UNESCO, Meeting of Experts on Ethno-Development and Ethnocide in Latin America, Final Report, San Jose, Costa Rica (December 7–11, 1981). Web. Accessed February 26, 2010. http://unesdoc.unesco.org/images/ 0005/ 000507/ 050786eb.pdf.

UNGA Resolution 1514 (XV), December 14, 1960. Web. Accessed July 23, 2011. www.un.org/documents/ga/res/15/ares15.htm.

UNGA Resolution 1541 (XV), December 15, 1960. Web. Accessed July 23, 2011. www.un.org/documents/ga/res/15/ares15.htm.

UN Permanent Forum on Indigenous Issues (UNPFII). Web. Accessed February 10, 2010. www.un.org/esa/socdev/unpfii/.

United States Public Law 103-150, 103rd Congress Joint Resolution 19, November 23, 1993. Web. Accessed March 22, 2010. www.hawaii-nation.org/publawall.html.

Vizenor, Gerald. "Genocide Tribunals." In Vizenor, *Native Liberty: Natural Reason and Cultural Survivance.* Lincoln, NE: University of Nebraska Press, 2009. 131–58. Print.

We Are Who We Were: From Resistance to Affirmation. Produced by the Hawaiian Patriotic League and Nā Maka o ka ʻĀina, 1998. DVD.

"Women Testify: A Planning Guide of Popular Tribunals and Hearings." Center for Women's Global Leadership, Rutgers University. Web. Accessed June 27, 2011. www.cwgl.rutgers.edu/globalcenter/womentestify/ch1.htm.

World Tribunal on Iraq. Transnational Institute, November, 17 2005. Web. Accessed June 27, 2011. www.tni.org//archives/mil-docs_wti.

~

Afterword: implementing the Declaration

MILILANI B. TRASK

The most significant initiative ever undertaken in the history of human rights transpired over a period of twenty-two years (1985–2007), during which time indigenous leaders from the seven global regions traveled to the United Nations to battle the most powerful states and governments of the world for the establishment of standards to safeguard the human rights and fundamental freedoms of the world's 370 million plus indigenous peoples. The debates that occurred during this time were far-ranging and much more substantive than those that occurred when the international human rights conventions were debated and adopted in the late 1950s and early 1960s. This was because notions of political and ethnic superiority that pervaded Western law during the colonial period had influenced the evolution of international human rights law. These racist perceptions, which were widely held by states and the UN system, were reflected in evolving international human rights law as distinctions between and among certain classes of human beings. Some human beings were "peoples" possessed of the right of self-determination and entitled to the human rights set forth in the UN human rights conventions. Other human beings, who were referred to as "minorities," "populations," and "people," were not "peoples" and consequently were not entitled to the protections of human rights law. The worlds' indigenous peoples fell into the latter category and were denied the collective right of self-determination until the adoption of the United Nations Declaration on the Rights of Indigenous Peoples (the Declaration) in 2007.

As a result of colonialism, indigenous peoples worldwide inherited a legacy of racism and discrimination, exclusion, xenophobia, marginalization, and forced assimilation.[1] The Declaration was drafted by indigenous advocates to address this colonial legacy.

---

[1] See *The Ethnic Question: Conflicts, Development and Human Rights* (Tokyo: United Nations University Press, 1990), and Conference against Racism, Racial Discrimination, Xenophobia and Related Intolerance, Declaration adopted in Durban, South Africa, September 8, 2001, para. 14.

No one ever thought that the time would come when indigenous peoples (those who had inherited a legacy of imperialism, who had suffered political disenfranchisement and been dispossessed of their lands territories and resources) would rise up, asserting basic human rights principles such as universality and non-discrimination and demanding equality and justice. But this is exactly what happened.

Of great significance also were the processes that were utilized in the standard-setting efforts that resulted in the passage of the Declaration. Unlike the international human rights conventions, which were drafted primarily by states, the Declaration from its inception was the product of indigenous advocacy, and consequently is reflective of indigenous history and experience. Many of the Declaration's provisions relate directly to, and address specifically, human rights violations that indigenous peoples and states continue to find problematic. These situations result in social disruption in our communities, political instability in states and continuing violence. If we are to overcome these problems and achieve the goals of peace and equity for our communities, security in the possession of our lands, territories, and resources, and our own cultural survival, we must now turn our efforts to implementing the Declaration.

The Declaration as a standard-setting instrument

On September 13, 2007, the UN General Assembly held a historic vote to adopt the United Nations Declaration on the Rights of Indigenous Peoples.[2] The Declaration is the most comprehensive universal human rights instrument explicitly addressing the rights of indigenous peoples, but it does not in actuality create any new rights. Rather, it was created to "elucidate" or clarify the human rights which indigenous peoples have always been denied. The Office of the UN High Commissioner for Human Rights has referred to the Declaration as "a 'harvest' that has reaped existing 'fruits' from a number of treaties, and declarations, and guidelines, and bodies of principle, but importantly from the jurisprudence of the Human Rights bodies that have been set up by the UN and charged with monitoring the implementation of the various treaties."[3]

---

[2] GA Res. 61/295 (Annex), UN GAOR, 61st Sess., Supp. No. 49, Vol. III, UN Doc. A/61/49 (2008).
[3] Statement of Craig Mokhiber, Office of the High Commissioner for Human Rights, Declaration on the Rights of Indigenous Peoples: Panel Presentation, United Nations, New York (October 26, 2006).

The Declaration affirms the principle of the universality of human rights by setting forth with clarity and brevity the individual and collective rights of indigenous peoples. These rights are addressed with specificity in the provisions of the Declaration. They include, but are not limited to, the right to self-determination and self-government (Arts. 3 and 4); the right to recognition and enforcement of treaties (Art. 37); the right to identity and membership (Arts. 33 and 35); the right to education (Art. 14); the right to subsistence and development (Arts. 20(2), 23 and 32); the right to live in freedom, peace, and security (Art. 7(2)); the right to practice their traditions and customs, and protect their cultural heritage and intellectual property (Arts. 11(1), 12, 13, 15 and 31); the right to maintain and strengthen their distinct institutions (Arts. 5, 18, 20(1), 33(2) and 34); the right to their lands, territories, and resources (Arts. 10, 25–30); the right to their traditional medicines and health practices (Art. 24(1)); the right to conservation and protection of the environment (Arts. 29, 32(3); the right to enjoy fully all rights established under international and domestic labor law (Art. 17); and the right to cross-border contacts and cooperation (Art. 36).

Following the template of indigenous advocacy

Indigenous peoples who are addressing issues with their states or with agencies and specialized bodies within the United Nations system can build upon the strong legal foundations that were laid by their predecessors during the debates that transpired when the Declaration was being drafted. This body of research and information can be found in the collective interventions of the global indigenous caucus. These documents contain not only the arguments advanced by indigenous peoples in defense of their collective and individual human rights, but are an excellent and comprehensive source of international human rights law underlying and supporting their positions. An additional advantage of utilizing these materials is that it demonstrates consistency on the part of indigenous advocates and ensures that efforts initiated by indigenous leaders in the formative years of the Declaration are carried to fruition by those who succeed them.

These interventions (which were ascribed to and endorsed by the vast majority of indigenous nations and peoples who participated in the process) were primarily the work of attorneys Paul Joffe and Dalee Sambo Dorough, who, in collaboration with other experts, worked diligently to assess and incorporate many diverse indigenous positions into a single global intervention bolstered by applicable international legal principles and jurisprudence. The global interventions address the most critical of issues raised during the debates, including the right of self-determination, rights relating to lands, territories, and resources, conflict resolution, and the right to restitution and redress. The global interventions are an excellent educational tool that can be used in our communities to provide our peoples with an understanding of their rights and relevant human rights law.

Collective interventions of particular importance include the following collective submissions and interventions.

1. Grand Council of the Crees (Eeyou Istchee) et al., Assessing the International Decade: Urgent Need to Review Mandate and Improve the UN Standard-Setting Process on Indigenous Peoples' Human Rights, UN Office of the High Commissioner for Human Rights (Joint Submission Indigenous Organizations in Consultative Status with ECOSOC, March 2004).

This document outlines the human rights obligations of the UN system and member states and discusses the arguments used by states to lower human rights standards where indigenous peoples are concerned. It presents the indigenous perspective and international law on matters of critical import to indigenous peoples including: collective rights (vs. individual rights), the use and meaning of the terms "peoples" and "indigenous peoples," the right of self-determination, issues relating to lands, territories, and resources, and the principle of territorial integrity.

2. Grand Council of the Crees (Eeyou Istchee) et al., "General Provisions" of the Draft UN Declaration on the Rights of Indigenous Peoples (Working group established in accordance with Commission on Human Rights resolution 1995/32, 62 Sess., Geneva, E/CN.4/2005/WG.15/CRP.2, 24 November 2005) (joint global statement by indigenous and human rights organizations).[4]

This document was created to counter racist arguments by states that (1) individual rights of citizens supersede collective rights of indigenous peoples; (2) that "national security" may be a limitation on indigenous

---

[4] Grand Council of the Crees (Eeyou Istchee) et al., "Indigenous Peoples' Right to Restitution," Working group established in accordance with Commission on Human Rights resolution 1995/32, 11th Sess., Geneva, E/CN.4/2005/WG.15/CRP.4, 24 November 2005.

human rights; (3) that provisions of the Universal Declaration on Human Rights relating to "morality," "public order," and the "general welfare in a democratic society" can be used to limit indigenous rights; and (4) that state constitutional law should be the law governing and defining indigenous human rights. This document has become increasingly important in post 9/11 times because of the tendency of states to use "national security" and "public order" as excuses to limit and/or deny indigenous human rights.

3.   Grand Council of the Crees (Eeyou Istchee) et al., "Indigenous Peoples' Right to Restitution," Working group established in accordance with Commission on Human Rights resolution 1995/32, 11th Sess., Geneva, E/CN.4/2005/WG. 15.CRP.4, 24 November 2005.

This document set forth the international law relating to the rights of indigenous peoples to restitution, and it distinguishes restitution from other legal concepts or terms, including "reparations," "compensation," and "redress." It also contains a comparison of existing texts and emerging texts on the right of restitution from the Organization of American States draft declaration, the African Charter on Human and Peoples' Rights, and the Indigenous and Tribal Peoples' Convention, 1989, ILO Convention No. 169. This joint indigenous statement was created to support the claims of indigenous peoples and communities for restitution for injuries resulting from colonization and its continuing negative impacts on indigenous communities.

4.   Grand Council of Crees (Eeyou Istchee) et al., Implementation of the Declaration on the Rights of Indigenous Peoples: Positive Initiatives and Serious Concerns, Expert Mechanism on the Rights of Indigenous Peoples, 2nd Sess. (joint global statement by indigenous and human rights organizations delivered August 12, 2009).

This document sums up recent positive developments relating to implementing the Declaration, including regional support from the Organization of American States (OAS), the Association of Southeast Asian Nations (ASEAN), the Inter-American Court, and various states including Belize, Bolivia, the Democratic Republic of the Congo, Denmark, and Greenland. It also exposes recent efforts of the "opposing" states (Australia, Canada, New Zealand, and United States) to reinterpret and redefine provisions and legal norms in the Declaration in ways that would circumvent the human rights of indigenous peoples or subject them to domestic law in these states. Indigenous peoples whose traditional territories lie within the boundaries of these states should examine this document because it provides a preview of how these states may respond to indigenous initiatives under the Declaration and how these states will interpret foreign domestic policy.

Applications of the Declaration within the UN system

The UN system is global and all-pervasive. Its undertakings impact indigenous peoples and communities within states, as well as regionally and internationally on a host of issues including many that are cross-cutting and critical to their cultural survival. Although the Declaration was actively developed and debated for years in the UN system, it would be a mistake to believe that the system understands the Declaration and that its agencies and specialized bodies are capable of, or want to, implement the Declaration.

In fact, the opposite is true. Only a few agencies have adopted policies to address indigenous rights and integrate the Declaration into their work.[5] Many agencies of the UN remain unaware of the Declaration or are not integrating the Declaration into their work. Indigenous peoples interfacing with UN agencies and specialized bodies should be aware that these entities do have a responsibility to address the human rights of indigenous peoples in all of their undertakings.

The Declaration itself underscores that the UN system has an "important and continuing role in promoting and protecting the rights of indigenous peoples." Its organs, specialized bodies, and agencies have an affirmative obligation to "contribute to the full realization" of the Declaration, including, *inter alia*, through the mobilization of "financial cooperation and technical assistance." The Declaration calls upon all UN bodies to "promote respect for and full applications of the provisions" of the Declaration. In undertaking this task, UN agencies are required to ensure "the participation of indigenous peoples on issues affecting them" (Preambular para. 20, Arts. 41 and 42 of the Declaration).

Former Special Rapporteur Rodolfo Stavenhagen addressed the obligations of these UN bodies in his 2007 report to the UN Permanent Forum on Indigenous Issues (the Forum), in which he noted that agencies should "refrain from supporting programs and projects which, either directly or indirectly, are or could be conducive to the violations of the rights of

---

[5] See the UNDP Policy of Engagement (2001), World Bank Operational Policy and Bank Policy on Indigenous Peoples (OP/BP 4.10).

indigenous peoples."[6] Special Rapporteur James Anaya also addressed the obligations of agencies and bodies of the UN in his 2008 report.[7] These advisory opinions and reports can and should be used by indigenous advocates who encounter UN agencies that are acting in conjunction with states to implement projects that violate the human rights of indigenous peoples.

In February 2008 the UN Development Group adopted its *Guidelines on Indigenous Peoples' Issues*. These guidelines were created to facilitate the efforts of UN bodies in integrating the provisions of the Declaration into their work and mainstreaming the rights of indigenous peoples into UN-supported programs at the country level. The guidelines were meant to help UN bodies operationalize the provisions of the Declaration in their mandates, and they have become an important tool for indigenous peoples trying to educate UN agencies on the Declaration while interfacing with them on the ground. In addition, the guidelines provide indigenous peoples with a template that they can easily follow when working within the UN system, because all agencies within the system are required to take a strategic approach to program development.

The guidelines assume that UN agencies know nothing about indigenous peoples or human rights law. Section I of the guidelines provides a background on the situation of indigenous peoples generally, and sets forth the international legal norms and standards that address indigenous peoples' issues (non-discrimination, gender equality, self-determination, collective rights, and the right to development). Section II of the guidelines consists of a graphic chart that synthesizes key issues relating to indigenous peoples and interfaces these issues with the applicable human rights principles that address them. For example, under the heading "Natural Resources," the graph explains how indigenous peoples view natural resources, what indigenous resource management systems are, and indigenous understanding of their guardianship role over resources, as well as indigenous understandings of sustainability.

The graph also identifies the applicable human rights of indigenous peoples relating to natural resources (subsistence rights, sub-surface and surface resource rights):

---

[6] Human Rights Council, Report of the Special Reporter on the situation of human rights and fundamental freedoms of indigenous peoples, Rodolfo Stavenhagen, UN Doc. A/HRC/6/15/ (November 15, 2007), para 72.

[7] Human Rights Council, Report of the Special Rapporteur on the situation of human rights and fundamental freedoms of indigenous peoples, S. James Anaya, UN Doc. A/HRC/9/9 (August 11, 2008).

free prior and informed consent relating to the licensing of development rights to resources, and the protection of heritage when natural
resources are developed). It cites the relevant international law from the
Declaration, the ILO Convention, and the CBD relating to these rights
so that agency staff and personnel can link their obligations to relevant
sources of the law. (p. 10)

Section III of the guidelines reviews the approach of the UN system to
strategic planning and program development, and sets forth the specific
programmatic implications for mainstreaming indigenous issues into the
planning process at every stage. Indigenous advocates who use the guidelines will find that they are applicable throughout the UN system and that
they are an excellent way to educate agencies and specialized bodies about
indigenous issues and human rights while ensuring that these agencies
integrate special measures for indigenous peoples at every stage of program or project development, whether it is economic, social, or cultural.
In addition, many indigenous peoples are using the guidelines as training
materials for their own people; in this way indigenous peoples and UN
staff can become familiar with a common approach to implementing the
Declaration when they work collectively on programs impacting indigenous communities.

Using the Declaration as an interpretive standard for
human rights conventions – making the Declaration binding

Under international law, declarations are not considered to be binding
on states. This means that declarations are "aspirational" statements, but
do not impose obligations or responsibilities on states. Conventions are
binding on states. This means that states are required to meet obligations
set forth in conventions and can be held accountable for human rights
violations where their actions breach provisions of the convention.

While this principle is generally accurate, it cannot be applied to the
Declaration on the Rights of Indigenous Peoples when it is used as an
interpretive standard for state obligations contained in human rights
conventions, and where the obligation, or alleged violation, pertains to
indigenous peoples. In these cases the provisions of the Declaration are
binding on states. This development in international law is extremely
important for indigenous peoples, because it means that indigenous advocates can use the Declaration's provisions when challenging state compliance with their binding human rights obligations under the human rights
conventions.

International treaty bodies have made it clear that whenever issues relating to human rights violations against indigenous peoples by states are raised they will utilize the Declaration as *the* interpretive standard by which to judge state compliance under the conventions. Treaty bodies have also begun to issue general comments relating to the applicability of the Declaration's provisions when interpreting state obligations under binding conventions.[8]

Treaty bodies have not been convinced by arguments advanced by states that the Declaration's provisions do not apply to them because they did not vote for its passage.

This argument was tried by the United States, but was rejected by the Committee on the Elimination of Racial Discrimination, which stated in its concluding observations that "While noting the position of the State party with regard to the United Nations Declaration on the Rights of Indigenous Peoples ... The Committee finally recommends that the declaration be used as a guide to interpret the State party's obligations under the Convention relating to indigenous peoples."[9]

In recent years, the UN system has made an effort to streamline its procedures in the field of human rights. A welcome advance has been the development of the Universal Periodic Review (UPR) mechanism that has facilitated the review of state obligations under several human rights conventions simultaneously. This new procedure means that indigenous peoples no longer have to monitor all of the conventions and their respective calendars, nor do they have to draft numerous shadow reports on state compliance with their many human rights obligations under different

---

[8] See Committee on Economic, Social and Cultural Rights, General Comment No. 21, Right of everyone to take part in cultural life (Art. 15, para. 1 (a), of the International Covenant on Economic, Social and Cultural Rights), UN Doc. E/C.12/GC/21 (December 21, 2009), para. 7; Human Rights Council, Report of the Independent Expert in the Field of Cultural Rights, Ms. Farida Shaheed, Submitted Pursuant to Resolution 10/23 of the Human Rights Council, UN Doc. A /HRC/14/36 (March 22, 2010), para. 9, n. 10, paras. 16 and 26; Committee on the Rights of the Child, Concluding Observations: Cameroon, UN Doc. CRC/C/CMR/CO/2 (January 29, 2010) (advance unedited version), para. 83; Committee on the Rights of the Child, Indigenous Children and their Rights under the Convention, General Comment No. 11, UN Doc. CRC/C/GC/11 (February 12, 2009); Committee on the Elimination of Racial Discrimination, Concluding Observations of the Committee on the Elimination of Racial Discrimination: Peru, UN Doc. CERD/C/PER/CO/14–17 (September 3, 2009), para. 11; Committee on Economic Social and Cultural Rights: Nicaragua, UN Doc.E/C.12/NIC/CO/4 (November 28, 2008), para. 35.

[9] Committee on the Elimination of Racial Discrimination, Concluding observations of the Committee on the Elimination of Racial Discrimination: United States, UN Doc. CERD/C/USA/CO/6 (May 8, 2008), para. 29.

conventions. Indigenous advocates may now check the reporting period for a state and prepare one report on behalf of their peoples that addresses all human rights violations against them, collectively or individually.

Conclusion

The drafting and passage of the UN Declaration on the Rights of Indigenous Peoples was a great achievement and accomplishment for the UN system, states, and indigenous peoples, nations, and communities who stayed the course, overcoming all odds in the face of great opposition. Now that the easy work has been done, we must commit ourselves to ensuring that the protections and provisions contained in the Declaration are operationalized and implemented. This commitment we must pass on to our children and grandchildren in the same way that we transmit to future generations the traditional knowledge and practices of our cultures. We do this because we accept our calling as guardians of the Sacred Earth and keepers of the light for our cultures, and because we know that the price we pay as human rights advocates is eternal vigilance.

INDEX

Lightning Source UK Ltd.
Milton Keynes UK
UKOW06f1206090916

282599UK00008B/260/P